*Dreams, Visions, and Spiritual Authority
in Merovingian Gaul*

Isabel Moreira

DREAMS, VISIONS, AND SPIRITUAL AUTHORITY IN MEROVINGIAN GAUL

Cornell University Press

ITHACA AND LONDON

Copyright © 2000 by Cornell University

First published 2000 by Cornell University Press

Printed in the United States of America

Librarians: A CIP catalog record for this book is available from the Library of Congress.
ISBN 0-8014-3661-3

Cornell University Press strives to use environmentally responsible suppliers and materials to the fullest extent possible in the publishing of its books. Such materials include vegetable-based, low-VOC inks and acid-free papers that are recycled, totally chlorine-free, or partly composed of nonwood fibers. Books that bear the logo of the FSC (Forest Stewardship Council) use paper taken from forests that have been inspected and certified as meeting the highest standards for environmental and social responsibility. For further information, visit our website at www.cornellpress.cornell.edu.

Cloth printing   10 9 8 7 6 5 4 3 2 1

For my parents

Contents

Acknowledgments

This book is the product not only of the past few years when it began to take its present shape, but of my undergraduate and postgraduate studies. It is a pleasure to finally be in a position to thank, in a formal manner, the many friends and scholars who have encouraged and advised me over the years.

My deepest debt is to Jill Harries, the advisor of my doctoral thesis at St. Andrews University. As a good-natured *episcopa*, she oversaw my shaky beginnings, offering advice and encouragement through to the completion of the work. I am also indebted to the fine faculty who taught ancient and medieval history at St. Andrews University. I particularly want to thank Simone McDougall and Lorna Walker for their support early on.

I have been fortunate to join an exceptionally collegial history faculty at the University of Utah. I owe much to the friendship and support of my colleagues and can hardly do justice to them here. However, I am particularly grateful to Glenn Olsen, Eric Hinderaker, Jim Lehning, and Dick Thompson; they read chapters, offered suggestions, and listened to my thoughts on matters medieval. A special thanks is reserved for Bob Goldberg, who kept me on schedule with writing, saw me through crises, and provided chocolate unconditionally. Linda Burns and her interlibrary loan staff at the Marriott Library combined industry with forbearance as I periodically swamped them with arcane bibliographic requests; it would be impossible to be a medievalist in Utah without them.

My book has also benefited from the advice and expertise of colleagues at various institutions. Bill Courtenay and Jane Schulenburg gave encouragement early on; Judith George read multiple chapters of the book in draft form; Bonnie Effros is a constant source of friendly advice on all things Merovingian. Frederick Paxton generously read and commented on the entire manuscript and directed me to important literature, for which I am very grateful. I also thank Lisa Bitel who made suggestions that greatly improved the manuscript. I would also like to thank John Ackerman and Joel Ray at Cornell University Press for their hard work turning the manuscript into a book. All shortcomings are, of course, my own.

Over the years I have received grants that enabled me to do research in the field. I am happy to have the opportunity to acknowledge them fully here: St. Andrews University for a postgraduate fellowship; the Institut für europäische Geschichte in Mainz for a two-year stipend and a travel grant to Poitiers; the University of Utah for Career Development Leave and a Research Assignment; and the Pontifical Institute for Medieval Study in Toronto for a Research Fellowship.

Finally, friends and family helped make this journey into authorship a pleasurable one. I warmly thank Colleen McDannell and John Hurdle, Megan Armstrong, Margaret Toscano, Ed and Marilyn Davies, Nancy Johnson, Anne Johnston, Anne Christie, Kay Harrison, Beverly and Mark Bassin, Maureen Nelson, Robert Summerfield, and my cat Joia who is always just herself. And finally, for their love and unfailing support, I thank my parents José Moreira and Valerie Cound Moreira, to whom this book is dedicated.

I.M.

Abbreviations

AASS	*Acta sanctorum* (Antwerp and Brussels)
AASS, OSB	*Acta sanctorum, Ordinis sancti Benedicti* (Paris)
AB	*Analecta Bollandiana* (Brussels)
ANRW	*Aufstieg und Niedergang der römischen Welt: Geschichte und Kultur Roms im Spiegel der neueren Forschung* (Berlin, New York)
BHL	*Bibliotheca hagiographica latina* (Brussels: Société des Bollandistes, 1992)
CC	*Corpus christianorum, Series latina* (unless Series graeca is noted) (Turnhout)
CPL	*Clavis patrum latinorum*. 3d edition (Turnhout: Brepols, 1995)
CSEL	*Corpus scriptorum ecclesiasticorum latinorum* (Vienna)
DACL	*Dictionnaire d'archéologie chrétienne et liturgie*, ed. F. Cabrol and H. Leclercq, 15 vols. (Paris: Letouzey et Ané, 1907–53)
Francia	Beihefte der Francia
GC	Gregory of Tours, *Liber in gloria confessorum*
GM	Gregory of Tours, *Liber in gloria martyrum*
HE	Bede, *Historia ecclesiastica gentis Anglorum*
HF	Gregory of Tours, *Historia Francorum*
HTR	*Harvard Theological Review*
HZ	*Historische Zeitschrift*
JEH	*Journal of Ecclesiastical History*
JTS	*Journal of Theological Studies*, new series
LHF	*Liber historiae Francorum*
Loeb	*Loeb Classical Library* (Cambridge Mass.)
MIÖG	*Mitteilungen der Institut für Österreichesgeschichte*
MGH, SRM	*Monumenta Germaniae historica, scriptores rerum Merovingicarum* (Berlin, Hanover, Leipzig)
MGH, AA	*Monumenta Germaniae historica, auctores antiquissimi*
PG	*Patrologia graeca* (Paris)

PL	J.-P. Migne, *Patrologia latina* (Paris)
RB	*Revue Bénédictine*
RHE	*Revue d'histoire ecclésiastique*
Settimane di Studio	Settimane di Studio del Centro italiano di studi sull'alto medioevo (Spoleto)
SC	*Sources chrétiennes* (Paris)
TU	*Texte und Untersuchungen zur Geschichte der altchristlichen Literatur* (Berlin)
VJ	Gregory of Tours, *Liber de passione et virtutibus s. Iuliani martyris*
Virt. mart.	Gregory of Tours, *De virtutibus s. Martini*
VM	Sulpicius Severus, *Vita s. Martini*
VP	Gregory of Tours, *Vitae patrum*
VPE	*Vitas sanctorum patrum Emeritensium*
VPJ	*Vita patrum Jurensium*
VR1	Venantius Fortunatus, *Vita s. Radegundis*
VR 2	Baudonivia, *Vita s. Radegundis*

Dreams, Visions, and Spiritual Authority
in Merovingian Gaul

Introduction

In the late fourth century, a story began to circulate which was destined to have a profound impact on the religious imagination of the middle ages. It was the story of a visionary's journey to heaven and hell. The visionary was purportedly the apostle Saint Paul of Tarsus, whose full account of his rapture to the "third heaven," mentioned briefly in the book of Acts, had been kept hidden in the foundations of the apostle's house. When it was discovered, so the story went, it was sent to the Catholic emperor Theodosius, who broke the seal and had it copied and published.[1] The work caught the popular imagination, and although it was not the first marvelous account of a visionary traveler, it was the most widely reproduced and embellished. Not everyone was convinced of the document's authenticity, however. Augustine of Hippo roundly condemned the piece as a fabrication and a crude interloper in the Christian tradition.[2]

Augustine's response to the *Visio Pauli* points to the extreme wariness and the ambivalence exhibited by some churchmen in the late fourth century when confronted with visionary tales. In the early Christian centuries, marginal Christian sects such as the Montanists, gnostics, and Donatists had claimed spiritual authority for their schisms on the basis of divine dreams and visions. Equally of concern to bishops of the fourth century was the persistence within the orthodox church of a Christian charismatic tradition of dreaming which pushed against the institutionalizing tendencies of clerical authority. Yet even in the fourth century, clerics were not entirely unwilling to affirm the spiritual authority of lay dreams. Most clerics prominent enough to have made an imprint on the literature that survived were vis-

[1] *Visio Sancti Pauli: The History of the Apocalypse in Latin, Together with Nine Texts*, ed. Theodore Silverstein (London, 1935), Studies and Documents, 4, ed. Kirsopp Lake and Silva Lake.

[2] Augustine, *In Johannis Evangelium tractatus ccxxiv* 98.8, CC 36 (Turnhout, 1954), ed. Radbod Willems.

ible in their communities because they were better educated and entertained broader ideas of Christian identity than did their flocks. Such men (and occasionally women) were immersed in an intellectual culture whose inherited religious influences favored dreams as a pathway to the gods. Thus most clerics who expressed opinions on such matters subscribed to what might be termed a middle-of-the-road position: some dreams might have spiritual meaning, and others probably did not. Even Augustine eventually modified some of his views about the divine nature of dreams. For Augustine, the proliferation of miracles and visionary reports at the North African shrines of the saints in the early fifth century suggested an arena in which dreams and visions could find a legitimate space within the Church: the cult of the saints. Yet in some essentials Augustine did not change; he believed there were limits on dreams and visions as legitimate means of achieving Christian gnosis, and he emphasized the rarity and spiritual exclusivity of the phenomena in that more intimate connection.

Scholars have responded to the challenge of these ambivalent opinions by suggesting that a roughly chronological development was taking place. The historiography of the first centuries of Christian dreaming posited shifts in access to the supernatural which are said to have occurred sometime between the second century and the late fourth. In his *Pagan and Christian in an Age of Anxiety*, E. R. Dodds claimed that as a result of the political and social "crisis" of the third century, prophecy went underground: "From the point of view of the hierarchy the Third person of the Trinity had outlived his primitive function." [3] That is to say, the clerical hierarchy was no longer as open as it had once been to permitting revelations by the Holy Spirit to determine the Church's course on matters of doctrine and practice. Since in the second century those revelations had had a very democratic air to them, with the Spirit speaking both to men and to women, to cleric and to lay, Augustine's restrictive argument seemingly articulated an erosion in the spiritual authority accorded the ordinary dreamer.

Though Dodds's emphasis on clerical agency in the third century was challenged by Peter Brown in *The Making of Late Antiquity*, both scholars agree on an essential point: Christians of the late fourth century saw their relationship to the supernatural differently than those of the second. While eschewing Dodds's premise that social and political malaise could be seen as a satisfactory explanatory model for religious change, Brown argues that between the second and fourth century there was nevertheless a shift in the locus of the supernatural, which he identified as coincident with the rise of the holy man. By the fourth and fifth centuries, it seemed, the Holy Spirit talked only to his special friends: ascetics, martyrs, and the clergy. [4]

---

[3] E. R. Dodds, *Pagan and Christian in an Age of Anxiety: Some Aspects of Religious Experience from Marcus Aurelius to Constantine* (Cambridge, 1965), p. 67.

[4] Peter R. L. Brown, *The Making of Late Antiquity*, 1976 Carl Newell Jackson Lecture (Cambridge, Mass., 1978), and his collected articles in *Society and the Holy in Late Antiquity* (Berkeley, 1982).

This privileging, or "professionalization," of certain classes of visionary (ascetics and the clergy), historians have argued, must thus have had the logical consequence of delimiting the other classes of visionary, most notably the "ordinary" Christian (that is, the Christian who had no claim by office or community consensus to a special spiritual status). Professional visionaries, according to this argument, squeezed out the ordinary Christian dreamer, who had been so active and whose visions had found such an important niche in the nascent Christian communities of the second century. The clerical hierarchy has generally been seen as the culprit when this shift is extended to the Merovingian age. By the sixth century, we are told, bishops often quashed the dreams of their flock or at any rate imposed their attitudes toward visions on a reluctant Merovingian populace.[5] According to such an argument, this was the demise of the ordinary dreamer, the victory of the clerical hierarchy which, as Dodds suggested, believed or wanted to believe that the Holy Spirit had outlived its primitive function. Or was it? This picture of a restrictive clergy intent on promoting the visions of only the spiritual elite stands in direct contradiction to the demographic variety of medieval visionaries, in Merovingian texts in particular. Gregory of Tours, for example, related how drunkards were the surprising recipients of divine dreams, even as he adhered to a strong rhetoric of spiritual "merit" to explain access to visionary phenomena. It is this dissonance which forms the basis for the discussion of visionary access in the first chapter of this book. There is no denying that clerical writers participated in promoting a restrictive language of merit. But was this rhetoric truly accompanied by restrictions on the ordinary dreamer's ability to voice the spiritual concerns prompted by his or her dreams and to have those in the religious hierarchy take these experiences seriously? I argue that the answer is no. For while asserting that only the "pure in heart" will see God, clerics and ascetics (often the same people at different stages of their careers) were far from seeking to legitimate a "meritorious" class of visionary. Rather, clerics were at pains to promote an inclusive view of the community of Christian believers. Furthermore, with regard to the laity, clerics must have been aware that their activities and authority were often served by more inclusive attitudes toward the bearers of significant dreams. Set in the longer history of a Christian community that believed the divinity could and did speak to his devotees, the evidence of Merovingian visionary accounts exhibits underlying continuities of belief and expectation with earlier centuries.

By the high middle ages, visionary literature and dream narratives were at the heart of the Christian tradition. This is not to say that religious leaders viewed dreams and visions uncritically in the middle ages, or that medieval

---

[5] Giselle de Nie, *Views from a Many-Windowed Tower: Studies of Imagination in the Works of Gregory of Tours*, Studies in Classical Antiquity, 7 (Amsterdam, 1987), p. 221, and Brown, who notes the presence of "oligarchies of bishops powerful enough to overshadow any other bearers of the holy," in "Eastern and Western Christendom in Late Antiquity: A Parting of the Ways," *Society and the Holy*, pp. 166–95.

visions reflected positively on the clergy and the monastic elite (often they did not). Rather, despite their often ambivalent and problematic nature, visions were entrenched in orthodox religious culture. The significance of the Gallo-Roman and Merovingian era (late fourth through eighth centuries) is clear by the Carolingian era and beyond, when visionary literature detailing journeys to hell and heaven was integral to the grammar of Christian eschatology. By this period visionary tales were being written all over Europe, and politically motivated dream literature became an important form through which the Christian subjects of Christian kings dealt with crises of leadership, reputation, and death.[6] Proceeding even further into the middle ages, we find an eleventh-century monk, Otloh of St. Emmeran, compiling a *Liber visionem*, a book of visions whose supernatural confirmation of Christian doctrine and soteriology, he believed, was a suitable means of edifying his monastic audience.[7] And by the twelfth, a pope was encouraging a nun in her visionary prophecies.[8] Such a world view would have been inconceivable without a history of clerical approbation, without the *Dialogues* of Gregory the Great, which lent authority to visionary accounts, and without the literary heirs of the *Visio Pauli* first penned in the West. In the Romano-Gallic and Merovingian centuries, dreams appear to have been brought, if not entirely uncritically, into the clerical "comfort zone." Furthermore, clerics drew heavily on the dreams and visions of the ordinary Christian in their writings on relics: miracle-books at shrines and inventions and translations of relics.

Clearly by the high middle ages the clergy had made its peace with the religious and spiritual potentialities of the visionary phenomenon. Yet how did this state of affairs come about? How did the clerical hierarchy come to permit dreams and visions such a prominent and accepted position in medieval religious culture? How and why, notwithstanding the rhetoric of exclusivity engineered in late antique hagiography, were peasants, women, and children accepted into the ranks of authentic visionaries? The answers are to be found in the slow process whereby clerics accommodated antique traditions of visionary access to a new palette of religious sensibilities—a process that was largely undertaken in the very early middle ages.

Some preliminary definitions are necessary to clarify the parameters of this study. First, it is important to indicate what constitutes the Merovingian period. In this book I focus on the fourth through eighth centuries, which includes the Gallo-Roman contribution to Merovingian culture. In order to address any topic in the Merovingian period, the scholar must make certain assumptions about the cohesion of the period, for the Gallo-Roman and

---

[6] Paul Edward Dutton, *The Politics of Dreaming in the Carolingian Empire* (Lincoln, Neb., 1994).

[7] *Liber visionem*, PL 146, cols. 341–88.

[8] Pope Eugenius III on Hildegard of Bingen's visions; see Barbara Newman, *Sister of Wisdom: St. Hildegard's Theology of the Feminine* (Berkeley, 1987), p. 9.

Merovingian centuries resist easy generalizations. Political boundaries were in constant flux, and expressions of culture and belief in Gaul, even under the Romans, were diverse. The Merovingian kings were Christian kings, but they had not formed the solid ideological alliance with the Church characteristic of the middle ages after Charlemagne. The clergy who wrote the hagiographic literature characteristic of the age changed in personnel and attitudes during the period. Nonetheless, hagiographic literature as genre—and the place of visions in that literature—was gaining momentum and developing as a cultural marker, even if not always in a linear fashion. The centrality of hagiography and cultic literature does in fact provide a measure of cohesion to the period, even if the period has become, as Walter Berschin expressed it, a *mare magnum* lacking orientation points.[9]

Most important for my aims here, the centuries between Augustine and the last Merovingians provide us with comparatively rich materials for understanding how the visionary experience became absorbed into clerical culture. In these centuries we can observe how visionary narratives maintained a central place in Christian expression notwithstanding the preference of some monarchical bishops to keep them at the margins.[10] In the second section of the book (Chapters 3–5) I approach the question of clerical attitudes toward dreams and visions from the perspective of clerical constructions of spiritual and religious authority. I do so by examining clerical responses to dream and vision narrative in specific contexts: as a prophetic instrument in the history of the Church, as a separatist threat in ascetic and monastic movements, as a pastoral concern, as a contributor to the cult of the saints, and as a literature that promoted clerical and liturgical efficacy in Christian soteriology. The utility of dreams and visions to clerical interests was thrown into higher relief because religious sensitivities and priorities changed sufficiently to accommodate new roles for the divine dream, especially at the tombs of the saints, and because after the seventh century the definition and scope of areas in which visions were accorded spiritual, religious, and doctrinal authority fell more securely under clerical control.

Throughout this book, I address dreams and visions—two phenomena which we today regard as discrete experiences—as a single phenomenon. With the exception of oneirological treatises, in regard to their authority dreams and visions were not distinguished in the narrative texts that have come down to us. Indeed, in the large majority of Merovingian narratives it is impossible to distinguish between the two experiences: a "vision" was

[9] Walter Berschin, *Biographie und Epochenstil im lateinischen Mittelalter*, 2 vols. (Stuttgart, 1986–88), introduces his second volume by asking the question "Wo beginnt das '"Merowingische'?" and poses the important question for any study of literature, "ob es richtig ist, Literaturepochen mit Dynastien zu verbinden" (p. 5).

[10] It is a movement echoed in modern scholarship; what was once regarded as a somewhat peripheral and "debased" emanation of medieval soteriology has begun to move to the center of historical inquiry. In Berschin's *Biographie und Epochenstil*, visionary literature is a distinct category of literature, a good indicator of the trend to bring it into the scholarly mainstream.

simply a "sight" which could be seen within or outside of a dreaming state. Dream images were described as *visiones*, and conversely *visiones* and *apparitiones* were described as occurring in dreams. At the same time, visions are described in Merovingian hagiography by a wide range of terminology: *somnia, visiones, revelationes, ostensiones, apparitiones*. The use of such terms, however, is primarily descriptive, and there is little to indicate that Merovingian authors were insisting on the formal categorization systems of late antiquity such as those of Macrobius and Chalcidius. In Macrobius' fivefold schema, for example, he recognized three veridical categories of dream and two that were "empty" or *vana*.[11] The three veridical types were the "enigmatic" dream (*somnium*) whose concealed or symbolic meaning required interpretation, the direct, prophetic dream (*visio*) which needed no interpretation, and the oracular dream (*oraculum*) in which an authority figure (priest, holy person) revealed the future to the dreamer.[12] However, in Merovingian writings the terms *somnium* and *visio*, which Macrobius used to distinguish between direct (theorematic) and allegorical (enigmatic) dreams, were used interchangeably, sometimes within the same vision narrative. Macrobius' system encompassed two types of dream that were not divine in origin but were produced by somatic or external causes: the *insomnium* was a nightmare in which daytime anxieties surfaced in sleep, and the *visum* (Gk. *phantasma*) was a dream in which malevolent powers (demons, incubi) invaded the vulnerable sleeper who hovered between sleep and wakefulness. By contrast, in Merovingian texts the term *visum* was sometimes used for dreams that were thought to be divinely inspired, although its Greek counterpart (*phantasma*) was never subject to such confusion. Though visionary terminology was used with great precision in the works of theorists like Macrobius, one must ask how far treatises of this sort reflected normal linguistic usage, even in their own day.

The *Vita s. Anstrudis* provides an example of how visionary terminology was used in Merovingian hagiography.[13] The author of the *vita* consistently related that the posthumous healing visions of Anstrudis' suppliants occurred in oppressive dreams. For Macrobius an oppressive sleep indicated a nonveridical dream caused by spectres. In the *Vita Anstrudis*, however, it was the veridical dream which suddenly oppressed and weighed on the sup-

[11] Macrobius, *Commentary on the Dream of Scipio* 1. 3, ed. F. Eyssenhardt, *Macrobius* (Leipzig, 1893). English introduction and translation by William Stahl Harris (New York, 1952).

[12] The corresponding Greek terminology was *oneiros, horama,* and *chrematismos,* respectively: Macrobius, *Commentary* 1. 3.

[13] *Vita s. Anstrudis abbatissae Laudunensis,* ed. Wilhelm Levison, MGH, SRM 6 (1913), 64–78. Anstrudis died c. 709. Levison ascribed the work to the later eighth century based on a passage toward the end of the text (chap. 31) in which the author noted the manner in which the saint's feast day was celebrated *secundum morem.* This passage appears in what I suggest is a later addition to the *vita* and is therefore not relevant for dating its biographic content, which may have been closer to the saint's time.

pliant: "oppressed by sleep, she saw in a dream God's servant Anstrudis" (*sopore depressa vidit in somnis Dei famulam Anstrudem*).[14] Similarly, when walking in the area of Hautvillers, Saint Nivardus of Rheims discovered that he could go no further because "the rushing in of a divine sleep began to weigh on him."[15] In light of the terminological vagueness of the Merovingian texts, then, the utility of our contemporary distinction between dreams and visions vanishes.

Hagiography and other types of cultic literature constitute the main written source for this book. Though notoriously difficult to evaluate, hagiography is the most abundant and eloquent source on the subject of dreams in the Merovingian period. While trying to be clear about the vagaries of this source material throughout the book, I have reserved the specific discussion of dreams in the hagiographic genre until Chapter 6. This may appear an unusual decision. My reason for doing it is as follows. Chapter 6 focuses on the normative aspect of hagiography—on the structured and dramatic use of dreams and visions. Thus it provides a useful counterbalance to Chapter 7 which examines the extraordinary record of the seventh-century visionary Aldegund of Maubeuge, whose visions were also eventually recorded in the hagiographic medium. There is no attempt in these chapters, or in the rest of the book, to suggest that some descriptions of visions were "truer" or more likely to have happened than others. All visions, regardless of their literary provenance, attest to the importance of the imaged discourse in Merovingian religious culture.

Hagiography is central to the study of dreams in the Merovingian period because no theoretical literature was written on the subject in that period. Furthermore, the phenomenological limitations of Merovingian descriptions of dreams hinge on the marginal use their authors made of the oneirological treatises which were common in antiquity. Dreambooks and oneirological treatises were read by pagans and Christians. Lists of dream icons and corresponding interpretation provided a prognostic guide for the curious and a resource for a caste of professional dream interpreters. The well-known *Oneirocriticon* of Artemidorus of Daldis is only the best known of this prolific genre.[16] More intellectually challenging offerings were found in philo-

---

[14] *V. s. Anstrudis* 24.

[15] *V. s. Nivardi* 7: "ita divinitus sompno irruente cepit opprimi." The "rushing in" of divine sleep, or divine possession, was common pagan and Christian vision thinking. Augustine addressed this "rushing in" in the context of ecstasy, pondering the question of whether the soul was infused with divinity within the body or externally. The Merovingian hagiographer's "oppressive sleep" motif was common usage as witnessed by other Lives written at the time. In Visigothic hagiography such as the *Lives of the Father of Merida*, veridical dreams occur in oppressive sleep.

[16] Artemidorus, *The Interpretation of Dreams: Oneirocritica*, trans. Robert J. White (Park Ridge, N.J., 1975). A barely Christianized work of this genre, the *Dream of Daniel*, was popular with christian writers in the middle ages because of its purported association with the prophet Daniel. Steven Fischer, *The Complete Medieval Dreambook: A Multilingual Alphabetical Somnia Danielis Collation* (Bern, 1982).

sophical and theological treatises, which pondered the nature of the soul and the intellect and other epistemological matters. The influence of Platonic and Neoplatonic thought on oneirology, including texts written from a Christian perspective, was profound. As I discuss in Chapter 1, the subject of dream taxonomies engaged some of the most prominent thinkers of antiquity, including Tertullian, Augustine, Chalcidius, and Macrobius. Yet although their influence on later Christian medieval philosophy was pronounced, especially from the twelfth century onward, in the early middle ages their works were not read primarily for guidance on Christian dreaming. The visionary theory that Augustine expounded in the twelfth book of his *De Genesi ad litteram* was widely copied but rarely read for its oneirology.[17] Augustine's treatise did not provide the kind of information clerics sought in their dealings with their flocks, nor did its terminology supersede the rather informal phrasing which prevailed in storytelling and other narrative forms. Medieval clerics were far more concerned with defining the parameters of religious authority than with conforming to ancient taxonomies.

It must be acknowledged that our sources present primarily one intellectual perspective—that of the clergy and others vowed to the religious life. It was the clergy who were at the forefront of oneiric documentation and interpretation. Clerics and oneiric theorizers had to deal with the incontestable fact that all humans dream, and that on occasion they dream vivid and ostensibly significant or "true" dreams. Dreaming could not be regulated; it could not be eliminated; and it could not be condemned since patristic and antique writings vouchsafed religious worth to the experience. Thus dreams needed to be tested for orthodoxy. One of the ways Christian oneirologists tried to achieve this was by devising dream etiologies which, it was hoped, could provide distinctions or categories of vision the interpretation of which could filter out demonic and somatic causes. Ultimately, however, vision etiologies could not be applied to produce consistent and satisfactory results. Another way to determine the spiritual value of a dream or vision was to assess the recipient's worthiness to receive such a precious gift. This was a favored but flawed solution since saints and sinners alike received divine dreams. Finally, the test of scripture could be applied to visions to protect orthodoxy and grant authority. This was well understood by Tertullian who, in the face of heretical visionary claims, still provided a space for them in Christian thinking and articulated a dictum whose spirit underlay clerical approaches to dreams and visions: "Conform to scripture."[18] The arbiter of scripture for the lay community was the cleric. Furthermore the text of a

---

[17] See Isabel Moreira, "Augustine's Three Visions and Three Heavens in Some Early Medieval Florilegia," *Vivarium* 34 (1996), 1–14, on how book 12 of Augustine's *De Genesi ad litteram* was excerpted in the early middle ages.

[18] "Omnem vero doctrinam de mendacio praeiudicandam quae sapiat contra veritatem ecclesiarum et apostolorum Christi et Dei." Tertullian, *De praescriptione haereticorum* 21.5, CC series latina 1 (Turnhout, 1954), ed. R. F. Refoulé, pp. 186–224.

dream or vision was interpreted by hagiographers and clerics using the same exegetical methods that they used for any other source of divine knowledge. This need to determine religious significance necessarily involved the clerisy, and it is clear from our sources that some clerics, if only by default, assessed dreams as part of their pastoral duties.

One consequence of the paucity of materials for reconstructing the intellectual history in the Merovingian age is that the era's visions were, until recently, accorded a relatively minor place in modern surveys of medieval visionary texts.[19] This situation has begun to change. In his magisterial study of visionary literature from Augustine to the thirteenth century, Claude Carozzi acknowledged the importance of the late Merovingian evidence, particularly the seventh-century *Vision of Barontus*, for the development and direction subsequent medieval visions were to take.[20] There are also some important studies on visions in late antiquity which are more focused in scope, such as those of Jacqueline Amat, Martine Dulaey, Giselle de Nie, and Patricia Cox Miller.[21] These and other studies illuminate the major

[19] Important scholarly contributions to the broad history of the phenomenon and its literatures are Peter Dinzelbacher, *Vision und Visionsliteratur im Mittelalter*, Monographien zur Geschichte des Mittelalters, 23 (Stuttgart, 1981); Ernst Benz, *Die Vision; Erfahrungsformen und Bilderwelt* (Stuttgart, 1969); and Steven F. Kruger, *Dreaming in the Middle Ages* (Cambridge, 1992).
[20] Claude Carozzi, *Le voyage de l'âme dans l'au-delà d'après la littérature latine (ve–xiiie siècle)*, Collection de l'école française de Rome, 189 (Rome, 1994).
[21] Amat, *Songes et visions. L'au-delà dans la littérature latine tardive* (Paris, 1983), provides a compendious examination of the literary and discursive threads of Christian dreaming in antiquity; Dulaey has focused on dreams in the thought of Augustine in her *Le rêve dans la vie et la pensée de saint Augustin* (Paris, 1973). The importance of dreams in the imaging of intellectual culture is addressed in Patricia Miller's *Dreams in Late Antiquity: Studies in the Imagination of a Culture* (Princeton, 1994); de Nie's *Views from a Many-Windowed Tower* exposed the imagistic nature of Gregory of Tours' thinking on dreams and other supernatural signs, and is an essential starting point for any study of Merovingian dreaming. For the Carolingian age, Hans Joachim Kamphausen, *Traum und Vision in der lateinische Poesie der Karolingerzeit* (Frankfurt, 1975) focuses on visionary phenomenology in Carolingian poetry and provides a short introduction to the Merovingian background. Paul E. Dutton has shown how close readings of political dream texts can illuminate an entire psychic stratum of a society in *The Politics of Dreaming* (Lincoln, Neb., 1994). A growing number of studies suggest a variety of approaches to the history of early medieval dreaming: literary and imagistic traditions, the intersection of Christian and Germanic ways of dreaming, journeys to the afterlife and the geography of the otherworld, visions as near-death experiences, and so on. Also important are Jacques Le Goff, "Christianity and Dreams (Second to Seventh Century)," in his *The Medieval Imagination*, trans. Arthur Goldhammer (Chicago, 1985), pp. 193–231, first published in 1977 in *Pour un autre Moyen Âge* pp. 299–306; Elizabeth Petroff, *Medieval Women's Visionary Literature* (Oxford, 1986); Mircea Éliade, *Myths, Dreams, and Mysteries: The Encounter between Contemporary Faiths and Archaic Realities* (New York, 1975), first published as *Mythes, rêves et mystères* (Paris, 1957); Peter Dinzelbacher, *Vision und Visionsliteratur im Mittelalter* (Stuttgart, 1981); Lisa Bitel, "In Visu Noctis: Dreams in European Hagiography and Histories, 450–900," *History of Religions* 31 (1991), 39–59; and Michel Aubrun, "Charactères et portée religieuse et sociale des 'Visiones' en occident du vie au xie siècle," *Cahiers de Civilisation Médiévale* 23 (1980), 109–30. In addition to numerous articles by Maria Pia Ciccarese (see bibliography) and Claude Carozzi's *Le voyage de l'âme*, which are given full consideration in Chapter 7, see also the articles in *Scede Medievali* 19 (1990).

authors and texts of the age: Sulpicius Severus, Gregory of Tours, Gregory the Great, the *Vision of Fursey*, and the *Vision of Barontus*. In addition to these well-known texts, I have also sought to include, especially in Chapter 6, dreams and visions described in the cruder mass of hagiographic texts produced in this period, many of which were anonymous productions of uncertain date and unclear provenance. (The date and justification for the use of these texts is in the notes, and no attempt has been made to correct Merovingian Latin spelling and grammar.) This book focuses on the ways Christians understood the place of visions in their relationship with the divine, and how spiritual authority was mediated through dream accounts. In view of this focus, I have not limited my discussion to visions of otherworldly travel but rather I include dreams and visions reported in a variety of contexts. These centuries saw profound social, religious, and literary changes as Germanic peoples and ideas were incorporated and adopted into a late Roman society that "lurched," as Peter Brown has expressed it, toward new modes of thinking.[22] These were the centuries when antique traditions of dreaming were Christianized and to some extent clericalized. To bypass the developments in these centuries imperils a surer understanding of how dreams and visions came to be given spiritual authority in the Christian middle ages.

[22] Peter R. L. Brown, *The Cult of the Saints: Its Rise and Function in Late Antiquity* (Chicago, 1981).

Part 1

VISIONARY ACCESS

I *Visionary Access in Christian Antiquity: The Making of Two Traditions*

In *Pagan and Christian in an Age of Anxiety*, E. R. Dodds claimed that in response to changing attitudes toward the supernatural at the end of the second century and the political and social turmoil of the third, high-ranking clerics came to reject the view that the Church should be governed by prophetic advice emanating from ordinary Christians. Instead, a divinely guided hierarchy would henceforth govern the Church on behalf of the entire Christian community. Of the Holy Spirit's fate Dodds wrote: "He was too deeply entrenched in the New Testament to be demoted, but he ceased in practice to play any part in the counsels of the Church." [1] In recent years much of Dodds's picture of religious change in the second and third centuries has been challenged, yet his essential point still stands: second-century thinkers and those who lived in the closing years of the empire saw their relationship to the supernatural very differently. [2] In the second century it was still possible for a pagan author to acknowledge the help of the gods alongside other friends in the dedication of a book, thanking them especially for his "vivid and recurrent visions of the true inwardness of the Natural Life." [3] For

---

[1] Dodds, *Pagan and Christian*, pp. 67–68.

[2] In *The Making of Late Antiquity* (Cambridge, Mass., 1978), Peter Brown dismissed the idea that the social and political malaise of the third-century "crisis" can be held as a solitary explanation for religious change between the second and fourth centuries. His review of Dodds's *Pagan and Christian* and W. H. C. Frend's *Martyrdom and Persecution in the Early Church* (Oxford, 1965), titled "Approaches to the Religious Crisis of the Third Century A.D.," *English Historical Review* 83 (1968), 542–58, anticipated much of his argument in the book. From the age of the Antonines to the rise of holy man in the fourth century, Brown sees not a pessimistic intellectual descent but rather a "shift in the *locus* of the supernatural" (p. 11). Conversely, Robin Lane Fox has de-emphasized the importance of these years as a religious watershed: see *Pagans and Christians* (San Francisco, 1986), p. 748 n. 25.

[3] Marcus Aurelius, *Meditations* 1.17, trans. Maxwell Staniforth (Harmondsworth, 1964); see also 7.67.

the Christians of late antiquity, however, the divinity spoke primarily to ascetics, martyrs, and sometimes the clergy.[4]

However one might choose to characterize the causes of this shift, it is important that the change from a largely unrestricted idea of access to the supernatural in the second century to an insistence on the privileging of a restricted class of holy visionary in the fourth should be seen in a proper light.[5] The literature in which dreams were presented to the Christian in late antiquity differed from that used in earlier centuries. Depiction of the dreams and visions of individuals in late antiquity and the early middle ages occurred primarily in the very specialized literature of hagiography. Seminal examples of this literature, especially the Lives of the desert saints, had a twofold impact on Christian views of the holy. First, the activities of ascetic heroes as portrayed in hagiography contributed to expectations of what the saintly life entailed. Second, hagiographic literature established the linguistic conventions whereby that holiness was expressed. Reading the fourth-century Lives of holy ascetics it is clear that a new class of "repositories" of the holy had emerged from desert hermitages in the third and fourth centuries. The supernatural battles which these holy individuals provoked were unlike any that ordinary Christians were likely to experience, and their rewards were likewise extraordinary.[6] Hermit saints had visions of demons fighting naked at night, and of angels who administered communion to them with the words "Life everlasting shall be yours, and imperishable prophecy."[7]

These reclusive heirs of the prophet Daniel were removed both geographically and spiritually from the Christian community, and in their *vitae* their exploits were embossed with a language of privilege and entitlement. Yet we must not be led astray by hagiographic enthusiasm and the language of merit which accompanied it. The privileging language of ascetic literature exposed

[4] Brown, *Making of Late Antiquity*, p. 12. The works of Peter Brown have been essential to scholarly discussion of this phenomenon in antiquity. Especially noteworthy in addition to the book are his articles reprinted in *Society and the Holy in Late Antiquity*: "The Rise and Function of the Holy Man in Late Antiquity," "Relics and Social Status in the Age of Gregory of Tours," and "Eastern and Western Christendom in Late Antiquity: A Parting of the Ways." Although they are important for discussions of the supernatural in antiquity, when projected into the sixth century Brown's ideas have tended to obscure rather than clarify the religious dynamics of the Merovingian age. See R. Van Dam, *Saints and Their Miracles in Late Antique Gaul* (Princeton, 1993), pp. 4–5.

[5] Le Goff, "Christianity and Dreams," uses the term "democratization" of dreams, a phenomenon he locates at the end of the fourth century, on the strength of the rather atypical Synesius of Cyrene. I prefer "open access" to dreams, since in a Christian context the notion of democratic access removes the sense that divine dreams were believed to be a divine gift. The emphasis in the sources is not on right of access but on eligibility of access.

[6] By "ordinary" I mean the Christian who had no special claim to spiritual authority by virtue of office or way of living. Obviously, the Christian who was granted a dream or vision considered to have spiritual meaning was by that experience rendered somewhat extraordinary. No economic distinction is intended by the term.

[7] Paphnutius, *Histories of the Monks of Upper Egypt* 23, and *Life of Onnophrius* 34, trans. and intro. T. Vivian (Kalamazoo, 1993).

a rhetoric which ostensibly excluded the ordinary Christian from personal connection with the divine. Yet just because this literature did not reflect the visionary experience of ordinary Christians, we should not conclude that such experience had ceased to exist. It is important to acknowledge that behind the hagiographic rhetoric of privilege and merit more inclusive ideas of visionary access continued to thrive. It is especially important that we keep this in mind as we look at the place of dreams and visions in the late antique and Merovingian context. A strong tradition of unrestricted access to the supernatural through dreams and visions persisted into the early middle ages in ways which were vital to the medieval understanding of the visionary phenomenon. For though a rhetoric of merit was increasingly adopted by a medieval church which was anxious to delimit the ranks of authorized visionaries, we must accept that the language of merit functioned more as an economy of explanation than as a description of reality. In describing the Lives of the saints, hagiographers promoted a model of spiritual exclusivity to which they did not adhere elsewhere in their writings. The persistence of the idea that the ordinary Christian dreamer could have divine and significant dreams, as we shall see below, challenges Dodds's contention that the third person of the Trinity had gone "underground." Rather, I wish to emphasize that in late antiquity, two important traditions of access to the supernatural coexisted, and the ambivalences inherent in them were transmitted to churchmen and authors in the early medieval West.

It is a significant and curious feature of Merovingian writings that while they insist on the necessity of spiritual merit for access to supernatural dreams and visions, the texts are alive with humble, dirty, and rascally inhabitants of Gaul who were apparently ennobled by divine favor. This Merovingian writers were only occasionally willing to explore. For example, Gregory, the sixth-century bishop of Tours, related a story about an extraordinary event that took place in Silvinus' monastery near Tours. It so happened that while temporarily incapacitated from performing the Mass, the priest Venantius looked up into the church rafters to see an apparition of an aged cleric descending a ladder. The apparition proceeded to celebrate the divine office on his behalf. Gregory noted that it was a vision "which no-one merited to see except him; why the others did not see the vision, we do not know." [8] Venantius was a man whose exceptional purity was extolled in a number of Gregory's stories, and who experienced a number of startling revelations during his lifetime. It was not a mystery for Gregory that such a man should be so spiritually privileged. What mystified Gregory was the misfortune of the many clerics and lay people gathered in church who saw nothing that day. Why had they been excluded from the vision? Clearly it was a ques-

---

[8] Gregory of Tours, *Vitae Patrum* 16.2, ed. Bruno Krusch, *MGH, SRM* 1.2 (Hanover, 1885): "quod nullus videre meruit nisi ipse tantum; reliqui vero cur non viderint, ignoramus." Gregory of Tours, *Life of the Fathers*, trans. by Edward James, Translated Texts for Historians, 1, 2d ed., (Liverpool, 1991).

tion which gave Gregory pause. Yet despite Gregory's claim not to know the answer, he provided the only one that made sense to him: Venantius had "merited" the vision.

Gregory's explanation of visionary access through a discourse of spiritual merit was a line of thinking that would have been readily understood by his audience. Early medieval Christians, reared as they were on the Lives of the saints in which the "pure in heart" saw beyond the visible to the spiritual, expected their holy men and women to be privileged in this way. Saints were by definition those who had transcended the boundaries of spiritual blindness; their lives were blessed by God and, in the words of Athanasius, visions were often a reward for their hardships. Hagiography enshrined this discourse of privilege, so that by Gregory's time the rhetoric of merit had become an insistent if not very consoling mantra.

Yet even to Gregory the difficulties evident in such a simplistic correlation must have been clear. Many of Gregory's stories and those of his contemporaries attested to a God who both revealed and concealed; to a God who granted access to divine and supernatural sights on a basis not confined to human assessments of spiritual worth. Bishop Ambrose of Milan explained to the Emperor Theodosius in the spring of 390, "Our God admonishes us in many ways, by heavenly signs, by the warnings of the prophets, and he wills that we understand even by the visions of sinners." [9]

In Gregory's tales of sixth-century Gaul, visions of sinners abound. Drunkards, thieves, children, and even women witnessed magnificent sights and supernatural spectacles. Ruefully, Gregory acknowledged that he, the bishop of Tours and guardian of St. Martin's tomb, himself the recipient of supernatural dreams in his youth, was not worthy to see the celestial source of lights shining from the oratory of the Virgin at Marsat. [10] It was a moment of sad reflection as Gregory failed to measure up to the meritorious model to which he subscribed.

Yet what is striking about Gregory's account is not that his stories failed to uphold the idea that visionary access was based on spiritual merit, but

---

[9] Ambrose, *Ep.* 51, written in April 390. Letters translated by Sister Mary Melchior Beyenka, *Ambrose: Letters*, Fathers of the Church, vol. 26 (New York, 1954).

[10] Gregory of Tours, *Liber in gloria martyrum* 8: "credo a caligine peccatorum meorum," ed. Krusch, *MGH, SRM* 1.2 (1885), p. 43 (hereafter, *GM*). Gregory related a drunkard's vision in his *Historia Francorum* 2.7, ed. Bruno Krusch and Wilhelm Levison, *MGH, SRM* 1.1 (1937–42). On another occasion Gregory explained a supernatural occurrence thus: "The earlier miracle was seen by only a few people, but this one appeared to all the people. In that earlier miracle there was evidence of power, but in this one there was a reinforcement of grace. That earlier miracle was kept secret to avoid ostentation, but this one was made manifest to everyone for glorification." Gregory of Tours, *Glory of the Confessors* 20, trans. by Raymond Van Dam, Translated Texts for Historians, 4 (Liverpool, 1988). Other cases of visions seen by some but not others include Bishop Severinus of Cologne, a "vir honestae vitae et per cuncta laudabilis" who heard choirs singing in heaven at St. Martin's death when his archdeacon did not. Gregory explained the archdeacon's exclusion: "Sed credo, eum non fuisse aequalis meriti, a quo haec non merebantur audiri." *De virtutibus s. Martini* 1.4, ed. Krusch, *MGH, SRM* 1.2 p. 140 (hereafter, *Virt. Mart.*) See also *GM.* 1 ("pure in heart") and 49 ("merit of the martyrs").

that despite information counter to this explanation, much of it provided by Gregory himself, Gregory still thought that they did. That conviction needs some explanation, since it suggests that the idea of visionary access rooted in merit was so entrenched by the sixth century that even in the face of indications to the contrary, merit remained the dominant explanatory motif. It is the purpose of this chapter to fathom this dissonance; to examine the Christian traditions underlying visionary access in order to set in context the Merovingian insistence upon the merit of the visionary.

The first place one might expect to find an answer on this issue is in the many oneirological and oneirocritical manuals and treatises surviving from antiquity. The study of dream manuals, however, is a false start, for pagan oneirologists focused on interpreting predictive dreams (*oneiroi*) rather than "god-sent" dreams (*chrematismoi*), and the oneirologist's skill was in determining meaning from various categories of *oneiroi* in which the dreamer's status and identity influenced the reading of the dream.[11] Such manuals did not limit the dreaming community in any way, except to differentiate interpretation according to the social status of the visionary; for the pagan gods had a highly developed sense of the respect due to social station. Pagans believed that human dreaming was open to divine infiltration. With the exception of those engaged in certain specific cults, most Romans attributed the supernatural component of the phenomenon to a rather weak sense of divine powers which were believed to inhabit the atmosphere. These powers were theoretically available to all.

In contrast to pagan prolixity on oneirology, Christian treatises on dreams and visions were rare, and they proposed little that was not borrowed or speculative. Tertullian's late second-century treatise *De anima*, which was the most extensive antique examination of dreams from a Christian perspective, is a good example of the way pagan ideas saturated the field of Christian oneirology.[12] There are more citations to classical authors in the treatise than there are to the Bible.[13] Furthermore, Tertullian's treatise was tainted for its subsequent Christian audience by its author's heresy, and the treatise does in fact contain some very idiosyncratic opinions.

[11] Artemidorus of Daldis' *Oneirocriticon* differentiated interpretations according to the social status of the dreamer. See Michel Foucault's analysis in *The History of Sexuality*, vol. 3, *The Care of the Self*, part 1 (New York, 1986); also L. H. Martin, "Artemidorus: Dream Theory in Late Antiquity," *The Second Century* 8 (1991), 97–108. For his Latin audience Macrobius rendered the categories thus: "somnium" and "visio" related to the allegorical and direct ("theorematic") categories of "oneiros" respectively. The god-sent "chrematismos" was termed "oraculum," and he further distinguished in the "enhypnion" (nonsignificative dreams), the nightmare ("insomnium"), and spectres or ghosts ("visum"). *Commentary on the Dream of Scipio*, in *Macrobius*, ed. F. Eyssenhardt (Leipzig, 1893); trans. with notes by William Harris Stahl (New York, 1952).

[12] Tertullian, *De anima*, ed. Jan Hendrik Waszink (Amsterdam, 1947); reprinted in *Tertulliani Opera pars 2. Opera Montanistica*, CC 2 (Turnhout, 1954), pp. 780–869; trans. Peter Holmes, *Ante-Nicene Christian Library* (Edinburgh, 1870.)

[13] Amat, *Songes*, p. 39.

In the early fifth century, Augustine investigated the visionary phenomenon in a treatise which was essentially an epistemological exercise, larded with clinical observations of the sort that passed for science in his day. Carefully distancing himself from the work of his North African compatriot Tertullian, he ignored those issues about divine dreams that were most central to his community. For example, Augustine offered no suggestion as to how dreams and visions could contribute in a positive way to Christian spirituality. Consequently Augustine's ruminations on visionary phenomena, though important to the intellectual tradition of the later middle ages, were eventually relegated to the philosophical backwaters of early medieval writing.[14]

If we focus on the intellectual literature of antiquity, then, we are assailed by lists of pagan authorities with little indication as to how dreams and visions were to be incorporated within the Christian tradition. Thus it is to a different genre of literature that we must turn if we are to fathom the assumptions underlying Christian attitudes on the issue of visionary access. We have to catch our sources unawares, as it were, if we wish to uncover a discourse which was rarely explicit but which nevertheless underlay much of patristic thought. We can do this by looking at Christian exegesis on the book of Genesis. For it is in the realm of biblical commentary that our sources best reveal their authors' attitudes. There we will find evidence for the persistence into the early middle ages of a discourse which promoted an alternative to the merit solution.

Adam's Sleep in the Garden of Eden

When the early church fathers tried to uncover and fashion a purely Christian theology of spiritual dreams, they naturally turned to the Bible. Both the Old and New Testament revealed a God who favored the medium of dreams, visions, and invisible voices to guide his chosen people.[15] By the time of Jacob and Daniel, the prophetic model had been established, and Christian commentaries identified these prophets as foreshadowing Christ. In order to tease out strands of the Christian discussion of visionary access we must

[14] Augustine's *De Genesi ad litteram* was widely copied in the early middle ages, but not for the discussion of visions in book 12. See Moreira, "Augustine's Three Visions." On Augustine's contribution to Christian dream theory see Dulaey, *Le rêve*.

[15] The New Testament emphasis on visual rather than auditory revelations has been ascribed to the influence of Hellenism. G. Bjorck, "Onar idein. De la perception du rêve chez les anciens," *Eranos Jahrbuch* 44 (1946), 306–14, argued that for the Jews the privileged sense was hearing, whereas for the Greeks it was sight. The patent oversimplification of this thesis was noted by H. Urs von Balthasar, *La Gloire et la Croix*, vol 1 (Paris, 1968), pp. 261–62, but the idea remains interesting. Most injunctions in the Old Testament are imparted by the voice of God, unaccompanied by a visible presence, which was often considered to be fatal. On the vision of God in the Old Testament and in rabbinical teaching see Kenneth E. Kirk, *The Vision of God: The Christian Doctrine of the Summum Bonum* (London, 1931), pp. 10–22, esp. pp. 11–12.

look not to the prophets but to the first human dreamer, Adam. Adam's experience began outside the historical tradition that made prophets out of Joseph and Daniel, and thus the emblematic significance of his sleep was open to discussion.

In Genesis 2.21–23 it was related that as God made woman, Adam had slept in the Garden of Eden: "So the Lord God caused a deep sleep to fall upon the man, and while he slept took one of his ribs and closed up its place with flesh." [16] Upon waking, Adam began to prophesy. The Genesis story had great resonance for Christian oneirologists, and they alluded to it regularly. The Genesis account signified that Adam's sleep was part of the primordial plan for humanity and that in addition to being a necessity occasioned by the weakness of the body, Adam's sleep was a prophetic sleep antecedent to the Fall. In the early centuries of the Common Era, Jewish and Christian exegetes alike pondered the meaning of this text.[17] What exactly had been the nature of this paradisiacal sleep, and what did it signify for the human condition after the Fall? Church fathers answered the question in different ways according to their interpretation of the theological "place" of dreaming. Though no single Christian opinion on this matter prevailed in the early Christian centuries, still it is possible to distinguish two distinct, although not strictly antithetical, philosophies which underlay contemporary discussion of dreams.

The first view held that dreams and visions were a natural, divinely sanctioned and, in theory, universally accessible channel for the Christian to experience direct and personal communication with the divine. It was a commonly held opinion in antiquity that dreams provided relatively open, unrestricted access to divine powers. Those who held this opinion found

---

[16] In the Vulgate and the *Vetus Latina* the Hebrew "thardema" was translated as "sopor," sleep. However, the Greek Septuagint translation rendered Adam's sleep as "ecstasy," and it is with this reading that most Christian commentators were familiar. See Monique Alexandre, *Le Commencement du livre Genèse I–V*, Christianisme antique, 3 (Paris, 1988) pp. 282–83. The Latin text of Genesis 2.21 used by Augustine reads in part: "Et iniecit Deus mentis alienationem super Adam, et obdormivit." See John Hammond Taylor, *Ancient Christian Writers*, vol. 42 (New York, 1982), app. 2, p. 330.

[17] Philo of Alexandria's writings are the heart, if not always the direct source, of much subsequent Christian exegesis on Genesis. In his *Allegorical Interpretation of Genesis*, 2. 19 ff., Philo developed an allegory or myth of perception based on Adam's sleep: the woman taken from Adam's side represented the origin of active sense perception. Adam's sleep was the beginning of perception for "when the mind wakes up perception is quenched." The active sense perception represented by the woman closes off mental perception and stimulates talk, sight, and the "active" senses. Philo, naturally enough, adhered to the prophetic, restrictionist view of visionary access: "But whether thou wilt find God when thou seekest is uncertain, for to many he has not manifested himself." *Allegorical Interpretation* 3.47. Philo also authored a work entitled *De somniis*, originally the second part of a longer treatise. Unfortunately, the first part of the work where he discussed dreams and visions which were directly heaven-sent, is no longer extant. See Philo, 1 and 5, in *Loeb*, vols. 229, 275, trans. F. H. Colson and G. H. Whitaker (Cambridge, Mass., 1929, 1934). On Philo's own search for God see Kirk, *Vision of God*, pp. 38–46. Waszink, *De Anima*, p. 14, finds no evidence that Tertullian had direct knowledge of Philo's work. See also Amat, *Songes*, p. 115, on Tertullian and Philo.

their stance reflected in Adam's sleep in the Garden of Eden. Adam was the image of Everyman and thus, it might be reasoned, the model for the earthly sleeper whose dreams continued to have in them something of the divine.

This unrestricted model reflected the view of the many Christians who believed that the Spirit would continue to guide the Christian community as it had done for the apostles. For these hopeful Christians, prophetic dreams and visions enabled new revelations to be communicated by divine powers as Christians matured in their spiritual understanding. For those who believed with St. Paul that the Christian message first imparted to the faithful was a simplified version, milk for those not yet ready to eat meat, the adult diet of Christian revelation was awaited with frank anticipation.[18]

The second approach to visionary access was to insist that divinely inspired visions were restricted to specific people, times, and places. This view was also reflected in interpretations of Adam's sleep. Adam, the first human, was regarded as a special case, a proto-prophet and thus a prototype for Christ. According to this reading, only a special, God-chosen person could be endowed with divinely issued dreams and visions and provide, on behalf of the wider community, a special link with God.

In modern scholarship these two philosophies of visionary access are generally presented as a chronological development, with the unrestricted model of the early Christian centuries giving way to more restricted evaluations of access in the fourth century.[19] I will argue that viewed from the perspective of sixth- and seventh-century literature, neither tradition entirely supplanted the other. In the remainder of this chapter I show how the two traditions were explored by Christian thinkers in late antiquity. The existence of a dual tradition and the conflicts inherent in it shaped the way dreams and visions were approached by those with spiritual authority in early medieval communities.

Early Christian Communities: Open Access

In fulfillment of the prophecy of Joel 3.1–5, the early Christian community was promised that "your daughters shall prophesy, your young men shall see visions, and your old men shall dream dreams (Acts 2.17)". This was prophecy was often fulfilled in succeeding centuries, much to the consternation of the clergy. But the delight of the early Christians in their assurance of divine favor was palpable. Theirs was a Saviour, they boasted, "who confers understanding, manifests mysteries, announces seasons, rejoices in the faithful."[20]

---

[18] 1 Corinthians 3.2–3.

[19] This is the implication of Dodds's observation that the Holy Spirit went underground in the third century, and Brown's focus on the rise of the holy man in the fourth.

[20] Letter to Diognetus 11.5 trans. Kirsopp Lake, *Apostolic Fathers,* 2, Loeb, vol. 25 (Cambridge, Mass., 1913), p. 375.

In this second-century community a slave named Hermas was seized by "a spirit" to know his transgressions and those of his community. One of the interesting things about Hermas the visionary was that he was not yet fully immersed in his new faith when his visions began.[21] Yet his vision instructed him to send copies of his vision book to prominent Christians and to reveal his visions before the Christian assembly: "In this city you shall read it [the little book] yourself with the elders who are in charge of the Church."[22] In doing this Hermas was doing what the righteous man was emboldened to do, for "when the man who has the Divine spirit comes into a meeting of righteous men who have the faith of the Divine Spirit, and intercession is made to God from the assembly of those men, then the angel of the prophetic spirit rests on him and fills the man, and the man, being filled with the Holy Spirit, speaks to the congregation as the Lord wills."[23] Thus it was the descent of the Spirit which made a prophet, and not necessarily an unblemished life. Hermas was informed that there was nothing special about him that he should have been honored with such signs of divine favor: "It is not because you are more worthy than all others that a revelation should be made to you, for there were others before you and better than you, to whom these visions ought to have been revealed."[24] Elsewhere, however, Hermas was told to "test, then, from his life and deeds, the man who says he is inspired." And so as early as the second century, even within a community that was open to the spiritual contribution of the layperson, we see that two perspectives found voice. In Hermas himself, however, we appear to have an heir to the tradition of Joel, in which the spirit alighted "even upon the menservants and maidservants" (Joel 2.29; Acts 2.18).

The problems inherent in extensive divine revelation quickly arose to confront church leaders. As Christianity rapidly spread among the heterogeneous peoples of Rome's Mediterranean empire, novel conceptions concerning the Christian life and afterlife were introduced by Christian converts steeped in the traditions of the religious communities to which they had formerly belonged. With the passing of the first apostolic generation, church

[21] Hermas, we are told, suffered from "double-mindedness" or spiritual doubt. When asked by an angel to identify the beautiful, aged lady in his vision, his first response was to identify her as the Sibyl before being informed that she represented "the Church." *The Shepherd of Hermas*, Vision I.i.3, trans. and intro. G. F. Snyder (London, 1968); also trans. Kirsopp Lake, Loeb, vol. 25 (Cambridge, Mass., 1913). Lady Church's warning against the "double-mindedness" of apostasy was of particular concern as persecution loomed upon the horizon. On the impact of the Roman oracular tradition on Christianity see Bernard McGinn, "Teste David cum Sibylla: The Significance of the Sibylline Tradition in the Middle Ages," in *Women of the Medieval World: Essays in Honor of John H. Mundy*, ed. Julius Kirschner and Suzanne Fonay Wemple, pp. 7–35 (Oxford, 1985), and Fox, *Pagans and Christians*, pp. 168–261.

[22] *Shepherd of Hermas*, Vision II.iv.3. The four visions section was probably appended at a slightly later date. Amat, *Songes*, p. 10, strongly argues for the influence of this work on the later Donatist passions.

[23] *Shepherd of Hermas*, Mandate 11.9. See J. Reiling, *Hermas and Christian Prophecy: A Study of the Eleventh Mandate* (Leiden, 1973), which focuses on the importance of "congregational prophecy."

[24] *Shepherd of Hermas*, Vision III.iv.3.

leaders were confronted by marginally Christian groups whose reliance on divine revelation through dreams and visions threatened the spiritual authority of church leaders and who also advanced new scriptures and new interpretations of scripture. In some communities dreams and visions suggested new and more elaborate systems of spiritual elitism and particularized salvation, with the consequence that they distanced themselves not only from ordinary Christians but also from the clergy who ministered to them. Church leaders, primarily the monarchical episcopate, affirmed that definitive authority on questions of faith and religion was restricted to the writings and sayings of the first apostolic generation.[25] Episcopal authority, the bishops avowed, rested on their fidelity to the apostolic tradition and their mission to preserve and interpret it.[26] Consequently, they argued, the new prophecies of Christian sectarians carried no weight in the face of scripture.

The earliest visionary challenge to the Church's version of scripture and exegesis came from the myriad gnostic sects that mushroomed in the early centuries. Gnostic Christians rejected the static, conservative tendencies of the Catholic movement in favor of a self-renewing faith guided by special knowledge imparted in dreams and visions. The apostles, they argued, had continued to receive visionary infusions after Pentecost in order to be spiritually capable of fulfilling their apostolic duties.[27] Likewise the apostles' successors must be open to fresh revelation, they maintained, enabling them to attain greater authority in spiritual matters than the original apostles.[28] Turning their critical eyes to the story of creation, they found in the story of Adam's sleep confirmation of their distrust for the God of the Old Testament. For as the author of one gnostic text explained, it was not sleep but forgetfulness which God imposed upon Adam in Eden: "It is not the way Moses wrote and you heard. For he said in his first book, 'He put him to

[25] See Elaine Pagels, "Visions, Appearances and Apostolic Authority: Gnostic and Orthodox Traditions," in *Gnosis: Festschrift für Hans Jonas*, ed. B. Aland (Göttingen, 1978), pp. 415–30. That Christ "appeared" to the disciple in corporeal form rather than in a vision was considered important evidence for the doctrine of Christ's bodily resurrection. "Apparitio," then, was the usual term to describe the Pentecostal sightings. Ambrosiaster's commentary on 1 Cor. 15.7, *CSEL* 81.ii, p. 166, makes this point clear: "Deinde apparuit Iacobo. Singulari Iacobo apparuit et Petro. Quod ideo putum factum, ut multifaria adparentia fidem resurrectionis firmaret."

[26] Pagels, "Visions, Appearances," pp. 416–17; Hans F. Campenhausen, *Ecclesiastical Authority and Spiritual Power in the Church of the First Three Centuries*, trans. J. A. Baker (London, 1969), originally *Kirchliches Amt und geistliche Vollmacht* (Tübingen, 1953).

[27] On gnostic visionaries see Pagels, "Visions, Appearances," pp. 415–430. Christ's disciples, which according to gnostic tradition included Mary Magdalene, required additional visionary infusions in order to make them spiritually capable of fulfilling their apostolic duties. *Letter of Peter to Philip*, ed. Marvin W. Meyer and Frederik Wisse, in *The Nag Hammadi Library in English*, ed. James M. Robinson, 3d ed. (San Francisco, 1988), pp. 431–37. In the *Dialogue of the Saviour* (*Corp. Gnost.* 3.5), three disciples, Matthew, Mary Magdalene, and Judas Thomas, were chosen to receive special visions disclosing secrets of the cosmos, and were further taught to discriminate between temporal visions and the eternal vision of God. *Nag Hammadi Library*, p. 251; see Pagels, "Visions, Appearances," p. 422.

[28] Thus Jesus' earthly ministry was only the first step in a continuous process of humanity's spiritual maturing; the teachings of Jesus through the medium of visions were perceived as a wellspring of divine knowledge and revelation. Pagels, "Visions, Appearances," p. 422.

sleep' but it was in his perception." [29] One religious community held that it had Adam's own account of his visionary ascent.[30] In none of these gnostic traditions was knowledge of the divine through visions accessible to all. The gnostics considered themselves an elite and their philosophy was imparted only to the initiate. It was precisely the ability to handle visions and assess them correctly which distinguished the gnostic. For that reason, though many Christian theologians recoiled from gnostic visionary claims, they did not disagree fundamentally with the gnostics on the issue of visionary access.

Though early church fathers expended considerable quantities of ink disputing with the abhorred gnostics, these alien-thinking groups were in many ways less threatening than Christian movements whose theology appeared to be completely orthodox. The Christian sect which claimed to speak with the Spirit and which drew most of the Church's fire in the early centuries was Montanism.

In the isolated regions of Phrygia, in the second century, a self-styled prophet named Montanus, accompanied by two prophetesses, Maximilla and Priscilla, began to preach. Emboldened by the Holy Spirit which they believed spoke through them, they promulgated a set of moral directives that included eschewing marriage and promoting a rigorous purity of life.[31] Recapturing the New Testament's sense of the imminence of the last days, the priestess Maximilla proclaimed that she would be the last prophet before the heavenly Jerusalem descended upon their little Phrygian village of Pepuza.[32] For, as these new prophets understood it, the Holy Spirit had finally descended as promised by Christ, and the end of times was near.

Montanist revelations and interpretations did not set out to oppose Chris-

[29] *The Apocryphon of John* 2.1, ed. Frederik Wisse, *Nag Hammadi Library*, p. 111. Similarly, in the *Tripartite Tractate* ed. Harold W. Attridge, Elaine E. Pagels and Dieter Mueller, *Nag Hammadi Library* pp. 75–76, dreams were described as impeding thought or mental acuity. These views are a complete reversal of Judaeo-Christian tradition which follows Philo's observation that "it is when the mind has gone to sleep that perception begins." *Allegorical Interpretation* 2.25. In its use of the term "ecstasy," the Greek version of Adam's sleep becomes something more than restfulness or imagination for the mind; it becomes a mode of perception—of vision.

[30] *The Apocalypse of Adam*, *Nag Hammadi Library*, pp. 277–86. This account is probably only one of many that circulated in gnostic circles. The sixth-century pseudo-Gelasian decretal condemns a text entitled "poenitentia Adae," which is evidence that Adamite apocrypha were long-lived. *PL* 62, 537–40.

[31] According to Tertullian, *On Modesty* 21.7, the Paraclete proclaimed it would not pardon sin (as was the practice of the Church), lest such action encourage further sin. *De pudicitia*, ed. Munier and Micaelli, SC 394, 395 (1993); also ed. Eligius Dekkers, pp. 1279–1330, CC 2 (Turnhout,1954). On Montanus see Eusebius, *The Ecclesiastical History* 5.16, trans. Kirsopp Lake and J. G. L. Oulton, *Loeb* 2 vols. (1926–32); Fox, *Pagans and Christians*, pp. 405–10; Timothy D. Barnes, *Tertullian: A Historical and Literary Study* (orig. 1971; Oxford, 1985), pp. 42–48, 77–84, 130–42, 329; Pierre de Labriolle, *La Crise montaniste* (Paris, 1913); and Campenhausen, *Ecclesiastical Authority* pp. 178–212. Montanus flourished c. 170. See also F. C. Klawiter, "The Role of Martyrdom and Persecution in Developing a Priestly Authority of Women in Early Christianity: A Case Study of Montanism," *Church History* 49 (1980), 251–61.

[32] Epiphanius, *Panarion* 48.2.4, ed. Ronald E. Heine, *The Montanist Oracles and Testimonia* (Macon, Ga., 1989), p. 3.

tian doctrine. Even their detractors recognized that Montanist views largely conformed to Christian teaching, and, at least initially, their views found powerful allies in the Church.[33] Their revelations did not threaten the fabric of the scriptures or the Church's organization, but rather they challenged its sense of historical timing. Their conviction that the Holy Spirit called the Church to the dawning of a new, more rigorous age of spiritual observance was rooted in the gospel. Had not Paul envisaged a time when Christians would progress to a mature spiritual understanding; when childish things would pass away? Montanus' call for Christians to prepare for the final days was congruent with the promises of scripture, although there is evidence that already in the second century certain communities were being warned that the end of times was not imminent.[34] It was not, therefore, primarily on scriptural grounds that the Church faulted the sect but rather because of its visible nonconformity.

The gnostics had kept their activities strictly to themselves. But the Montanists, mindful of the urgency of their timetable, encouraged their members to travel to populous communities, cities and military camps to spread their teachings.[35] Both inside churches and outside them, their combination of exhortation and ecstatic fervor drew public attention to their cause. Later, admittedly unsympathetic sources indicated that during these ecstatic trances they spoke in tongues, in words which were "unintelligible, and frenzied, and totally obscure." These spiritual mumblings were then interpreted by another member of the community.[36]

Whatever our later sources' distaste for such public display, it was evidently a potent attraction. Even allowing that orthodox writers may have exaggerated the disorderliness of their frenzy, it was this public, popular aspect of their presence in the community which drew most fire from their adversaries. How was it possible, orthodox opinion asked, that the Holy Spirit could inhabit and seemingly possess the bodies of these so-called prophets? Was not their claimed possession by the Spirit in fact possession by a demon?[37]

In response to orthodox attacks on their ecstatic trances, the new prophets and their supporters sought scriptural justification for their activities, which they believed they found in Adam's sleep in the Garden of Eden. It is important to note that both sides of the dispute relied on the Greek translation of

---

[33] Origen, *On the Epistle to Titus*: "Indeed some have properly raised the question whether those who have the name of Cataphrygians [Montanists] ought to be called a heresy or a schism." *Montanist Oracles*, trans. Heine, p. 9.

[34] *Shepherd of Hermas*, Vision III.viii.9. When Hermas asked his angelic guide whether the end of times was near he was referred back to his vision of a tower (the Church) being built, but not yet near completion.

[35] Origen, *Contra Celsum* 7.9, trans. Frederick Crombie, *Writings of Origen*, vol. 2, Ante-Nicene Christian Library 23 (Edinburgh, 1872).

[36] Ibid.

[37] Eusebius, *Ecclesiastical History* 5.16–17.

Genesis 2.21, which stated that God imposed an "ecstasy" upon Adam.[38] Montanists believed that Adam's ecstasy was the prototype for their own experiences—the possession of the soul by the Spirit during which the soul was necessarily removed from a full exercise of its own faculties (*amentia*). Their reading of Adam's ecstasy as a Spirit possession was entirely in keeping with a common understanding of the term, and in many circles, including gnostic Christian circles, the text had been traditionally understood in that way. However, confronted by Montanist claims, orthodox authors closed ranks and asserted that true prophecy did not entail ecstatic possession. Epiphanius of Cyprus, writing in the fourth century, assembled a mountain of scriptural evidence designed to undercut many common understandings of the term "ecstasy."[39] Adam's ecstasy, he maintained, did not entail an "ecstasy of wits and thoughts," for upon wakening Adam knew what was past and present, and he prophesied the future: "These were not the words of a man in ecstasy, nor of one not in full possession of his faculties, but the words of a man possessing a sound mind." The ecstasy experienced by Adam, he argued, was not the same thing as the frenzied possession reported of Montanus and his associates and thus was not an admissible precedent for the prophetic movement.

Though the debate about Montanism centered on the public, visible aspect of their ecstatic trances, Montanist prophets also relied on private dreams. According to one (possibly spurious) source, Christ came dressed as a woman to one of the prophetesses in her sleep.[40] Likewise, during the persecution of Christians in the second and third centuries, Montanist-inspired passions of the martyrs, especially in North Africa, set great store in dreams that were related to their companions and then published for wider public consumption; for "of greater repute are those things newly revealed, all the more for their being new, according to the abundance of grace decreed for the last periods of time."[41] The Montanists' private revelations through dreams were less easily refuted by orthodox writers than their waking vi-

---

[38] In Greek and early Latin editions, Adam's "deep sleep" was rendered as "ecstasy." See n. 16 above.

[39] Epiphanius, *Panarion* 48.4.4 ff. Epiphanius noted the variety of meanings attached to the word (amazement, fear, different state of perception), but he focused on only one: madness (48.4.6). Epiphanius wrote his critique of Montanist revelations over a century after the dispute began, yet still theological impulse was to amass scriptural ammunition to dismiss Montanist visionary claims.

[40] Epiphanius, *Panarion* 49.1. Perhaps not a genuine oracle; see D. E. Groh, "Utterance and Exegesis: Biblical Interpretation in the Montanist Crisis," in *The Living Text*, ed. D. E. Groh and J. Jewett (New York, 1985).

[41] *Passio SS. Perpetuae et Felicitatis*, ed. and trans. W. H. Shewring (London, 1931). There is much in this text to suggest that it was influenced by Montanism, contra H. Leclercq, "Perpétue et Felicité," cols. 393–444, *DACL* 14.i. (1939). See also Fox, *Pagans and Christians*, pp. 401–3. For a literary and psychological study of Perpetua's visions see Peter Dronke, *Women Writers of the Middle Ages: A Critical Study of Texts from Perpetua (d. 203) to Marguerite Porete (d. 1310)* (Cambridge, 1984).

sions and trances, perhaps because of wide acceptance of dreaming as a medium for divine communication.

The Church's experience with the Montanist movement taught it to be suspicious of visionary claims calling for a new and more rigorous asceticism. Clerical calls for moderation in ascetic practices (couched in cautions to avoid pride) echoed in future confrontations with visionary ascetics, and helped to solidify the arguments against the millenarian views that continued to circulate in the Mediterranean world. Although ultimately condemned by Rome, the Montanist movement continued to find adherents into the third century, especially in North Africa. As the Church grappled with the sporadic persecutions to which the Roman authorities subjected them, the bravery of Montanist martyrs was chronicled in vision-rich passions. Their most famous and vocal adherent was Tertullian, whose views on the importance of dreams, visions, and ecstasy were very influential in the early medieval period.

With the loss of Tertullian's treatise *On Ecstasy*, we must rely on his treatise *On the Soul* (*De anima*) for his views.[42] Although designed to refute pagan and heretical ideas on the subject, Tertullian's discussion of dreams relied perforce on pagan works and ideas whose traditions promoted the value of dreams as a means of divine communication.[43] Stoic ideas were especially favored in his work.[44] For Tertullian dreams were a gift from God to be added to *naturalis oraculum* or foresight, and he noted that veridical dreams were attested in *tota saeculi litteratura*.[45]

As a Montanist, Tertullian was sympathetic to the view that the activity of the Spirit was to be seen in the contemporary church. "For seeing that we acknowledge spiritual 'charismata,' or gifts, we too have merited the attainment of the prophetic gift. . . . We have now amongst us a sister whose lot it has been to be favoured with sundry gifts of revelation, which she experiences in the Spirit by ecstatic vision amidst the sacred rites of the Lord's day in the church; she converses with angels, and sometimes even with the Lord; she both sees and hears mysterious communications."[46] Likewise

---

[42] The treatise was written around the first decade of the third century, possibly as early as 206–207. Barnes, *Tertullian*, p. 55. Waszink dated the treatise between 210 and 213. *De anima*, CC 2 (1954), pp. 780–869. On Tertullian's dream theories see Amat, *Songes*, pp. 93–104, and Dulaey, *Le rêve*, pp. 55–56.

[43] *De anima* 46.2–3. There were skeptics in the ancient world, of course. Tertullian cites Aristotle and Epicurus as examples, but points out that some dreams must be true if only to satisfy the laws of probability and chance.

[44] Like the Stoic, Tertullian regretted the sleeper's lack of control over emotions—in dreams the sleeper experienced strong feelings such as fear or joy and thus in sleep fell short of the Christian and Stoic ideal of impassivity. Yet at the same time he held that sleep is necessary for the health of both body and mind and so could not be considered either irrational or unnatural. *De anima* 43.7, 45.6. Hence no soul is naturally free of dreams: "Dum ne animae aliqua natura credatur immunis somniorum" (49.3.). On Stoicism in Christian thought see Marcia Colish, *The Stoic Tradition from Antiquity to the Early Middle Ages*, vol. 2, Studies in the History of Christian Thought, 35 (Leiden, 1985), pp. 9–29.

[45] *De anima* 46.10–11.

[46] *De anima* 9, trans. Peter Holmes, *Ante-Nicene Christian Library* (Edinburgh, 1870).

in their dreams, combined with ecstasy, the Christian was enabled to know God. Tertullian's Pentecostal view in which Christians were given the gift of prophetic dreams is reflected in his reading of Adam's prophetic sleep. In his *De anima* he wrote: "Thus in the beginning was sleep set alongside ecstasy: 'And God sent an ecstasy upon Adam and he slept.' Sleep came upon the body for rest, ecstasy came to the soul to prevent it from rest."[47] Prevented from rest, the soul entertained dream images that were open to divine communication. Tertullian therefore accorded to dreams a very special place in Christian life, and he believed that through such means the faithful had been given access to knowledge of divine things.[48]

Considering further Tertullian's reading of Adam's sleep in the Garden of Eden, we encounter Adam's significance as archetypal dreamer. Adam's ecstatic sleep and subsequent awakening was a divine mystery prefiguring Christ's death and resurrection and thus, by extension, humanity's salvation: "For if Adam was a figure of Christ, then Adam's sleep was Christ's death . . . a sleep from which he ultimately awoke, just as Christ was resurrected."[49] He continued: "This is why sleep is so salutary, so rational, and is actually formed into the model of that death which is general and common to the race of man. . . . If you only regard it as the image of death, you initiate faith, you nourish hope, you learn both how to die and how to live, you learn watchfulness, even as you sleep."[50]

Adam thus foreshadowed the lot of Everyman who in sleeping and waking daily experienced in symbolic form death and resurrection. Tertullian believed this mystery was a gift from God, for "God willed . . . to set before us . . . by daily recurrence the outlines of man's state, especially concerning the beginning and termination thereof."[51] The superficial inactivity of the sleeping body provided the Christian with a daily reminder of the beginning and end of human life,[52] and the wakefulness of the soul in dreams opened a gateway to divine communication.

Tertullian, however, was very aware of the dangers of accepting certain types of visionary experience. He warned that dreams did not always come

---

[47] *De anima* 45.3: "Sic et in primordio somnus cum ecstasi dedicatus: 'et misit deus ecstasin in Adam et dormiit.' Somnus enim corpori provenit in quietam, ecstasis animae accessit adversus quietam, et inde iam forma somnum ecstasi miscens et natura de forma."

[48] See Waszink, *De anima*, p. 6.

[49] *De anima* 43.10: "Si enim Adam de Christo figuram dabat, somnus Adae mors erat Christi." See also Plato, *Timaeus* 29.3, and Clement of Alexandria, who examined Plato's discussion in *Republic* 7 on sleep and death as signifying the descent of the soul, and saw in awakening an allegory for the Lord's resurrection. *Stromates* 5.14, ed. A. Le Boulluec and P. Voulet, SC 278 (1981).

[50] *De anima* 43.

[51] *De anima* 43.11: "Voluit enim deus, et alias nihil sine exemplaribus in sua dispositione molitus . . . humani vel maxime initii ac finis lineas cotidie agere nobiscum."

[52] The currency of such a belief is not hard to understand. From a purely observational standpoint, a sleeping person appeared to be in a state which resembled death: the body was immobile, breathing shallow, and the "activity of the soul" in dreams was not apparent. It was commonly believed that so deep a sleep could descend upon a man that he could be mistaken for dead.

from God; they also came from diabolical spirits and from the natural activity of the soul. He also denounced gnostic Christians who privileged postapostolic visionary revelations over scripture, and urged their submission to the authority of presbyters and bishops.[53] But within the parameters of the orthodox Christian community, he advanced expansive ideas of visionary access:

> But from God who has promised indeed, "to pour out the grace of the Holy Spirit upon all flesh, and has ordained that his servants and his handmaids should see visions as well as utter prophecies," must all those visions be seen as emanating, which may be compared to the actual grace of God, as being honest, holy, prophetic, inspired, instructive, inviting to virtue, the bountiful nature of which causes them to overflow even to the profane, since God, with grand impartiality, "sends his showers and sunshine on the just and on the unjust." . . . and almost the greater part of mankind get their knowledge of God from dreams.[54]

It was an opinion which, as we have seen, Ambrose echoed almost two centuries later.[55] But Tertullian's confidence in dreams and visions as a source for continued inspiration in the Church was not shared by all; his Montanist leanings alienated many later thinkers from his works. Augustine, for example, never cited him as an authority on dreams. Nevertheless, Tertullian's argument was an important one. As the first of his species, Adam was the image of Everyman, the archetype for the Christian sleeper whose dreams continued to have in them something of the divine. His writings supported an unrestricted or universalist model of relatively open access to divine dreams. (It is important to note, however, that Tertullian was not the originator of this interpretation of Adam's sleep. It was fairly common in the second century and echoes can be found in the early middle ages.[56])

With the fourth century, peace finally came to the Church. The Emperor Constantine was converted to Christianity and won his famous victory over the pagan general Maxentius after seeing a vision of the Cross in the sky.[57] The persecution of Christians ceased, and as Romans flocked to the religion of their emperor, attention focused on the professionally holy: the clergy and the monks of the desert. The problem of heresy did not disappear, of course. By the fourth century, the challenge of the second-century brand of Christian gnosticism had been transformed though not eliminated. Valentinian gnos-

---

[53] On Tertullian against gnostic visionaries see Pagels, "Visions, Appearances," pp. 428–30.

[54] *De anima* 47.

[55] See n. 9 above.

[56] *The Treastise on the Apostolic Tradition of St. Hippolytus of Rome, Bishop and Martyr*, ed. Gregory Dix (London 1968) 3.36.6: "Whereby he made the dawn of another day at the beginning of his sleep, fulfilling the type of his resurrection."

[57] Eusebius, *Life of Constantine*, 28, trans. Ernest Cushing Richardson, *Nicene and Post-Nicene Fathers*, Second Series, vol. 1 (Grand Rapids, Mich., 1904). Fox, *Christians and Pagans*, pp. 613–19, contributes to the debate surrounding the historicity of Constantine's vision.

ticism continued to be a scourge to Arian and Catholic authorities, especially on the eastern frontiers of the empire, into the fifth century.[58] Another group, the Manichees, held the attention of the Church in the fourth century. This sect followed the teachings of their founder Mani, a visionary executed by the Persian government in A.D. 276.[59] He claimed to be an "apostle" of Christ who had received direct revelation concerning the nature of God and Man, and the division of the cosmos into good and evil, light and darkness. Although relatively little is known about the secrets of the Manichees, their dualism was inspired by a postapostolic revelation that ran counter to the teachings of the orthodox church. The most vigorous opponent of the Manichees in the late fourth century was Augustine of Hippo. Having spent some years as an adherent of the sect himself in his youth, Augustine was well placed to challenge their views. It was in the context of Manichaean error that Augustine first came to a critical assessment of dreams and visions. However, Augustine soon moved beyond antiheretical polemic to research the phenomenon from a position more central to Christian concerns.

Augustine: Restricted Access

Although Augustine was to return to the subject at various times in the latter part of his career, the first work in which he made an in-depth study of the visionary experience was the final book of his *On the Literal Interpretation of Genesis*.[60] The completion of the work was much anticipated by his friends and the clergy. Evodius, the bishop of Uzalis and Augustine's longtime friend, wrote long letters asking obscure questions which Augustine at first answered and then put off by referring Evodius to his forthcoming publication.[61] When it finally appeared, the disappointment of his correspondents was profound. Rather than providing specific guidelines for the Christian response to the visionary experience, Augustine had fashioned an

---

[58] Giovanni Filoramo, *A History of Gnosticism*, trans. Anthony Alcock (Oxford, 1990), p. 171.

[59] On Mani and Manichaeism see Peter Brown, *Augustine of Hippo: A Biography* (London, 1967), pp. 45–60; W. H. C. Frend, "The Gnostic-Manichaean Tradition in Roman North Africa," *Journal of Ecclesiastical History* 4 (1953), 13–26; Samuel N. C. Lieu, *Manichaeism in the Later Roman Empire and Medieval China* (Manchester, 1985).

[60] *De Genesi ad litteram*, CSEL 28, ed. Joseph Zycha (Vienna, 1894), pp. 3–345; trans. with notes, John Hammond Taylor, *Ancient Christian Writers*, vols. 41, 42 (New York, 1982). See also Taylor, "The Text of Augustine's *De Genesi ad litteram*," *Speculum* 25 (1950), 87–93.

[61] In 414, just before Augustine's treatise was complete, Evodius wrote two letters to Augustine concerning visions, of which only one survives, *Ep.* 158, and Augustine's replies, *Epp.* 159, 162. *S. Aureli Augustini Hipponiensis episcopi epistulae III*, ed. Alois Goldbacher, pp. 488–97, CSEL 44 (Vienna, 1904). Evodius had been with Augustine in Italy and converted to Christianity just before him. They established a monastic community in Thagaste upon their return to North Africa until each in turn was called to episcopal office. Their correspondence reveals a fraternal friendship.

epistemological theory of vision, or perception, which owed much to Neo-platonic mysticism. Only occasionally did it address dreams and visions as a concrete concern to the Christian community. Still, Augustine's position as an authority on the subject was assured by the work, and in the final years of his life his thoughts returned often to the issue, most notably in a letter to Paulinus of Nola commonly known as *On the Care to Be Had for the Dead* and in the final chapters of the *City of God*.[62]

It is in his letter to Paulinus that we come closest to seeing the essential difficulties which the visionary phenomenon posed to the Church. In addressing the issue of the care of the dead, Paulinus and his contemporaries were familiar with stories in which the dead returned to the living in dreams and apparitions, demanding proper burial.[63] In his letter to Paulinus, Augustine owned that he was somewhat baffled by the problems these stories posed. On the one hand, he was very skeptical that dreams and visions could be the vehicle for the dead to reappear to the living for whatever purpose. Most reports of seemingly prophetic dreams were, he argued, coincidences which were later remembered, as opposed to the many uncoincidental dreams that were forgotten. But this argument did not explain those cases that were accepted as genuine by Christian tradition.

Approaching the question of the visions from the dead from the point of view of the departed saint, Augustine questioned the proposition which such visions implied. He questioned whether, having once experienced the delights of heaven, the dead would willingly return to the cares of the world. But even if the dead *were* willing to forgo such pleasures temporarily, Augustine had to believe that they could not. Poignantly, he offered a personal perspective: "[T]o say nothing of others, there is my own self, whom my pious mother would no night fail to visit. . . . Far be the thought that she should, by a life more happy, have been made cruel."[64] Monica must surely have appeared to him if there was any way in which she could. Yet, as Augustine admitted, the weight of orthodox opinion was against such categorical assertions. "These things if we shall answer to be false, we shall be thought impudently to contradict the writings of certain faithful men, and the senses of them who assure us that such things have happened to themselves." Augustine's solution was to aver that such cases may be explained as the work of angels; that perhaps occasionally to bolster faith, God sent prophetic and revelatory visions in which the special dead seemed to appear

[62] *De cura pro mortuis gerenda*, ed. Joseph Zycha, *CSEL* 41 (Vienna, 1900), pp. 619–60; *PL* 40 (1845) 698–708.

[63] The question of whether the souls of the dead visited the living in their dreams was regularly discussed by early Church writers. The tenacity of this belief in Christian circles derived from pagan reverence for the *manes*. Ultimately, however, the strength of such ideas was rooted, as Augustine was aware, in the psychological need of the bereaved and the influence of a heavy conscience on the imagination.

[64] Augustine, *De cura* 16.

to the living.[65] Such cases, he emphasized, were not of a usual nature. He cited examples from the Old Testament to show that God occasionally revealed knowledge of supernatural things to the prophets, but only on a need-to-know basis. Martyrs were another caveat to the rule. They were privileged to receive divine visions before martyrdom (a commonly held belief) and to benefit the suppliants at their tombs thereafter. This concession to the natural order of things is made, Augustine supposed, to increase the Christian faith for which they died, although whether the martyrs themselves appeared, or angels who took upon themselves the outward appearance of the martyrs, he could not decide.

While accepting that the saints *could* appear to the benefit of the Christian community, Augustine reasoned that such events must be rare, and confined to the experience of exceptional individuals. Yet he did not eliminate the crowd in their witness of the extraordinary. He allowed that St. Felix of Nola had appeared to the inhabitants of Nola as he defended their city from barbarian attack. To eliminate the possibility that the ordinary Christian could witness and thus benefit from such a supernatural episode would be to impoverish the meaning of the miracle as instruction to the faithful. Consequently Augustine was more concerned to restrict the class of veridical apparition than to restrict the identity of the visionary recipient.

Augustine reveals his views on visionary access most tellingly in his commentaries on Adam's sleep in the Garden of Eden. For Augustine, Adam's ecstatic sleep and prophecy indicated his special status, and enabled him to "participate with the host of angels and, entering into the sanctuary of God, understand what was finally to come." [66] We may suppose that when Augustine envisaged Adam seeing events to come, he believed Adam's vision concerned the final days of human history and not specifically the Fall. Augustine believed that Adam's vision encompassed the beginning and the end of human experience, and that he came to know in his ecstasy the contours of the end of history just at that moment when he was participating (albeit passively) in the beginning of earthly existence.

In an earlier work, *Against the Manichees*, Augustine had likewise called attention to the prophetic aspect of Adam's sleep, as signifying "hidden wisdom." To accomplish this interpretation he suggested that sleep itself is a channel into the "realm of intelligence," a falling away from earthly, mundane reality with its obfuscations and distractions, to enter into a realm of

[65] Ibid. Augustine proposed that the visions of martyrs and other deceased could be angels who donned the outward appearance or image of the person recognized by the beholder. The righteous dead were thereby no longer fatigued by the cares of the world. See Augustine's further discussion in his *Treatise on the Soul and Its Origin*, ed. Carolus Urba and Joseph Zycha, CSEL 60 (Vienna, 1913), pp. 301–419; trans. Peter Holmes and Robert Ernest Wallis, *A Select Library of Nicene and Post-Nicene Fathers, St. Augustine*, vol. 5 (Edinburgh, 1887), pp. 309–71.

[66] Augustine, *De Genesi ad litteram* 9.19.

higher knowledge, the realm of the intellect.[67] Sleep provided the state in which the soul was removed from bodily senses and thus contemplated what was "interior and hidden."[68] Thus for Augustine, Adam's dream fit the paradigm of the special case, of God's chosen recipient of arcane knowledge.

In Augustine, then, we see an influential Church leader expressing the supremacy of the restricted model of visionary access. This clear shift in exegetical interpretation between Tertullian in the second century and Augustine in the early fifth fits neatly with the idea of a shift in the religious values in late antiquity which has been often proposed but which must now be reassessed.[69]

In the first two or three centuries A.D. a number of Christian groups claimed that the full, mature message of Christ was being imparted to them through the Holy Spirit's gift of revelation. This charismatic assurance sat well with the Pentecostal beginnings of the Christian community, to which these sects invariably appealed. However, supplemental messages of this genre were rarely sufficiently tactful of clerical institutions and practices to be endorsed by clerics and Christian communities that embraced these free thinkers were generally marginal or rapidly became so. An alternative view of visionary access developed in which divine visions were restricted to specific people, times, and places. It has long been argued that this was the position favored by the monarchical bishops after the Montanist scare of the second century. The Christian hierarchy thus began to question the divine origin of most dreams, honoring instead a quality of "uniqueness" in the experience of the apostles of the primitive Church who had preached and written under the guidance of the Holy Spirit. These apostolic writings, it is maintained, were regarded by the bishops as sacred and inviolable. In their view, the Spirit would continue its work in guiding the Church in its historical mission, but must not be regarded as a source of new teaching. Though this strictly dispensationalist interpretation of episcopal thought has been rightly challenged in recent years, nevertheless we can acknowledge that because the clerical conception of redemption was bound to a historical schedule, the implication of unrestricted community access to divine guidance was particularly unsettling and foreboding.[70] Fueled by clerical concerns about maintaining spiritual and thus other types of authority in their communities,

[67] Augustine, *Two Books on Genesis against the Manichees* 2.12, trans. Roland J. Teske, Fathers of the Church, 84 (Washington, 1991).

[68] Essentially what Augustine described here in Adam's sleep was a state of ecstasy, and by the time he came to write his *Literal Interpretation of Genesis* he was using a translation of Genesis which employed the equivalent Latin term.

[69] Dodds, *Pagan and Christian*, and Brown, *Making of Late Antiquity*. Dissenting is Fox, *Pagans and Christians*, who stresses the early history of the moral visionary model and its continuity into later centuries.

[70] James L. Ash, "The Decline of Ecstatic Prophecy in the Early Church," *Theological Studies* 37 (1978), 227–52, reviews the history of the dispensationalist position. Ash attributes the currency of this view to Protestant historians and proposes an alternative model of the second-century decline in prophecy to one in which the episcopate "captured" prophecy.

partisans of what may be termed the restrictionist movement preached the dangers of according unrestricted spiritual sanction to the dreams of their flock. As we have seen, Augustine is a good example of this line of thinking.

Still, even in the late fourth and early fifth centuries there were clerics who were very receptive to ideas of broad access to prophetic dreams. Synesius of Cyrene, bishop of Ptolemias from c. 410, wrote in his treatise *On Dreams*: "Let all of us devote ourselves to the interpretation of dreams, men and women, young and old, rich and poor, private citizens and magistrates, inhabitants of the town and of the country, artisans and orators. No one is privileged, either by sex, age, fortune or profession. Sleep offers itself to all: it is an oracle always ready, and an infallible and silent counsellor."[71] Admittedly Synesius was in some respects a special case. He was a Neoplatonist when he wrote the treatise and only avowed Christianity when he was hastily thrust into episcopal office. Thus it might be argued that *On Dreams* was the work of a pagan and should not be considered valid for assessing Christian views. Yet Synesius was not unrepresentative of many clergy at the turn of the fifth century who were schooled in classical and philosophic learning before being co-opted into the Christian leadership. One might argue, rather, that Synesius' determined confidence in the oracular nature of dreams would have been shared by the many other bishops whose culture changed more slowly than their avowed religion. Synesius' view that no dreamer was more privileged than another was clearly in counterpoint to the privileging ideas of his contemporary Augustine—although Synesius, like many devotees of philosophic schools advocated a sober lifestyle to enhance interpretive abilities.[72] Thus at the turn of the fifth century both universal and restrictive ideas of access were current among the Christian elite.

I have outlined these two ideologies in ways that suggest a polarization of Christian opinion which if consistently applied might have led to a rupture within the Church. But neither of these positions was rigidly defined or unquestioningly adopted by the clergy; as we shall see, most clerics hovered between the two and set about, on a case-by-case basis, to mediate between disparate views on the subject. Church theologians likewise tended to mediate rather than dichotomize. But the ramifications of the two ideologies for the Christian community did provide an undercurrent of tension which explains the often discordant tones of patristic and hence Romano-Gallic and Merovingian opinion. The rhetoric of merit which we encountered in Gre-

---

[71] Synesius, *De insomniis* 16, PG 66, 1281–1320. Trans. Naphtali Lewis, *The Interpretation of Dreams and Portents in Antiquity* (Wauconda, Ill., 1996); see also Jay Bregman, *Synesius of Cyrene. Philosopher-Bishop.* (Berkeley, 1982).

[72] *De insomniis* 14: "The best profit we are able to obtain is to render the spirit healthy, and elevate the soul; also it is religious exercise which renders us apt at divination. Many in their desire to foresee the future have renounced the excesses of the table so as to live sober and temperate lives; they have kept their bed pure and chaste: for the man who desires to make his bed like the tripod of Delphi will carefully refrain from rendering it a witness of nocturnal debauches; he prostrates himself before God to pray."

gory of Tours' discussion of visions derives, I maintain, from his adherence at an intellectual level to the restricted philosophy of divine dreaming filtered through the privileged medium of hagiography. But had the alternative tradition of more universal access to divine dreams disappeared? Had the third person of the Trinity gone underground, as Dodds maintained? The answer is no. Indeed the unrestricted or extended access view was reiterated throughout the middle ages.

Pope Gregory the Great: Between Two Traditions

Turning to the writings of Pope Gregory I at the beginning of the seventh century, we find that at different times he articulated both the restricted and unrestricted argument. Much had happened in the intervening centuries. The western Mediterranean world had been indelibly altered by the infusion of Germanic peoples and customs. The Church suffered disruptions and hard times but emerged into the sixth and seventh centuries with new strengths, especially in the expansion of the cult of martyrs and saints under ecclesiastical auspices.

Pope Gregory wrote two important and widely read works that touched on dreams and visions. In the first, the *Dialogues*, he used copious dream and vision anecdotes, combined with some rudimentary philosophical observations on the nature and activities of the human soul, to support the Christian belief in the life of the soul after death.[73] With its lively accounts of admonitory dreams and deathbed visions, the work was conceived as a didactic undertaking. In his massive commentary on the book of Job, a less accessible work, Gregory considered the place of dreams and visions in the wider context of God's historical plan for humanity.[74] Because Gregory's works are so different, both in style and in approach, it is not easy to render clearly his thinking on this subject. Rather we are left to balance against each other seemingly conflicting reminiscences of ancient debates.

Gregory was familiar with the thinking of both Tertullian and Augustine. Yet he was not simply reproducing earlier opinions when, at the beginning of the last book of his *Dialogues*, he discussed the consequences of Adam and Eve's transgression in the Garden of Eden: "In paradise he had habitually enjoyed converse with God and in purity of heart and loftiness of vision mingled with holy, angelic spirits. After falling from that noble state he also lost the inner light which enlightened his mind." Although mankind had lost

---

[73] Gregory the Great, *Dialogues*, SC 251, 260, 265, ed. Adalbert de Vogüé (1978–80); English translation by Odo John Zimmerman, Fathers of the Church, 39 (New York, 1959).

[74] Gregory the Great, *Moralia in Job*, CC 143, 3 vols., ed. Marc Adriaen (Turnhout, 1979–85); *Grégoire le Grand: Morales sur Job*, SC 32 (1952), 212 (1974), 221 (1975), ed. and trans. A. de Gaudemaris and A. Bocognano, intro. R. Gillet; *Morals on the Book of Job*, in 3 vols., by J. Bliss (Oxford, 1844–50).

the remembrance of paradise which Adam had enjoyed, Christians had been given a new life redeemed by Christ and thereafter guided by the Holy Spirit as a pledge of mankind's eventual inheritance.[75] It was against the background of this activity of the Spirit among the faithful that the many recent dreams and visions concerning the afterlife of the soul were being revealed. The Spirit's descent upon the Christian community at Pentecost, Gregory believed, was being mirrored in the Spirit's renewed activity as the end of times approached; the world of the Spirit was moving closer. Reflecting upon Redemptus' apocalyptic vision described at the close of book 3, with its signs that the things of the earth are slipping from man's grasp, Gregory saw mankind's duty clearly: to seek after the things of heaven with a new urgency.[76]

The millenarian atmosphere which flared up periodically in Italy as elsewhere in response to political and social crises must account at least in part for Gregory's attitude toward the visionary experience. Reports of supernatural visions had a dual significance: individually, a vision communicated a personal message; collectively, visions reported in large numbers suggested that the divinity was communicating a broader message to humankind. In pondering the eschatological significance of the visions be recorded, Gregory drew upon a familiar metaphor: society's death and resurrection portended in Adam's sleeping and awakening.

Pope Gregory explained to his deacon Peter that if the present life is like a dark night, and the life to come is the approaching day, there is a period before dawn, a "transitional hour," when darkness blends into light.[77] This morning twilight provided the image for the blending of the end of the present world with the beginning of the future world which, he believed, was even then occurring.[78] Gregory reprised the metaphor in his *Moralia in Job* where he associated night with the present life, and affirmed that he who longs for the approach of morning knows that his sight is imperfect.[79] For the Lord "visits us at dawn" and illuminates our darkness with the light of knowledge of himself.[80] The dawn approaches imminently, for "though

---

[75] Christ sent the Holy Spirit "as a pledge of our inheritance." *Dial.* 4.1. The coming of the Holy Spirit to the disciples is described in Acts 2.1–4. Whereas Augustine juxtaposes the Genesis account, in which mankind loses its spiritual vision, with Paul's rapture to the third heaven (the vision of a privileged Christian sage), Gregory emphasizes humankind's Fall as being redeemed by the Spirit's activity in the whole Christian community. Gregory's interest was in spiritual vision as a universal charism, rather than in analyzing the celestial path by which the individual soul would attain that vision.

[76] *Dial.* 3.38.

[77] *Dial.* 4.43.2: "Sed quemadmodum cum nox finiri et dies incipit oriri, ante solis ortum simul aliquo modo tenebrae cum luce conmixtae sunt."

[78] *Dial.* 4.43.2: "ita ut huius mundi finis iam cum futuri saeculi exordio permiscetur." The image works not only because of the ancient simile in which sleep is the image and a kind of anticipation of death, but because it also complies with the traditional idea concerning the optimal hour for experiencing a divinely inspired vision.

[79] *Mor. in Job* 23.39.

[80] *Ibid.*, 8.48.

heaven and earth abide henceforth and forever, still they are at this present time of themselves hastening on to nought." [81]

Gregory, who knew and absorbed much of Tertullian's thinking, would have been aware of this traditional metaphor which so aptly explained why as the things of the earth slipped away, revelatory dreams and visions were becoming such a rich and regular source of information on the nature of the life to come.[82] However, Gregory applied the metaphor to make a point that was different from Tertullian's. Tertullian used the metaphor to describe the fate of the individual soul as it confronted death. Gregory applied it to a wider canvass, to depict the eschatological fate of Christian society. This interpretation explained why so many individuals were being made aware of the supernatural world, and it supported the wide demographic base of Gregory's vision recipients.

Yet Gregory balanced his illustration of extended access to the supernatural with a parable involving a pregnant woman in a dungeon, whose meaning supported the opposing view. Before looking in greater detail at the parable, it is important to consider the context in which the discussion arose. Book 4 of Gregory's *Dialogues* opens with a discussion of the two foundations for religious belief. The first is experiential knowledge (*scire experimento*), which was imparted to humanity by the Holy Spirit to substitute for its lost memory of paradise.[83] To this appeal based on human experience Gregory added an allegory which focused on a second basis for religious belief: deference to a higher, external authority. The allegory drew its inspiration from a famous story in Plato's *Republic*, a work which was popular in antiquity and in the middle ages.[84]

In Gregory's garbled version of the story, a pregnant woman cast into a dungeon without light gave birth to a child who, because of the darkness, had never experienced sight. On hearing his mother describe things she had seen before her confinement, the child might doubt that her description was

---

[81] *Ibid.*, 5.63.

[82] It is not clear whether Gregory knew Tertullian's *De anima*. The positive attitude toward sleep expressed by Gregory and Tertullian, in which the daily physical experience of sleeping and waking stimulated daily contemplation on the end of human life and the resurrection to follow, is striking. It is no coincidence that the work of these two authors who chose to take up this theme should also be marked by a correspondingly high regard for the spiritual importance of dreams.

[83] For this first proposition, Gregory drew directly on Augustine's treatise *De fide rerum invisibilium*, CC 46 (Turnhout, 1969), ed. M. P. J. Van den Hout. Augustine's treatise had appealed to the universal human experience of real but invisible social and family ties such as the bonds of love and friendship, to show how we all believe in things we cannot see. Gregory adds the specific example of a young man's belief that his parents were truly his parents, even though he did not remember his conception and birth. In the *Moralia* Gregory returned to the theme of mankind's loss of vision as a consequence of the Fall (5.61).

[84] Augustine, *De fide*; Plato, *Republic* 7.1–2, trans. P. Shorey, Loeb 276 (Cambridge, Mass., 1935). De Vogüé discusses the history of this Platonic simile and Gregory's use of it in "Un avatar du mythe de la caverne," in *Homenaje a Fray Justo Perez de Urbel*, vol. 2 (Burgos, 1976), pp. 19–24.

real since he had no experience of them. Gregory suggested that humanity is born into a like darkness, a spiritual darkness, requiring belief in the experiential knowledge of the other world to be furnished by its spiritual parents. In this story Gregory addressed those who were not confident in their faith and asserted that they, like the little boy, should put their trust in the superior knowledge of their elders, *maiores*, who have experience of otherworldly knowledge through the Holy Spirit.[85]

The interpretation of the story depends on the identity of the *maiores* with whom Gregory identified the mother, for upon their word rests the ultimate authority on the realm of the invisible. Possible contenders includer the biblical holy men, the doctors and saints of the early church, and the Mother Church itself. G. Cracco has argued that the *maiores* are those in the present world who are imbued with the Spirit and who, with spiritual vision, testify to the invisible world around us.[86] Adalbert de Vogüé prefers that the mother in the story represents the faith of humanity which transmits the memory of primaeval happiness and the community of the Church, that is, the saints who testify to the future life by means of the Holy Spirit.[87] The *maiores* are "ceux qui nous précèdent par le temps et par le savoir."[88] In support of this view de Vogüé points out that most of Gregory's visionaries are not saints or holy men and so contemporary saints could not have been Gregory's intended meaning.[89] De Vogüé is surely wrong in limiting Gregory's *maiores* to historical figures who testify to the past and future life. Gregory's use of Plato's allegory referred just as clearly to the invisible world which was contemporaneous with the present life, but which because of mankind's spiritual blindness cannot be seen. This was the sense of Augustine's treatise *De fide rerum invisibilium* which Gregory used alongside Plato, and which stressed precisely this issue as well as its relevance to the afterlife.[90]

But de Vogüé is right about the prominence of lay visionaries in the *Dialogues*. Gregory did not confine genuinely inspired dreams to the experience of the saints; as becomes clear in a survey of the *Dialogues*, he credited the visions of laymen, minor clergy, and monks in roughly equal numbers. This belief signals a universalist element in Gregory's understanding of visionary access not articulated otherwise in his work. Gregory's visionaries were not necessarily saints, and they were imbued, for whatever reason, with temporary access to an imaged vision of spiritual significance, a spiritual insight perceived as external. That spiritual vision was a charism, a gift enjoyed by the faithful whether they be historical or contemporary figures. Gregory in-

---

[85] *Dial.* 4.1.5.

[86] G. Cracco, "Gregorio e l'oltre-tomba," in *Grégoire le Grand*, ed. J. Fontaine, R. Gillet, and S. Pellistrandi; (Paris, 1986), pp. 255–66.

[87] De Vogüé, *SC* 265, p. 20 n. 3.

[88] Ibid., p. 21, n. 5.

[89] De Vogüé, "Grégoire le Grand et ses 'Dialogues' d'après deux ouvrages récents," *Revue d'histoire ecclesiastíque* 83 (1988), 288.

[90] Augustine, *De fide*.

cluded himself when he wrote that those of "us" who have received the Spirit do not doubt the existence of the invisible life.[91] Elsewhere he alluded to the cave imagery again in order to assert that the breath of liberty is nigh.[92]

Gregory's writings struck a chord with the audience for which he wrote. His *Dialogues* especially was greatly admired and quickly disseminated. The eschatological context in which his vision accounts were framed had important repercussions for medieval attitudes toward dreams. Admonitory dreams and visions, in their collective strength alongside other supernatural phenomena or signs, were henceforth linked to the expectation of the final days. And although Gregory's account of the life of St. Benedict in book 2 of the *Dialogues* presented the reader with a model of the visionary saint, the wider picture presented by his works reflected what by the seventh century was the prevailing situation: the community of ordinary Christians had an important role as participant and witness to supernatural events, especially those which supported the values of clerical culture.

[91] *Dial* 4.1.4: "Quotquot ergo hunc Spiritum, hereditatis nostrae pignus, accepimus, de vita invisibilium non dubitamus."
[92] *Mor. in Job* 5.66: "standing at the entrance of our cave."

2 Daniel's Heirs: Visionary Ascetics in Gaul

Christian asceticism, in both its eremitic and cenobitic forms, had its genesis in the eastern Mediterranean world.[1] From perhaps as early as the mid third century, hermits and their disciples abandoned the secular world (largely urban) to pursue solitary lives of contemplation in the deserts of Egypt, Palestine, and Syria.[2] There, a distinctive wisdom literature was produced, based on the sayings of holy men whose principles shaped monastic rules for spiritual living.[3] In the East also, hagiographies exalting the spiri-

[1] Essential introductions to asceticism and monasticism in the East are: Derwas James Chitty, *The Desert a City: An Introduction to the Study of Egyptian and Palestinian Monasticism under the Christian Empire* (Oxford, 1966); Hugh Gerard Evelyn-White, *The Monasteries of the Wadi 'n Natrun*, vol. 2, *The History of the Monasteries of Nitria and Scetis* (New York, 1932); Peter Nagel, *Die Motivierung der Askese in der alten Kirche und der Ursprung des Mönchtums*, TU 95 (Berlin, 1966); A.-J. Festugière, *Les moines d'Orient*, 4 vols. (Paris, 1961–65); Philip Rousseau, *Pachomius: The Making of a Community in Fourth-Century Egypt* (Berkeley, 1985); Susanna Elm, *Virgins of God: The Making of Asceticism in Late Antiquity* (Oxford, 1994); John Binns, *Ascetics and Ambassadors of Christ: The Monasteries of Palestine, 314–631* (Oxford, 1994); and Hubertus Lutterbach, *Monachus factus est. Die Mönchwerdung im frühen Mittelalter*, Beiträge zur Geschichte des alten Mönchtums und des Benediktinertums, 44 (Münster, Westfalen, 1995).

[2] Christians were only one group among many which sought refuge in the desert from taxes, persecution, and family obligations. According to Jerome, Anthony had a precursor in Paul of Thebes, who was said to have lived in the desert since the persecution of Decius. *Vita s. Pauli*, PL 23, 17–30.

[3] Eastern ascetic literature is vast, and much is unpublished or inaccessible. Anonymous collections of sayings were widely disseminated in many different versions. Perhaps more than any other source they illuminate the pithy culture of desert monasticism. See *Les sentences des pères du désert: les apophthegmes des pères (recension de Pélage et Jean)*, ed. Jean Dion and Guy Oury, intro. by Lucien Regnault (Sablé-sur-Sarthe, 1966); *Les sentences des pères du désert: Série des anonymes*, ed. Lucien Regnault (Sablé-sur-Sarthe, Begrolles-en-Mauge, 1985); Helen Waddell, *The Desert Fathers* (Constable & Co. 1936); and William Bousset, *Apophthegmata. Studien zur Geschichte des ältesten Mönchtums* (Tübingen, 1923). Some ancient authors combined traditional sayings with their own insights, for example Palladius and Evagrius. See Cuthbert Butler, *The Lausiac History of Palladius*, 2 vols., Texts and Studies, 6.i–ii (Cambridge, 1898–1904); Antoine and Claire Guillaumont, intro., trans., and commentary, *Évagre le Pontique Traité practique ou le moine*, SC 170, 171 (1971).

tual focus of holy lives established the pattern and aspiration for the religious life for all Christians. Thus when ascetics and their disciples began to establish themselves in Gaul, the character of the monastic movement they produced there, as in the West generally, was profoundly influenced by eastern values and eastern monastic models.

In Gaul the ascetic life was primarily defined in a cenobitic environment, although its ideals were eremitically inspired and hermits were sometimes attached to or associated with these foundations.[4] Rhône valley monasticism, which produced some of the most influential promoters of the ascetic life in Gaul, was primarily cenobitic and Basilian.[5] As spiritual "relay stations" for eastern influence in Gaul (the phrase is Prinz's), the monastic centers of Lérins, Marseilles, and Lyons were particularly influential in determining the cenobitic future of Gaul. Cassian of Marseilles, like countless others, was of eastern origin and had trained in the Egyptian desert before arriving in Gaul. He was particularly influenced by the ascetic writings of the eastern monk Evagrius Ponticus and transmitted Evagrius' thinking to the West.[6] Others such as the north Gallic nobleman Honoratus, his brother Venantius, and his friend Caprasius traveled to the East to examine desert living firsthand. After his brother's death, Honoratus returned to found the island monastery of Lérins, which attracted many young men from northern Gaul.[7] Their vision of the contemplative life, the literature which they brought with them, and the literature which they produced in Gaul determined the flavor of monastic living in the West. Consequently, Gallic ascetics were reared on eastern values, eastern preoccupations, and eastern metaphors. They saw demons as Ethiopians in a country where there were none; they imported camel-hair shirts to wear and eastern herbs to eat; they sought the "desert" in the dense woods of Gaul and Germany; one young man even tried to im-

---

[4] Friedrich Prinz, *Frühes Mönchtum im Frankenreich. Kultur und Gesellschaft in Gallien, den Rheinlanden und Bayern am Beispiel der monastischen Entwicklung 4. bis 8. Jahrhundert*, 2d ed. (Darmstadt, 1988), pp. 112–17, distinguishes between and suggests contact points between Rhône valley and Aquitainian monasticism.

[5] The adoption of eastern rules by western monasteries disseminated eastern ascetic principles throughout Gaul. Lérins's rule has not survived, but based on the rules of foundations it influenced we know that the eastern rules of Basil, Pachomius, and Macarius (the latter possibly a version of the *Regula Magistri*) were influential. See V. Desprez and Adalbert de Vogüé, *Règles monastiques d'occident iv–vie siècle d'Augustin à Ferréol*, Vie monastique, vol. 9 (Bégrolles-en-Mauge, 1980).

[6] On the impact of Evagrian and Neoplatonic thought on western asceticism see Pierre Courcelle, *Late Latin Writers and their Greek Sources* (Cambridge, Mass., 1969) pp. 227–32; [translated from the French by Harry E. Wedeck, *Les Lettres Grecques en occident de Macrobe à Cassiodore*, 2d. ed. (Paris, 1948)]. Cassian of Marseilles, who had probably met Evagrius in Egypt, wrote the *Institutiones* (420–424) and *Conlationes* (426), which synthesized eastern influences for a western audience. *Jean Cassien, Institutions cénobitiques*, ed. Jean-Claude Guy, SC 109 (1965); *Jean Cassien, Conférences*, ed. Eugene Pichery, SC 42, 54, 64 (1955–59).

[7] Honoratus, founder of Lérins before 410, became bishop of Arles in 426. The account of his life, the *Sermo de vita s. Honorati*, ed. Marie-Denise Valentin, SC 235 (1977), was written by his episcopal successor Hilary of Arles.

itate Symeon the stylite, standing on a column through an icy winter in the forests of Trier until he was ordered down from it by his bishop.[8] Nevertheless, despite the intentionally mimetic quality of Gallic monasticism, ascetics in Gaul faced different challenges from those of their eastern brothers, and in adapting to new religious and political realities they set a different tone.

The visionary ascetic in Gaul was likewise profoundly influenced by eastern models. The Gallo-Merovingian visionary inherited a tradition in which monks and hermits were privileged seers, and yet the images and language by which they came to express that distinctiveness developed in these early centuries to reflect a more highly clericalized culture. As a result, the preoccupations of ascetic visionaries changed the spiritual culture of Gallic clerics too.

Visions and the Ascetic Life

In patristic and medieval sources there was general agreement that a life of renunciation and asceticism was a life pleasing to God. A life of renunciation would be hard, but as Athanasius noted of St. Anthony of Egypt, asceticism bore spiritual fruit and "visions are granted as a compensation for its hardships."[9] Visions might be the reward for the monk's fidelity to God, yet his life of sacrifice was also seen as validating those visions. In the Christian world the spiritual status of the visionary played an important role in his or her credibility, just as once in pagan oneirology the secular status of the dreamer determined the scope of the vision.[10] Among Christians, as Peter Brown so memorably put it, the holy man was the professional in a world of amateurs, who derived his spiritual and supernatural authority by virtue of a life of renunciation lived twenty-four hours a day.[11]

In the constellation of ascetic renunciations, fasting and celibacy were held to be sacrifices of particular significance and were often linked to prophecy

---

[8] On Ethiopians and Egyptians as emblems of the demonic see Franz Joseph Dölger, *Die Sonne der Gerechtigkeit und der Schwarze. Eine religionsgeschichtliche Studie zum Taufgelöbnis*, Liturgiewissenschaftliche Quellen und Forschungen, 14 (Münster, Westfalen, 1971; orig. pub. 1918), pp. 52–57; on eating imported herbs (St. Hospicius of Nice) see Gregory of Tours, *Historia Francorum* 6.6, ed. Bruno Krusch and Wilhelm Levison, *MGH, SRM* 1.1 (1937–42) (hereafter *HF*); on the stylite of Trier (St. Vulfolaic) see *HF* 8.15; on wearing camel-hair shirts see Sulpicius Severus, *Vita s. Martini* 10.

[9] Athanasius, *V. Antonii* 66, *PG* 26 (1887) 835–976, a reprint of Bernard de Montfaucon's 1698 edition; quoted translations are from Robert T. Meyer, *St. Athanasius, Life of St. Anthony*, Ancient Christian Writers, 10 (Westminster, Md., 1950).

[10] The status of the dreamer was an ancient determinant in dream interpretation. See Foucault, *Care of the Self*, part 1.

[11] Brown, *Making of Late Antiquity*, p. 6. See also Brown's study of the ascetic holy man, "The Rise and Function of the Holy Man in Late Antiquity," in Brown, *Society and the Holy*, pp. 103–52, first published in the *Journal of Roman Studies* 61 (1971), 80–101. Brown's reconsideration of this article appears in chapter 3 of his *Authority and the Sacred: Aspects of the Christianization of the Roman World* (Cambridge, 1995).

and divine dreams.[12] The seventh-century bishop Isidore of Seville, for example, noted that prayers penetrated heaven more easily through fasting. As he remarked in a chapter on abstinence, "Through fasting even the hidden things of the heavenly mysteries are revealed and the secrets of the divine sacrament are disclosed. For in this way Daniel was worthy to know, by an angel revealing it, the sacraments of the mysteries."[13] Thus for monks the example of the prophet Daniel provided a positive emblem for their visionary hopes, for in Daniel divine communication through visions had been linked to the ascetic life from the very start.[14]

Of course fasting was expected of all Christians at certain junctures in the liturgical year, but monks were more strictly bound to these rhythms. At the same time, the connection between fasting and visions troubled theologians, and their reservations filtered into ascetic literature. It was forbidden to Christians to seek actively after revelations by fasting, for that would be akin to pagan divination. Yet monks must fast. The main premise of the monastic life was that asceticism was necessary to restrain the body and train the soul; some monks even advocated dry fasts in their attempts to quell bodily desires.[15] However, purity of heart, not dreams and visions, was the ascetic's goal, and so fasting, though encouraged, was to be practiced in moderation. Alongside other asceticisms, fasting was preeminently the external means by which the monk developed internal discipline.[16] Any desire for unusually rigorous fasting was interpreted as a sign of dark forces at work; monks were warned that demons "encourage the weak to feats of fasting and those who are weighted down with illness to sing standing on their feet for long periods."[17] Visions might be the reward, but they could not be the goal of

[12] Rudolph Arbesmann, "Fasting and Prophecy in Pagan and Christian Antiquity," *Traditio* 7 (1949–51), 1–71.

[13] "1. Facilius per ieiunium oratio penetrat coelum. 2. Per ieiunium etiam occulta mysteriorum coelestium revelantur, divinique sacramenti arcana panduntur. Sic namque Daniel, angelo revelante, mysteriorum sacramenta cognoscere meruit." Isidore of Seville, *Sententiarum* 2.44, "De abstinentia," *PL* 83, 537–738.

[14] Anthony's visions and asceticism were likened to those of Daniel by Athanasius, *V. Antonii* 82.

[15] Evagrius Ponticus, *Praktikos* 91; intro., trans., and notes by John Eudes Bamberger, *Evagrius Ponticus: The Praktikos, Chapters on Prayer* (Kalamazoo, Mich., 1981). The Origenist Evagrius Ponticus was Bishop Nectarius of Constantinople's archdeacon when an illicit attraction to a married woman caused him to abandon the city and seek the ascetic life, first in Jerusalem, then at Nitria (Egypt), and thence to the seclusion of the Cells. Evagrius' teachings were known in the West and influenced Western asceticism. See Courcelle, *Late Latin Writers*, p. 229. On the dietary assumptions behind dry fasts see Aline Rouselle, *Porneia: On Desire and the Body in Antiquity* (Oxford, 1988), chap. 10. On Evagrius' teachings on visions see Antoine Guillaumont, *Aux origins du monachisme chrétien. Pour une phénoménologie du monachisme*, Spiritualité Orientale, no. 30 (Bégrolles-en-Mauges, 1979), pp. 144–47; on his teachings generally see pp. 185–212. See also Phillip Rousseau, *Ascetics, Authority, and the Church in the Age of Jerome and Cassian* (Oxford, 1978), pp. 251–53.

[16] Philip Rousseau, "Cassian, Contemplation, and the Coenobitic Life," *Journal of Ecclesiastical History* 26 (1975), 113–26.

[17] Evagrius, *Praktikos* 41. Translations of Evagrius' works are Bamberger's.

the hermit's hardships. So Athanasius, following well-established tradition, taught that the visions of the semiliterate hermit Anthony were directly linked to his commitment to the ascetic life, an ideal state pleasing to God.

Celibacy, unlike fasting, could not be practiced too rigorously by the monk; this renunciation too was linked with prophetic knowledge. Patristic writers believed that the Old Testament prophets (whom they also viewed as the first monks) were blessed with prophetic gifts because they lived the unsexed "angelic life." [18] Sex and sexual thoughts were distractions which alienated the Christian from true contemplation of the divinity and thus must be set aside if the monk was to enjoy the *vita angelica*. Through fasting and celibacy, alongside other monastic virtues (which with the rise of cenobiticism came to include communal living), the monk prepared for the beginnings of prophetic contemplation and prayer.

Prayer was at the heart of the monk's life and ideally should be practiced continuously. Sulpicius Severus noted of Martin of Tours that he was praying even when he appeared to be doing something else.[19] The primary purpose of this prayerful contemplation was spiritual and mental illumination. Sometimes this contemplation resulted in visions which could range from the Augustinian "intellectual vision" (sudden interior illumination or perception of the divine, with its momentary sense of unity with the divinity, effected without images) to the "spiritual" or "imaginative" visions of the imaged kind. Evagrius Ponticus (c. 345–399), whose works were widely read in Gaul, warned monks against the latter: "When you are praying, do not fancy the divinity like some image formed within yourself." [20] However, all monks could hope for the vision of God in the next life: "By true prayer a monk becomes another angel, for he ardently longs to see the face of the Father in Heaven." [21]

Counterbalancing this rosy picture of the visionary monk, however, was another equally crucial component of the ascetic life: demons. As witnessed by ascetic literature, the life of the monk, especially the holy man, was one of perpetual confrontation with demonic powers.[22] Holiness was tested by

---

[18] See John Bugge, *Virginitas: An Essay in the History of a Medieval Idea* (The Hague, 1975), pp. 41–47. "In early monastic thought it is clear that virginity remains a prerequisite for true Christian *gnosis*" (p. 44). Also see P. Suso Frank, Ἀγγελιχὸς βιος. *Begriffsanalytische und begriffsgeschichtliche Untersuchungen zum "engelgleichen Leben" im frühen Mönchtum*, Beiträge zur Geschichte des alten Mönchtums und des Benediktinerordens, 26 (Münster, Westfalen, 1964), pp. 57–61.

[19] Sulpicius Severus, *Vita sancti Martini* 26 (hereafter *VM*), ed. Carolus Halm, *Sulpicii Severi libri qui supersunt*, CSEL 1 (Vienna, 1866); *Sulpice Sévère, Vie de Saint Martin*, ed. Jacques Fontaine, *SC* 133–35 (1967–69).

[20] Evagrius, *153 Chapters on Prayer* 66; intro., trans., and commentary by Bamberger, *Evagrius*.

[21] Evagrius, *153 Chapters on Prayer* 113.

[22] For demons in Merovingian hagiography see František Graus, "Hagiographie und Dämonenglauben—Zur ihren Funktionen in der Merowingerzeit," in *Santi e Demoni Nell'Alto Medioevo Occidentale (Secoli V–XI)*, Settimane di studio 36, vol. 1 (Spoleto, 1989), pp. 93–120.

these conflicts of will and strategy with the devil and his minions, and the danger of being susceptible to demons prompted much fearful self-examination by the visionary monk. One of the favorite tricks of demons, ascetic literature warned, was to generate delusive visions which endangered even the holiest of minds.[23] Evagrius Ponticus advised his monks, "See to it that the evil demons do not lead you astray by means of some vision. Rather be wise: turn to prayer and call upon God to enlighten you if the thought comes from him, and if it does not, ask him to drive away from you the deceptive one quickly."[24] Demons were notorious for using truth to deceive the faithful. Adepts in demonic struggles were schooled to question visions, engage apparitions in dialogue, and distinguish divine truth from what was merely the demonic appearance of it. Those who achieved these aims were accredited with spiritual discernment. Yet demonic phantoms haunted even the most cautious of contemplatives, and ascetic rigor alone was insufficient to keep demons at bay. "Such a one comes to believe that no hostile force is at work in him, aware as he is that there are no impure disturbances of his flesh, and that on the contrary he experiences only purity. So he draws the conclusion that the apparition is divine in origin. But in truth it is produced in him by the demon."[25]

The tension between the ascetic's supposed access to divine visions and his susceptibility to the attacks of demons lay at the crux of the ascetic tradition. Holy men lived in spiritual symbiosis with their demons, and that relationship became embedded in the literature that disseminated ascetic values. Demons ensured that no visionary "reward" could go unexamined, yet it was precisely the ascetic's familiarity with and confrontation of demons which made his or her visions more trustworthy. For the modern reader of ascetic literature, the infusion of the holy life by the demonic suggests that demons were reified vehicles for the expression of the monk's internal conflicts. Though demonic agency was perceived to underlie any obstacle to the monk's spiritual ambitions, real or imagined, it is also clear that monks believed in demons as real presences which preyed on the fragile imagination.

Ultimately, demons had advantages over monks. Monks had to sleep, but demons did not, and nights were long and dark in the middle ages. Nocturnal spectres and phantoms beguiled dreamers with visions of repudiated delights: family meals, conversations with friends, and the presence of women. Alternatively, they induced fright in the dreamer by sending him nightmares in which, as Evagrius related, he fought off armed men, trembled on precipices, and encountered snakes and other fearful animals.[26] In St. Columba's poetic language: "These are the ones who by the ugli-

---

[23] Isidore, *Sententiarum* 3.6. Indeed, bringing dreams had been the demon's function in antiquity.
[24] Evagrius, *153 Chapters on Prayer* 94.
[25] Ibid. 73.
[26] Evagrius, *Praktikos* 54.

ness of their faces and the clattering of their wings would be quite pleased to frighten fearful men whose fleshy eyes are unable to gaze upon beings of such a nature." [27]

Nightly vigils offered protection from these imaginary dangers. Later sacramental collections preserve prayers such as the following that were said in monastic dormitories to dispel fears of satanic illusions during sleep: "Bless, O Lord, your servants' sleeping place. You who do not sleep, who protects Israel, protect your servants of this house who rest after their work from the illusions of a satanic phantom; that awake they may meditate on your teachings, and while sleeping they may feel your presence in their sleep, you who appeared in dreams to Jacob leaning on the ladder." [28] Likewise at vespers prayers were offered that with God's protection the monks might overcome the "nocturnal frauds of the insidious ones." [29] Satanic phantoms were dangerous because they led the monk into sinful thoughts. Sexually arousing dreams, especially wet dreams, though not considered a sin of volition in patristic thought (unless they were encouraged), reminded the monk nevertheless of his sinful nature and physical urges and provoked shame. [30] The monk Paphnutius did not dare undertake the divine experiment suggested to him by an angel to test his chastity—to take a naked and beautiful virgin to bed with him; thus learned that the inner demon of sexual desire was more dangerous than any "external" demons. [31]

Yet monks were not without consolations for their pains, as we have noted. Angels brought assurances to the contemplative. "Then the angels will walk with you and enlighten you concerning the meaning of created things," the monks were promised, and "though we are impure [the Holy Spirit] often comes to visit us." [32] Yet how could the monk distinguish between dreams and visions that were products of the Holy Spirit and those attributable to other causes? If demonic delusions could so easily masquerade as divine or angelic apparitions, how could they be recognized for what they were?

While Christian philosophers attempted to address this concern by elaborate theoretical expositions on the subject of dreams and visions, ascetic literature taught a rudimentary etiology. Visions came from God, from the

[27] St. Columba, *Altus Prosator* ll.78–84, trans. Harold Isbell, *The Last Poets of Imperial Rome* (Harmondsworth, 1971), p. 272. James Francis Kenney, *The Sources for the Early History of Ireland*, vol. 1 (New York, 1929), pp. 263–65.
[28] "Benedic domine hoc famulorum tuorum dormiturio, qui non dormis neque dormitas, qui custodis israel, famulos tuos huic domui quiescentes post laborem custodi ab inlusionibus fantasmatice satane, vigilantes in preceptis tuis meditentur, dormientis te per soporem sentient, qui iacob somnis apparuisti innixum scale." *Liber Sacramentorum Gellonensis* no. 468 (2862), ed. Antoine Dumas, *CC* 159, 159A, p. 453.
[29] *Lib. Sac. Gell.* no. 338 (2140): "ut nocturni[s] insidiatori[bu]s fraude<s>." See also no. 338 (2137).
[30] Augustine, *De Genesi ad litteram* 12.15; Isidore, *Sententiarum* 3.6.
[31] Cassian, *Conferences* 15.
[32] Evagrius, *153 Chapters on Prayer* 80, 62.

Devil, or from the self. The latter cause was generally linked to permanent or temporary mental and physiological conditions: mental illness, hallucinations, severe sickness, an incontinent or inappropriate diet. It was in distinguishing between visions sent by God and those sent by the Devil that monks had to be most alert. Once again, ascetic literature offered some advice. Pachomius discerned true visions from false based on the experience of ecstasy.[33] It was a view with which Augustine was in sympathy.[34] Evagrius advised his monks to combat the assault of demons with prayer.[35] The experienced monk also had at his disposal diagnostic tools by which to judge a vision in the form of ritual dialogue. St. Anthony had advised:

> When any phantom appears, do not promptly collapse with cowardly fear, but whatever it may be, first ask with stout heart, "Who are you and whence do you come?" And if it should be a vision of the good, they will reassure you and change your fear into joy. If, however, it has to do with the Devil, it will weaken on the spot, seeing your steadfast mind; for to simply ask "Who are you and whence do you come?" is an indication of calmness. Thus did the son of Nave inquire and learn; and the Enemy did not escape detection when Daniel questioned him.[36]

Anthony's advice was predicated on the visionary's psychological response to a vision and the need to control it: demonic visions inculcated fear, divine visions brought joy, but the monk must be impassive, cool, and in control. Yet even a cursory reading of visionary literature in antiquity shows this rudimentary classification to have been valueless. Divine visitations were routinely reported to have brought fear and trembling in their wake, and some demonic visions offered comfort—at least initially. Questioning apparitions (even those apparently authentic), overcoming fear, taking charge of the experience were hard even for seasoned monks. Moreover, even if the monk had the presence of mind to draw on his training and interrogate the apparition as St. Anthony had advised, much was still left to the judgment of the individual. Ultimately only a life of holiness, humility, and prayer could provide protection against demonic delusions.

Furthermore, claims to visionary experience created potential conflict between monks and clergy. Clerics had good reason to be somewhat skeptical of the goings-on in some monastic communities. The ideal of the illiterate hermit, touting divinely inspired wisdom to confound even academics, was fraught with problems. Deficiency of learning or subordination of learning to "divine inspiration" exposed the monk to error, and in extreme cases to

---

[33] For Pachomius' views on ecstasy see Bousset, *Apophthegmata*, p. 237, n. 1., and Guillaumont, *Aux origins*, p. 143.

[34] Augustine, *De Genesi ad litteram* 12.13.

[35] Evagrius, *153 Chapters on Prayer* 94.

[36] Athanasius, *V. Antonii* 43.

heresy. One of the sayings that circulated among monastic communities was that when a monk asked Anthony "How do you ever manage to carry on, Father, deprived as you are of the consolation of books?" the holy man replied, "My book, sir philosopher, is the nature of created things, and it is always at hand when I wish to read the words of God." [37] These were fine sentiments, but dangerous too. The following story was likewise related with approval. "One of the brethren owned only a book of Gospels. He sold this and gave the money for the support of the poor. He made a statement that deserves remembrance: 'I have sold the very word that speaks to me saying: "Sell your possessions and give to the poor."'" [38] This was precisely the kind of story that stirred the gravest of clerical concerns. Claims to divine inspiration, especially if couched in the language of dreams and visions, could be dangerously misinformed without the yardstick of scripture.

Another area of clerical concern about ascetic communities was their vulnerability to the claims of charismatic leaders within their midst. Occasionally individuals sought to extend their personal influence by claiming to have received special powers and favors. At St. Clarus' monastery, for example, the monk Anatolius produced a fine robe, which he said had been given to him by angels, and he wanted to be acknowledged as a prophet. [39] As long as the abbots of communities kept such outbursts under control, they remained internal matters. But some ambitious ascetics looked beyond their compounds for support. Some claimed to be prophets. Others proclaimed the need for renewed dedication to the apostolic life. When these calls were accompanied by populist appeals, they rapidly became of concern to the clergy who, in the West, were far less likely than their eastern counterparts to tolerate such free agents of the holy. [40]

Popular religious movements were legion in the early middle ages. In the late fourth century, for example, a Spanish layman, Priscillian, attracted an earnest following with his call to strict asceticism and was eventually executed for his pains. [41] In the sixth century, a man from Bourges who had a rather mystifying encounter with some flies donned animal skins and took up a life of prayer. Eventually he was accused of claiming to be Christ, and of traveling around with a woman named Mary who was not (as he claimed) his sister. He attracted many of the clergy as well as "common folk" who fancied themselves saints, and he prophesied and healed the sick until the

[37] Evagrius, *Praktikos* 92.
[38] Ibid., 97. See also Gregory of Tours, *Vitae Patrum* 6.4.16 and 5.6.5.
[39] VM 23.2–3.
[40] Brown, "Eastern and Western Christendom," pp. 184–85.
[41] On Priscillian see Henry Chadwick, *Priscillian of Avila: The Occult and the Charismatic in the Early Church* (Oxford, 1976); Clare E. Stancliffe, *St. Martin and his Hagiographer: History and Miracle in Sulpicius Severus* (Oxford, 1983), pp. 278–96; and Ralph W. Mathisen, *Ecclesiastical Factionalism and Religious Controversy in Fifth-Century Gaul* (Washington, D.C., 1989), pp. 11–18.

bishop of Le Velay had him killed.[42] These were extreme cases, of course, but they underscored the dangers which the combination of supernatural claims and the ascetic mantle could bring.

Nevertheless, the connection between the ascetic life and its spiritual rewards appeared to privilege ascetics as dreamers of holy dreams. The cult of the holy man fed into a general perception that visions were a natural part of the hermit's discourse with the divinity, and that holy men dispensed their wisdom in the language of dreams. In this, the holy man put commentators in mind of the prophet Daniel, and the holy man's followers saw themselves as heirs to this prophetic tradition. Importantly, the clergy were often among the fervent admirers of these holy professionals and were often responsible for recording their deeds. Clerics at every level of the hierarchical spectrum were inspired by the monks of the Egyptian desert, and in Gaul they were themselves likely to have been disciples of a holy monk. However, it was the responsibility of the higher clergy, whatever their background, to oversee and instruct their flock. Clerical office and its sacramental offerings needed to command respect and awe from Christians under their charge, including monks, if they were to be effective for salvation. The reputation of holy solitaries for forging connections with the divine gave these "friends of God" a spiritual attraction which certainly pulled uncomfortably at the fringes of episcopal authority. Their claims to have special access to the divine sometimes cut into the bishop's role as guide for his flock and thereby fed into antagonisms that were deeply embedded in the history of separatist monastic communities.

Yet the clergy always held the trump card. All claims had to be subject to the litmus test of scripture and the traditions of the Church. In their institutionalized authority in matters of scripture, sacraments, and tradition, the clergy had the power to assess visionary hermits on behalf of the wider Christian community.

Monastic and Clerical Spiritual Culture in Late Antique Gaul

The last two decades of the fourth century were years of tremendous change for the Gallic church. It was a time when the newly introduced monastic life (at this juncture little more than loosely organized eremitism) was expanding rapidly. Hermitages and monasteries for men and for women were springing up just outside the major cities of Gaul, and disciples flocked to learn spiritual wisdom from ascetic holy men whose lives and miracles

---

[42] Gregory of Tours, *HF* 10.25. Ralph W. Mathisen, "Crossing the Supernatural Frontier in Western Late Antiquity," in *Shifting Frontiers in Late Antiquity*, ed. Mathisen and Hagith S. Sivan, pp. 309–20 (Aldershot, 1996), sees "exploitation of the supernatural" as a safety valve for those with limited influence to express their views.

could not be hidden despite their pursuit of solitude. As Élie Griffe romanti-
cally expressed it, it was as if a fresh breath had passed over Gaul, purifying
the air and vivifying souls.[43] The episcopal infrastructure of Christian Gaul
was already largely in place by this time, with major bishoprics having been
founded by the mid third century. By the late fourth century Gallic clerics
were expanding their missionary horizons beyond their urban and suburban congregations to the rural and marginal populations which still resisted
Christianization, but they were only just beginning. Sulpicius remarked of
the decades when Martin began to preach in the Touraine that there were
many who had not heard the name of Christ. Yet, Sulpicius asserted, by the
time he knew Martin, "there was not a single place which was not filled with
a great number of churches or monasteries."[44] About two thousand monks
and consecrated virgins were reported to have attended Martin's funeral (an
impressive number whose likely accuracy has been defended[45]). Monks from
these early monasteries, such as Martin and his disciples, were often the first
to reach the outlying populations, and their Christianizing efforts were supported by and contributed to episcopal aims.

The relationship between bishops and ascetics, and between clerical and
ascetic spiritual culture, has been the subject of much scholarly interest in recent years. The trend has been to soften the sometimes antipathetic nature of
the relationship, which had been characterized by Cassian's famous injunction that monks should "avoid bishops." It is indisputable that in some dioceses bishops and monastic communities nurtured longstanding grievances.
Monastic communities' desire for spiritual autonomy and clerical concern to
supervise such communities inevitably caused friction and occasionally confrontation. However, openly antipathetic statements about the clergy, which
had once been common in Mediterranean monasticism, rarely found a sympathetic home in the literature of the early medieval West. Western audiences
warmed to hagiographies that advocated respect for the clergy. For example,
Athanasius, bishop of Alexandria, wrote of St. Anthony that "renowned man
that he was, he yet showed the profoundest respect for the Church's ministry
and he wanted every cleric to be honored above himself."[46] The works of
Evagrius, archdeacon turned monk and exile, on the ascetic life (translated
into Latin by Rufinus and later by Gennadius) advised like respect for the

---

[43] Élie Griffe, *La Gaule chrétienne à l'époque romaine*, vol. 2 (Paris, 1964–65), p. 367.

[44] *VM* 13.9 "ut iam ibi nullus locus sit qui non aut ecclesiis frequentissimis aut monasteriis
sit repletus."

[45] Sulpicius, *Ep.* 3.18. ed. C. Halm, *Sulpicii Severi libri qui supersunt*, CSEL 1 (1866). Christian Courtois, "Die Entwicklung des Mönchtums in Gallien vom heiligen Martin bis zum
heiligen Columban," in *Mönchtum und Gesellschaft im Frühmittelalter*, ed. Friedrich Prinz,
pp. 15–16, Wege der Forschung, 312 (Darmstadt, 1976). The article was originally published in Settimane di studio 4 (1957), pp. 47–72. Courtois emphasized that his article was
not simply about numbers but about a social phenomenon which was "a true epidemic of
conversions."

[46] *V. Antonii* 67.

sacramental ministry of the clergy: "One is to love the priests after the Lord, in as much as they purify us through the holy mysteries and pray for us."[47] Western hagiographies drew on the inspiration of such immensely popular and widely disseminated literature. Thus the larger picture was one of general cooperation, with most monastic communities being founded by or rapidly brought under the protection of the local bishop. St. Martin's earliest community, Ligugé, was founded in 360 or 361 under the protection of Bishop Hilary of Poitiers. When Martin became bishop of Tours he founded a community of eighty monks, later named Marmoutier, across the river from the city and retired there whenever his episcopal duties could spare him. According to his hagiographer, in time Marmoutier provided neighboring cities with ascetic bishops, many of them young nobles who had applied themselves to lives of humility and mortification, "for what city or church would not desire a priest from Martin's monastery?"[48] The model of monks becoming bishops was even more pronounced at the island monastery of Lérins off the coast of the French Riviera, which in the fifth century produced so many monastically trained bishops that it has been termed the "nursery" monastery of the Gallic church.[49] Martinian monasticism and Rhône valley monasticism were different from the start. The monastic culture of Lérins, Arles, Lyons, and Marseilles was intimately allied with eastern-style cenobiticism mediated through Cassian's *Institutiones* (Institutes) and *Collationes* (Conferences), whereas Martin's model was initially eremitic. Yet it must be remembered that the distinction between eremiticim and cenobiticism is artificially rigid. Hermits lived in varying degrees of contiguity to cenobitic institutions, and some solitaries, like Martin, eventually adoptd communal living.

As ascetics infiltrated the Gallic episcopate, so did their ascetic values. In what has been termed the "ascetic invasion of the City by the Desert," monastic-style spirituality became the religious aspiration of both clerics and the Christian laity.[50] Some bishops with monastic backgrounds brought monastic interests and concerns into the episcopate. When in the early sixth century Bishop Caesarius of Arles drew up rules for his monastic foundations, he wrote into them protections against future episcopal encroachments; they could not ultimately be upheld, but it is significant that he

[47] Evagrius, *Praktikos* 100.
[48] *VM* 10. 9: "Quae enim esset civitas aut ecclesia, quae non sibi de Martini monasterio cuperet sacerdotem."
[49] In addition to terming Lérins a nursery ("pflanzstätte") because of the monk-bishops produced there, Prinz also terms the monastery an exile monastery ("flüchtlingskloster") because so many of the northern Gallic aristocracy fled there to undertake the ascetic life. *Frühes Mönchtum*, pp. 47–62. Mathisen, *Ecclesiastical Factionalism*, esp. pp. 76–85, notes the political motivations behind the Lérins phenomenon.
[50] Robert Austin Markus, *The End of Ancient Christianity* (Cambridge, 1990), pp. 199–211. Markus notes Caesarius of Arles' elevated ambitions for his congregation. See also William Klingshirn, *Caesarius of Arles: The Making of a Christian Community in Late Antique Gaul* (Cambridge, 1994).

tried.[51] Even at the end of the sixth century the abbot Eugendus of Condat remained sufficiently wary of the combination of clerical office and monastic leadership that he personally eschewed ordination and undertook to discipline his monks away from the clerical view.

The flow of ascetics into the clerical arena was matched by a reverse flow of clerics into the monastic sphere. Not all ascetics were, like Martin, reluctant to take on clerical office, and conversely many ascetics started out as clerics.[52] Monasteries needed clerics who could provide sacramental services, and these monastic clerics appear to have gained some additional authority in the process. Monastic clerics brought pastoral ideals to the ascetic communities they joined so that increasingly ascetics too were expected to use their influence and supernatural powers in public ways. As Philip Rousseau has noted, Western monks who became bishops drew their spiritual authority from both their ascetic ideals and their pastoral activities, reflecting "an awareness in the holy man that a wider public has need of his gifts." Martin's pastoral miracles should be seen in this context.[53]

The remainder of this chapter will focus on hagiographic portraits of two very different visionary ascetics: Martin of Tours as portrayed in Sulpicius Severus' *Vita Martini*, and Eugendus, abbot of the Jura monasteries whose anonymous Life was the last of three abbatial portraits forming the composite *Lives of the Fathers of Jura*. Generally speaking, ascetic *vitae* make for very problematic source material; our information on individual monks and hermits is often from much later sources.[54] So I have chosen here to examine the Lives of two ascetic visionaries who have been well studied, and whose authors were contemporary or near-contemporary to their subjects. Their Lives embody many of the trends which we have observed: Martin the reluctant bishop who brought his own brand of ascetic spirituality to the world of the clergy, and the abbot Eugendus who in the face of opposition within his community deployed visionary accounts larded with biblical motifs to cement and consolidate leadership in his monastic community. In Eugendus' *vita* we see precisely that reverse flow of hierarchical concerns into the aspirations and imagination of the ascetic. Thus these two monks and their different careers offer us different views of the role of visions within the ascetic community.

[51] Caesarius of Arles obtained a papal privilege from Hormisdas; see *S. Caesarii Opera omnia*, vol. 2, ed. G. Morin (Maredsous, 1937–42), pp. 125–26.

[52] Walter Guelphe, "L'érémitisme dans le sud-ouest de la Gaule a l'époque Mérovingienne," *Annales du Midi* 98 (1986), 293–315.

[53] Philip Rousseau, "The Spiritual Authority of the 'Monk-Bishop': Eastern Elements in Some Western Hagiography of the Fourth and Fifth Centuries," *JTS*, n.s., 23 (1971), 380–419, esp. 416.

[54] Some regional studies on ascetics in Gaul include Guelphe, "L'érémitisme"; Jean Heuclin, *Aux origines monastiques de la Gaule du Nord: ermites et reclus du ve au xie siècle* (Lille, 1988); and Joseph-Claude Poulin, *L'idéal de sainteté dans l'Aquitaine carolingienne d'après les sources hagiographiques (750–950)* (Quebec, 1975), which is essential also for the Merovingian period.

St. Martin of Tours: Ascetic Bishop

Little is known of Martin's life that is not dependent on the publications of his disciple Sulpicius Severus, and it is Sulpicius' interpretation of Martin's spirituality and deeds which is presented to us in his writings: a *Vita Martini* completed before the saint's death in 397, three letters written after the saint's death which were widely circulated, and finally a book of "dialogues" which favorably compared Martin's asceticism and "virtus" with that of renowned eastern ascetics.[55] Thus it is important to consider all aspects of Martin's life, including his relationship to the supernatural through dreams and visions, through the filter of Sulpicius' broader perspective and agenda. Sulpicius' renditions of Martin's visions, as will become evident, were carefully constructed to reflect and promote his own particular message in terms of iconic images, cultural referentiality, and audience receptivity.

Sulpicius Severus: The Author as Visionary

Martin's hagiographer was a Gallo-Roman nobleman, born in Aquitaine c. 360, who converted to the ascetic life in his prime and, following the example of his friend Paulinus of Nola, dissolved much of his patrimony to live a life of ascetic poverty.[56] He did not join Martin's community but rather, in a pattern familiar at the time for wealthy individuals, established an ascetic community on his estate. The exact location of his community at Primuliacum is unknown, but it was probably not far from Toulouse.[57]

Sulpicius took as his model for the ascetic life the aged Martin, whom he came to know three or four years before the saint's death. The resulting hagiography, based on his conversations with Martin and the recollections of others who had known him, provided his readers with a saint whose life, works, and miracles eventually defined the Gallic saintly ideal. It was a portrait of holiness whose roots lay in the ascetic and hagiographic tradition made famous by Athanasius' *Life of St. Anthony*.

It is not surprising that Martin, as Sulpicius depicted him, was a visionary

[55] Sulpicius' *VM* was written c. 396, the letters soon after Martin's death in 397, the *Dialogues* c. 404–6, and the *Chronicle* c. 403–6; see Stancliffe, *St. Martin*, pp. 71–85 on dates. Latin text ed. Carolus Halm, *CSEL* 1 (1866). Translations are mine unless otherwise indicated. Citations to the *Dialogues* follow the tripartite division. The literature on Martin of Tours and Sulpicius Severus' writings is enormous. Indispensable are: Fontaine, *Sulpice Sévère, Vie de St. Martin*, SC 133–35; Stancliffe, *St. Martin*; Rousseau, *Ascetics, Authority*; and Prinz, *Frühes Mönchtum*, pp. 19–46. For the history of Martin's cult in medieval Tours see Sharon Farmer, *Communities of St. Martin: Legend and Ritual in Medieval Tours* (Ithaca, N.Y., 1991).
[56] Our best source for Sulpicius' life is his own work, especially the *Dialogues*. See also Gennadius, *De viris inlustribus* 19 in E. Richardson, *TU* 14, 1 (Leipzig, 1896), pp. 57–97.
[57] See Stancliffe, *St. Martin*, p. 30.

saint. Eastern hagiography gave a literary context for ascetics endowed with the "gift of visions." But Sulpicius also knew from experience that saints or angels could appear to the monk in dreams, for, as he related in a letter to the deacon Aurelius, Martin himself had once appeared to him in a dream. In the description of Sulpicius' dream which follows, especially its images and its epistolary context, we are alerted to Sulpicius' method, and thus to the way we should read his rendering of his subject's visions.

In the early morning hours of the day of Martin's death, Sulpicius related that he was visited by the saint in a dream.[58] The deacon Aurelius had just left him after a short visit, and Sulpicius sat alone in his cell brooding upon the Day of Judgment and on his sins. Exhausted by grief, he took a nap. "Sleep then came over me—a light and uncertain sleep as is common in the morning hours, indecisively suspended over the limbs, such as is not the case in any other kind of sleep; the kind of sleep in which almost awake, you know yourself to be sleeping."[59] Suddenly, Sulpicius saw the holy bishop Martin, dressed in a white toga, face alight, with eyes like stars and his hair blazing red. He was able to recognize Martin from his outward appearance, without actually being able to look at him (an experience he admits to be difficult to explain). Martin's appearance, though recognizable, was transfigured by his proximity to the divinity, for his smile and blessing echoed the iconography of ancient theophanies, while his white toga indicated the rank and purity of God's chosen.[60]

Martin's handing Sulpicius a book was a gesture fairly common in dreams, the book usually representing the Word of God or alternatively the Book of Life in which the names of the elect were recorded.[61] Yet this book was neither of these, but rather Sulpicius' own composition, the *Life of St. Martin*. Jacques Fontaine notes Sulpicius' irreverence in proffering his own publication. Was it perhaps a gesture that pointed to Sulpicius' self-

[58] Sulpicius, *Ep.* 2, "Ad Aurelium Diaconum."

[59] *Ep.* 2: "somnus obresit—qui, ut semper matutinis horis levior incertusque, ita suspensus ac dubius per membra diffunditur ut, quod in alio sopore non evenit, paene vigilans dormire te sentias." That is to say, when sleep is not so heavy that the mind succumbs to the body's need for rest. It is clear that Sulpicius was aware of ancient dream theory which proposed that the morning hours were optimal for receiving a divine dream (although most often this kind of sleep is described as occurring at dawn). His use of the word *obresit* (*sic*) recalls the ancient belief that divine sleep is an externally imposed weight which temporarily incapacitates the body but makes the mind receptive to divine dreams. References to the *VM* throughout are from Fontaine's edition in the *Sources chrétiennes*.

[60] Fontaine, *Vie*, vol. 3, pp. 1191 ff., comments on the Roman aspect of Martin's appearance, in his white toga like a candidate for consulship. In his versification of the *VM*, the sixth-century poet Venantius Fortunatus imagined Martin's senatorial company in the court of heaven, a theme perhaps originally suggested by this vision, Fortunatus, *Vita sancti Martini* 3, ed. Fridericus Leo, *MGH, AA* 4.1 (Berlin, 1881). Victricius of Rouen, *De laude sanctorum* 12, ed. J. Mulders and R. Demeulenaere, CC 64 (1985) pp. 69–93, likewise described the saints wearing senatorial garb.

[61] Rousseau, "Monk-Bishop," p. 380, notes the figure of Moses holding the Tablets of the Law as a possible iconographic influence.

appointed role as prophet of a Martinian apocalypse?[62] Perhaps. However, if we look not at the iconography of the vision but rather at the context in which the vision occurred, the pious parody which this scene poses need not have been as presumptuous as Fontaine suggests.

Sulpicius had drifted into sleep troubled by his thoughts on the Day of Judgment and his sins. These were depressing thoughts, for although he had written the biography of the saintly Martin, he had not yet taken upon himself the rigors of full discipleship. In the dream, then, and in answer to his anxieties, Martin offered back to him, with spiritual irony, the portrait of a life which Sulpicius' own skill had crafted. To a certain extent Martin endorsed Sulpicius' book by this action, but more important, by returning to him Sulpicius' own record of his life, he challenged Sulpicius to follow him. This interpretation is confirmed in the end of the letter where Sulpicius revealed to Aurelius the meaning of the vision. "He has shown us, by means of the vision, that heaven is open to his followers, and he has taught us where we should follow him."[63] Since this was the message of Martin's life as portrayed in Sulpicius' hagiography, Sulpicius interpreted the vision as a message of hope and faith which he, with his depressing thoughts about sin, had yet to fully accept.

Martin then blessed Sulpicius in the dream. Sulpicius recalled that he stood transfixed, intent on the light as if he could not satisfy his desire to see Martin's face, until suddenly Martin was transported to heaven, traversing the immense vastness of the air until he was out of sight. Martin's rapid movement heavenward broke Sulpicius' trance. On seeing his friend Clarus ascend heavenward after Martin, Sulpicius tried to follow but found that he could not move his limbs.

The exact meaning of Sulpicius' vision of Martin is open to interpretation, but in order to understand Sulpicius as a narrator of dreams, one must consider the epistolary medium in which he documented it. Sulpicius' dream brings us closer to his inner life than any other passage in his writings. He recorded the experience itself with a great amount of care and attention, as he did his account of his emotional reaction. Sulpicius' account exposed to his reader, Aurelius, his most personal fears and his most cherished hopes. Yet he related it in the form of an open letter to be read by a larger audience than its intended recipient. The public audience of this personal account explains the narrative's iconographic sophistication, with its intentional association to ancient theophanies. Though the psychological integrity of the account impresses one with the conviction that the dream is not simply a literary creation, the account nevertheless suggests many biblical and classical images, and exposes the oneirological understanding of its author. Sulpicius' care-

---

[62] Fontaine, *Vie*, vol. 3, pp. 1195–96.
[63] Sulpicius, *Ep.* 2.17.

fully crafted description alerts us to the importance of visions as "text," for though the account is as close to the reporting of an authentic experience as we come in early medieval sources, nevertheless it has multiple layers of meaning which have been worked out by the dream's author. Its audience, ostensibly private, is in fact very public, and its message, although coded as a private message to Sulpicius, reveals a broader message intended for all Christians. Furthermore, Sulpicius' dream reminds us that such is the nature of all our visionary sources, that between the dream itself and the written form in which it is available to us, there is a long process of mental rumination, some of it private, and some of it public through the transforming nature of oral tradition and communication. Martin's own visions would have been related to Sulpicius perhaps by Martin himself, and certainly by his disciples who told them among themselves. But by the time they were written down by Sulpicius, much of their meaning had already been decided.[64] It was then left to Sulpicius to determine context and suggest iconographic juxtapositions which gave them the meaning they ultimately acquired.

Imagining the Christian, Imagining Christ

Sometime between 370 and 372, when the disheveled, dirty, ragged abbot of Ligugé entered the city of Tours as its newly elected bishop, the stage was set for tensions that were to characterize the remainder of the bishop's life. Popular fervor and clerical admiration for Martin as a proven miracle-worker and reputed holy man had swept him into office, against the wishes of a few who may have wanted different qualities in a prospective bishop. According to his hagiographer, Martin's critics cited his lowliness and uncouth appearance as objections to his holding such a high office.[65] Underlying these criticisms, however, were serious concerns about what or who a bishop should be; about the "dignity" of the office and the competence with which its considerable religious and political authority would be wielded. Certainly in Sulpicius' portrait of subsequent events, the religious divisions epitomized in Martin's rocky election set the stage for a particularly fraught episcopal reign. Yet though Martin's episcopate was marked by a number of crises, for Sulpicius the central issue was spiritual authority. It was around this dramatic issue that Sulpicius constructed his biography of the saint.

For Sulpicius, true spiritual authority was to be found only in those who, whatever their social or religious rank, dedicated their lives to God through asceticism (*askesis*). The true bishop was at heart a monk—someone like Martin, who prized the contemplative life and who, when he was suddenly

---

[64] Rousseau, "Monk-Bishop," pp. 404, 405 n. 1.
[65] Hermits were not necessarily of low class. See Guelphe, "L'érémitisme," pp. 301–2.

and unwillingly catapulted into high office, strove to maintain his ascetic values and integrate them into the episcopate.[66] "It was thus," Sulpicius noted, "that, full of authority and grace, he fulfilled his episcopal functions, for he abandoned neither his monastic resolve nor his monastic virtues."[67]

To Sulpicius, then, Martin's ascetic training made him a better bishop, an incarnation of early Christian apostolic leaders whose wisdom, leadership, and religious authority had rested upon charismatic inspiration. Like those early leaders, he was guided by divine wisdom, by visions and celestial visitations. Sulpicius contended that Martin, in contrast to bishops who by tradition held the title "vir apostolicus," was "vere apostolicus," truly an apostle of Christ.

Sulpicius meticulously described Martin's voluntary privations; his abstinence, fasts, vigils, and prayers, his eating and sleeping only as nature required.[68] He also described the saint's intimacy with the world of the supernatural: his vision of Christ, conversations with angels, and confrontations with demons. Martin's struggles with supernatural powers testified to his powers as a holy man. Conversely Martin's asceticism gave authority to his claims to have spoken with angels. To appreciate the full significance of Martin's example, however, we must consider the light in which these activities were seen by the bishops of his day and examine those visions and encounters with the supernatural which, in their insistent promotion of ascetic values, could be interpreted as threatening to the authority of the clergy.

Though Martin was at heart a monk, as Sulpicius claimed, he was also a bishop. Bishops oversaw their flock through the apostolic authority vested in them by tradition and by the sacraments. Yet Sulpicius had no confidence in the spiritual value of high office per se, even though it brought with it potential for immense religious and political power. Episcopal office which in secular terms denoted ecclesiastical authority could be, and often was, he believed, the antithesis of spiritual authority. Thus Sulpicius set about distancing Martin's spiritual authority from his tenure in episcopal office.

One way in which Sulpicius did this was by emphasizing the lengths to which Martin had gone to eschew sacerdotal office. As a young man, Martin had protested strenuously against the desire of Hilary of Poitiers to ordain him as deacon, being finally induced from his sense of humility to accept the humblest order of exorcist.[69] When Martin was elected to the important see of Tours, he had to be taken there as if a prisoner. In Sulpicius' eyes, no mere bishopric could honor such an exceptional man. Although

---

[66] On eastern monasticism and the ascetic tradition as background to Martin's ascetic life see Stancliffe, *St. Martin*, pp. 233–41; Rousseau, "Monk-Bishop," and *Ascetics, Authority*, pp. 143–65.

[67] *VM* 10.2: "plenus auctoritatis et gratiae, inplebat episcopi dignitatem, ut non tamen propositum monachi virtutemque desereret."

[68] Ibid., 26.2.

[69] Ibid., 5.1–2.

there must have been important episcopal support for Martin at the time, Sulpicius contrasted the unified desire of the people to elect him bishop with a small coterie of bishops who opposed his election, depicting this opposition as a demonic plot, foiled by a miracle.[70]

With the exception of Martin's resurrection miracles performed while a monk, it was as bishop that Martin performed his most memorable miracles in Sulpicius' Life. He destroyed pagan temples with celestial aid, cured a paralytic in Trier, rid a slave and a cook of ferocious demons, and cured a leper with his kiss.[71] When the bishop slipped on some uneven steps and injured himself very badly, an angel appeared to him and washed his wounds.[72] At each turn, Martin was supported and protected by divine aid. In contrast to the propensity in later Gallic hagiography to highlight the authority of the bishop, there were no miracles or visions in Martin's Life which sought to cast a special luminance upon episcopal office per se. Rather Sulpicius depicted Martin's community activities as relying on his authority as an ascetic.[73]

Sulpicius laid great weight on Martin's successes as a missionary. As he razed pagan temples Martin was protected by angels, sometimes bearing celestial arms. But Sulpicius attributed Martin's successes to powers that long preceded his tenure as bishop. Martin's earliest conversion of pagans occurred when as a monk he was instructed in a dream to visit and convert his parents. On his journey he converted a brigand intent on killing him by speaking to him of the word of God. These early conversions of pagans could thus be interpreted as merely expanding in scope when he became a bishop. Preaching, another clerical preserve, was also an important aspect to Martin's Christianizing efforts, although sometimes overshadowed in Sulpicius' narrative by the more dramatic razing of pagan temples.

In describing Martin's powers, Sulpicius betrayed his own antagonistic attitude toward the ecclesiastical establishment. In the Life he took a defensive stand against the episcopal hierarchy; bishops, he tells us, were Martin's persecutors. Furthermore, he denounced the bishops for paying court to secular princes, especially to the emperor Maximus, accusing them of debasing episcopal honor to mere clientship of the emperor. By the time he wrote the *Dialogues* some three or four years after the Life, Sulpicius' position had hardened as his own work came under clerical attack. Indeed it is hard to find any redeeming aspect to the Gallic episcopate in Sulpicius' later works.

Martin's visions were perhaps the most striking way Sulpicius expressed and developed contrasting images of authority—ascetic versus cleric. Mar-

[70] Ibid., 9.
[71] Ibid., 12–18.
[72] Ibid., 19.
[73] Rousseau, "Monk-Bishop," 406–7, notes that whereas early monk-bishops such as Ambrose, Martin, and Augustine were portrayed combining clerical and ascetic authority, eventually the authority of a holy man's clerical office would supplant his ascetic authority.

tin's most famous vision was of Christ at Amiens. It was said that while still a catechumen, Martin came across a beggar outside the city of Amiens. The winter cold was fierce, and no one stopped to help him. Martin took pity on the beggar's plight, but having only one covering himself, took his sword (he was still in the army) and cut his cloak into two pieces, giving one half to the beggar. That night, Christ appeared to him in a dream, dressed in Martin's half cloak. Christ commented to his angelic entourage, "Martin, who is still only a catechumen, has clothed me in this garment."[74] Martin's Christ, therefore, came to him not as Pantocrator, not as king of heaven, but as a Christ of poverty, of suffering and humility. It was an image to which Martin was faithful his entire life.

In Sulpicius' Life of the saint, there was another occasion when Martin was confronted by an image of Christ, a false, demonic image whose appearance echoed and acted as a foil to the genuine Christ vision of his youth. Sulpicius related that one day, when Martin was in his cell, the Devil appeared before him in the guise of Christ. The apparition wore a kingly robe, with a diadem on his head and golden slippers on his feet, and demanded to be recognized as the Christ. But Martin, enlightened by the Holy Spirit, retorted, "The Lord Jesus did not say that he would come in a purple robe and wearing a shining diadem. I will not believe that Christ has come unless he appears in the garment of the passion, displaying the wounds of the Cross."[75] Martin rejected the vision, as Sulpicius tells us, because of his powers of discernment granted through the Holy Spirit. However, Martin's remark on contrasting images of Christ (as king and as beggar) was clearly intended to comment on broader issues of Christian devotion. The vision was intended as a cipher for distinguishing between different kinds of Christian—the humble and the prideful. The humble were, of course, the monks and ascetics who, like Martin, gave up their worldly goods and status in order to follow a life of holy poverty. But who were the prideful? Some commentators have suggested that the rejected image of the false Christ, bejeweled and regal, represented a rejection of imperial power.[76] Though the vestments described are certainly imperial, it is the finery and splendor of episcopal office which surely underlies the criticism. In Sulpicius' *Dialogues*, Postumianus complained about the effects of sacerdotal office on even the

---

[74] "Martinus adhuc catechumenus hac me veste contexit." Ibid., 3.3. A similar story is told in Regnault, ed., *Les sentences des Pères*, no. 1358.

[75] VM 24.7: "non se . . . Iesus Dominus purpuratum nec diademate renidentem venturum esse praedixit; ego Christum, nisi in eo habitu formaque qua passus est, nisi crucis stigmata praeferentem, venisse non credam."

[76] Stancliffe, in *St. Martin*, p. 240, n. 65, draws attention to the possible parallel between this demonic imperial figure and Hilary of Poitiers' *Contra Constantium Imperatorem* 5, SC 334, ed. A. Rocher (1987). See also Fontaine, *Vie*, vol. 3, pp. 1022–28. Thomas F. Mathews, *The Clash of the Gods: A Reinterpretation of Early Christian Art* (Princeton, 1993), notes that "to dress Christ as an emperor was to make him a devil. Or a fool" (p. 178).

humblest of men as they embraced the sartorial splendor of the office.[77] For Sulpicius, the contrast of images represented a contrast of spiritual values. On the one hand were the higher clergy, with their fine education and their fine clothes —the image of ecclesiastical authority—and on the other were poverty-stricken monks, beggared for their love of Christ. Sulpicius, himself of aristocratic family, gave up all his possessions to lead a life of Christlike, Martinlike poverty; it was the humble Christ, happy with a beggar's garb, whom Martin and Sulpicius followed.

For an ascetic audience, the spiritual message behind these iconographic differences was clear. The claims of powerful bishops to represent Christ may, like the words of the Devil, deceive the faithful, while the humble monk lives truly in Christ's image. But this polarization is more than simply another jibe against the clergy by a bitter Sulpicius. It is a plea for a particular type of spiritual life, one in which Christians are free to follow Christ (and Martin) by taking on a life of poverty and suffering, a spiritual vocation which, in the aftermath of the persecution of Priscillianists, Sulpicius saw to be under attack.

Sulpicius' design was to promote the monastic life and ideology, and Martin was the model. Monasticism was a relatively new movement in Gaul, and its introduction was not smooth. In the eyes of some Gallic bishops, Martin's enthusiastic asceticism smacked of Priscillianism. Sulpicius tried to head off criticism by insisting that Martin practiced only moderate asceticism, but suspicion nevertheless remained.

One of the stories Sulpicius told about Martin suggests that conversion to the ascetic life, like baptism, was purgative in nature. One day, as some of the brothers in Martin's monastery were standing outside his cell, they heard him being upbraided by the Devil for having received into the community monks who had transgressed since baptism.[78] Martin retorted that by desisting from further sin and undertaking a better life in the monastery, the transgressors' faults were absolved. The Devil continued to argue for a stricter code of conduct in which God's mercy was not available to the lapsed. Martin then made his famous boast that if the Devil himself renounced his evil deeds, Martin would guarantee his salvation.[79]

Set within the framework of a demonic apparition, and hence in the traditional literary mold of confrontation between the saint and the Devil, the issues raised by this episode are precisely the type which dogged early ascetic communities. An important issue of the day was the question of ascetic rigor.

[77] Sulpicius, *Dialogi* 1.21, ed. C. Halm, *Sulpicii Severi libri qui supersunt*, CSEL 1 (1866).
[78] *VM* 22.3.
[79] Ibid., 22. See Fontaine, *Vie*, vol. 3, p. 970 ff. and Stancliffe, *St. Martin*, pp. 194–95. Martin's boast that he could save the Devil if he repented shows the influence of Origenist thinking, which was popular among ascetics in the East. By the time Sulpicius wrote the *Dialogues* he was aware that this view had been condemned, and he retracted his position.

Sulpicius wanted to distance Martin from too great a rigor by attributing demonic inspiration to those who expressed the desire for an overly strict definition of souls eligible to be saved. Sulpicius was interested in juxtaposing Martin's orthodoxy with the potential disruption inherent in the strict values of Priscillianism.

The primary focus of the supernatural conversion, however, was its discussion of rehabilitating the lapsed while at the same time maintaining within the monastic community certain standards of Christian purity. In Christian antiquity the office of baptism was often reserved for the later stages of the Christian's life because the consequences of sin for salvation were considered far greater after baptism than before. St. Anthony memorably rebuked the demons who tried to tally his faults from birth, but permitted them to count them from the time of his baptism.[80] The lapsed discussed in this conversion, however, had been guilty of serious wrongdoing, probably to the extent of having committed "capital" or "mortal" sins.[81] Martin was essentially proposing that entry into the monastic life was like baptism, a commitment to the pursuit of spiritual perfection, and that by the undertaking of the ascetic life, one's post-baptismal sins were washed away. Martin's stance in this episode forged a philosophy of the role of the monastery in society, offering a definition of monasticism that focused on the ongoing nature of the pursuit of spiritual perfection. Martin's decision to admit into his community the grievously imperfect, therefore, charted a role for monasticism within the Christian community which could be set alongside ecclesiastical ritual (baptism) as a purgation and hence a route to salvation.

Asceticism, Heresy, and the Gallic Clergy

What had triggered much of the ascetic-cleric tension in Gaul was the Priscillianist affair.[82] Priscillian was the charismatic leader of a layman's movement which advocated a life of strict abstinence. Based on the Council of Saragossa (c. 380) we know that initially his movement was associated with nothing more serious than some dubious practices which included unrelated men and women attending bible-readings, Sunday fasts, nonconsumption of the eucharist, mountain retreats, walking barefoot, and virgins taking the

[80] Athanasius, *V. Antonii* 65.

[81] Fontaine, *Vie*, vol. 3, p. 972. For example, the Council of Valence in 374 excommunicated those guilty of mortal crimes. *Concilium Valentinum* 4, ed. C. Munier, in *Concilia Galliae a.314–a.506*, CC 148 (Turnhout, 1963), pp. 35–42.

[82] Sulpicius addresses Martin's role in the Priscillianist affair in his *Dial.* 3.11–13, and in his *Chronicle* 2.46–51. On the Priscillianist affair and its impact on the fourth-century Church in the West see Chadwick, *Priscillian*; Stancliffe, *St. Martin*, pp. 278–96; and Mathisen, *Ecclesiastical Factionalism*, pp. 11–18.

veil before the canonically prescribed age of 40.[83] However, Priscillian had enemies. After some initial problems in Spain, Priscillian attracted sufficient support among the Spanish and Gallic episcopate to be elevated to the bishopric of Avila in 381 (largely for his own protection). Shortly thereafter he was deposed from his see by an opposing faction of bishops, who accused him of, among other things, overzealous abstinence and holding beliefs akin to those of the gnostics and Manichees.[84] After traveling through southern Aquitaine, where he and his ideas attracted an enthusiastic following, he continued on to Rome and thence to Milan where he obtained the support of the Emperor Gratian, and he and his followers were reinstated in their bishoprics. But after Gratian's death the imperial usurper Magnus Maximus (383) ordered an episcopal Synod to be convened at Bordeaux, where Priscillian's teachings were in fact condemned as heretical in 384–85. Having appealed successfully to an emperor once before, Priscillian proceeded to appeal to the new emperor in Trier. So did his enemies, and soon Priscillian saw his case moved to the secular courts where he found himself on trial no longer for heresy but for sorcery, a capital crime. He was found guilty of the charge, and in 385 he was executed along with some of his male and female followers.

The Priscillian affair appears to have had more to do with church politics than with theology.[85] Indeed, it is quite possible that Priscillian's views were no more unorthodox than those of many churchmen of his time, including Martin himself, to whom Sulpicius attributed beliefs of dubious orthodoxy.[86] Martin was drawn into the affair not as a defender of Priscillian's orthodoxy but as a voice for leniency on behalf of a fellow bishop. On hearing of Priscillian's unhappy fate, Martin and his followers protested the execution by refusing to enter into communion with those bishops who had been responsible for his death. The rift which his decision threatened among the Gallic clergy alarmed the anti-Priscillian bishops, who once more appealed to the emperor Maximus, demanding that Martin be made to com-

[83] For these and other accusations against Priscillian's followers see Chadwick, *Priscillian*, p. 14. Chadwick also observes of Priscillian that "his followers did not set high value on mystical visions of light or of demonic powers. Nor did they speak with tongues." Yet Priscillian believed that the Spirit continued to guide lay Christians, men and women, through revelations. See Chadwick, "Priscillian of Avila: Occult and Charisma in the Ancient Church," *Studia Patristica* 15:1. (1984), 3–12. On Priscillianist apocrypha see Donatien de Bruyne, "Fragments retrouvés d'apocryphes priscillianistes," *Revue Bénédictine* 24 (1907), 318–35.
[84] Priscillian actually denounced Manichaeism and gnosticism, but the labels were often used as umbrella terms for as yet unnamed heresies. Sulpicius termed Priscillian's heresy gnosticism. Sulpicius, *Chronica* 2.46, ed. C. Halm, *Sulpicii Severi libriqui supersunt*, CSEL 1 (1866). On the association of Priscillianism with Manichaeism see Mathisen, *Ecclesiastical Factionalism*, pp. 13–14, and contra, Raymond Van Dam, *Leadership and Community in Late Antique Gaul* (Berkeley, 1985), pp. 101 ff.
[85] Stancliffe, *St. Martin*, pp. 278, 282–83.
[86] Sulpicius attributed to Martin Origenist views (*VM* 23) and millenarian views (*Dial.* 2.14), both of which were condemned by orthodox churchmen.

ply. The emperor then delivered to Martin an ultimatum. If Martin agreed to join in communion with his fellow bishops and help consecrate Felix as bishop of Trier, the emperor would not execute some of Gratian's followers for whom Martin had been appealing, and he would recall military tribunes already sent out to Spain to root out remaining Priscillianists. In order to save lives, and to prevent a witch-hunt, which according to Sulpicius intended to identify Priscillianists only by their pale faces and ascetic garb, Martin complied.[87]

The Priscillianist affair shook the Gallic church. Bishops were seen to have used secular authorities to murder other bishops, and ascetic communities modeling themselves on the holy men of the Egyptian desert found themselves in danger of being hounded as heretics.[88] Martin was shaken by the events, and Sulpicius informs us that thereafter he kept aloof from episcopal synods and gatherings.[89] The memory of these events, coupled with some further assaults on the monastic way of life in Sulpicius' lifetime, ensured that in his Martinian works the friction between ascetics and the ecclesiastical establishment was made central to the Life. This is especially evident in Sulpicius' accounts of Martin's visions.

In his *Dialogues* Sulpicius related one vision that commented directly on the aftermath of the Priscillianist affair. After being coerced into communion with the Felician bishops, Martin left the city of Trier in profound sorrow. Once in the countryside, he retreated from his fellow travelers a little way to sit in solitude in a clearing in the woods. In that solitude, Martin grieved, first condemning himself for his actions and then defending them. Then an angel appeared before him with the following message: "With reason, Martin, do you struggle with yourself, but you had no other way out. Recover your strength, regain your steady character, otherwise you risk not only your reputation but also your spiritual health."[90]

This tale pointed to crises in two areas of Martin's life. The first was the public impact which this defeat might have on his reputation (*gloria*)—a reminder that his life as a bishop was a very public one—and the second was a personal crisis occasioned by spiritual self-doubt. In the public arena, Martin was humiliated. In confronting the bishops and the emperor as any holy man was expected to do, he had gambled on his reputation, but the move had backfired, for in agreeing to commune with the Felician bishops he was publicly retracting a position he regarded as righteous. Holy men were not accustomed to losing out in confrontation scenes with secular potentates. Martin had bravely confronted the Caesar Julian as a catechumen, as Sulpi-

---

[87] *Dial.* 3.11.
[88] Stancliffe, *St. Martin*, pp. 282–83.
[89] *Dial.* 3.13.
[90] *Dial.* 3.13: "Merito . . . Martine conpungeris, sed aliter exire nequisti. Repara virtutem, resume constantiam, ne iam non periculum gloriae, sed salutis incurras."

cius tells us, announcing that he would no longer fight in the imperial army. More recently he had snubbed the present emperor at a banquet. Yet this bishop with a mighty reputation in the prime of his life had been made to capitulate and act in opposition to his beliefs. The long journey back to Tours, where he had to confront his congregation and clergy, must have been a terrible ordeal.

Yet Martin's encounter with the angel in the forest deflected some of the political ramifications of his capitulation. In Sulpicius' account, the angel identified Martin's inner turmoil as the greater source for concern. Martin sat in solitude in the forest, drawn away from the company of his followers—echoing Jesus in the garden of Gethsemane—and confronting the spiritual and psychological disintegration of self-confidence to the point where salvation itself was imperiled. The angel did not give his approval for what Martin had done. (Sulpicius no less than Martin believed that his action in communing with these bishops was wrong.) However, the angel assured Martin (and the readers of Sulpicius' story), that there was divine acceptance of his compromise. Whether the angel who comforted Martin was intended to be understood as a supernatural being or as a kindly voice among the bishop's entourage, Sulpicius' narration of this conversation in the language of a vision accomplished an important function in the Life. The vision's achievement was in expanding the significance of Martin's capitulation, from a personal episode to the broader issue of spiritual integrity.

Talking with Demons and Angels

At the beginning of this chapter we noted the importance of the holy man's way of life, which alone gave authority to his visions. But the spiritual authority of a holy man could also be greatly enhanced by his charismatic wisdom. The balance between the authority accorded to visions and to the holy life was a precarious one: dreams and visions were problematic authorizers of sanctity.

According to Sulpicius, dreams, visions and conversations with angels guided Martin's deeds and illuminated his inner life. He was also beset by demons who presented themselves as messengers from God and who tried in other ways to impede his holy mission. Good angels and bad angels were theologically equal but opposite counterweights in the cosmos, yet Martin's case shows that when it came to Christians' dealings with them, visions of demons were judged very differently than visions of angels.

A holy man battling against demons raised no eyebrows among an audience in late antiquity, for demons were everywhere. Christians abjured the Devil and his forces upon baptism, and were cautioned to be ever alert to those habits, practices, and weaknesses that were signals of demonic possession. It was conventional for Christians to identify demonic agency in those human forces that threatened the Christian good. Whether opposition was political, spiritual, or personal, the human face of the demonic was familiar in the Christian community.[91] On the road to Milan, having set out in response to a dream instructing him to convert his parents to the Christian life, Martin was accosted by the Devil in human form. "Wherever you go, or whatever you set out to do, the Devil will always oppose you," he was told.[92] Martin retorted, "The Lord is my Helper; I will not fear what Man may do to me." The confrontation made explicit the human face of malevolence, and alerted the reader of the Life to the fact that demonic agency operated behind Martin's spiritual conflicts.[93] It was also a signal of Martin's special powers as a holy man, for this demonic abuse had beset him from the time of his decision to lead a holy life, a common juncture for intensification of such attacks. Martin was depicted as a Christian hero involved in a lifelong struggle with Satan, ready to pitch his battle lines wherever the Devil made his appearance—in dreams, visions, in his cell, or on the open road.

Martin was also well known for having divinely inspired dreams and visions. From his youth, he was attentive and responsive to his dreams. Not long after his conversion he was chided in a dream that he should return to Pannonia to convert his pagan parents, which he did although with limited success.[94] Also in a dream Martin saw his vision of Christ dressed in the halfcloak which he had given to a beggar at Amiens.[95] This dreamed vision did not make Martin proud, we are told, but enabled him to recognize God's goodness. Although he was not yet baptised, Martin had fulfilled Christ's call to serve the poor, which early Christians saw completed in conversion to the ascetic life. In later life, Sulpicius recorded, Martin was often visited in his cell by angels who conversed with him.[96] Some of the accounts must have originated with Martin. Others were reported by outsiders, such as the monks who while standing outside his cell heard Martin conversing with angels within. On one occasion, Sulpicius and fellow monk Gallus waiting for an audience outside Martin's cell, heard murmurings within. After a couple of hours Martin emerged and revealed that he had been speaking with saints Agnes, Thecla, and Mary. Then "he described to us the face and clothing of each. Indeed he confessed to being visited by them frequently, not just on

[91] Historians have been intrigued by what such episodes reveal about the mentality of an age which sees the Devil so clearly in its fellow man. Fontaine brought two strands together when he suggested that Satan is a personal facet of the spiritual perception of the believer, while at the same time the Devil's depicted deeds can often be seen to conform to historical events. *Vie*, vol. 1, pp. 194–95. See also Stancliffe, *St. Martin*, pp. 194–96.

[92] *VM* 6.2.

[93] Another potent agency of evil in the *vita* was paganism. The Devil appeared often as an embodiment of the pagan forces that Martin strove to convert in his missions, including the gods identified as Mercury, Venus, and Minerva. Ibid., 22.1.

[94] Ibid., 5.3; 6.3.

[95] Ibid., 3.3.

[96] Ibid., 21.1.

that particular day. Indeed he admitted that often he saw the Apostles Peter and Paul." [97]

Unlike his confrontations with demons (which could always be seen in a personal, interior, figurative sense), stories of conversations with saints and angels did raise eyebrows among his contemporaries. Angelic visitations posed issues of spiritual authority in ways which demonic visions did not. This is not to say that tales of Martin's explosive encounters with the Devil and his minions received uniform acceptance. Martin, it seemed, saw demons everywhere, sitting on the shoulder of the wicked Count Avitianus, sitting on the back of a disturbed cow, or calling from the crags around his cell announcing the arrival of his enemy Brictius. The reports of such goings-on, not surprisingly, aroused suspicion and disbelief in some quarters. But the individual who claimed to speak daily with prominent saints and described their appearance in such matter-of-fact detail was a different kind of threat to established authority.

Martin's most outspoken critic was a presbyter of Tours named Brictius, a one-time disciple who now ridiculed Martin's visionary life as the ravings and delusions of a senile old man. [98] Brictius seems not to have been alone in his skepticism. Sulpicius admitted as much when he owned that he and the monks of Marmoutier likewise had difficulty believing in such mystical events. What is not clear in the accounts we have of Brictius' criticisms is how far they purposefully rejected Martin's visionary mentality, and how they were simply part and parcel of Brictius' opposition to Martin on other grounds. It has been suggested that Brictius' attacks were motivated by his belonging to a faction in the Tours clergy, possibly Felician, which opposed Martin. [99] This seems likely in view of his election to the See of Tours on Martin's death. But it is also clear that tales of Martin's visions repelled some among the clergy. Coming from a man with little education, Martin's communication with angels, demons, and the ghostly shades of the deceased seemed too close to superstitions of the pagan *rustici* to invite respect from the cultured clergy.

Whatever the precise reason, Brictius' attack on Martin as a credulous and demented old man stung Sulpicius to defend Martin's visionary experiences. Already in the Life, written before Martin's death, Sulpicius had begun to address these issues. He gave prominent space to anecdotes that showed Martin debunking false visionary claims and exercising his powers of spiritual discernment. He declared that Martin, like Anthony before him, was gifted with that spiritual sight, that power of discerning between good and

---

[97] *Dial.* 2.13: "Referebat autem nobis vultum adque habitum singularum. Nec vero illo tantum die, sed frequenter se ab eis confessus est visitari. Petrum etiam et Paulum Apostolos videri a se saepius non negavit."

[98] *Dial.* 3.15: "per inanes superstitiones et fantasmata visionum ridicula prorsus inter deliramenta senuisse."

[99] Mathisen, *Ecclesiastical Factionalism*, p. 20.

evil spirits, which enabled him to penetrate the external appearance of any phenomenon and spy its spiritual origin. Such a vision, a gift of the Holy Spirit, was endowed to those pure of heart and honed by a life of obedience and asceticism. The exercise of this gift was what separated saints like Martin from the deluded would-be prophets who were all too common at the time. Sulpicius' portrayal of Martin's visionary life was dedicated to making this distinction clear. Martin's visions occurred at a time when there was much alarm at the imminent coming of the Antichrist and the associated rise of false prophets. In Spain a young man had claimed first to be Elijah, and then Christ, and a Spanish bishop named Rufus had believed in him, worshiping him as if he were God. For that reason, Sulpicius adds, the bishop was deposed. In the East, another man claimed to be John the Baptist and was believed by many.[100] By contrast, Martin was an exposer of false prophets such as the charlatan Anatolius.

At Clarus' monastery, close to Marmoutier, the would-be prophet Anatolius tried to convince his fellow monks that he spoke regularly with angels and that messengers came and went between himself and God. He presented himself to the community in a white tunic of remarkable brightness, claiming that it had been conferred on him by Christ as a sign of his God-given power. The man's claims caused consternation in the community, and so Clarus decided to take him to Martin to have his claims assessed. In the course of the journey, even before they had reached Martin, the white tunic disappeared, along with the man's presumption. So great was the Martin's reputation for discernment that the mere threat of being brought into his presence was enough for the demonic *fantasma* to be unmasked.[101]

Sulpicius' belief in the spiritual health of his subject is clear. However, Sulpicius also acknowledged that there were dangers in endowing visionary claims with spiritual authority, which could lay the Christian open to demonic delusion. But Martin, he averred, could be relied upon to discern the true spiritual origin of visions, in contrast to some other church leaders. In the final analysis, Sulpicius' position was entirely orthodox. He never claimed that Martin's spiritual authority derived from his prophecies or visionary encounters. Rather it was through the pattern of Martin's daily life, his integrity as a bishop, and his virtues as a monk that Martin could be considered righteous: "For if Martin had not lived this inestimable life and if he had not had this excellence, then he never would have been endowed with such glory among us." [102]

* * *

Sulpicius' Martin was a visionary ascetic—a hermit monk of the eastern kind who fought with demons, spoke with angels, communicated with saints, and was rewarded with a vision of Christ. Yet despite Sulpicius' trans-

[100] *VM* 24.1–3.
[101] Ibid., 23.
[102] *Dial.* 2.13: "Nam nisi inaestimabilem vitam adque virtutem Martinus egisset, nequaquam apud nos tanta gloria praeditus haberetur."

parent antagonisms toward the clerical establishment, his *Vita Martini* provided a model of sanctity which eventually informed not only monastic but also episcopal and even female ideals of sanctity.[103] Though the model was shaped in conflict, the sharp edges of religions rancor dulled as time went on.

Ultimately, Martin's reputation benefited from clerical sympathies for monks and the ascetic life. This perspective was obscured in Sulpicius' works, but it should be remembered that Sulpicius was hardly an impartial observer of the tensions which rent the Church in his day, and his personal bitterness toward many in the ecclesiastical establishment soured his view of their spiritual purity. Nor was Sulpicius interested in relinquishing his rancor when attempts were made to resolve the disputes that occasioned the division.[104] He lamented the continuing turmoil in the Church which did not allow ascetics to be left in peace.[105] It was not only in his defense of Martin but also because of personal bitterness that Sulpicius criticized the clergy.

One should be cautious, therefore, about the extent to which the role of asceticism, with its visionary component, was really brought into question by Gallic clerics in this period.[106] Sulpicius focused on the tension between the two paths to God. That view was not an objective reflection of contemporary sentiment. Polarizing the two evils of Priscillianism and the tainted episcopate was, however, an extremely effective way for Sulpicius to open up a middle ground for the acceptance of ascetic spirituality and the centrality of the monastic life to the Gallic Church. As we have noted, evidence is strong that in the fourth and fifth centuries monasticism was actively encouraged and flourished under clerical and episcopal patronage. Martin's first monastery was founded under the patronage of Hilary of Poitiers. His own disciple, the disaffected Brictius, went on to episcopal office, a vocational pattern of monk turned cleric which was even more pronounced in other parts of Gaul, especially in the Rhône Valley.[107] In the following years,

---

[103] On Martin as a model for female sanctity see Fortunatus, *Vita Radegundis*, ed. Bruno Krusch, *MGH, SRM* 2 (1888), pp. 364–77. Farmer, *Communities of St. Martin*, pp. 20–29 notes that Sulpicius' *VM* offered a model for cooperation between the episcopate and monasteries, even if it did not always live up to its promise in subsequent centuries.

[104] Both the *Dialogues*, which is outspoken in its criticism of the Gallic clergy, and the *Chronicle*, which records the tensions between monks and clerics, were written after the official termination of the Felician dispute at the Synod of Turin in 398. See Stancliffe, *St. Martin*, p. 290.

[105] *Dial.* 1.2, 2.8.

[106] This is not to say that Sulpicius' sense of contemporary hostility towards monasticism did not have a legitimate basis. There were very scathing attacks on ascetic communities by a certain Vigilantius. But the attack was soundly rebuffed and the pamphleteering did not prevent monastic communities from continuing to grow and flourish in Gaul. Vigilantius' attack is known through its rebuttal by Jerome, *Contra Vigilantium*, PL 23, 339–52. Stancliffe cites evidence of persistent hostility between clerical factions well into the second decade of the fifth century which seem to align to pro- and antiascetic parties. *St. Martin*, pp. 288–89.

[107] On Rhône valley monastic communities see Ian Wood, "A Prelude to Columbanus: The Monastic Achievement in the Burgundian Territories," *Columbanus and Merovingian Monasticism*, ed. H.B. Clarke, British Archeological Reports: International Series 113 (1981), 3–32; Prinz, *Frühes Mönchtum*, pp. 47 ff., esp. 59–62; and Gérard Moyse, "Les origines du monachisme dans le diocèse de Besançon (Ve–Xe siècles)," *Bibliothèque de L'École des Chartes* 131 (1973), 21–104 (on the Jura monasteries, 56–70).

ascetic ideals were rapidly incorporated into the episcopal ideal for bishops other than Martin. Saintly bishops were expected to promote monasteries in their dioceses. In the 470s Constantius of Lyons extolled Germanus of Auxerre for providing two paths to God, the first through his monastic foundations and the second through his sacerdotal office.[108]

Meanwhile, monks were striving to achieve positions of authority in monastic affairs. As we shall see in the case of Eugendus, visionary abbots developed their own idioms of religious authority.

St. Eugendus of Condat: Ascetic Abbot

Eugendus (St. Oyend) was abbot of the Jura monasteries at the turn of the sixth century (490-c. 510). His *vita* is the third in the anonymous *Lives of the Fathers of Jura*, which recorded the lives of three saintly abbots of the Jura monasteries including the founding brothers Romanus and Lupicinus.[109] Writing shortly after Eugendus' death, the author drew on early traditions about the founding abbots and on personal knowledge of Eugendus.

The first Jura monastery of Condat had eremitic beginnings. About the year 435, Romanus, imitating St. Anthony, left his family home to live in the wilds of the Jura mountains, keeping the company only of wild beasts. His brother Lupicinus joined him after Romanus appeared to him in a night-vision (*per visionem nocte*). Soon the two brothers were living in the wilds "like two doves in a nest."[110] In time, disciples gathered around them. Romanus founded a monastery at Condat and his brother later founded a community eventually known as St. Lupicien, both modeled on the eremitic communities of the Egyptian desert. This type of monastic organization was probably known to them through the example of the Gallic monasteries of Lérins and Lyons, where monks lived in individual cells, assembling primarily for prayer and meals,[111] and from hagiographic accounts including the *Life of St. Anthony* and the *Life of St. Martin*. However, by the fifth

---

[108] Constantius, *Vita Germani ep. Autissiodorensis* 6, ed. R. Borias, SC 112 (1965).

[109] *Vita patrum Jurensium*, ed. François Martine, SC 142 (1968); BHL 7309, 5073, 2665. Based on internal evidence and supporting documentary material, Martine accepts the hagiographer's contention that he was a contemporary of Eugendus and dates the composition to a decade after Eugendus' death in 512–14, c. 520 (pp. 53–57). For a discussion of the authenticity of the VPJ see Martine's introduction (pp. 14–44), which refutes Krusch's contention that the work was a Carolingian fabrication. *MGH, SRM* 3 (1896). See also Prinz, *Frühes Mönchtum*, p. 67. n. 124. A number of monastic foundations were associated with Romanus and Lupicinus: Condat, La Balme (for their sister), Lauconnum (St. Lupicien), and Romainmoutier.

[110] *VPJ* 12.

[111] The monastery did not take on the fully developed communal aspect of a monastic community until the time of Eugendus, who rebuilt the monastery after its destruction by fire. Ibid., 170.

century theirs was a model of ascetic community which was diverging from trends elsewhere in Gaul.[112]

The contemplative Romanus oversaw his monks with gentleness. Still, life must have been hard in the mountains, for soon the monks were clamoring to leave. They claimed to be beset by monstrous *phantasmata*.[113] One of the monks, a saintly deacon named Sabinianus, suffered horrific nighttime abuse from the Devil. First the Devil beat him about the head with stones and tried to set his cell on fire, and then the Devil, who up to that point had appeared in human form, changed into the guise of two very chaste young girls. The girls' modesty was soon changed to lasciviousness, however, as they began to remove their clothing. Sabinianus, while able to avoid looking at them and going so far as to chastise the Devil, could not escape another terrible beating.[114] These demonic encounters echoed the ascetic motifs of the desert monks, whose Lives were read by the Jura monks.

Like their eastern forebears, Romanus' monks lived lives of prayer and contemplation. However, unlike Anthony and Martin, none of the monks at Romanus' monastery was reported to have had visions of Christ and his angels. Romanus' brother Lupicinus had visionary capabilities, however, which were deemed miraculous. His hagiographer reported that Lupicinus could project himself through visions into the minds of those for whom he prayed.[115] Still there was clearly no strong tradition of angelic visions associated with the two brothers at the time the compiler-hagiographer wrote in the sixth century. By contrast, visions impregnated with biblical language and imagery flowered riotously in the Life of Eugendus.

Eugendus headed his monastery at a time when it had developed from an eremitic organization to become an established cenobitic complex. Because of this evolution the monastery needed a new type of leader, someone who could govern large numbers of monks through good example and consensus. New values of leadership replaced the old: leadership, discipline, and authority were all needed, not just claims for personal sanctity. The community was becoming increasingly institutionalized and its relations with the outside world were becoming more clearly defined.

---

[112] Markus, *End of Ancient Christianity*, pp. 213–14. See also Dorothee König, *Amt und Askese. Priesteramt und Mönchtum bei den lateinischen Kirchenvätern in vorbenediktinischer Zeit*, Regulae Benedicti Studia, Supplementa 12 (St. Ottilien, 1985), pp. 228–31; and Lutterbach, *Monachus factus est*, pp. 63–68.

[113] *VPJ* 51.

[114] Ibid., 54–6. Sabinianus' abuse mirrors the torments endured by Anthony of Egypt, whose *vita* was an important source of inspiration to the monastery's first abbots. *V. Antonii* 4. On another occasion Sabinianus encountered a demonic serpent in a canal. The serpent slipped into the icy water and the monks were afraid to continue their work. Sabinianus, however, recognizing the serpent as the Devil, had the brothers make the sign of the Cross over his hands and feet and continued his work in the water. *VPJ* 57–58.

[115] Benedict of Nursia was accredited with a like ability by Gregory the Great. *Dialogues* 2.22.

It was said that in his childhood, Eugendus' holy life was presaged in a vision in which he was taken to the threshold of the monastery so that he could diligently scan the eastern sky, just as once the patriarch Abraham had done.[116] This vision occurred, the hagiographer maintained, so that it could be said of Eugendus figuratively (*typice . . . dicebatur*), "This shall be your inheritance."[117] As Eugendus stood there, people joined him one by one until a crowd surrounded him, including the saintly abbots Romanus and Lupicinus. Then Eugendus saw the heavens open in the east and a pathway, shining with light, like a crystal ladder descended to the place where he was, and choirs of angels dressed in white came towards him. He and the others were so struck by the sight that they could not talk. Then the angels carefully mingled with the assembled mortals, and gathering them up and uniting them to themselves, they ascended with them once more to heaven. As they ascended, the angels sang a phrase which Eugendus heard again when he entered the monastery a year later, "Ego sum Via et Vita et Veritas." As the vision receded, the star-studded sky closed, leaving Eugendus alone. He woke up in terror and related the whole to his father, who knew it to be a sign of his son's monastic future.[118]

The childhood presaging of a saint's holy career was a common motif in the Lives of the saints. What made this vision so striking was its use of Old Testament imagery to predict the sort of abbot Eugendus would become. The vision promised that, like Abraham, Eugendus would be a leader and the patriarch of a fine dynasty dedicated to God and, metaphorically speaking, begotten by his seed. Like Abraham, Eugendus was told to look at the skies to learn that his progeny would be numerous like the stars. Then a shining path, like Jacob's ladder, descended from heaven, permitting angels to mix with monks, a reminder that monks lived the angelic life.[119] The call "I am the Way, the Life, and the Truth" suggested that Eugendus's life, like Christ's, would offer a path to salvation.[120] Although at the time of the vision Eugendus was still a young boy under his natural father's care, his spiritual parentage was established by his association with the holy founders of the monastery. In an image beloved of monastic writers, Eugendus' followers enveloped him the way bees crowd a honey-grape. The mystical image of bees and honey suggested the spiritual progeny which would be generated from his spiritual powers.

Eugendus entered the monastery of Condat a year after this momentous

---

[116] *VPJ* 121.

[117] Ibid.: "sic erit semen tuum." See Genesis 15.5.

[118] *VPJ* 123–24.

[119] Genesis 28.12–13. Visionary ladders and other means of spiritual ascent are discussed by Éliade, *Myths, Dreams*, pp. 99–122, and Walter Cahn, "Ascending to and Descending from Heaven: Ladder Themes in Early Medieval Art," in *Santi e Demoni nell'alto medioevo occidentale (secoli v–xi)* vol. 2, pp. 697–724, Settimane di studio 26 (Spoleto, 1989).

[120] Adapted from John 14.6.

vision. The next watershed in his monastic career occurred when the abbot under whose direction he had been living, Minausius, became ill and designated Eugendus as his successor. Eugendus was still relatively young, and his appointment appears to have met with opposition.[121] After his installation as abbot, a second vision, like the first, intimately linked Eugendus' leadership with the future prosperity of the monastery. Eugendus was "struck" by a very clear revelation.[122] During the night, he saw a vision of the former abbots Romanus and Lupicinus, accompanied by the monastic elders who had lived in their time. After receiving the abbots' blessing, Eugendus saw the present abbot enter the room clothed in a white *pallium* with purple stripes. Romanus took from Minausius his belt of office and set it around Eugendus' waist. He then took the *pallium* from the abbot's shoulders and likewise clothed Eugendus with it. Romanus then declared that those signs of abbatial office were now Eugendus'. Then the elders suddenly dashed their lamps against the walls. A voice spoke to Eugendus through the darkness, telling him not to be sad for the loss of this present material light, but to look to the east where he would soon be aided by divine light. On turning to look in that direction he saw the light of dawn creeping in until a ray of daylight streamed toward him. He came out of the vision and jumped from his bed in joy. What the vision predicted, we are told, soon came to pass.

The meaning of the vision was clear to the monks of Eugendus' day. The reigning abbot's tokens of office were placed upon Eugendus by the community's founder in a spiritual representation of their approval for the transmission of abbatial authority to the saint. The passing of these symbols of office from one abbot to another strengthened the idea of spiritual continuity from Romanus to Eugendus. The extinction of the light was explained by the author as representing those who from jealousy sought to take away from Eugendus those powers already vested in him—a clear reference to the troubles which surrounded Eugendus' appointment as abbot. The temporary darkness may have alluded to an interim period during which his appointment was thwarted.[123] (It appears that some disaffected monks left the monastery at this time, complaining of Eugendus' youth.) The light of dawn approaching from the east might then be interpreted according to the hagiographer's subsequent attestations to the saint's healing powers and the many prodigies witnessed thereafter. These signs manifested Eugendus' spiritual powers, and soon, we are told, his reputation was such that the clergy were happy for any contact with him. The *pseudofratres* who had been Eugendus' detractors were, from that time on, regarded as degenerate wretches.

---

[121] Eugendus' predecessor as abbot is not named in the *VPJ* but in a later abbatial list. In the catalogue of the abbots of St. Oyend, he is called Minausius. See Martine, *SC* 142, pp. 75–76.
[122] *VPJ* 134: "evidentissima revelatione percellitur." For what follows see 135–37.
[123] Ibid., 138.

This important vision, which was intended to lend a supernatural aura to Eugendus' elevation to abbatial office, and which foretold his short-term persecution, fits into a category of visions which was to become very popular in Gallic hagiography. Political conflicts or embarrassments were transformed through the idiom of visions into opportunities for resolution.

Visions were important also in explaining a monastery's acquisition of relics. According to the hagiographer, one summer day as Eugendus sat sleeping under a tree, he dreamed that three men came toward him. He asked them who they were and they revealed themselves to be the apostles Peter, Paul, and Andrew. They declared their desire to stay with the Condat community. Eugendus awoke from his dream to see approaching two of his monks who had been away from the monastery for two years. With them they brought relics of the three apostles who had greeted Eugendus in his dream.[124] This simple story, a popular one in hagiography, was meaningful because it conveyed in a recognizably human form the very real presence of the saints which was believed to reside in the tangible remains in the monastery's keeping. The apostles' courteous greeting, coming as it did in advance of their relics, added to the sense of the saints as honored guests who came willingly to grace Eugendus' community. The story reflected well on the sanctity of the future abbot and the holy benefits accorded to the community under his direction.

In the final vision we learn of the profound debt owed by the monks of the Jura monasteries to the example of St. Martin as related by his hagiographer.[125]

One day, as Eugendus slept on his pallet, exhausted from weeping, a great brightness enveloped him. It was St. Martin, who asked Eugendus what he wanted. Eugendus related his concern about the fate of two brothers who were away from the monastery. Martin comforted Eugendus by reminding him that when the brothers had left he had prayed to Martin, commending them to his care. Martin was able to assure Eugendus that the two were safe and that indeed one of them would arrive at the monastery the following day, putting to rest his concern for their well-being.

The dreamed vision is striking in its reminiscence of Sulpicius' account of his own vision of Martin. Like Sulpicius, Eugendus fell asleep exhausted from his tears. He displayed concern not only for the monks under his charge, but about the critics in the community who had accused him of exiling the brothers. Eugendus' vision of Martin as an exceptionally bright

[124] Ibid., 153–55.
[125] The Jura monasteries were profoundly influenced by oriental monasticism as relayed by Cassian's writings and by the monastic practice of Lérins, Marseilles, and the Rhône valley monasteries, especially those in the Lyons diocese where Romanus lived for a time (either at *Insula Barbara* or Ainay). See Prinz, *Frühes Mönchtum*, pp. 68–69. The Jura monasteries were also marked by their veneration of St. Martin, as is evident in the *VPJ* and in the early eremiticism at Condat.

light also reminds us of Sulpicius' description of the saint who emitted a great light. It does not seem unlikely, therefore, that the author had Sulpicius' letter to the deacon Aurelius in mind when he related this tale. Martin was certainly an important saint for the monks at Condat in Eugendus' time, and there are many echoes of the *Vita Martini* in the *Lives of the Fathers of Jura*.[126] Particularly important was the issue of monks holding clerical office, which reflected on the nature of leadership within monastic communities. Eugendus, we are told, believed it was better for an abbot not to hold sacerdotal office since it did not give a proper example to the young monks, and furthermore, in a passage very reminiscent of Sulpicius' *Dialogues*, Eugendus remarked that many seasoned monks who led spiritually mature lives became secretly puffed up when sacerdotal office was conferred upon them.[127] Eugendus' comments harked back to traditional ascetic wariness of clerics, for which Martin was a very clear example. Ultimately, however, Martin's example is a telling foil to Eugendus' Life. Martin provided a model of spiritual leadership in Sulpicius' eyes precisely because he rejected overt symbols of authority. Eugendus, with his visions emphasizing abbatial leadership, is quite distant from the reluctant Martin.

In ascetic biographies, visions were a compelling way of communicating ideas about the nature of spiritual authority and leadership. In the examples of Martin and Eugendus, their hagiographers used visions to present, explore, and resolve problems which monastic leaders sometimes faced when confronted by pressures internal or external to the monastic community. In Sulpicius' *Vita Martini* visionary stories became barely disguised vehicles for commentary on ideological, political, and leadership issues. Martin's visions elevated the virtues of monasticism and asceticism, contrasting them with the worldliness of the ecclesiastical establishment. Yet this rejection of leadership and personal authority ill fitted the direction in which the monastic community was going. There was a real need for leadership in monasteries. Increasingly, stories were told which reflected on the abbot's responsibilities, not simply as spiritual guide but as disciplinarian. Gregory of Tours' story about the late abbot of Randan, who tried to govern his monks through persuasion rather than by command, is an example. When the abbot had a vision of hell with wretches immersed in a fiery river spanned by a narrow bridge, and asked the meaning of the vision, he was told, "From this bridge will be hurled headlong anyone who is discovered to have been lacking in authority over those committed to his charge."[128]

Eugendus' example of abbatial leadership within the monastic arena registers a changing of religious ideals. Monasteries had to be run harmoniously

---

[126] For instance, Martin's miracles were extolled, including one in which a flask of his oil was untouched by the conflagration which gutted the monastery. *VPJ* 161–64.

[127] Ibid., 133–34.

[128] Gregory of Tours, *HF* 4.33.

for the good of the souls within them. Discipline was a kindness when so many were vulnerable. Leadership and ranks of authority within the monastery had to be clear and respected. And at the apex of the monastic life, abbots and their officers required legitimate avenues for leadership.

As concepts of leadership and religious authority evolved, it was not surprising that dreams and visions became legitimating vehicles for airing those ideas. Biblical images like that of the patriarch embracing his chosen people grafted a new language of spiritual authority onto older conventions, and created a new idiom of spiritual leadership.

* * *

Clerical opinion had never denied the monk's attainment of spectacular spiritual experiences. To do so would have been to deny a long tradition within Christian spiritual life. Nor did clerics deny that the ascetic life, with proper safeguards of clerical supervision, was punctuated by visionary rewards. Many clergymen fostered monastic communities and held up individual hermits as exemplars of the holy life. And, despite episcopal anxieties about individual monastic communities or self-styled prophets, bishops were generally supportive of monastic communities in their dioceses, founded them occasionally, and, by the fifth century, increasingly were themselves former monks. Such former monks brought to their office a love of the cloister and a respect for the contemplative life.

What the cleric did not do, however, was suggest that ascetics were privileged dreamers. Monks were not regarded as a special class or caste of spiritual dreamers, nor were they encouraged to think of themselves as such. The clergy, after all, were appointed by God (with the help of the citizenry, the clergy, and sometimes secular powers) to lead the entire religious community—cleric, lay, and monastic. In the Cyprianic tradition of divinely guided clerical leadership, divine dreams and visions might visit the clergy, especially the higher clergy, to empower them to direct God's people.[129] And ordinary Christians too, who lived according to precepts formulated for them by the church leadership under the guidance of the Holy Spirit, had occasional glimpses of those higher powers. Monasteries had scribes to record the visions of their holy monks. The clergy likewise had opportunities to publish supernatural events. But who would preserve the experiences of lay men and women by recording them? This was the province of the clerics, and

---

[129] Cyprian of Carthage believed that the activity of the Spirit through admonitory dreams and visions in the Christian community worked primarily through its clerical leaders, like himself, although he did accept the visions of some children in his congregation, perhaps because their youth suggested innocence. Cyprian of Carthage, Letters (1–81), trans. Sister Rose Bernard Donna, Fathers of the Church, vol. 51 (Washington, D.C., 1965). See Letters 11, 16, and 39. See Amat, Songes, pp. 104–12. Fox, Pagans and Christians, pp. 410–11, notes that "approved visions now had an obedient tone."

as we shall see in subsequent chapters, once they accepted the dreams of visions of particular lay men and women as authentic they were not slow to record them. In accepting that the dreams of ordinary Christians could have divine significance the clerisy perpetuated an ancient tradition that held that divine dreams were potentially available to all.

Part 2

VISIONS AND AUTHORITY IN
THE MEROVINGIAN COMMUNITY

In the short term, the upheavals caused by the barbarian invasions of the
western Roman provinces in the fifth century benefited few. But it has long
been recognized that the reputation and leadership of the episcopate did
benefit over the long term. Through acts of personal courage in difficult
times, through makeshift diplomacy and hard-headed negotiations with barbarian leaders, but above all through a strong sense of the underlying continuity of Christian history and tradition, the higher clergy maneuvered themselves into positions of administrative authority in Gallic towns and spiritual
authority among their congregations.[1] A bishop's success as spiritual leader
within his diocese often depended on his ability to muster external resources
or powers. Some of these secular powers he inherited from Christian antiquity, others he acquired as regional politics allowed, but as Friedrich Prinz
and other historians of the Merovingian episcopate have emphasized, it is
anachronistic to try to separate out the bishop's secular powers from his religious powers in this period.[2] In early medieval Gaul spiritual and temporal
authority went hand in hand.[3]

[1] Bishops rallied their frightened flocks to counter the barbarian threat—for example Bishop
Anianus of Orleans before Attila. *Vita s. Aniani Ep. Aurelianensis, MGH, SRM* 3, ed. Krusch
(1896), pp. 104–17. The clergy did not always emerge unscathed from these encounters; in the
Vita s. Aniani we learn that the priest Memorius, his subdeacons, and twenty newly baptized
"innocents" were decapitated on a mission to Attila on behalf of Bishop Lupus of Troyes.
[2] Friedrich Prinz, "Herrschaftsformen der Kirche vom Ausgang der Spätantike bis zum Ende
der Karolingerzeit. Zur Einführung ins Thema," introduction to *Herrschaft und Kirche:
Beiträge zur Entstehung und Wirkungsweise episkopaler und monastischer Organisationsformen*, ed. Prinz (Stuttgart, 1988).
[3] Friedrich Prinz, "Die bischöfliche Stadtherrschaft im Frankenreich vom 5. Bis zum 7.
Jahrhundert," *Historische Zeitschrift* 217 (1974), 1–35, examines episcopal assumption of secular roles and powers in Gallic cities. See also Prinz, *Herrschaft und Kirche*, and Jean Durliat,
"Les attributions civiles des évêques mérovingiens: L'exemple de Didier, évêque de Cahors
(630–55)," *Annales du Midi* 91 (1979), 237–54.

This is not to say that the bishop's episcopal authority went unchallenged. Some bishops had to fight hard against local opposition to remain in office, and some had difficulties enforcing their authority even in religious matters in their dioceses.[4] Yet by the sixth century, for which Gregory of Tours has given us such a illuminating account of his fellow bishops and their class, the clerical hierarchy was sufficiently well entrenched in the religious and political fabric of Frankish Gaul for the institution to weather occasional instances of incompetency, politicking, and corruption.[5]

In the fifth and sixth centuries Gallic bishops wielded local power and gained political visibility through their exercise of civil roles in the towns. In the sixth century, bishops were granted fiscal rights and immunities by the early Merovingian kings and were delegated administrative powers including a judicial role. By the seventh century they enjoyed a significant degree of autonomy in some portions of the Frankish kingdoms (primarily Neustria and Burgundy), with their power now issuing from personal wealth and political connections.[6] As Friedrich Prinz has highlighted, the distinction between power delegated to bishops in late antiquity and power which issued from personal wealth and status placed late Merovingian bishops in a different relationship to central royal authority.[7] Even the most securely tenured bishop, however, had to negotiate competing interests within his diocese, including the diocesan clergy whose local connections made them vulnerable to factionalism, the laity comprising city officialdom, aristocratic families, and the military officers of the Frankish kings. One of the ways Gallic bishops were able to rise above these local concerns, and realize a vision of their office within the context of the universal Church was by promoting ideal images of the Church, its clergy, and its role in the community. Clerics claimed this ideal by exercising spiritual authority in visible ways before

---

[4] Bishop Cautinus of Clermont, for example, was unable to enforce his order of excommunication against a suspected matricide. See Ian Wood, "The Ecclesiastical Politics of Merovingian Clermont," *Ideal and Reality in Frankish and Anglo-Saxon Society*, ed. Patrick Wormald, Donald Bullough, and Roger Collins, p. 52 (Oxford, 1983).

[5] Essential on the Merovingian bishops are Georg Scheibelreiter, *Der Bischof in merowingischer Zeit* (Vienna, 1983); Prinz, *Frühes Mönchtum*; Prinz, "Die bischöfliche Stadtherrschaft"; Martin Heinzelmann, *Bischofsherrschaft in Gallien. Zur Kontinuität römischer Führungsschichten vom 4. bis zum 7. Jahrhundert. Soziale, prosopographische und bildungsgeschichtliche Aspekte*, Beihefte der Francia 5 (Munich, 1976); D. Claude, "Die Bestellung der Bischöfe im Merowingische Reiche," *Zeitschrift der Savigny-Stiftung für Rechtsgeschichte, kanonistiche Abteilung* 49 (1963), 1–75; Bernhard Jussen, "Über 'Bischofherrschaften' und Prozeduren politisch-sozialer Umordnung in Gallien zwischen 'Antike' und 'Mittelalter,'" *Historische Zeitschrift* 260 (1995), 673–718; and essays by Prinz, Heinzelmann, and Reinhold Kaiser in Prinz, *Herrschaft und Kirche*.

[6] Reinhold Kaiser, "Royauté et pouvoir épiscopal au nord de la Gaul (VIIe–Xe siècles). Résultats d'une recherche en cours," in *La Neustrie: Les pays au nord de la Loire de 650 à 850; colloque historique international*, ed. Harmut Atsma, Beihefte der Francia 16, vol. 1 (Sigmaringen, 1989).

[7] Prinz, "Herrschaftsformen der Kirche," p. 8.

their congregations and asserting the centrality of their office and its ambitions to all their constituents.

Visions which appeared to suggest that these activities were framed by supernatural concord were naturally an important means by which churchmen could legitimate political and religious objectives. In order for dreams and visions to have a place in shaping episcopal politics, two things were necessary. First, bishops had to have a strong sense of how episcopal identity was defined in ideal terms and how it could function in practical terms in the Merovingian political climate. Second, ecclesiastics needed a firm belief in the place, authority, and usefulness of divinely sent dreams in addressing to matters of faith and in guiding the historical mission of the Church.

In striving after an episcopal ideal, bishops looked to forge religious identity which was sustainable and which would make them appear effective pastors and intercessors. As Christ's representatives on earth, bishops were expected to be celibate, above reproach morally and doctrinally, and faithful to the traditions of the Church. Shored up by these inner virtues, the good bishop demonstrated leadership within his community and in his dealings with those outside it. The bishop's integrity in these areas was most visibly displayed by his successful assumption of episcopal office, which, despite any indications to the contrary, had to be seen as the will of the Holy Spirit. Assumption of episcopal office generated certain expectations of the incumbent: the consecrated bishop was expected to renounce secular ambitions and detach himself from family ties. By becoming the defender of his flock, especially the poor and disadvantaged, he was expected to find a new constituency, a new family whose interests he must shield against the predations of Frankish nobles. As a religious teacher, providing Christian instruction and liturgy for his flock, he was also expected to protect his community from its doctrinal enemies. This was by no means an easy ideal for most bishops to live up to. One has only to read the works of Gregory of Tours to note how many fell short of the mark. Those who achieved the ideal, or appeared to, surely had angels on their side—as many of Gregory's stories were designed to show.

Thus, the dreams and visions which had bishops as their subject in the Merovingian era were often intended to comment, positively or negatively, on this episcopal ideal. In some cases, visionary accounts were used to affirm a bishop's reputation for holiness when his worthiness was brought into question. Visions could also be used to render intelligible, in religious terms, occasions when individuals fell short of the ideal. Whether told of bishops or by them, visionary stories about bishops were rarely neutral, and could either enhance or harm reputations. Dreams and visions were thus capable of becoming an imaged rhetoric of virtue and merit which was integral to a bishop's authority in religious matters and his ability to speak on behalf of the supernatural protectors of the community, the saints.

At the same time that dreams and visions were told about the higher clergy by interested third parties, some bishops successfully employed this imaged rhetoric for their own purposes. In recent years there has been important research uncovering the historical motives and tensions that underlaid conventional Christian rhetoric, especially in hagiography.[8] Yet this rhetoric was not the exclusive preserve of later hagiographic spin doctors; some bishops were successful in using dream and vision accounts as a present means to communicate broader designs. This was possible because bishops spoke to a Christian culture which had long understood dreams to be a legitimate way in which God spoke to his people and to his Church.

The three chapters which follow comment in different ways on the intersection of dreams and visions with arenas of religious authority in Gaul. In Chapter 3 we will see how a well-connected bishop, Gregory of Tours, understood the agency of dreams and visions in articulating and refining his sense of the bishop's office. Chapter 4 examines healing dreams which were said to have occurred at the shrines of the saints, and which were given some public recognition by the clergy through the publication of miracle books. Finally, in Chapter 5, tales of visionary journeys to the otherworld are examined for their ability to legitimate and promote the soteriological efficacy of clerically dispensed liturgical offerings. Each of these contexts reveals Merovingian churchmen operating with different degrees of assurance. Seen together these chapters depict a clergy that found ways, on a case-by-case basis, to permit a Christian culture of dreaming to develop and flourish, while maintaining episcopal authority.

[8] Paul Fouracre, "Merovingian History and Merovingian Hagiography," *Past and Present* 127 (1990), 3–38.

3   Gregory of Tours:
   A Visionary Bishop

In the writings of Gregory of Tours, historians of the sixth-century Merovingian episcopate have an enviable source of information. The prolific writings of a bishop who was well connected, often well informed, and combined a delicious curiosity about his peers with a desire to record his times for posterity provide an insider's view of the ecclesiastical politics of his day. Yet at the same time it is undeniable that our view of the sixth-century episcopate has tended to be dominated by the perspective of this one man. Historians generally overcome this shortcoming by emphasizing or debating Gregory's representativeness of the Gallic episcopate as a whole. Yet how representative was Gregory of the views of his day? As we examine him as a source for so many of the stories of divine dreams and supernatural visions in the sixth century, we must bear this question always in mind. It is not enough to observe that many of Gregory's stories were told to him by episcopal colleagues and others of his wide acquaintance, for a story retold by a second party inevitably becomes the "property" of its most recent narrator.

In this chapter I focus on the insights we have into the oneiric beliefs of Gregory, who not only recorded visions of others but claimed to have had them himself. What social and religious experiences and assumptions went into making this visionary bishop, and how did his views intersect with the religious norms of his day? And how did Gregory's role as bishop of an important city and guardian of St. Martin's cult determine the way he understood the oneiric dimension of his office? As will become clear, Gregory's sense of the duties and responsibilities of his office and the scope of oneiric authority extended beyond the Christian population in his diocese to encompass the entire community.

The Making of a Visionary Bishop

Gregory was born into a distinguished Gallic family of the senatorial aristocracy around the year 539.[1] He was educated by his paternal uncle Gallus, bishop and saint of Clermont, and by Gallus' archdeacon and successor, Avitus, of whom he wrote fondly that it was he, "second only to the psalms of David, who has led me to the words of evangelical preaching, and to the stories and epistles of apostolic virtue."[2] Although Gregory lived his adult life in Tours, he retained strong connections with his Clermont relatives and with the cults they propagated there. Relatives on both sides of his family had occupied prominent Gallic bishoprics including the See of Tours. A number of Gregory's male relatives were already venerated as saints during Gregory's lifetime, and Gregory's accounts of their lives and deeds helped broaden the basis for and perpetuate their veneration.[3]

Before we consider the contribution of Gregory of Tours as a uniquely prolix and colorful narrator of visionary tales, it is important to consider the broader cultural context in which his views were developed. There were two major influences on Gregory's visionary thinking, representing two spheres of authority in his life. The first was the world of his extended family with their stories and traditions. The second was the intellectual milieu to which Gregory aspired—the world of the pan-Mediterranean Christian intelligentsia, to which Gallic bishops still in the sixth century, rightly or wrongly, believed they belonged.

Our most intimate view of Gregory's attitude toward dreams is in passages where he recalled and fashioned family stories told about himself and others during his youth. Gregory lost his father when he was quite young, and was brought up by his mother Armentaria, his paternal uncle Gallus,

[1] Gregory's works are in *MGH*, *SRM* 1.1 and 1.2, ed. Bruno Krusch and Wilhelm Levinson (1937–42). On his biography and episcopate see Luce Pietri, *La ville de Tours du IVe au VIe siècle: naissance d'une cité chrétienne* (Rome, 1983), pp. 247–64; Gabriel Jacques Jean Monod, *Études critiques sur les sources de l'histoire mérovingienne*, 2 vols. (Paris, 1872–75); Raymond Van Dam, *Leadership and Community*, and his *Saints and Their Miracles in Late Antique Gaul* (Princeton, 1993); and Martin Heinzelmann, *Gregor von Tours (538–594): "Zehn Bücher Geschichte." Historiographie und Gesellschaftskonzept im 6. Jahrhundert* (Darmstadt, 1994). Gregory's birth date is calculated by his *De virtutibus sancti Martini* 3.10 (hereafter, *Virt. Mart.*), where he mentions his birth as being thirty-four years before his consecration to the bishopric of Tours in 573. On Gregory's claim to senatorial rank and its significance in the sixth-century context see Frank D. Gilliard, "The Senators of 6th Century Gaul," *Speculum* 54 (1979), 685–97, and for an alternative interpretation, Brian Brennan, "Senators and Social Mobility in Sixth-Century Gaul," *Journal of Medieval History* 11 (1985) 145–61.

[2] "Qui me post Davitici carminis cannas ad illa evangelicae praedicationis dicta atque apostolicae virtutis historias epistolasque perduxit." *Liber Vitae Patrum* 2, *SRM, MGH* 1.2 (1885) ed. Bruno Krusch pp. 661–744 (hereafter, *VP*). English translations of the *Liber Vitae Patrum* are from Edward James, *Gregory of Tours, Life of the Fathers*, Translated Texts for Historians, Latin Series 1 (Liverpool, 1985).

[3] On the saints promoted by the family of Gregory of Tours see Van Dam, *Saints and Their Miracles*, pp. 50–81.

and Avitus of Clermont. Evidently the young Gregory was raised on stories about his family. Armentaria was probably the source for many of these stories, but some accounts of such illustrious forebears as his great-grandfather Gregory of Langres may have been common knowledge. Told as prognostications, the stories often hinged on angelic promises communicated in dreams.

When the plague arrived in Gaul in 543, Gregory was probably no more than four years old, yet the devastation and fear it caused in the area was remembered long after. Gregory's uncle Gallus was said to have prayed fervently that his city of Clermont be spared. When an angel appeared to him in a vision promising that his prayers had been heard and that his city would not be touched, Gallus instituted rogations, setting out in procession to the church of St. Julian of Brioude sixty-five miles away. As a consequence of his prayers, we are told, the inhabitants were spared.[4] Gregory may have learned this story from Gallus himself as he was growing up in his household. At the same time he learned the expected role of a bishop in time of crisis: girding his flock, dissipating fear by confronting the horror with purposeful action, and expecting a sign or vision as an appropriate divine response. It is worth noting that Gregory organized rogations in a similar fashion in Tours in the face of another terrible epidemic a few years later, indicating that he had learned directly from his uncle's vision and responsive action.[5]

Gregory's mother too had a story to tell of those terrible times. As the plague approached Clermont, signs and marks appeared on the homes and churches of the area. Armentaria had a vision one night in which it seemed to her that the wine in their cellars had turned to blood. In her dream she wept, believing that she and her family were to be victims of the plague. An apparition promised her that if she kept the vigils of St. Benignus whose feast day was on the morrow, she would be spared. St. Benignus was a family cult instituted by Gregory's grandfather and namesake Gregory of Langres. Armentaria carried out the instructions of the vision, and Gregory recalls that whereas neighboring homes were marked, theirs remained unmarked.[6]

With a strong family tradition of storytelling in which supernatural forces protected and advised in dreams, it is not surprising to discover that Gregory learned early to respect the oneiric dimension of his world. He related his own first visionary experience as having occurred when he was a "young boy."[7] He must have been very young, for his father was still alive. Gregory's

---

[4] *HF* 4.5.

[5] Ibid., 10.30.

[6] See de Nie, *Views* pp. 261–62.

[7] *Liber in gloria confessorum* 39, ed. Bruno Krusch *MGH, SRM.* 1.2 (hereafter, *GC*). Gregory was at the age when he was just learning to read, as the vision story makes clear. Elsewhere Gregory states he was eight years old when he began to learn to read with Nicetius of Lyons. *VP* 7.2.

father Florentius often suffered from fevers and pains. One night a "person" appeared to Gregory asking if he had read the book of Joshua. The young Gregory replied that thus far he had learned only the letters of the alphabet and did not even know of the existence of such a book. The person then instructed him to break a splinter from a piece of wood, to write Joshua's name on it, and to place it beneath his father's pillow as a protection. The following morning Gregory shared his dream with his mother, and she instructed that the directions be carried out. The remedy worked, and Gregory's father regained his health for another year until he was once again afflicted. Again the apparition appeared to Gregory, this time asking if he had read the book of Tobit. Once again Gregory acknowledged that he had not. The apparition instructed him to do what Tobit's son had done for him, namely catch a fish and burn its entrails in front of his father. Gregory related this second vision to his mother, and the instructions were carried out as before with the same success. It is worth noting that Tobias' action on behalf of his father Tobit was not quite as the angel related it in Gregory's vision. Tobias burned the heart and liver of the fish to banish the demon that had killed his prospective wife Sarah's previous husbands (Tobit 8.2–3), whereas his father's blindness was cured by Tobias' anointing of Tobit's eyes with the fish's gall (Tobit 11.11–13). The unifying thread of association was not, as one might expect, the incidence of blindness, for this was not the affliction suffered by Gregory's father. Rather, the underlying cause of the sickness, a demon, was the link to Tobit's blindness. Since in exegetical works on Tobit the fish in the story was interpreted as Christ, the *piscis magnus*, the angelic advice might have been interpreted as a Christian remedy for possession by demons.[8] It is difficult to speculate at what juncture the dream became associated in Gregory's mind with the story of Tobit. Was it a partially remembered school story? Or was the biblical association made by his elders, or even by himself at a more mature age? Whatever the answer, Gregory's story emphasized that dreams spoke the language of scripture (even if he was mistaken in the details), and that Scripture was the *medicamentum* which must be applied to the suffering psyche.

Gregory's earliest experiences of significant dreaming thus occurred at a formative stage in the development of his religious ideas. Dreams had become at once an option for resolving family crises and a means of situating the guidance of angels within the intimate orbit of personal affairs. Gregory had also discovered firsthand that dreams were important for effecting cures with divine help. It was perhaps as a result of this belief, and thus expectation, that healing visions are among the most common in Gregory's corpus of visionary narratives.

[8] On this exegetical reading see Quodvultdeus, *De promissionibus et praedictionibus Dei* 2.39, ed. René Braun, *Opera Quodvultdeo Carthaginiensi episcopo tributa*, CC 60 (1976) pp. 1–223.

As another crisis loomed in his mid-twenties, Gregory chose again to rely on the advice of a dream. Gregory wanted to write. Notwithstanding his pride in his illustrious family, he was troubled by a "rusticity" in his writing style. His voluminous works show the drive of a vocational writer, but one senses that he was always looking over his shoulder at his friend Venantius Fortunatus, whose poetry combined rare artistic talent with the benefit of a sound education at Ravenna. The conflict between his desire to record the miracles of the saints which he believed was God's will, and his fears of inadequacy produced a crisis which he described as an intermingling of self-doubt and desire.[9] Gregory's anxiety was resolved finally by a dream that came upon him while he observed the cures taking place at noontime in the basilica of St. Martin.[10] His mother Armentaria appeared to him and asked him why he was so slow to write down what he saw. Gregory responded that since he was not learned in literature it would be shameful of him to attempt such a project; would that Severus, Paulinus, or even Fortunatus were there to describe those events! His mother then both encouraged and chided him in the dream: his language was more easily understood by the people than that of the learned, she insisted, and should he fail to record the events, it would be a divine charge against him.[11]

Armentaria's reference to literary style and elitism in the dream reflected a longstanding concern that the form of Latin spoken by clerics, because it was often beyond the understanding of their flock, impeded their effective communication of the Christian faith. A century earlier, Julianus Pomerius, inspired by Augustine's *De doctrina christiana* 4.28, had expressed these concerns in Gaul: "[A] teacher of the church should not parade an elaborate style, lest he seem not to want to edify the church of God but to reveal what great learning he possesses. . . . Such should be the simplicity and straightforwardness of the bishop's language: though this may mean less good Latin, it should be restrained and dignified so that it prevents no one, however ignorant, from understanding it." He went on: "[A] good Latin style is one that expresses briefly and clearly the things to be understood . . . the prudent-minded are pleased not by the ornamental but by the forceful; for things have not been provided for the sake of words, but words have been devised to express things." [12]

Gregory took the dream very seriously as his authority to write; as he stated in the preface to his *De virtutibus S. Martini*, he would not have undertaken the work had he not been warned to do so two and three times

---

[9] *Virt. Mart.* 1, praef.: "Maeroris, cur tantae vitutes, quae sub antecessoribus nostris factae sunt, non sunt scriptae; terroris, ut agrediar opus egregium rusticanus."

[10] de Nie, *Views* (1987), p. 215, discusses Gregory's imprecision about this dream.

[11] See Erich Auerbach, *Literary Language and Its Public in Late Latin Antiquity* (New York, 1965), pp. 25–66, on the *sermo humilis*.

[12] Julianus Pomerius, *De vita contemplativa* 1.23.1; 3.34.2, PL 59, 415–520. Translation by M. J. Suelzer, *Ancient Christian Writers* (Westminster, 1947).

by a vision.[13] We should take this claim seriously. Gregory's desire to write was legitimated by the dream's emphasis on his obedience and his pure, spiritual motives. The dream enabled him to substitute for one kind of authority to write (a polished style and impressive erudition—embodied by other Martinian writers, Sulpicius Severus, Paulinus of Périgeux, and Venantius Fortunatus) another, higher register of authority (a dream ordering him to glorify St. Martin's miracle).

Gregory's accounts of his youthful visions and the importance of vision stories in his family's lore indicate the importance of family history in influencing the perspective of the dreamer. Gregory learned early to explore his dreams openly and to think of them as imaged commentaries on his experience. Giselle de Nie writes that, "since Gregory regarded a certain type of dream-reality as spiritual reality, he was always looking for it, expecting it."[14]

In late antiquity the Christian intelligensia, especially bishops, recounted dreams as storytelling devices, while also regarding them as windows on spiritual truths. This tradition provided a cultural context which, in addition to family predisposition, determined Gregory's attitude towards dreams. We see the lives of this class in their letters, their poems, and occasionally their devotional writings. These literary outpourings were often affective in nature, exposing spiritual restlessness in the language and imagery of dreams, and they partook of a literary culture that relied on shared cultural references, shared images, and shared metaphors.

In his *Cathemerinon*, the fourth-century Spanish writer of hymns Prudentius wrote movingly and poetically of dreams. In tones reminiscent of Tertullian, Prudentius described mankind's biological rythms of sleeping and waking as portending figuratively the darkness of sin and the light of Christ's deliverance. In his "Hymn at Cockcrow" he explained that "the sleep that is given to us each night is like the sleep of death. Like the terrible night, our sins make us lie asleep and snoring. . . . Come O Christ, and invade our sleep; break the chains that darkness has forged. Free us from our habits of sin; fill us with the new light of day."[15] Such sentiments had become convential expressions in late antiquity.

Prudentius lent his poetic voice to Christian teaching. For example, he subscribed to the view that divine dreams were the preserve of the just. He wrote in his sixth hymn, "Before Sleeping": "How deep are the mysteries that Christ reveals to the just while they are sleeping soundly, how clear and quieting. . . . In such sleep honest men rest their minds without worry so that their souls can travel across Heaven's length and breadth." Prudentius ended

---

[13] *Virt. Mart.* 1, praef.: "Quod non praesumerem, nisi bis et tertio admonitus fuissem per visum."

[14] de Nie, *Views*, p. 298.

[15] Prudentius, *Liber Cathemerinon* 1, ll. 25–28, "A Hymn at Cockcrow," in *The Last Poets of Imperial Rome*, trans. by Harold Isbell (Harmondsworth, 1971), p. 154.

the hymn with the admission that for most Christians such dreaming visions are not likely: "But we deserve none of this because error fills our hearts." [16] Gregory of Tours, who was much preoccupied with issues of merit and purity in the visionary, knew Prudentius' works and would have found in them much to confirm his views.

In Italy in the 370s we find another writer of hymns who used the images of sleep to convey the emotional toll of the human condition. Ambrose, bishop of Milan, lost his younger brother Satyrus not long after he assumed episcopal office. Satyrus had already given his family a fright when he was shipwrecked on a return trip from Africa. Good Christian that he was, Satyrus had tied a piece of consecrated host in a neckerchief around his neck and thrown himself into the waves and upon God's mercy. He swam to shore safely. This much-beloved brother succumbed to illness not long after, however, and Ambrose's grief was intense. Ambrose quickly wrote a funeral oration for the interment, but then worked further on the piece until he had a carefully crafted reminiscence of his brother, and a treatise on belief in the resurrection. [17]

In the first part of the work, Ambrose consoled himself with the image of his brother who came to him in his sleep. Sleep is sweet, he proclaimed, because in its images the memory of Satyrus was restored to him. In his meditation on mortality, Ambrose never suggested that his vision of his brother was a supernatural event. His brother, he declared, returned to him, but not as a sentient being. Ambrose well understood the principle expounded by Augustine some years later that sleep brings the dreamer into the realm of the imagination in which images are formed by the memory. [18] Ambrose's vision of his dead brother brought consolation. But it was also a poetic vision, a reminiscence which drew on both pagan and Christian antecedents for its language and for its cultural milieu. [19] Ambrose, like Prudentius, saw in the language of dreams a poetic means of expressing emotion, desire, consolation, and faith. Yet Ambrose also reported visions which he interpreted in a literal and concrete way. For example, he claimed to have been directed in a vision to discover and elevate the remains of the martyrs of Gervasius and

---

[16] Prudentius, *Cath.* 6, ll. 73–76, 113–18.

[17] Ambrose, *De excessu fratris*, in *Sancti Ambrosii opera, pars septima*, CSEL 73, ed. O. Faller. Translated by H. de Romestin, *St. Ambrose: Select Works and Letters*, a Select Library of Nicene and Post-Nicene Fathers 10 (Edinburgh, 1989), pp. 159–97. On the philosophic context of the work see Goulven Madec, *Saint Ambroise et la Philosophie* (Paris, 1974), pp. 27–36. On Ambrose's attitudes to dreams see Amat, *Songes et visions*, pp. 212–17, and Dulaey, *Le rêve*, pp. 65–68.

[18] Augustine, *De Genesi ad Litteram* 12.6.

[19] On consolation literature see Charles Favez, *La consolation latine chrétienne* (Paris, 1937); in the Merovingian context see Judith George, "Variations on Themes of Consolation in the Poetry of Venantius Fortunatus," *Eranos* 85 (1987), 53–66, and *Venantius Fortunatus: A Latin Poet in Merovingian Gaul* (Oxford, 1992), pp. 85–106. On Ambrose's sources see Pierre Courcelle, "De Platon à saint Ambroise par Apulée. Parallèls textuels entre le 'De excessu fratris' et le 'De Platone,'" *Revue de Philologie* 87 (1961), 15–28.

Protasius in his church in Milan; nor was this the only occasion when martyrs made a timely and welcome appearance in the bishop's career.[20]

In Gregory's own century, his good friend Venantius Fortunatus, an author only slightly less prolific than Gregory, rarely described dreams and visions even in his religious works. He made no mention of the visions of St. Radegund and her nuns in his hagiographical account of the saint.[21] Yet in other hagiographical works which concerned figures much more distant in time, Venantius was not averse to reporting dreams.[22] In the manner of Ambrose and Prudentius, Venantius was comfortable alluding to dreams in a poetic manner and saw dream images as a means of bringing loved ones closer. "If Sleep comes over me, let even dreams tell you of me, for dreams are wont to behold those truly of one spirit," wrote Fortunatus to his sorely missed friend Dynamius of Marseilles.[23] Venantius' example of restraint reminds us that no single clerical oneiric culture prevailed in the sixth century. Yet the admissibility of dreams both as a vehicle for divine injunctions and as a poetic Christian motif was entirely congruent with contemporary norms. Gregory's stories participated in a late antique culture of dreaming which legitimated a public role for dreams in matters of political import and recognized dreams as a valid cipher of supernatural authority.

Episcopal Office and Spiritual Authority: Shaping an Ideal

In addition to the civil powers that bishops had inherited in the towns as a result of the political and social disruptions of the fifth century, and the grants of the early Merovingian kings in the sixth, there were also values intrinsic to their office which authorized their moral leadership in the community. One was the history and tradition of an office supposedly inherited from Christ's disciples—the handing down of office from one individual to another, generation by generation. The legitimate conveyance of episcopal office through the Spirit's descent at ordination and consecration brought

---

[20] Ambrose, *Ep.* 22; Paulinus of Milan, *Vita sancti Ambrosii* 14, *PL* 14, 27–46. The remains were discovered in the church of SS. Nabor and Felix, and were translated to a new basilica (the Ambrosian basilica) which Ambrose wished to consecrate with relics. The Bolognese martyrs Vitalis and Agricola supernaturally revealed the location of their relics to Ambrose, who deposited them in a basilica in Florence.

[21] Venantius Fortunatus, *Vita s. Radegundis.* There are two Lives of Radegund of Poitiers, the first by Venantius Fortunatus written sometime after 587 (hereafter *V. Rad* 1) and the second by the nun Baudonivia written a generation later, but before 605 (hereafter *V. Rad* 2), both edited by Krusch, *MGH, SRM* 2 (1888), pp. 358–95. Radegund's visions were described by Baudonivia, pp. 377–95; those of her nuns are in Gregory of Tours, *HF* 6.29.

[22] For example, Fortunatus related that Clovis had received a vision before his battle against the heretics (Visigoths). Venantius Fortunatus, *Liber de virtutibus s. Hilarii* 20, ed. Bruno Krusch, *MGH, AA* 4.2 (1885), pp. 7–11.

[23] Venantius Fortunatus, "Ad Dynamium Massiliensem," *Carmina* 6.9, ed. Fridericus Leo, *MGH, AA* 4.1 (1881); translated by Judith George, *Venantius Fortunatus: Personal and Political Poems*, Translated Texts for Historians 23 (Liverpool, 1995), p. 55. For commentary on the poem see George, *Venantius Fortunatus: A Poet*, pp. 141–43.

with it an expectation that the bishop was in harmony with the supernatural forces that directed episcopal tradition. These supernatural aids often came in the guise of former bishops of the district who appeared to the living as ghosts: the returned dead.[24] To be effective, episcopal office had to transcend the barriers between the present world and the "other" world. Bishops demonstrated their sacred power and spiritual legitimacy by controlling supernatural powers. To a significant degree, their worthiness to do this was rooted in their claims to moral superiority in setting the highest example of the Christian life. The underlying purpose of many of Gregory's stories was to illustrate their special relationship with the supernatural.

However, in asserting spiritual authority over their flock and exercising control over the supernatural realm, bishops also came into conflict with alternative claimants to such powers: Germanic kings whose tradition imbued them with sacral powers, alternative Christian communities such as heretics, and non-Christians.

The Chosen: Visions and Episcopal Election

One of the more revealing ways that supernatural visions spoke to concerns about episcopal office was in the transfer of apostolic authority from one bishop to the next.[25] Early in its history the Church established an enabling ritual, election, whereby the bishop was vested with spiritual authority both by virtue of his place as a human link with the apostles and by the independent activity of the Holy Spirit. The early Church established the requirement that bishops be elected to their office by a combination of clerical election and popular support (though judging by those cases we know about in the Gallo-Roman and Frankish church, bishops generally met *in camera* with the townsfolk waiting outside).[26] Only by such means could apostolic authority perpetuate itself and shield the bishop from an accusation of simony. Yet under both the Christian Roman emperors and their Germanic successors the reality was that many bishops came by their positions through patronage and royal appointment.[27] Indeed Merovingian councils moved to formalize royal interest in episcopal election.[28] Consequently, those who were elected by some sort of spontaneous popular action were not always

[24] On apparitions of dead bishops as authority figures and rulers see de Nie, *Windows*, p. 287, and Adriaan H. B. Breukelaar, *Historiography and Episcopal Authority in Sixth-Century Gaul: The Histories of Gregory of Tours in Their Historical Context* (Amsterdam, 1994), pp. 240–45. On the return of the dead to the living in the middle ages see Jean-Claude Schmitt, *Ghosts in the Middle Ages: The Living and the Dead in Medieval Society*, trans. Teresa Lavender Fagan (Chicago, 1998) (originally *Les revenants. Les vivants et les morts dans la société médiéval* [Paris, 1994]).
[25] Geoffrey Barraclough, "The Making of a Bishop in the Middle Ages," *Catholic Historical Review* 19 (1933–34), 275–319.
[26] HF 2.13.
[27] On royal motivation see Kaiser, "Royauté et pouvoir épiscopal," 143–60.
[28] Royal consent was articulated at Orleans in 549. See Wood, "Ecclesiastical Politics," pp. 42–43; *Conc. Aurelianense* 10.

the most successful candidates. And even hagiographic literature, which excelled in the art of finessing, could not always obscure the rancor attendant on unpopular episcopal appointments.[29]

Appointments that bypassed the clerical scrutiny of election were also liable to bypass ecclesiastical procedures regarding preparation for office. In the high middle ages the interval between episcopal election and consecration, that is to say between the partial and full assumption of official powers, was a subject of practical and philosophic debate.[30] Yet a Gallic bishop was in a different position; he *could* be a private citizen one day and a bishop the next.[31] For the sake of procedure, ecclesiastical grades could be conferred in rapid succession, but credibility remained a problem. In such cases, stories of supernatural intervention smoothed deficiencies in the transition. Thus episcopal elections were often moments when visions might occur and the Holy Spirit appear.

The Holy Spirit's activity was reported, for example, in the events leading up to the election of bishop Rusticius of Clermont.[32] On the death of the previous bishop, Venerandus, there was great community dissent over the choice of the next bishop. One Sunday as the bishops met to decide the issue, a veiled woman dedicated to God interrupted their deliberations to proclaim that none of their candidates was pleasing to God: "Behold, the Lord will choose a bishop for himself today." When a priest of Clermont happened to enter the room, the woman cried out that this was the man she had been shown in her vision (*per visionem*). "Here is the one whom God elects! Behold the man who is destined to be your bishop! This man is to be consecrated as bishop!" Rusticius was then proclaimed by all the people as the worthy and just choice. In the atmosphere of unrest prevailing in Clermont, and in view of the factionalism that had developed over the choice of bishop, it might seem truly the working of the Holy Spirit that an alternative candidate acceptable to both sides presented himself. The woman who proposed the compromise was a religious woman, a *mulier . . . velata atque devota Deo*. Like Rusticius, she was an outsider to the election process and thus a credible, if surprising, mouth piece for the Holy Spirit.

In another Clermont election, a timely vision removed an unworthy episcopal candidate from the running.[33] After the death of Sidonius Apollinaris, a priest who hoped to step into his shoes as bishop of Clermont held a ban-

---

[29] *Vitae* which provide evidence for factious elections include *Passio s. Leudegarii episcopi et martyris Augustodunensis* I., ed. Bruno Krusch, *MGH, SRM* 5 (1910), pp. 249–322, and *Passio S. Praeiecti et martyris Arvernensis*, ed. Bruno Krusch, *MGH, SRM* 5 (1910), pp. 212–48. See Wood, "Ecclesiastical Politics," and Fouracre, "Merovingian History."

[30] Robert Benson, *The Bishop-Elect: A Study in Medieval Ecclesiastical Office* (Princeton, 1968) discusses the stages by which the bishop's powers were conferred by the Church and by the monarchy in the middle ages.

[31] Wood, "Ecclesiastical Politics," p. 45, notes that though laymen were sometimes appointed directly to the early Merovingian episcopate, such appointment was not very common.

[32] *HF* 2.13.

[33] Ibid., 2.23.

quet for the townsfolk intending to canvass support. This priest, portrayed by Gregory of Tours as an arrogant criminal, may nevertheless have had substantial backing in the community. As he presided over the feast which all the townspeople attended, he was offered a cup of wine by the cupbearer. As the priest drank his wine, the cupbearer revealed a dream he had "seen." In the dream, he saw himself attending a trial presided over by a judge who, on the advice of Sidonius Apollinaris, summoned the living priest to account for his crimes. At the completion of the story, the priest fell down dead and was very hastily buried. Foul play seems certain.[34] The public narration of the dream, however, legitimated the removal of this unwanted man and paved the way for Sidonius' successor, Aprunculus, a former bishop of Clermont then living in exile.

The story also asserted the rights of the clergy over the laity to influence episcopal elections. We find an echo of these concerns in the Life of the seventh-century bishop, Praejectus of Lyons. Before Praejectus assumed the office, another clerical candidate named Garivald, sensing his support among the clergy slipping, sought to buy the support of the laity with gold and silver. Praejectus' hagiographer commented of the laity that "by force they suppressed all the clergy."[35] The Holy Spirit could not always be relied upon to intervene before the election of a scoundrel. As related by Gregory, the election of Priscus to the bishopric of Lyons, with his pushy wife Susanna, precipitated a scandalous episcopal reign during which women ran in and out of the episcopal residence as if they lived there and those loyal to Priscus' predecessor were "persecuted." Priscus even threatened to have his predecessor's cape (perhaps already being venerated as a holy relic) cut up to make socks for himself.[36] Here was a case where factional interests dominated the religious governance of a community and determined the bishop's posthumous reputation. In all such cases the stories are told from a unilateral political perspective. There were often very good reasons why the community or the clergy promoted one candidate above another, or why they resented bishops appointed for them over their heads, not the least being the channeling of community resources and patronage in new and unwelcome ways.[37]

Visionary stories provided a form of continual assessment of a bishop's career. The deceased St. Tetricus was said to have appeared to Pappolus, bishop of Langres, upbraiding him for despoiling his diocese. "What are you

[34] de Nie, *Views*, offers a different intepretation: "When the dream is intended for a third party and is so communicated, it functions as criticism or as a curse" (p. 292); she suggests the priest died of fright (p. 281).

[35] *Passio Praeiecti* 13, in Paul Fouracre and Richard A. Gerberding, *Late Merovingian France: History and Hagiography, 640–720* (Manchester, 1996), p. 282.

[36] HF 4.36; VP 8.5.

[37] The *vitae* of seventh-century episcopal saints as presented and commented upon in Fouracre and Gerberding, *Late Merovingian France*, provide good examples of the mutually reinforcing cooperation between local and royal interests.

doing here, Pappolus? Why do you befoul my diocese? Why do you rob the Church? Why do you scatter the flock which was entrusted to my care? Off with you, resign your bishopric, leave this neighbourhood and go somewhere else far away!" Pappolus died soon after of a heart attack. He was succeeded by Mummolus "the Good," who discovered that Lampadius, a former deacon, had embezzled from alms given for the poor and had illicitly appropriated church lands for his own use. Evidently the church in Langres was in financial trouble, and tensions were perhaps exacerbated when Pappolus tried to collect money on his visitations. Tetricus, the former bishop, who had dismissed Lampadius as deacon, was thus not blamed for the financial problems Pappolus inherited, appearing rather as an avenging spirit.[38]

Fortunately, the wrath of some avenging bishops could be appeased. Some bishops were astute enough to pour money into homegrown cults and into shrines for their predecessors. A story told of Cautinus, deacon and then bishop of Clermont (551–71), relates that while he was lying in bed one night he heard chanting issuing from the church. He went to his window and noticed the church shining with a bright light. Inside the church there was a crowd of people dressed in white, holding candles and chanting psalms around the tomb of Stremonius (the first and hitherto neglected bishop of Clermont). Cautinus watched the spectacle for a long time, and at dawn he ordered that the tomb of Stremonius be surrounded by a railing and white shrouds, and that it be venerated as a saintly shrine.[39] It is clear that Cautinus was permitted to witness this spectacle so he might institute a cult at the site of the tomb, but there was also a political agenda. Cautinus' elevation to the bishopric had not been supported initially by the clergy of Clermont. who had elected instead a priest named Cato. Cautinus, however, was King Theudebald's choice, and he was duly installed. As Raymond Van Dam has proposed, in instituting the cult of the first bishop of the city and relating the miraculous vision, Cautinus wanted to show respect for his adopted city and reconcile the clergy to his unpopular appointment.[40] The origins of the cult of St. Praejectus of Lyons lie in similar circumstances; the martyr's murderers promoted his cult in a bid for reconcilation with the bishop's family.[41]

The case of Cautinus' appointment was not without personal resonance for Gregory of Tours, who was appointed bishop over the head of the Tours clergy and was later brought to trial on the charge of treason.[42] Although the charges were dismissed, Gregory was silent about the actual circumstances of his appointment. His support for Cautinus against the properly elected

---

[38] *HF* 5.5.

[39] *GC* 29. On Cautinus' disputed appointment see *HF* 4.5–7.

[40] Raymond Van Dam, *Gregory of Tours, Glory of the Confessors*, Translated Texts for Historians, 4 (Liverpool, 1988), p. 43.

[41] For a discussion of this case see Fouracre, "Merovingian History," and Fouracre and Gerberding, *Late Merovingian France*, pp. 254–70, esp. 270.

[42] *HF* 5.49. One of Gregory's accusers was fellow metropolitan bishop, Bertram of Bordeaux.

Cato may have been rooted in his own sensitivity about his royal appointment to the episcopate.[43] Gregory, of course, was a fine example of how a bishop could consolidate his position by adopting and promoting the cult of his predecessors. However, the struggle between the diocesan clergy and congregation to elect and the royal court to appoint new bishops proved a constant disruption in Merovingian ecclesiastical politics. Those bishops who could not find a way of reconciling their subjects to their leadership reaped years of rancor and disapprobation. Sometimes the community eventually got its way, however, removing unwanted bishops in ways having nothing to do with the Holy Spirit.

Amplified Virtue

Though the transfer of secular office holders to positions of clerical leadership often brought worthy candidates into service, it also had problematic consequences. Newly appointed bishops came to their offices with preconsecration ties and obligations—familial, dynastic, and economic. Though celibacy was only recommended for the minor clergy, by the sixth century it was expected of the episcopate. (Male virginity was probably very rare.) In a poem to Bishop Felix of Nantes, Venantius Fortunatus praised Felix's vow of chastity, which he viewed as underscoring the bishop's commitment to the Church: "You married the Church and chose the happier vow." [44]

Bishops such as Felix had wives and offspring before their elevation to episcopal office. Their wives were expected to take a vow of continence alongside their husbands so that the married couple's relationship would henceforth be that of brother and sister, as was required by conciliar law.[45] These bishops' wives (*episcopae*) had a recognized social and religious status, and were expected to serve as spiritual models for the community.[46] Whereas a woman wanting to lead a religious life was prohibited from leaving her husband without his permission, a married man's acceptance of epis-

---

[43] Venantius Fortunatus, *Carmina* 5.3., ed. Fridericus Leo, *MGH, AA* 4.1 (Berlin, 1881).

[44] Felix was bishop of Nantes from 549 to 582. Fortunatus, "Ad Felicem episcopum Namneticum in laude," *Carm* 3.8.29.

[45] See *Concilium Turonense* (567), 13 (12), "Episcopus coniugem ut sororem habeat," CC 148A (1963), p. 180. On celibacy and the clergy see Christian Cochini, *Apostolic Origins of Priestly Celibacy* (San Francisco, 1990); Suso Frank, Ἀγγελιχος βιος, on the connection between virginity and the angelic life; and Brian Brennan, "Deathless Marriage and Spiritual Fecundity in Venantius Fortunatus' *De Virginitate*," *Traditio* 51 (1996), 73–97. On the angelic life and sexual abstention as an asocial state see Peter Brown, "The Notion of Virginity in the Early Church," *Christian Spirituality: Origins to the 12th century*, ed. Bernard McGinn, John Meyendorff, and Jean Leclercq World Spirituality, vol. 16 (New York, 1985) pp. 427–43, and Brown, *The Body and Society: Men, Women, and Sexual Renunciation in Early Christianity* (New York, 1988).

[46] On the role of bishops' wives see Brian Brennan, "'Episcopae': Bishop's Wives Viewed in Sixth-Century Gaul," *Church History* 54 (1985), 311–23; he considers the social position of *episcopae* to have been more positive than does Suzanne Fonay Wemple, *Women in Frankish Society. Marriage and the Cloister 500 to 900* (Philadelphia, 1981), pp. 131–35.

copal rank was often a unilateral decision. Occasionally, frustrated wives tried to implore or seduce their husbands into resuming conjugal relations. In such cases, the wife had the authority of scripture on her side, as one of the wives implored: "Why do you close your ears and refuse to hear Paul's precepts where he wrote, 'Return again to one another, so that you be not tempted by Satan.'"[47] Although on this occasion the wife's wishes prevailed, generally such appeals did little good. Episcopal celibacy was promoted on the basis of canon law and Catholic custom, not on St. Paul's concession to human weakness.

Visions further authorized this custom. Gregory related how one wife's seduction attempt was foiled by a vision. The presumptuous wife entered the bishop's chamber while he was sleeping and as she approached his bed she saw a lamb of great brightness resting upon his breast. Terrified by the vision, she left her husband to sleep in peace.[48] Gregory's interest in this story can well be imagined. The vision confirmed Catholic practice to be divinely sanctioned even against the rather tolerant message of scripture. The lamb symbolized the bishop's innocence and Christ's protection of his vow. The vision indicated that episcopal celibacy should be advanced as a state pleasing to God, and the chaste bishop's protection by a divine apparition emphasized the bishop's special status among the clergy.

Visions of this sort also provided supernatural testimony to the moral expectations of the office. The bishop may have once belonged to the secular realm, it was implied, but in his new office supernatural protection was extended to him to fulfill its expectations. Episcopal office sanctified the man who held it, and supernatural visions promoted the myth of clerical merit against the assaults of the cynical.

To a certain extent Gregory's insistence on the moral probity of bishops must be seen in light of the value of ascetic ideals. Gregory was eager to show that the ascetic ideal could be encompassed within episcopal office. Though he did not devote much attention to monks and hermits in his works, when he did they were generally portrayed sympathetically. Gregory described his grandfather Gregory, bishop of Langres, as living a life of abstinence and prayerfulness so profound "that while in the midst of the cares of the world, he shone like a new hermit."[49] At the same time, the hermit did not have the same spiritual authority as the bishop in Gregory's eyes, and episcopal control over the activities of monks and recluses was jealously guarded.[50] He be-

---

[47] *HF* 1.44, quoting 1 Cor. 7.5: "Cur obduratis auribus Pauli praecepta non audis? Scripsit enim, 'Revertimini ad alterutrum, ne temptet vos Satanas.'"

[48] *GC* 77.

[49] *VP* 7.2: "ut in medio mundi positus, novus effulgeret heremita."

[50] Helen Robbins Bitterman, "The Council of Chalcedon and Episcopal Jurisdiction," *Speculum* 13 (1938), 198–203. Bishops in the Carolingian period could not interfere in abbatial election. Merovingian bishops had rights and a supervisory role over monasteries, especially nunneries. Caesarius of Arles' exemption from episcopal control for St. John's in Arles was an exception; Radegund of Poitiers, whose convent followed Caesarius' rule, was unable to gain the same privilege.

lieved that the real challenge of episcopal office was to combine both the ascetic and pastoral ideals.

Rival Claims to Authority

King Guntramn's Dream

If Daniel was the model for the hermit who both dreamed and interpreted his own visions, Joseph was the model for the bishop who interpreted the dreams of kings. Augustine wrote of Joseph, "And so Joseph, who understood the meaning of the seven ears of corn and the seven kine, was more of a prophet than Pharoah, who saw them in a dream; for Pharoah saw only a form impressed upon his spirit, whereas Joseph understood through a light given to his mind." [51] It was an ancient belief that kings, rulers, or others in positions of secular or military authority might be addressed by God, even those who were not of the Hebrew or Christian faith: "God has revealed to Pharoah what he is about to do." [52] Professional dream interpreters of the Roman world, whose traditions and literature were rooted in the values of ancient Mesopotamia, expected kings and emperors to dream on matters concerning the fate of the entire community. Both Artemidorus in the second century and Macrobius in the fifth believed that the status of the dreamer was an important component in determining a dream's significance. This belief was reflected in a fivefold classification of enigmatic and allegorical dreams which circulated in antiquity: personal, alien, common, public, and cosmic. [53] The dream of a king was more likely to bear on the fate of the community he ruled than would the dream of a minion; if God wished to communicate things relating to the commonwealth of the kingdom, he would do so by means of the dreams of kings. [54] Thus for Gregory and his contemporaries there was nothing strange in kings and princes having dreams whose import might affect the entire kingdom. However, according to both pagan and Christian tradition, the king was merely a vehicle, not an interpreter of dreams. That role fell to God's representative who attended on the king, just as Joseph had attended on Pharoah. Though Gregory never acted officially

[51] Augustine, *De Genesi ad litteram* 12.9.
[52] Genesis 41.25, 28.
[53] The personal dream involved oneself, the alien involved others, common dreams involved both the dreamer and others, public dreams referred to events in the public arena including the fate of a city, and the cosmic dream centered on events such as eclipses and earthquakes. On social status in Artemidorus's *Oneirocriticon* see Foucault, *Care of the Self*; for the fivefold classification see Macrobius, *Commentary* 3.2–3, and Chalcidius, *In Timaeum* 256, ed. J. H. Waszink, in *Timaeus a Calcidio translatus, commentario instructus*, Corpus Platonicum Medii Aevi, Plato latinus 4 (London, 1962).
[54] E. R. Dodds, *The Greeks and the Irrational* (Berkeley, 1951), pp. 107–9. The status of the dreamer determined not only the public scope of the dream's interpretation, but also the way the content of a given dream might be explicated. A dream that might bring good fortune to a master might bode ill if dreamed by a slave.

as a dream interpreter for a king, in recording visions on royal affairs and providing background information in his *History* he provided the framework for interpretation. Political visions, therefore, had their place in the Merovingian world, and bishops had a role in establishing their meaning for posterity.

Perhaps the most telling political vision related by Gregory was a dream told by King Guntramn, the underlying theme of which accorded with a dream of his own. Gregory and Guntramn were seated at dinner when the king, contemplating retribution, began to accuse the bishop of Marseilles, Theodore,[55] of having been complicit in his brother King Chilperic's murder: "If I do not succeed in avenging Chilperic's death before this year is up, I ought no longer to be held a man." Gregory tried to deflect this proposal by pointing out that Chilperic was responsible for his own fate through having behaved treacherously. Gregory continued:

> "Let me tell you, moreover, that everything which subsequently happened I saw in a dream. In my dream vision I saw (*per visionem somnii inspexi*) Chilperic with his head tonsured, as if he were being ordained as a bishop. I saw him carried in on a throne, which was quite unadorned except that it was covered with a plain black cloth. Lighted lamps and tapers were being borne before him." That is what I said, and the King answered: "I, too, saw a vision (*vidi . . . visionem*) in which Chilperic's death was announced. Three bishops led him into my presence and he was bound with chains: the first was Tetricus, the second Agricola and the third Nicetius of Lyons. Two of them said: 'Undo his fetters, we beseech you, give him a good beating and let him go.' Bishop Tetricus, on the contrary, opposed them with great bitterness. 'That is not what you must do!' he said. 'For his sins this man must be cast into the flames.' They went on arguing among themselves like this for a long time, and then far off I perceived a cauldron which was boiling fiercely, for there was a fire lighted beneath it. Poor Chilperic was seized: they broke his limbs and they threw him into the cauldron. I wept to see what happened. He was dissolved away and quite melted (*liquefactus*) in the steaming water, and soon no trace at all of him remained." As the King said all this to our great astonishment, the meal came to an end and we rose from our seats.[56]

With this abrupt conclusion to the narrative, Gregory left the task of determining the full significance of the two dreams to his audience; perhaps their meanings seemed more immediately evident at the time than they do today. Certainly the immediate purpose of Gregory's vision was accom-

---

[55] In 582 the claims of the pretender Gundovald were supported by the Austrasian regents for the young Childebert II and perhaps by Chilperic. In 585, after Chilperic's death, Gundovald reasserted his claims but was killed by Guntramn's army. Theodore of Marseilles (through whose port Gundovald came and went) supported the claims of the pretender Gundovald against Guntramn, thus inciting the king's enmity. Gregory, however, relates that Theodore was a man of great sanctity. HF 8.12.

[56] HF 8.5, trans. Lewis Thorpe (Harmondsworth, 1974).

plished, namely, to deflect Guntramn from blaming Theodore of Marseilles for Chilperic's death. Chilperic's death was cast as divine retribution for his sins. As Giselle de Nie has written of Gregory's vision, "the attention . . . is directed away from the actual physical event to its spiritual causes, which are alone regarded as important." [57] Yet the images of the visionary event do in fact throw light on the unease which Chilperic's reign had engendered among the clergy, and thus provide a window on the tensions between royal and episcopal power in the Merovingian kingdom.

Historians tend to focus on the extent to which churchmen "usurped" or were conceded secular powers in the early middle ages. Yet interestingly, Gregory's dream is a vision of a king who had tried to encroach on episcopal culture. Unlike his brother Guntramn, Chilperic was presented by Gregory as resenting the bishops, complaining that they, not kings, exercised power in his realm. [58] Yet clerical interests evidently held a fascination for him, and, perhaps because of his obsessive focus on them, it seemed to Gregory that he tried to become like them; he added new letters to the Latin alphabet in an attempt to promote writing, attempted debates on theological subjects, and even embarked on the forcible conversion of Jews in his lands. [59] What these measures had in common was their identification with clerical expertise. Chilperic wanted to be both king and bishop. In the process, the king became identified in Gregory's imagination with the very powers he had tried to usurp. [60] Hence the dominant motif in Gregory's vision is the Christian liturgy. To Gregory, Chilperic's tonsured head and candle-lit procession were reminiscent of a bishop's ordination ceremony (*quasi episcopum ordinari*), except that there was nothing positive in the image. The black throne and the funeral tapers suggest a man condemned. Chilperic's ordination was a diabolical inversion of the rite, reaping death, not salvation. In the eyes of many of Gregory's peers, Chilperic's was a fitting fate for a king who had alienated so many clergymen. In life Chilperic was perceived as being disrespectful of the Church. He had murdered two of his sons— Merovech and Clovis—and caused no end of trouble for the Merovingian kingdoms by his ruthless machinations. He had even had Gregory tried for treason. According to Gregory, he was "the Herod and Nero of our time."

Guntramn's vision of his royal brother is interesting primarily for its use of archetypal imagery. Chilperic was thrown into a cauldron of boiling water, a common chthonic image in Germanic, Celtic, and Pictish lore, and known in Christian images of the afterlife as well—perhaps a faint reminis-

---

[57] See de Nie, *Views*, p. 285–87, for a discussion of this vision.

[58] *HF* 6.46.

[59] On Chilperic's decree that no distinctions be made in the persons of the Trinity, and on his adding new letters to the alphabet, see *HF* 5.44; on baptizing Jews see 6.17.

[60] In this quasiclerical vision of Chilperic there may also have been a hint of ancient imperial rhetoric. Did Chilperic, like Constantine, want to be Christ's bishop in the secular realm? The sacral nature of Merovingian kingship would have promoted such identification.

cence of Indo-European ideas. Guntramn's vision of bishops casting the king into the pot provides a Christian dimension to the vision, yet a savage one. The bishops mutilated the body, breaking Chilperic's legs like a victim of torture (or like Christ?). The destruction of Chilperic is complete when the body melts away so that nothing of him remains at all. However, the vision may also have been interpreted as an image of the political disintegration of Chilperic's house: the death of his sons and the blight brought upon a dynasty headed by an impious man. Such an interpretation would fit with the overall tenor of Gregory's politics. Gregory related other visions pertaining to the fate of Chilperic's royal house. One night, in his sleep, he had a vision of an angel which flew over St. Martin's church. "Woe! And more woe!" the angel cried, "God has stricken Chilperic, and all his sons. Of all those who have issued from his loins, not a single one has survived ever to rule over his kingdom."[61] Gregory's holy friend Salvius of Albi had another vision portending the same fate. "I see the naked sword of God hanging over that house."[62]

At the time when Gregory and Guntramn had their visions, soon after Chilperic's death in 584, Chilperic's dynasty did indeed seem defunct. In 587 Guntramn and his nephew Childebert entered into a treaty under whose terms, if Guntramn predeceased him, Childebert would eventually inherit the entire kingdom.[63] Chilperic's third wife, Fredegund, however, was pregnant when her husband was killed and gave birth to a boy, Chlothar. Guntramn was suspicious of the boy's legitimacy, and at first seized the young heir's inheritance. Guntramn's vision of Chilperic's complete destruction might therefore be seen as a divine decree which could be used to justify his political ambitions. However, when Chlothar was about six years old, he was baptized, with Guntramn sponsoring as godfather. Childebert protested, fearful that Guntramn might support the boy's claims to a portion of the kingdom in the future. Guntramn was inclined to give certain cities to Chlothar in the future, but had no intention of nullifying the treaty.[64] However, years later, Chlothar did in fact succeed to the kingdom as Chlothar II, unifying it under his rule, and fathered one of the great Merovingian kings, Dagobert I. Chilperic's house, then, was not quite as defunct as it appeared in the mid-580s.

Gregory's and Guntramn's visions also provided commentary on the nature of power and authority, royal and sacred. Chilperic was viewed by Gregory as an archetypal wicked king who challenged the rights and authority of the Church. In some respects that view was justifiable in light of the more cooperative model of episcopal involvement in the royal fisc established by

[61] HF 5.14.

[62] Ibid., 5.50.

[63] Treaty of Andelot, November 28, 587. HF 9.20. For an overview of the dynastic struggles after Chlothar I's death see Edward James, The Franks (Oxford, 1988), pp. 162–82.

[64] HF 9.20.

Chilperic's predecessors. Yet Gregory's vision hints at another dimension of clerical anxiety. As a Germanic king with the tradition of sacral kingship behind him, Chilperic may have wanted to exercise royal power in sacred matters in ways which conflicted with the Church's desire to control the sacred. Before the time of the Arnulfings when the Church claimed to make and unmake kings, it did not seek to legitimate the sacral power of kings which it viewed as dangerously pagan. Of all the Merovingian kings Gregory knew personally, Guntramn was the only one to whom he attributed supernatural powers, and that was because he was a pious (if occasionally ruthless) man. Gregory believed accounts which claimed that a fringe cut from Guntramn's cloak cured a quartan ague, and that the possessed were brought to confess their crimes through repetition of his name.[65] Because of his charity, vigils, and fasting, Gregory commented of him that "he might well have been taken for one of our Lord's bishops, rather than for a king." [66] Guntramn openly gave the bishops their due and his pious activities conformed to Christian patterns of devotion. By contrast, Guntramn's vision of Chilperic escorted by three bishops who condemn him in the afterlife was precisely the kind of vision that appealed to Gregory: holy bishops wielding retributive powers and seated in judgment upon kings.[67]

Visions of Orthodoxy: Jews, Arians, and Schismatics

While bishops had defined responsibilities to the Christian community, they also took upon themselves the responsibility of shielding their flocks from those outside it. Bishops actively placed themselves as intermediaries between the impressionable Christian community and the "dangerous" orbit of non-Christians whose company their flock was encouraged to eschew. Metaphorically speaking, bishops were the doorkeepers between the world of the Christian laity and the "outer darkness."

This dual responsibility of the higher clergy is reflected in the dreams and visions recorded by them. In regard to the Christian community, bishops needed to investigate the dreams and visions of their constituents with precision and sensitivity so as not to disrupt the interior world or values of their own community. When confronted by visions that spoke of the non-Christian, bishops saw merely another facet of the same responsibility.

Indeed, nowhere is clerical willingness to intervene in the mental world of the Christian community so pronounced as when they related stories touching on those outside it. A small but significant corpus of visionary tales relates to groups relegated to the margins of Merovingian society, specifically Arians, schismatics, and Jews. In promoting visions relating to (and condemning) clearly identified marginal groups, clerics displayed great cer-

[65] Ibid., 9.21.
[66] Ibid., 9.2.
[67] See de Nie, *Views*, p. 287, for a discussion of dead bishops as rulers of the kingdom.

tainty. When confronted by those who did not share their beliefs, or current Christology, clerics benefited from long rhetorical and psychological conditioning. In polycultural communities, such as still existed in parts of southern Gaul in the fifth and sixth centuries, knee-jerk reactions to heresy were part of the cleric's acculturation to his own Christian identity.

Some bishops attempted to translate their ideological isolation into something more permanent than the mere overseeing of conciliar prohibitions. Such efforts are most clearly seen in episcopal dealings with the Jews in their communities, and in the imaginative world of dreams and visions which the bishops regulated.

The Jews were a familiar presence in Merovingian Gaul.[68] Jewish settlement in southern Gaul, which long preceded Christianity there, was concentrated in and around the port of Marseilles, where, in common with the rest of the empire, Jews had traditionally enjoyed certain basic rights as Roman citizens. Until the end of the fourth century, Jews in the Empire were permitted to live according to Jewish law and were entitled to seek compensation if their property was destroyed by Christians. In Gaul, Jews experienced a relatively peaceful although restricted coexistence with the Christian population until the third quarter of the sixth century, first under the Visigoths and then under the Franks. The concerns of the Christian clergy centered primarily on regulating social contact between Christians and Jews. The prohibitions spelled out by the Council of Agde (506) were typical: Jews and Christians could not intermarry, nor could they eat together, and should Jews desire to convert to Catholicism, they needed eight months of preparation before baptism.[69] Yet for all this, Jews and Christians were sometimes friends or acquaintances: Sidonius Apollinaris in the fifth century, for example, was friendly with a Jew whose learning he greatly respected,[70] Gregory of Tours indulged in futile debates with them,[71] and some Merovingian

[68] On the history of the Jews in this period see Bernhard Blumenkranz, *Juifs et chrétiennes dans le monde occidental 430–1096* (Paris, 1960); Solomon Katz, *The Jews in the Visigothic and Frankish Kingdoms of Spain and Gaul* (New York, 1940); Bernard S. Bachrach, *Early Medieval Jewish Policy in Western Europe* (Minneapolis, 1977); John Michael Wallace-Hadrill, *The Frankish Church* (Oxford, 1983), pp. 390–403; and Michel Rouche, *L'Aquitaine des Wisigoths aux Arabes 418–781; naissance d'une région* (Paris, 1979).

[69] On the prohibition against eating together see *Concilium Agathense* (506) 40 (repeated verbatim in the *Concilium Veneticum* [461–91] 12). On intermarriage prohibitions see the *Concilium Aurelianense* (533) 19; *Concilium Claremontanum* (535); *Conc. Aurel.* (538) 14(13). On preparation for baptism see the *Concilium Agathense* 34. The preparation time appears to have been dispensed with during the mass conversions under the Merovingians. Jews were also prohibited from walking with Christians publicly on certain days. See *Conc. Aurel.* (538) 33 (30); *Concilium Matisconense* (581–83) 14. In a late Merovingian council it was prohibited for Christians to be sold to Jews (indicating a measure of affluence among the Jewish community). See *Concilium Clippiacense* (626–67) 13. For councils, see C. Munier, *Concilia Galliae a. 314–a. 506*, CC 148 (1963), and C. de Clercq, *Concilia Galliae a. 511–a. 695*, CC 148 A (1963).

[70] Sidonius Apollinaris, *Ep.* 3.4; 6.11; 8.13, ed. C. Luetjohann, *Epistulae et Carmina*, MGH, AA 8 (1887).

[71] HF 6.5.

kings and nobles actively courted and protected them. In Gregory's works, however, is reflected the rising tensions between the Christian and Jewish communities in the sixth century. In 576 Bishop Avitus of Clermont initiated mass expulsions of some Jews and the forcible conversion of over five hundred others in his city.[72] Gregory enthusiastically supported the efforts of his former teacher by commissioning a poem to commemorate the occasion, but was not in a position to emulate him in Tours, presumably because Tours did not have the Jewish population of cities to the south.[73] Still, Gregory familiarized himself with Christian literature on the subject; he tells us, for example, that he had read a work by Prudentius against the Jews (no longer extant). He decried Jewish "stubbornness" in his writings, and he impugned the character of bishops whose contacts with Jews were perceived to be too friendly.[74] (The role played by such accusations in the ecclesiastical politics of the period has been explored in a number of important works.)[75] Yet Gregory yearned for greater involvement in efforts to convert Jews, and the pen was his natural recourse.

Gregory hurriedly commissioned Venantius Fortunatus to put into verse the news arriving from Clermont of mass conversions, perhaps, as has been suggested, to be read publicly in Clermont to bolster Avitus' support in the community.[76] In his own writings, Gregory likewise conducted an offensive against the Jews by relating vision accounts which postdated the conversions in Clermont. Christian visions of Jews and their miraculous conversion to Christianity were small but significant cameos which underscored the broader aspirations of some Merovingian bishops.

Gregory told two visionary tales that concerned the conversion of Jews. The first was a historical tale which was already circulating in the East and which would have a long history in the medieval West.[77] Gregory related

[72] Ibid., 5.11, 6.17. For example, Gregory records the civil unrest caused by the "obstinacy" of a faction of Jews who resisted the attempted conversion, going so far as to attack one of their number who *did* convert.

[73] Gregory commissioned Fortunatus to write the poem "De Judaeis conversis per Avitum episcopum Avernum," *Carm.* 5.5.

[74] See Gregory's comments on Cautinus, *HF* 4.12: a bishop should only have dealings with Jews if conversion to Christianity was the intent behind the association. On the role of "judaizing" in ecclesiastical politics see Wood, "Ecclesiastical Politics," and Brian Brennan, "The Conversion of the Jews of Clermont," *JTS* n.s. 36 (1985), 321–37.

[75] Wood, "Ecclesiastical Politics"; Brennan, "Conversion."

[76] Brennan, "Conversion"; *HF* 5.11; Fortunatus, "De Judaeis conversis." There have been a number of important studies on Avitus of Clermont's forced conversion of the Jews and its political background: Wood, "Ecclesiastical Politics"; Brennan, "Conversion"; Walter Goffart, "The Conversions of Avitus of Clermont, and Similar Passages in Gregory of Tours," in *To See Ourselves as Others See Us*, ed. J. Neusner and E. S. Frerichs, pp. 473–97 (Chico, Calif., 1985). See also A. J. Zuckerman and B. S. Bachrach, "The Political Uses of Theology: The Conflict of Bishop Agobard and the Jews of Lyons," *Studies in Medieval Culture* 3 (1970), 23–51.

[77] See a similar story in Evagrius' *Historia ecclesiastica* 4.36, PG 86.2, 2770, set in Constantinople at the time of Bishop Mena (536–52). On the later medieval tradition of this tale see John M. McCulloh, "Jewish Ritual Murder: William of Norwich, Thomas of Monmouth, and the Early Dissemination of the Myth," *Speculum* 72 (1997), 698–740.

how it once happened that in the East, the son of a Jewish glassworker took his lessons with Christian boys, and also took communion with them. When his father found out, we are told, he threw the child into his furnace. The mother's cries brought Christians to the rescue, and on beating back the fire the boy was found to be unharmed and reclining "as if on soft feathers." When asked how he had escaped harm, the boy replied that the woman he had seen in the basilica with an infant on her knee (the Virgin Mary) had covered him with her cloak and protected him from the fire. The boy's father was then promptly thrown into the furnace in his son's stead and burned to death. The boy and his mother were baptized and, Gregory tells us, many Jews were converted by this example.[78]

The story is interesting for a number of reasons. First, there is the centrality of the Virgin Mary as intercessor and protector of those who partake in the Christian mysteries. (The maternal aspect of this protection was inspired by an image of the Virgin and child in the Church.) The Virgin protected all recipients of the eucharist, even a young Jewish boy whose first step towards Christianity was his unreflective copying of his friends. The protection afforded the boy by the ritual act of communion simply underscored for a Christian audience the importance and miraculous nature of the sacrament. Furthermore, the story promised supernatural protection for those who converted. The Virgin was the protector of the Christianized Hebrew boy, just as once a man "like a son of the gods" had once protected Daniel and the other Hebrew boys in the fiery furnace.[79] In telling this familiar story of supernatural protection, Gregory may have been warning Jews who might, like the father in the story, seek revenge against those who presented themselves for baptism. As Gallic bishops could attest from individual cases, social unrest or the threat of violence sometimes accompanied conversions in tightly knit communities, and this story, indeed, may have been intended as a direct comment on the violence which erupted in 576 when a Jew converted at Clermont.[80]

Gregory's second miraculous story involved healing at a Christian shrine. The martyr Domitius, we are told, appeared in a dream to a Jewish suppliant at his shrine and, on his request, healed both his hip and his unbelief.[81] We are not told why the Jew anticipated a cure at the Christian shrine, but his conversion to Christianity was a necessary component of the tale to explain why his prayers were answered by the martyr ahead of the prayers of other (Christian) suppliants at the shrine.

The story of Domitius' apparition conformed to a traditional rhetoric in

---

[78] *GM* 9.

[79] Daniel 3.25. Christians believed themselves to be the true children of God through the spirit, rather than, as the Jews, heirs only in the flesh.

[80] *HF* 5.11.

[81] *GM* 99.

which even the natural enemies of Christianity could not deny its power. The healing and conversion of the Jew in the story was an image of the Christian community's belief in its privilege in the eyes of others, aided by the unquestioned efficacy of its rites. Supernatural confirmation of episcopal conversion politics likewise advanced the central role of the bishop as community leader, and established the *locus dramatis* as the church and shrine controlled by the bishop. Church councils promoted the view that conversion of the Jews would be inevitable if only they would listen, if only they could approach closely enough to sacred places.[82] It was hoped that proximity to Christian centers of power could accomplish the conversions that only a few bishops such as Avitus dared to enforce, and which secular rulers were generally reluctant to oversee.[83]

Gregory's use of visions to pose the Jewish question to his Christian readership, to suggest preferred models of action and interaction, appears at first sight to be relatively passive, written as they were against the backdrop of more invasive tactics carried out in other cities. It is possible to see the vision narratives as a nonconfrontational medium, open to a bishop like Gregory who could not express his ambitions in a more active way. Ironically, however, stories of this kind, repeatedly read and copied, expressed archetypes of evil whose power was far longer lasting than the displacements of Jews by Avitus. Perhaps the recognition by Gregory and future writers that visions and other miraculous events could be a useful and subversive medium to influence religious opinion was the most far-reaching consequence of the struggles of the year 576.[84]

Repudiation of non-Christians in visions centered more on questions of allegiance, custom, and style of life than on doctrinal difference. None of the visions described above attempted to address questions of disputed theology between Christians and Jews. No pathway except the miraculous was offered for the conversion of individual Jews, underscoring the belief of Merovingian clerics that conversion was an event, not a process.[85]

[82] Non-Christians were allowed (perhaps even encouraged) to attend church services: "Ut episcopus nullum prohibeat ingredi ecclesiam et audire verbum Dei, sive gentilem, sive haereticum, sive iudaeum, usque ad missam catechumenorum." *Statuta Ecclesia Antiqua* (A.D. 475) 16 (84), ed. C. Munier. *Concilia Galliae a. 314–a. 506*, CC 148 (1963). Non-Christians, like catechumens, were dismissed before the distribution of the host.

[83] HF 6.17. Ecclesiastical control of mass conversions was paramount. Goffart, "Conversions of Avitus," has emphasized the fundamental difference in Gregory's attitude toward Avitus' activities and the short-term and disruptive consequences of King Chilperic's own attempts at the mass conversion of the Jews.

[84] Gregory's contemporary Fortunatus, later bishop of Poitiers, recorded how Germanus of Paris appeared to a Jewish woman named Anna in the form of a "new Moses" with radiating horns. *V. Germani Parisiensis* 7 (22), ed. Krusch, MGH, AA 4.2 (1885), pp. 11–27, and MGH, SRM 7, ed. Levison (1920), pp. 372–418.

[85] Recent conversion literature focuses on conversion as process rather than event, but this is a modern perspective. See Ramsey MacMullen, *Christianizing the Roman Empire A.D. 100–400* (New Haven, 1984). In describing Jewish conversion as miraculous event, Gregory specifically made no differentiation between Jewish and Christian experience.

Gregory of Tours is also our souce for visions which had Christological issues as their subject. Reflections on the human and divine nature of Christ were readily represented in visual form. Gregory related that in the cathedral at Narbonne there was an icon of Christ wearing only a loincloth.[86] On three occasions a "persona terribilis" appeared in a dream to the priest Basileus stating that whereas the congregation were all clothed, Christ was left naked, and adding that he should be covered with a curtain. After the priest failed to obey the dream the first time, and the second, the apparition struck him with blows and threatened him with death should he fail again. The priest, Gregory tells us, had not understood the dream. After he reported his dream to the bishop, however, the picture was covered.[87]

The priest's dream indicates a sensitivity toward both the respect due to the Christ figure (the terrible person of the vision points to the congregation who are better and more respectably clothed) and also to changing attitudes which had made such visual representations of Christ undesirable. One has only to refer to the mosaics in the Arian and cathedral baptisteries in Ravenna in which Christ is devoid even of a loincloth to witness the dimensions of iconographic change.[88] The exposure of the body in the Narbonne painting represented Christ's humanity; yet the vision seems to indicate that acknowledgment of Christ's divinity had suffered as a result. Thus, the issue of whether Christ should be portrayed in devotional art scantily covered with a loincloth, or more fully clothed, related to deeper considerations of Christ's soteriological function and experience. The bishop's acceptance of the priest's dreams mirrored his acknowledgment of the theological problems underlying them. And the priest's account of the apparition's outrage was possibly one way a member of the lower clergy could share his reservations about a painting, perhaps present in the church for a considerable period, and clarify its inappropriate nature without calling the bishop's orthodoxy into question. Gregory of Tours, who is our source for this account, leaves the story without further comment. Gregory's vision accounts refuting Arianism, however, touched closer on his own interests.

Further afield, Arian Visigoths in Spain carried on intermittent religious

---

[86] See K. Wessel, "Der nackte Crucifixus," *Rivista di archeologia cristiana* 43 (1967), 333–45, and Robert Austin Markus, "The Cult of Icons in Sixth-Century Gaul," *JTS* n.s. 29 (1978), 151–57. On icons in this period generally see Anna D. Kartsonis, *Anastasis: The Making of an Image* (Princeton, 1986), pp. 28–39, 127; N. H. Baynes, "The Icons before Iconoclasm," *HTR* 46 (1951), 93–106; and Peter Brown, "A Dark Age Crisis: Aspects of the Iconoclastic Controversy," in Brown, *Society and the Holy*, 251–301. Even Gregory's own preface to the story "reads like a half-apology, half-justification of something still a little suspect." Markus, "The Cult of Icons," 153.

[87] *GM* 22.

[88] Baptismal scenes in which Christ appears completely naked may be seen in the dome of the Arian baptistery in Ravenna. A more complex version appears in the dome of the cathedral baptistery there. Sixth-century art such as church paintings and mosaics are virtually nonexistent in Gaul, but descriptions of their appearance sound very like those which exist from the sixth century at Ravenna.

persecutions against the Catholic Christians by their territories.[89] Gregory felt he knew their measure: "The people there are heretics: they witness these great deeds but are not motivated to believe. They never cease skillfully to reject the sacraments of the divine teachings with the chattering of wrong interpretations. But the power of the Lord destroys and disorders his opposition."[90]

Arianism was essentially a foreign heresy for Gregory; we get no impression from his writings that in his time Arianism posed an internal threat to Gallic Catholicism. Gregory's knowledge of Arianism came predominantly through disputes with Spanish envoys who stopped at Tours on their way to the royal courts of Paris and Soissons. (Religious friction between Gaul and Spain did not prevent dynastic marriages taking place, which provided a regular source of information and irritation to the bishop.)[91] When King Leovigild's envoy Agilan met with Gregory, what started out as a theological dispute on the nature of the Trinity rapidly disintegrated into a shouting match.[92] In this, as in his other disputations, Gregory showed himself to be an inferior theologian who allowed personal animosity and frustration to take over when he had exhausted reasoning. But it was with genuine concern that he asked Chilperic's ambassadors, returned from Spain in 582, for news of how the Catholics there were holding out, and with grief that he learned of new heretical arguments.[93] In short, Gregory at Tours stood as an orthodox sentinel on the diplomatic route to the Frankish court, and no Arian envoy appears to have made the journey twice!

In view of the frustrating and ineffectual nature of Gregory's disputations with Arians, it is not hard to appreciate the attraction which miracles and visions held for him. A revelation provided divine proof of the truth of Catholic Trinitarianism. As the barbarians abandoned their siege at Bazas, a mir-

---

[89] On the Visigoths in Gaul see Edward A. James, "Septimania and Its Frontier: An Archeological Approach," in *Visigothic Spain: New Approaches*, ed. Edward James, pp. 223–41 (Oxford, 1980), and Herwig Wolfram, "The Goths in Aquitaine," *German Studies Review* 2 (1979) 153–68. General works include Roger Collins, *Early Medieval Spain: Unity in Diversity, 400–1000* (London, 1983); Jocelyn N. Hillgarth, *Visigothic Spain, Byzantium and the Irish*, (London, 1985); and, on the Arian episcopate, Ralph Mathisen, "Barbarian Bishops and the Churches in *barbaricis gentibus* during Late Antiquity" *Speculum* 72 (1997), 664–97.

[90] *GM* 25: "Est enim populus ille hereticus: qui videns haec magnalia, non conpungitur ad credendum, sed semper callide divinorum praeceptionum sacramenta nequissimis interpretationum garrulationibus non desinit inpugnare; sed virtus Domini diversam partem distruit et confundit." Translation by Van Dam, *Glory of the Martyrs*.

[91] Dynastic marriages between Franks and Visigoths were often contentious and sometimes tragic. The most successful alliance was between King Sigibert and Brunhild, an Arian Visigothic princess who converted to Catholicism on her marriage. *HF* 4.27. Brunhild's sister Galswinth was murdered shortly after her marriage to Chilperic. *HF* 4.28. Brunhild's daughter Ingund married the Visigothic king Leovigild's son Hermangild, whom she converted to Catholicism, and who as a result became the focus of a rebellion against his father. *HF* 4.38; 5.38; 6.40; 6.43; 8.28.

[92] Ibid., 5.43.

[93] Ibid., 1.18, 40.

acle was seen to occur in the cathedral; three drops (*tres guttas*), brighter than crystal, were seen to fall from the vault by a stunned congregation.[94] The priest, Peter, had the presence of mind to catch the drops which joined together, three into one, to make a single very beautiful gem. The gem appeared clear (*apparet clara*) to those who were pure, and dark (*videtur obscura*) to those who had sinned, and Gregory saw in the fusion of the three drops a divine refutation of Arianism.[95] Yet it must also be remembered that the story of the gem of Bazas was set in a remote past, when Visigothic and Vandal invaders stood outside Gallic cities. Gregory reported no contemporary refutations of Arianism in dreams or visions, and thus one must conclude that the doctrinal threat of proselytizing Arians was too far removed to penetrate his dreams and those of his flock.

What do all these visions refuting the religious value of other belief systems reveal about the central theme of this chapter, namely the role of the higher clergy in promoting the value of visions? With the exception of those visions concerning the Jewish community which did reflect contemporary episcopal activities, the visions we have examined had little relevance to the real spiritual perils awaiting the Christian flock. Arianism could hardly be termed an immediate threat to the cities of Gaul by the late sixth century. It is true that Gregory held to the formulaic convention of prefacing his *History* with a declaration of Catholic Trinitarian faith, an important indicator that Catholic orthodoxy could not be assumed; still, the everyday business of religion as digested in dreams and visions did not focus on reassurance on the nature of the Trinity. The same point can be made about Christological differences between East and West, perhaps epitomized by the Narbonne icon vision.[96] Gregory was poorly informed about religious matters in the East and showed little interest in the theological disputes between Rome and Constantinople in which other Gallic bishops were involved.[97] In common

[94] Gregory identifies them as Huns, although it is more likely that they were Visigoths. See Van Dam, *Glory of the Martyrs*, p. 34, n. 18.

[95] *GM* 12: "patuitque evidenti ratione, contra iniquam et Deo obibilem Arrianam heresim, quae eo tempore pullulabat, haec acta." For another miraculous refutation of Arianism, see ibid., 79–80.

[96] Van Dam, *Glory of the Martyrs*, p. 42, n. 26, suggests that the Greek name of the priest, Basileus, may suggest the quarter from which this new sensibility arose. Still, Greek names were not uncommon in the south where Greek saints and martyr cults were popular. See Eugen Ewig, "Die Verehrung orientalischen Heilige im spätrömischen Gallien und im Merowingerreich," *Francia* 3:2 (1979), 393–410.

[97] Views vary on Gregory's grasp of political events outside Gaul and especially in the East. Averil Cameron has suggested that the diversity of Gregory's information on some topics may merely have reflected conflicting traditions rather than errors, "The Byzantine Sources of Gregory of Tours," *JTS* n.s. 26 (1975), 421–26, reprinted in Averil Cameron, *Continuity and Change* (London, 1981). Some bishops in Gaul were involved in eastern controversies. Avitus of Vienne wrote two books against the Eutychian heresy and kept current with developments in the Acacian Schism: Avitus of Vienne (c. 450–c. 519), *Contra Eutychianam heresim libri II*, ed. R. Peiper, *MGH, AA* 6.2, pp. 15–29. Fortunatus, later bishop of Poitiers, identified himself with Rome and Chalcedon in the wake of the Three Chapters controversy and praised Justin II for upholding of the Council of Chalcedon in his poem "Ad Iustinum et Sophiam Augustos," ed. Fridericus Leo *MGH, AA* 4 (1881), pp. 275–78, ll. 23–26.

with many sixth-century writers, Gregory avowed the Nicene Creed,[98] but otherwise, apart from occasional reports on political events in the East, Gregory was far more concerned with religious events close to home.

Gregory's vision accounts are not in any sense theologically profound. Religious divergence was intensely personalized, repudiating the heretic rather than the heresy, eschewing the abstract in favor of the concrete. Gregory's use of visions wedded Christian doctrine to supernatural authority, which in its turn gave authority to the visionary medium. In Gregory's writings vision accounts were not tools for shaping of the religious attitudes of those on the margins. Instead they had everything to do with shaping Christians' attitudes about themselves.

* * *

Though to the modern reader Merovingian tales of supernatural dreams and visions reflect many of the concerns which we know to have been central to the higher clergy, it is important to realize that stories of this kind are not primarily mimetic of a well-defined and securely established institution. Neither episcopal office nor the storytelling culture in which visionary narratives found a place were static in aim or design. For someone like Gregory, visionary stories and storytelling were a dynamic enterprise. They had broad moral implications and they had to do with reputation. Likewise, episcopal ideals were evolving in these centuries as bishops were forced to adapt to new political circumstances, new allies, new enemies, new ambitions, and new ways of seeing themselves. Bishops published dreams and visions in order to influence fellow Christians to share and endorse their "vision" of themselves—a vision in which bishops, aided by supernatural protectors, exercised religious and political authority.

Finally, bishops cultivated a vision of themselves in which spiritual merit was rewarded by supernatural manifestations. But manifesting spiritual merit was a more serious business for Merovingian bishops than simply being an expression of their hope of seeing dreams and visions. The authority of a bishop in religious matters relied substantially on his reputation for holiness. The ideal bishop had to be above reproach in both his private and public life. But in the merciless politics of Merovingian *kirchenpolitik*, reputation was an all-too-fragile commodity. Hence the value of dream and vision narratives. Insinuations challenging a bishop's orthodoxy on his reputation for corporeal purity could be deflected by visionary affirmations of virtue.

[98] *HF* 1, Praef.

4   *Dreams and Visions*
at the Shrines of the Saints

Visions experienced at the site of a saint's relics, "at the feet of the saint," occupied a special place in the miraculous repertoire which clerics recorded to promote widespread recognition of the efficacy of their shrine.[1] By their very nature as healing visions, by their context of association with holy relics, and as events recorded within the kindly sphere of clerical approbation, visions at the shrines were viewed differently from those revealed in other contexts. Dreams and their dreamers acquired some credibility by virtue of the context in which they were received: dreamers had motive (desire for physical or spiritual healing) and opportunity (vigils and prayers before holy relics), and the dreams themselves had identifiable agency (the shrine's saintly patron). Shrine guardians, be they clerics or monks, were responsible for nurturing the saintly presence through public ritual and private observance. When petitioners' dreams were accompanied by miraculous healing, it was seen as evidence that the saint was supernaturally "present" at the shrine.

Record-keeping and publication of visions were entirely in keeping with the public, community context of shrine activities. In the Gallo-Roman and Merovingian era popular shrines drew pilgrims from far and wide. Individual petitions and collective thanksgiving combined at the altars which held the saints' remains, and over the course of many generations individual Christian communities carved a spiritual history and identity for themselves infused by reminiscences of their patron saint's bounty.[2]

---

[1] *Virt. Mart.* 4.14: "ante pedes sancti."

[2] On the cult of the saints and their relics in Gaul see Hippolyte Delehaye, *Sanctus. Essai sur le culte des saints dans l'antiquité,* Subsidia Hagiographica, 17 (Brussels, 1927); Van Dam, *Saints and their Miracles,* and *Leadership and Community,* pp. 177–300; Arnold Angenendt, *Heilige und Reliquien. Die Geschichte ihres Kultes vom frühen Christentum bis zur Gegenwart* (Munich, 1994); and Brown, *Cult of the Saints,* who notes the importance of community par-

The self-appointed guardians of the holy places were monks and cler-ics.[3] Monasteries acquired healing relics by gift, by trade, and sometimes by theft.[4] Occasionally a monk from among their own number had a sufficient reputation for holiness that his tomb became the site of healing miracles, as was recorded of the abbot Martius. As Gregory related, "That his holy tomb was made famous by the divine miracles that were manifested there can be attested by the crowd of sick people who visit it. They go to the tomb sick and immediately return home cured."[5] Though some monasteries were will-ing to manage the crowds who flocked to their relics, others preferred to regulate access, sometimes restricting visits to certain days of the week or month in an effort to preserve the quiet of their precincts.[6]

Clerics directly identified the power and blessings of their office with the sacrifices of martyrs past, and they were not above "discovering" martyrs when they were lacking. The Merovingian clergy busied themselves with cultic matters, dedicating altars, churches, and cathedrals to the saints, read-ing the saint's *vita* on his or her "birthday" (*dies natalis*), and organizing processions and vigils in which the whole community could join. Thus the clergy kept the saint as constant exemplar and cultic focus before the eyes of their flock. As guardians of the shrines, clerics had multiple responsibilities: correct observance of the saint's day, maintaining the fabric of the tomb or shrine, and regulating the tension between display and retention, between

---

ticipation in the cult of the saints, and the processions which move from town to suburban cemeteries creating a "therapy of distance" (p. 87).

[3] Individual relics were sometimes in private ownership, but private ownership of public shrines is unlikely, although sometimes the sources are not very clear. The matron who took the body of the recluse Lupicinus to Trézelle despite local opposition was petitioned personally for future access to the relics and their healing powers. *VP* 13.3.

[4] Monasteries acquired relics through gift: the relic of the True Cross was obtained by Sulpi-cius Severus for Primuliacum by the gift of Melania the Younger to Therasia, wife of Paulinus of Nola, and thence to Bassula, Sulpicius' mother-in-law. Radegund obtained a fragment of the Cross from the Emperor Justin II and his wife Sophia through diplomatic gift. Trade of relics for prayers was implied in every gift. Pious theft of relics is witnessed in the theft of St. Martin of Tours' body from Candes by the men of Tours under the noses of the men of Poitiers. *HF* 1.48. On changing attitudes to the disbursement of relics, see John M. McCulloh, "From An-tiquity to the Middle Ages: Continuity and Change in Papal Relic Policy from the 6th to the 8th Century," in *Pietas. Festschrift für Bernhard Kötting*, ed. Ernst Dassman and Karl Suso Frank, pp. 313–24, Jahrbuch für Antike und Christentum, Ergänzungsband, 8 (Münster, 1980). For monastic theft of relics from the ninth through eleventh centuries, see Patrick J. Geary, *Furta Sacra: Thefts of Relics in the Central Middle Ages*, rev. ed. (Princeton, 1990), pp. 56–107.

[5] *VP* 14.4, trans. Edward James. The paralytic Chaidulf was cured by kissing the cloth which covered the holy abbot Senoch's tomb. *VP* 15.4.

[6] At Radegund's convent in Poitiers, the relic of the True Cross was displayed on Wednesdays and Fridays until the seventeenth century when the practice was discontinued. See also *GM* 5 on the eastern origins of the practice. Saints with foresight ordered that their burials be at a dis-tance from the main body of the community where their remains could be visited more easily. The Jura monk Romanus asked to be buried outside his monastery so that women (who would otherwise have been refused access) could visit his tomb. *VP* 1.6. Radegund was buried in the funerary church of St. Mary outside Poitiers' city walls—not in her convent where her own cloistered nuns could have had access to her. *GC* 104.

full and restricted access to the relics of the saint. Clerics might strive to lend appropriate gravity to those occasions when the saint's remains were displayed, but popularity (the presence of people) was paramount to the successful cult center. There were no processions without the people, no miraculous healings without plentiful cripples, no joyful masses of thanksgiving without the alleviation of troubles which weighed upon and were prayed for by the entire congregation. It is this popular aspect of cultic veneration which has attracted so much scholarly interest, for nowhere do ordinary people make such a concerted appearance in the sources as when they are praying to, begging favors from, and thanking saints for their largesse. And as the sources bear witness, dreams at the shrines of the saints were, for many, the currency in which their most intimate hopes were realized.

That dreams had long been associated with shrines, and especially healing shrines, is axiomatic. In the Christian tradition as in the pagan, dreams were believed to be one of the preferred vehicles through which divine therapy was offered to those in physical or mental distress. Externally visible afflictions are those most commonly described in medieval sources, but less immediately visible anxieties must also have found relief at the shrines. The social and religious stresses which propelled the suppliant to seek help were legion and are common in every age: environment, political upheaval, economic distress, familial disintegration, sickness, disappointed ambition, guilt, and grief.

The popularity of saintly cults in Gallic communities suggests that the shrines were filling a genuine need. Without suggesting that the depressing economic and political conditions which prevailed in fifth- and sixth-century Gaul were in any way responsible for the origins of saintly cults there, I do suggest that they explain in part why some shrines flourished. In short, it would be hard to disagree too vehemently with the picture which Gregory of Tours presents of the social and economic ills of the sixth century. Historians of climate confirm that weather conditions were unfavorable to abundance in these unhappy centuries. Bad harvests and the resulting hunger bred malnutrition and susceptibility to disease, and imported epidemics.[7] Economic desperation was compounded by political anomie, by the internecine warring of the Merovingian kings who were responsible for chronic social violence and who levied the punitive taxes which were an oft-cited source of discontent.[8] In Gregory's writings we see the sick and dispossessed

[7] Samuel Dill, *Roman Society in Gaul in the Merovingian Age* (New York, 1966), pp. 254–62. Bubonic plague devastated western Europe in the sixth and seventh centuries. See J. R. Maddicott, "Plague in Seventh-Century England," *Past and Present* 156 (1997), pp. 7–54.

[8] On taxation in the sixth century see *HF* 9.30; on clerical immunity see *HF* 10.7. See also Walter Goffart, "Old and New in Merovingian Taxation," *Past and Present* 96 (1982), 3–21; Goffart, "Merovingian Polyptychs: Reflections on Two Recent Publications" *Francia* 9 (1981), 57–77; and Robert Fossier, *Polyptyches et censiers* (Turnhout, 1978).

gathered in great numbers at the altars and tombs of Gallic churches hoping
for miraculous solutions to the legacy of social ills. Fear and desperation undoubtedly encouraged receptivity to signs of supernatural intervention, and
it is possible that shared anxieties about survival surfaced in community-
wide adherence to the saints as archetypal emblems of relief, and in a conviction in the religious and social relevance of lucid and vivid dreams.

In this chapter I want to look at the way in which the power of the saints
permitted the clergy and their congregation to funnel visionary experience
into legitimate, ecclesiastically sanctioned channels. First, I will look at
how the clergy constructed a Christian reading of the pagan Gallic landscape
through dreams and visions, and thereby discovered the optimal complec-
tion of devotion at Christian shrines. In order to accomplish this reading,
however, the clergy had to eradicate undesired elements in the pagan culture
of therapy at shrines, while reading into it the genesis of the Christian culture which strove to supplant it. This effort included regulating the memorialization of lay and clerical visions in permanent form. Altars, oratories,
churches, and even large monastic complexes were built in the Merovingian
age at the explicit behest of dreams. Second, I examine the shrine's records,
the *libri miraculorum*, in which dreams and visions were accorded legitimate
and privileged space.

Since every aspect of cult observance was under clerical supervision and
clerics were largely responsible for giving shape to the surviving documentation on visions, our sources permit a fairly complete view of the way clerical interests were codified and asserted by sanctioning dreams and visions
in legitimate contexts in the Christian community.

Imprints on the Landscape

Reading the Gallic Landscape

Gallic bishops often labored under singular difficulties in promoting reverence for the saints in their dioceses. The early history of the Christian community in Gaul was unclear, and the resting place of its martyrs was uncertain. Bishops had a fine line to tread. On the one hand, they were committed
to excising pagan interlopers from Gaul's martyr history where, on insufficient historical grounds, ancient tombs were held to be those of Christian
martyrs. On the other hand, they hoped to recover, and often rediscover, the
martyrs and bishop-missionaries whose blood and effort could help them
forge the Christian identity of their dioceses. In this realm of uncertainty
there was great scope for supernatural assistance.

The Gallo-Merovingian clergy placed themselves at the center of the
cult of the saints. Always wary of an independent religious building project
within their territories, clerics emphasized the sacred or supernatural com-

ponent in the recovery and repair of sacred sites. As leaders of the Christian community, bishops were often visited in their dreams by the forgotten martyrs of their dioceses, who registered their distress at the neglect of their tombs. Some dream requests were modest: a petition for a suitable covering for a tomb which was broken or exposed to the elements.[9] However, even modest requests might lead to greater things. In an apparition, St. Genesius of Clermont made known the whereabouts of his tomb to a poor man who had lost his oxen. The tomb had become uncovered and Genesius wanted the marble lid to be replaced. Genesius explained that he had left the present world a martyr. Persuaded by a miracle and reports of cures (rather than by the oxherder's testimony), Avitus, the incumbent bishop of Clermont, built a church over the remains of his predecessor and ordered that a festival be celebrated there in the saint's honour.[10] Variations on this vision narrative account for many examples of tardy cult initiation and veneration in Merovingian writings.[11]

Once the identification or discovery of relics had been accomplished, visionary apparitions provided the clergy with the kind of information essential for establishing a cult: the date of the saint's death (the feast day upon which the saint would be commemorated) and perhaps enough of the circumstances of the martyrdom to provide material for a small devotional reading. Vitalina, a martyr totally unknown before she appeared in a vision, proclaimed her holy identity, and "after this, the virgin showed herself to many and she both presented requested benefits, and . . . proclaimed the date on which her death should be commemorated."[12] Vitalina is a good example of the preoccupation often displayed by medieval saints with the circumstances of their veneration on earth.[13]

Once saints' tombs were recovered and cults established, further visions emphasized the continuity of interest, or investment, of the saint in his or her shrine. If the saints could heal the sick and release captives and the possessed, then it was little wonder that they could be counted upon to protect their shrines. Sometimes saints relied on earthly proxies to get a job done,

---

[9] *GM* 64; *GC* 18, 34, 103.

[10] Episcopal incumbents were expected to venerate the memory of their predecessors, encouraging their reputation as saints and miracle workers. A glance down the episcopal lists confirms their success. Often the bishop took upon himself the task of recording the life of his predecessor or spiritual master. St. Honoratus of Arles' life, for example, was composed by Hilary, his successor as bishop, in the same year as Honoratus' death in 429 (*Sermo de vita s. Honorati*), and Hilary's biography in its turn was written by his disciple, Honoratus of Marseilles, in 477. See Prinz, *Frühes Mönchtum* pp. 49–50. The importance of *vitae* in this process is underscored by Gregory of Tours. *GM* 63. On St. Genesius see *GM* 66.

[11] See *GM* 50, 48, 62; *GC* 17, 79.

[12] *GC* 5: "Post haec multis per visum virgo ostensa est et beneficia petita praebuit et diem obitus sui, in quo commemoratio eius celebraretur, edixit."

[13] See, e.g., *GC* 103 (the Parisian virgin Criscentia) and *GM* 66 (Genesius of Clermont). See also note 15 below.

such as repairing a leaky roof. Some saints expected good housekeeping, bargaining with sinners to keep the site of their remains swept clean.[14] More often stories about saints and their shrines promoted the notion that the saints were self-sufficient. Saints singlehandedly protected their remains from theft and churches bearing their dedication from war. Sometimes they needed a little extra muscle. On one occasion, St. Stephen was seen in a vision appealing to the saints Peter and Paul to help preserve his relic-filled oratory at Metz from destruction by the Huns.[15] As the power of the saints was being uncovered, these and many other such stories promoted a discourse of Christianization in which bishops and their saints moved in concert in a seemingly unstoppable wave of conversion. Yet the labor of Gallic clergy and missionaries did not occur in a vacuum—it was always defined against non-Christian traditions.

Christians were newcomers in Gaul; the landscape they inhabited was a daily reminder of the past. Evidence of Gaul's non-Christian and pre-Christian history marked towns, villages, and countryside alike: mossy dolmens on windswept heights, ancient tombs with elaborate carvings, springs and groves which commanded the respect of locals in unsettling ways, and finally impressive temples built to Greek, Roman and oriental deities (properly Romanized, of course) all bore testimony to the long religious traditions of Gaul. In the north, Celtic gods of fertility and war cohabited with Germanic war gods, just as Celt and German west of the Rhine had lived together for centuries. In contrast to the nonmonumental picture of German religious sites portrayed by Tacitus, the Frankish peoples in the north set up visible compounds with altars substantial enough for Christian missionaries to require divine help in razing them.[16] These did not simply disappear with the conversion of the Frankish ruling house to Christianity in the late fifth century. Furthermore in southern Gaul, local sites of pagan worship, especially in the countryside, worried fourth- and fifth-century bishops. In those areas of Gaul which had been only superficially Romanized (primarily rural areas), indigenous religious practices continued unabated at sacred springs and groves.[17]

The existence of sacred sites and shrines at which non-Christian practices

---

[14] *Visio Baronti* 14; *GC* 90.

[15] On cleanliness see *GC* 90 and *GM* 32; on self-protection see *GM* 41, 47, 89, 91, and *HF* 2.6.

[16] Tacitus, *Germania* 9, ed. Karolus Müllenhoff, in *Germania Antiqua* (Berlin, 1973). On supernaturally aided razing of temples see *V. s. Martini* 13, 14, 15; *V. s. Radegundis* 2.2.

[17] In the north, in the modern *département de L'Oise*, pagan sacred springs (associated with popular religion) often took longer to Christianize than more prominent sites (associated with the Roman state religion). Michel Roblin, "Fontaines sacrées et nécropoles antiques, deux sites fréquents d'églises paroissiales rurales dans les sept anciens diocèses de L'Oise," in *La christianisation des pays entre Loire et Rhin (ive–viie siècle)* ed. Pierre Riché, pp. 235–51, Actes du Colloque de Nanterre (3–4 mai, 1974), Histoire Religieuse de la France, 2 (Paris, 1993).

continued is clear in the sources, though the religious identification of their adherents is subject to discussion.[18] One of the main problems in trying to assess activity at pagan shrines in Gaul is the inclusive nature of the terminology used to describe them in Christian written sources. "Paganus" and "rusticus" were interchangeable terms in this period,[19] and Christian authors were undoubtedly aware of the polemic value in using a single set of terms to describe all non-Christian worshipers. We should not assume that they were as ignorant of differences within the "pagan" community as their choice of vocabulary would suggest. Beyond such conscious rhetorical decisions was also the currency of custom by which Latin texts referred to the gods of the indigenous population by the names of Roman gods with whose functions they most nearly corresponded. Thus both by custom and design the sources have obscured our view of what the Christians faced in Gaul. While we may try, based on the known geographical distributions of peoples and their likely religious affiliations, to distinguish among Roman, Gallic, or Frankish shrines, we should not believe that Christian writers were laboring under anything like the same uncertainty.

Whatever the identity of these pagan shrines, they were designated in Christian polemic as demonic and thus a suitable target for Christian aggression. Episcopal sermons and church councils inveighed against superstition, augury, and false worship. We do not know beyond anecdotal evidence how consistently the clergy, beyond expressing disapproval for certain traditional sites of worship, were involved in the business of destruction. Some pagan temples and Jewish synagogues were destroyed by lay Christians whipped up into a fury by their clergy, but hagiography (our most consistent source) emphasized the lone entrepreneurial monk or cleric aided by warrior

[18] The problem of distinguishing religious "belief" or "identity" from cultic "practice" is problematic and much discussed for this period. On paganism and Christianization see Markus, *End of Ancient Christianity*, and his "From Caesarius to Boniface: Christianity and Paganism in Gaul," in *The Seventh Century: Change and Continuity*, ed. Jacques Fontaine and Jocelyn N. Hillgarth, pp. 154–72, Studies of the Warburg Institute, ed. J. B. Trapp, vol. 42 (London, 1992); Ramsey MacMullen, *Christianizing the Roman Empire A.D. 100–400* (New Haven, 1984); Clare E. Stancliffe, "From Town to Country: The Christianization of the Touraine 370–600," in *The Church in Town and Countryside*, pp. 43–59, Studies in Church History, 16 (Oxford, 1979); Yitzak Hen, *Culture and Religion in Merovingian Gaul AD 481–751* (Leiden, 1995); and Dennis Trout, "Town, Countryside and Christianization at Paulinus' Nola," pp. 175–86, and Richard Rothaus, "Christianization and De-paganization: The Late Antique Creation of a Conceptual Frontier," both in *Shifting Frontiers in Late Antiquity*, ed. Ralph W. Mathisen and Hagith S. Sivan, pp. 299–308 (Aldershot, 1996).

[19] Michel Roblin, "Paganisme et rusticité: un gros problème, une étude de mots," *Annales. E.S.C.* 8 (1953), 173–83. It has been argued that the use of the term "paganus" to denote non-Christians was influenced by the usage of Christian writers, and that this meaning survived alongside its original meaning as merely an inhabitant of the territorial area of the *pagus*. The "rusticity" of the "pagani" also came to have pejorative overtones, especially when "rusticity" was used to convey the idea of unpolished literary style and disrespect to the Christian religion, specifically to the saints. See discussions in Christine Mohrmann, "Encore une fois: paganus," *Vigiliae Christianae* 6 (1952) 109–21, and Michael Richter, "Linguistic aspects," in *The Church in Town and Countryside*, pp. 149–57, Studies in Church History, 16 (Oxford, 1979).

angels or by unexpected passivity in the locals. In the fourth and fifth centuries an ambitious monk or clergyman did not have to go far to find an ancient shrine to destroy, or "pagan" adherents to "convert." Even in the sixth century a story about St. Gallus relates that as a young deacon he accompanied King Theuderic to Cologne, and there, in company with another cleric, burned down a barbarian temple, fleeing from the fury of the worshipers to the safety of royal protection.[20] Miracles were told in hagiographies to explain how the saint, who risked martyrdom in this endeavor, not only evaded the fury of the people but converted them too. Yet the reality must often have been less edifying: St. Gallus could rely on the protection of the king for his actions, but no conversions are recorded as having resulted from them.[21] In the short term, conversions based on destructive acts could rarely have been as effective as our sources would have us believe. But this was not the point. Demolitionist Christians were looking for something more than conversions; they were seeking inner conviction of their Christian self-identity and hoping for external affirmation which could come only from the awe in the eyes of the enemy and from the presumed proximity of angels. Were these men confronting "imaginary pagans," seeking confrontation at sites which had long been abandoned? In some cases, perhaps. But we cannot dismiss the longevity of local topographic loyalties.[22]

In some cases the persistence of pagan observance was so strong that bishops had to resort to dreams as justification for changes in policy. In Dijon, for example, there was a huge sarcophagus which Bishop Gregory of Langres believed to be a pagan burial place. The *rustici* were accustomed to make petitions there which were speedily answered. In one case a young boy tried to steal a candle left on the tomb, but it was guarded by a huge serpent. Gregory was informed of these miracles, but refused to believe them and strenuously urged his flock to cease their worship there. Then, as Gregory of Tours relates, circumstances intervened; the martyr of God revealed himself to the blessed confessor and said: "What are you doing? Not only do you despise [this tomb], but you spurn those who honour me. Do not do this, I ask of you, but quickly prepare a roof to put over me." Shaken by this vision, Gregory went to the tomb and wept for a long time praying for God's indulgence for his ignorance.[23]

This story illustrates the problems bishops had in dealing with popular veneration at pagan sites. Gregory of Langres had evidently tried to prevent

[20] *VP* 6.2. Queen Radegund reportedly destroyed a Frankish fane close to her royal residence at Athies. *VR* 2.2.

[21] Immediate on-site conversions and community concord were hagiographic *topoi*. See *VM* 13–15; *VR* 2.2.

[22] Pagans, whether they were Gallo-Romans in the south or Franks in the north, were depicted trying to save their shrines from destruction. *VM* 13, 15; *VR* 2.2. For a critical evaluation of the value of hagiographic literature for discussions of paganism in Gaul, see Yitzak Hen, *Culture and Religion in Merovingian Gaul, AD 481–751* (Leiden, 1995), pp. 154–206.

[23] *GM* 50. Bishop Gregory of Langres, c. 506–539, was Gregory of Tours' great-grandfather.

devotion at this site through persuasion, telling his flock that they should not worship there. Having taken this stance, Gregory's volte-face was facilitated by his vision of the martyr. By revealing himself to Gregory in the vision, the martyr Benignus did more than set the record straight; he assigned responsibility for his cult to the bishop and the Church, thus ensuring ecclesiastical control of this powerful site.[24] This was the model for Merovingian ecclesiastical appropriation of pagan sites: the transfer of supernatural authority from local interests to that of the bishop, often by means of dreams and visions.

There is one final point to be drawn from the case of Dijon. Some sites were not identifiably Christian or pagan by their external appearance, or rather, perhaps, not so identifiable as to resist assimilation to new religious needs. Bishop Gregory of Langres could plead ignorance concerning the Christian inhabitant of the tomb because Christians were sometimes buried in pagan sarcophagi. Visual cues, if there were any, were sometimes not sufficiently distinctive to assign incontrovertible religious identity to a site. Similarly, the medical practices at healing shrines or watering places might have an ambiguous or neutral religious cast to them since they were open to Christian interpretation.[25]

If the visual distinction between pagan religious sites and their ancient or primitive Christian counterparts was not paramount, then what Christian bishops were trying to do was not eradicate offensive temples which reminded them of pagan worship but rather impose a religious reading of the landscape. Such a reading could not often be done on the basis of historical record or local memory, which was notoriously evasive and unreliable. Churchmen and monks needed a kind of divine infrared beam in the form of dreams and visions to detect pagan targets in the landscape. Ultimately, the right of acceptance or rejection of an established cult lay with the bishop, except in those rare cases where popular resistance was too strong, as in Dijon. However, the dreams and visions of churchmen smoothed the way, and prepared the Christian community to see or interpret their environs in ways sanctioned by the church.

Visiting the Christian Shrine

While the identity of Christian and pagan shrines was to some extent open to clerical construction, the activities centered on Christian shrines pointed to commonalities with pagan counterparts. Like pagan shrines, Christian shrines focused the attention of the populace as sites for religious processions, feasting, dancing, singing, and frivolity. Christian shrines were noted

[24] Ibid.

[25] On fourth-century watering sanctuaries and the character of St. Martin's thaumaturgy see Aline Rousselle, "From Sanctuary to Miracle-worker: Healing in Fourth-Century Gaul," in *Ritual, Religion and the Sacred*, ed. Robert Foster and Orest A. Ranum, pp. 95–127, Selections from the Annales, economies, sociétés, civilisations, vol. 7 (Baltimore, 1982).

for bringing joy (*laetitia*)—of the pious and ribald kind—to those who honored the saint.[26] Crowds from all ranks of society visited saints' tombs on their feast days in the hope of a blessing of some sort, like "happy bees around their familiar hive."[27] Others were there all year round. For example, *matricularii* (the poor registered to a particular shrine) could expect to benefit from the largesse of a hopeful or successful suppliant.[28] A deaf and blind mute named Anagild was supported by donations to St. Julian's shrine for an entire year.[29]

While the afflicted provided the object of the saint's compassion, Frankish royalty provided the models for the ideal of the pious pilgrim at the shrine. Queen Ultrogotha, a woman whose piety seems to be have been widely esteemed, was portrayed as seeking the shrine of St. Martin as once the Queen of Sheba had sought out the wisdom of Solomon.[30] Her activities there are described quite precisely. "She therefore abstained from eating and sleeping and sent very generous alms in advance; then she went to the holy place. She entered the church, and because she was frightened and nervous, she did not dare approach [the tomb] because her sins prevented her. Then she passed the night keeping vigils, praying and weeping profusely. At daybreak she presented many gifts and sought to celebrate a mass in honour of the blessed confessor." Three blind men miraculously recovered their sight, and her visit ended with her attendance at a general acclamation of the glory of God and his confessor Martin.

Although Ultrogotha's visit to the shrine did not include a therapeutic dream, in every other regard her awe-filled activities represented those of the ideal suppliant. In dreams and visions recorded at the shrines we see such activities, including fasting and gift-giving, being supernaturally reinforced.

Voluntary self-deprivation of basic human needs such as food and sleep was considered an appropriate sacrifice in antiquity. Furthermore, fasting and sleep deprivation enhanced the senses for receiving supernatural communication.[31] Such privations were intended to cleanse the mind of impurities of body and imagination. Sexual abstention was a commonly cited preparation for presentation at a shrine.[32] Jerome voiced his own concerns

---

[26] *VJ* 24, 25. Improper and immoderate *laetitia*, however, was the mark of an evil man. *VJ* 15.

[27] *VP* 7.6.

[28] In *VJ* 38, a sick girl's father gives food and drink to the *matricularii*.

[29] *VJ* 12.

[30] *Virt. Mart.* 1.12. Queens were often commended for seeking shrines or relics; Queen Radegund's seeking echoed that of the Empress Helena. Isabel Moreira, "Provisatrix Optima: St. Radegund of Poitiers' Relic Petitions to the East," *Journal of Medieval History* 19 (1993), 285–305, esp. 300.

[31] On asceticism and visions see Chapter 2. "Per ieiunium etiam occulta mysteriorum coelestium revelantur." Isidore, *Sententiarum* 2.44. Fasting should not be excessive lest it appear as a pagan or heretical attempt to induce visions. For the ideal fasting visionary see Fox, *Pagans and Christians*, pp. 385–8, 395. See also Arbesmann, "Fasting and Prophecy," pp. 32–71.

[32] As it was for the Asclepian cult, and other pagan mystery cults (Cult of Isis, Eleusinian mysteries, etc.). On sexual abstinence see Fox, *Pagans and Christians*, p. 347.

about his state of mind when approaching holy places: "Whenever I have been angry or had some bad thought upon my mind, or some evil fantasy has disturbed my sleep, I do not dare to enter the shrines of the martyrs. I quake with body and soul." [33]

Gift-giving was another prudent preparation for a visit to the shrine. The act of giving had two beneficiaries: the donor, who reaped the spiritual benefits of self-deprivation, and the recipient (the shrine itself or the poor). Almsgiving to the poor was an indirect form of giving to a church, and it had its roots in the ascetic tradition.[34] Queen Ultrogotha showed her generosity and her piety by giving gifts before as well as after her night spent at St. Martin's tomb. Such contributions were given in the hope of tangible and intangible benefits—as an act of piety intended to bring the donor into favor with Christ and his saints, or in the expectation of a miracle. As had been common in pagan shrines, gifts were sometimes promised with at least a certain degree of contractual understanding by both sides. One woman who did not receive the favor she expected took back the gift which she had given.[35] Conversely, St. Nicetius appeared in a dream to remind a peasant who had promised him two silver candlesticks and had delivered only one that he had not paid in full.[36] Thus both the supplicant and the saint kept accounts. Gifts were also commonly given as thanksgiving for benefits already received.[37] Examples are legion in Merovingian sources. For example, wax offerings were made to the shrine, sometimes at considerable cost, in the hope of the saint's intercession. They were perhaps molded to represent the limb for which healing was desired, or else comprised the height or weight of the suppliant.[38] Wax offerings were recyclable and were remolded for liturgical pur-

---

[33] Jerome, *Contra Vigilantium* 12, trans. Brown, *Cult of the Saints*, p. 11.

[34] Brigitte Beaujard, "Dons et piété à l'égard des saints dans la Gaule des Ve et VIe siècles," in *Haut moyen-âge. Culture, éducation et société*, ed. Michael Sot, pp. 59–67 (Nanterre, 1990), notes a change in sixth-century sources: "Mais au VIe siècle, dans biens des cas, les dons paraissent dissociés des pratiques ascétiques. Hors de tout effort sur soi-même, ils acquièrent une force intrinsèque. Ils deviennent un *remedium* capable d'amadouer Dieu lui-même et à tout le moins le saint auquel ils sont destinés. Ils sont pris dans une système de don et de contre-don chrétien" (p. 63).

[35] *GC* 66.

[36] *VP* 8.

[37] For a detailed study of many forms of votive offerings evidenced by hagiographic sources see Anne-Marie Bautier, "Typologie des ex-voto mentionnés dans des textes antérieurs a 1200," in *La piété populaire au moyen âge*, pp. 237–282, Actes du 99e Congrès National des Sociétés Savantes, Besançon, 1974, vol. 1 (Paris, 1977).

[38] *VR* 1.32. A young girl named Goda was cured after a candle was made and lit for her: "facta candela ad mensuram suae staturae." Bautier notes the earliest evidence for wax-limb offerings in the Christian West are tenth-century, although such offerings were common at pagan shrines in antiquity. "Typologie des ex-voto," pp. 237, 253. The examples she gives (pp. 240, 253) of Merovingian prohibitions of offering wooden limbs (from Council of Auxerre, 573–603, and the *Life of Eligius of Noyon*) and candles (*Life of Eligius*) should perhaps be interpreted as prohibitions made because these practices were occurring at pagan shrines, rather than as prohibitions against candles and wax limbs at Christian shrines—that is, prohibitions of context rather than of the materials themselves.

poses. One gift to St. Martin's tomb was two hundred pounds of wax.[39] Most gifts important enough to be recorded were of this generous nature. A certain Sabaricus presented a large gold cross to be suspended over the tomb of St. Symphorian.[40] St. Radegund offered her royal vestments, including gems, pins, and bejeweled girdles at various altars.[41] Substantial gifts allowed for necessary improvements to the shrines housing relics of the saints. An oft-noted need was widening entrances to tombs in order to allow better access by the faithful, or the removal of a saint's body from a wooden coffin to a stone sarcophagus.[42] Smaller gifts of food and drink were common and were given as alms for the poor.

Dreams that supported these activities provided supernatural justification for Christian practices which were reminiscent of pagan offerings, still common in Gaul. Even in minor ways, features that had characterized pagan shrines were transferred to new Christian settings. For example, it was reported of Julian of Brioude's tomb that animals who approached it were pacified.[43] While harmonious relations with the natural world were to become a staple in the saint's dossier, at St. Julian's shrine the memory of pagan animal sacrifices, for which the animals had to be willing participants in their ritual slaughter, was surely not far beneath the surface.[44]

An activity at Christian shrines which would have struck a pagan audience as very familiar was the practice of incubation. Incubation involved sleeping at a shrine in the expectation of a dream or vision of the divine or semidivine being to whom the shrine was dedicated.[45] Usually the expectation of the dream was that it would bring a cure or advice. At some pagan shrines, dormitories had been constructed to enable large numbers of petitioners to sleep in proximity to the shrine.[46] The Christian practice of spending the

[39] *Virt. Mart.* 4.15; see also 1.18.
[40] Fortunatus, *Vita s. Germani episcopi Parisiensis*, ed. Bruno Krusch, 34 MGH, AA 4.2, (1885) p. 14.
[41] VR 2.13, 14.
[42] VP 2. 4; 7.5. Tombs were moved by a miracle to permit access to St. Martialis' relics. GC 27. St. Julian's tomb was inaccessible to a monk until a dream advised him of a good time to approach it. VJ 28. A casket of relics shrank to fit inside the altar. VP 15.1.
[43] VJ 31.
[44] Ibid.: animals offered to the church are remarkably tame. Julian's tomb was close to a large pagan sanctuary dedicated to the worship of Mars and Mercury. In a manner which recalls the nature powers of pagan gods, Julian deployed thunder and lightning bolts to display his power. VJ 6, 13, 15.
[45] On the pagan practice of incubation see C. A. Meier, "The Dream in Ancient Greece and Its Use in Temple Cures (Incubation)" in *The Dream and Human Societies* ed. Gustave Edmund von Grunebaum and Roger Caillois pp. 303–18 (Berkeley, 1966); and Robert Karl Gnuse, *Dreams and Dream Reports in the Writings of Josephus: A Traditio-Historical Analysis* (Leiden, 1996), pp. 119–26.
[46] The great pagan healing shrines of antiquity were often elaborately constructed. According to Pausanias (*Descriptio Graeciae*), the facilities at the Asclepian shrine at Epidauros in the second century had been upgraded to include dormitories for incubation and new residences for women outside the complex. At Pergamum there were baths, a gymnasium, and a theatre. See Howard Clark Kee, *Miracle in the Early Christian World* (New Haven, 1983), chap. 3.

night at the shrine was certainly an extension of ancient models of behavior and interaction.[47] The issue is not whether Christians practiced incubation but rather to what extent the Gallic clergy endorsed the activity, or at least provided a favorable environment in their churches for curative dreams. Whether Christians approached the shrine, as the pagans did, with the clear intention of having a dream of the god, or kept vigils in the hope that some miraculous cure would occur, the fact was that nighttime at the shrine provided optimal conditions for such an event. "Incubation" sometimes happened by default, as it were. Napping at the shrine may not have been a choice but a necessity occasioned by the fatigue of sickness or long travel. Daytime siestas were common moments when visions occurred: Gregory of Tours saw a vision of his mother at noontime when he snoozed in St. Martin's basilica, and a heavenly voice spoke in a noontime dream to St. Rusticula "as she rested in St. Peter's basilica."[48] The sources make clear that vigils of the sick and travel-weary at the railings of the saint's tomb were often punctuated by periods of sleep, creating the perfect opportunity for dreams of the saint and ensuring that such visions remained an integral part of the drama of healing. The substitution of vigils at the tomb of the Christian saint for a couch before the shrine of a pagan god of healing thus did nothing to diminish the suppliant's avenues of recourse.[49] Indeed, although no permanent provisions were made for sleeping in churches (that is, no dormitories), pilgrims rested on bedding in the courtyards in front of churches. Those occasions when the saint deigned to appear to the sick supplicant were obviously noteworthy and sometimes public events; they remained an important way in which ordinary people encountered the power of the saint in dreams which were reported to, and given authority by, the clergy.

Concern to distinguish Christian from pagan practices was nowhere so clear as when it had to do with miraculous healings. Ultrogotha's visit to St. Martin's had culminated in the miraculous healing of three blind men who were present at the mass she had offered. Although the healings did not directly involve the queen's person, they were construed as the outcome of her laudable activities. It was the hope of miraculous healing which drew a large

[47] Gregory of Tours relates that "many people with fevers have slept by the tomb of the blessed Abraham and have been cured with the aid of heavenly remedies," *VP* 3.1. However, most overnight stays were described as vigils, the antithesis of sleeping. See also *Virt. Mart.* 1.22.

[48] *Virt. Mart.* 1, Praef.; *Vita Rusticulae sive Marciae abbatissae Arelatensis* 9, ed. J. Mabillon, *AASS, OSB* 2 (Paris, 1669), pp. 139–47; reprinted *AASS* Augusti ii. (1735), pp. 656–64; abbreviated ed., Krusch, *MGH, SRM* 4 (1902), pp. 337–51.

[49] Sleeping in churches was not uncommon in late antiquity—not just the hopeful in search of a cure, but also the priest or sacristan, who was often expected to live on the premises, guarding the sacred objects from theft or desecration. The priest Lucian was sleeping in his small church when he was told the whereabouts of St. Stephen's remains in a dream. Avitus of Braga, *Epistula ad Palchonium episcopum Bracarensem de reliquiis s. Stephani*, PL 41, pp. 805–16. On the issue of Christian incubation see de Nie, *Views*, p. 229, Dodds, *Anxiety*, p. 46; Dulaey, *Le rêve*, p. 186–88; and Le Goff "Christianity and Dreams," p. 209.

proportion of the visitors at a saint's shrine, and clergymen attached to a shrine were only too happy to encourage the mood of expectation that such hopes inevitably aroused. This they did not primarily from the cynical motive of an enlarged budget (useful though such resources were) but from a belief that miracles were signs of the saint's presence at the shrine. As Gregory noted of St. Martin: "For although he is unable to reveal himself to people in person, he is constantly displaying himself through his obvious miracles." [50] Miracles at a shrine assured the community that the saint was present with them and that the relics maintained a supernatural attachment to the saint in heaven. Indeed a saint's relics might be considered more powerful than when the saint when alive. "The virtue which comes from the tomb is much more worthy of praise than those things which a living person has worked in this world," wrote Gregory of Tours.[51] Dreams of saints at the site of their relics, authenticated by miracles, enhanced the message of holy presence in a deeply personal way.

Memorializing Dreams and Visions

While shrines were often the setting for dreams of the saints, dreams were also used to justify the building of shrines. Romans were accustomed to commemorating their religious experience in concrete form; altars, temples and modest shrines erected at the direction of dreams dotted the late antique landscape.[52] Wayside shrines to tutelary deities were positioned at road crossings, in grottos, and in fields open to the sky. They are still there.

In early Christianity, churches and martyries (*martyria*) were built in Palestine at the sites of the historical theophanies mentioned in the scriptures.[53] Scenes and events from the life of Christ, for example, were considered theophanies or epiphanies and were memorialized by religious edifices. Churches were constructed over the place of his birth, the garden of Gethsemane, the sepulchre where he was buried, the Mount of Golgotha, and the Mount of Olives from which he ascended to heaven after his resurrection.

---

[50] *Virt. Mart.* 2.40.

[51] *VP* 2 on St. Illidius.

[52] Pagan edifices and markers built at the behest of dreams were commemorated in inscriptions. At Convenae in Aquitaine, an inscription reads: "Erriapo Albinus Paulini f(ilius) ex viso posuit," and at Grand, another reads: "[Deo Apollini Gr]anno Consi[n]ius [Tri]bunus somno iussus." See P. Wiulleumier, *Inscriptions latines des trois Gaules*, 17th supplement to "Gallia" (Paris, 1963), p. 2, #4, and p. 169, #416; for other examples see p. 68, #186 a, b, and p. 157, #379. An altar dedicated to the goddess Diana in Italy bore the inscription: "Dianae sanctae T. Flaminius. Ariston ex monitu aram fecit." See I. C. Orellius, *Inscriptionum Latinarum selectarum amplissima collectio ad illustrandam Romanae antiquitatis*, vol. 1 (Turin, 1828), p. 291, #1444. See also Ramsey MacMullen, *Paganism in the Roman Empire* (New Haven, 1981), pp. 60–61.

[53] On the Palestinian evidence and the early use of the terms "theophany" and "epiphany" see André Grabar, "Les images des théophanies dans les martyria des lieux saints," in *Martyrium. Recherches sur le culte des reliques et l'art chrétien antique*, vol. 2 (Paris, 1946), pp. 129 ff.

Religious monuments were also built over sites associated with divine appearances recorded in the Old Testament: the Church of Mambre was built over the place where three angels appeared to Abraham. In addition to these monuments in Palestine commemorating historical epiphanies, broader interpretations of divine manifestation included sites where miracles, thaumaturgical epiphanies, and other phenomena had occurred. These were not geographically limited.[54] Parallels to memorialization of epiphanies were found in pagan mystery religions, including Mithraism and the cults of Isis, Dionysius, and Asclepius. The early Church had not invested in the memorialization of dreams and visions, but by the fourth and fifth centuries such restraint had evaporated.[55] Where once the pious built altars to Diana, they now built shrines to the memory of undocumented martyrs on the strength of dreams.[56] Such unregulated activity concerned Church authorities, who wanted to distinguish the Christian practice of erecting monuments dedicated to the memory of martyrs from the pagan "superstitious" worship of minor deities. Christian leaders were not opposed to their flock frequenting sepulchral martyr shrines. As Augustine explained to his friend Paulinus of Nola, Christian sepulchral "memorials" were intended, as their name suggested, to bring to the mind a recollection or memory of the martyr saint who lay buried there.[57] Yet, as ecclesiastical legislators under the influence of Augustine had clearly expressed over a decade earlier, the impetus to build shrines on the strength of dreams alone was liable to abuse. At the Carthaginian council of 401 the assembled bishops were eager to voice their concerns about the practice, and prohibited the specific action of erecting altars on the strength of "dreams and false revelations."[58]

In territories under Merovingian control, the practice of dedicating shrines to martyrs and saints on the prompting of dreams continued. However, conciliar prohibitions and episcopal disapproval evidently took their toll, for it is only occasionally that we have epigraphic or literary evidence of the survival of such practices (the epigraphic evidence is difficult to quantify . . .).[59] One such example from the fifth century is found in the choir of

---

[54] Ibid., pp. 129–39.

[55] Fox, *Pagans and Christians*, pp. 398–99.

[56] Examples of Christian buildings erected over pagan shrines to Diana include the unnamed monastic community outside Trier which had gathered around the aspiring stylite, Vulfolaic (*HF*, 8.15) and Columbanus's monastery at Annegray dedicated to St. Martin of Tours, cited by Katherine Scherman, *The Flowering of Ireland: Saints, Scholars, and Kings* (London, 1981), p. 177.

[57] Augustine, *De cura* 6. Isidore of Seville reiterates these concerns in *De ecclesiasticis officiis* 1.35 (34), ed. Christopher M. Lawson, CC 113 (1989).

[58] "Nam quae per somnia et per inanes quasi revelationes quorumlibet hominum ubicumque constituuntur altaria omnimodo improbentur." "De Falsis Memoriis Martyrum," *Registri Ecclesiae Carthaginensis Excerpta*, ed. C. Munier, CC 149 (1974), pp. 204–5.

[59] Most surviving Merovingian epigraphy is funerary, on the problems of which see Ingrid Heidrich, "Südgallische Inschriften des 5.–7. Jahrhunderts als historische Quellen" *Rheinische Vierteljahrsblätter* 32 (1968), 167–83. I would like to thank Bonnie Effros for this reference. On the epigraphic genre see Robert Favreau, *Les inscriptions médiévales*, Typologie des sources, 35 (Turnhout, 1979).

St. Ursula's church in Cologne. A certain Clematius restored a basilica for the Ursula and her virginal companions because he was "often warned by divinely inspired fiery visions" to do so. The basilica, the inscription states, was built in fulfillment of a vow which he made at that time.[60] Another inscription composed by Venantius Fortunatus commemorated the erection of a basilica by a nobleman named Leontius who had seen the martyr Eutropius of Saintes in his sleep.[61] It is even possible that the famous hypogeum at Poitiers, traditionally known as the crypt of the abbot Mellebaudus, is another example.[62] Other Christian examples exist for other parts of the former Roman empire, but on the whole it was rare for a vow made in response to a dream or a vision to be recorded epigraphically.

In literary, especially hagiographic, sources the connection between dreams, visions, and the decision to build was often more direct. A few hours after St. Radegund of Poitiers' death the tribune Domolenus, sick with a swollen throat, saw the saint in a dream, and she commanded him to build an oratory dedicated to St. Martin. He ordered it to be done, and he was healed.[63] Rusticula, abbess of the convent of St. John at Arles, began to build an enlarged church for her community intending to dedicate it to the Holy Cross, but a vision showed her a more magnificent building which she was to dedicate to the Cross: "Then a building of wondrous magnitude constructed in Heaven was shown to her in a vision and she understood this to mean that the Lord was commanding her to build something similar on earth. Joyfully she hastened to fulfill her Lord's orders faithfully and constructed a temple of sparkling beauty."[64]

Monastic founders often cited dreams and visions as the rationale for

[60] "Divinis flammeis visionib[us] frequenter / Admonit[us] et virtutis magnae mai / iestatis martyrii caelestium virgin[**] / imminentium ex partib[us] orientis /Exsibitus pro voto Clematius V. C. de / proprio in loco suo hanc basilicam/ voto quod debebat a fundamentis / restituit." Edmond Le Blant, *Inscriptions chrétiennes de la Gaule antérieures au viii siècle*, vol. 2 (Paris 1856, 1865), p. 569, #678B. See also his preface to volume 1, xcii–xciii. This text is not in the most recent works on Gallic inscriptions.
[61] "Quantus amor Domini maneat tibi Papa Leonti / quem sibi iam sancti templa novare movent / Eutropii illa etenim venerandi antistitis aula / corruerat senio dilacerata suo / nudatasque trabes paries vacuatas habebat / pondere non tecti sed male pressus aquis / nocte sopore levi cuidam veniente ministro / instauratorem te docet esse suum / pro mercede tui meruit magis ille monere." Le Blant, *Inscriptions chrétiennes* vol. 2, p. 363, #580. On Eutropius, bishop and martyr of Saintes, see *GM* 56. On the text, see note 60 above.
[62] Le Blant claimed that still discernible on the wall behind the altar was the word "monitus" (referring to an "admonitio" in a vision). Edmond Le Blant, *Nouveau recueil des inscriptions chrétiennes de la Gaule antérieurs au viiie siècle* (1892), p. 268, #253. However, I have been unable to confirm the presence of this inscription in modern studies of the crypt, which include Carol Heitz, "L'hypogée de Mellebaude à Poitiers" in *L'inhumation privilégiée du ive au viiie siècle en occident*, ed. Yves Duval and J.-C. Picard, pp. 91–96; Actes du colloque tenu à Créteil les 16–18 mars 1984 (Paris, 1986); and J.-P. Adam, G. Aubin, J.-F. Baratin et al., eds. *Les premiers monuments chrétiens de la France*, vol. 2, Sud-Ouest et Centre (Paris, 1996), pp. 302–9.
[63] *VR* 1.38.
[64] *V. s. Rusticulae* 8, trans. Jo Ann McNamara, John E. Halborg, and E. Gordon Whatley, *Sainted Women of the Dark Ages* (Durham, N.C., 1992). On the authenticity of the text see Pierre Riché, "La *Vita s. Rusticulae*: Note d'hagiographie mérovingienne," *AB* 72 (1954), 369–77.

choosing to build in a certain spot. St. John the Baptist instructed Odilia of Hohenburg on the site where she should erect a church.[65] Eparchius of Angoulême (sixth century), looking for a secluded spot to settle, walked outside the monastery walls of St. Cyran and lay down to sleep. Christ's voice spoke to him as he slept: "Eparchius stay here, do not go any further."[66] Nivardus, bishop of Rheims, was likewise given divine aid in choosing the site for his foundation of Hautvilliers. Nivardus was sitting beneath a great oak tree when he saw a vision which he interpreted to be mystical. An angel in the form of a white dove threw out three of its feathers, which then encircled the intended area. The dove finally came to rest in the upper branches of the tree, and when the monastery was built, Nivardus dedicated a church to St. Peter and all the apostles on the site of the tree, with its trunk incorporated into the altar.[67]

Though it was not uncommon for the saints to be guided by visionary means in hagiography, ancient Christian proscriptions against active divination dictated a passive role for most Christians in their communication with the divine.[68] Active solicitation of visions was not unknown, however, and specific cult information was sometimes sought by such means. In one case a church was built in clear and open anticipation of a vision of this type. The bishop of Cologne, Eberigisilus, had learned of the martyr Mallosus who was reported to have been martyred in Birten, but the whereabouts of whose relics were unknown. Undeterred, the bishop built a church in the martyr's honor, "that it might be known, if anyone received a vision of the martyr, the body could be translated there."[69] Soon after, a deacon at Metz learned in a vision the whereabouts of the martyr's remains and, guided by the vision's instructions, was able to point out the burial place. The story is a reminder of the close and incestuous association between dreams of saints and the relic *inventiones* which brought their presence to light.

Finally, the places where visions were received sometimes became sacred sites in their own right. The nuns at St. Aldegund's convent, for example, remembered that a miraculous cure was effected at the very site, in front of the altar, where Aldegund had once had a vision.[70] The vision of Nivardus cited

[65] *Vita s. Odiliae abbatissae Hohenburgensis*, ed. Wilhelm Levinson, MGH, SRM 6 (1913), pp. 24–50, 17. This is a late Carolingian *vita* of a Merovingian saint, but perhaps based on earlier traditions.
[66] *Vita et virtutes Eparchii reclusi Ecolismensis* 8, ed. Bruno Krusch, MGH, SRM 3 (1896), pp. 550–64.
[67] *Vita Nivardi episcopi Remensis, auctore Almanno monacho Altivillarensi* 8, ed. Wilhelm Levison, MGH, SRM 5 (1910), pp. 157–71.
[68] Exceptions to this rule were martyrs who appear to have been considered a special case, as in the Perpetua's request for a dream concerning her brother Dinocrates. *Passio SS. Perpetuae et Felicitatis*, ed. and trans. W. H. Shewring (London, 1931).
[69] GM 62: "ut scilicet, cum aliquid revelationis de martyre acciperet, in ea beatos artus, Domino annuente, transferret . . . praestolans Domini misericordiam, quid iuberet de martyre revelari."
[70] *Vita s. Aldegundis*, ed. J. Mabillon, AASS, OSB 2 (1688), pp. 806–15.

above likewise made a connection between the place where a vision occurred
and a sacred spot; the tree where the dove came to rest was fashioned into
an altar for the monastery. Thus we see in Merovingian Gaul that the practice of memorializing visionary theophanies was similar to practices current
in the East.[71]

Dreams and Visions in Shrine Documents

As we have seen, shrines were constructed where once there had been
none, and existing shrines were rededicated to the new pantheon of Christian saints. Visions announced the coming of the saints to their new neigh-
borhoods and showed them overseeing the construction of their cultic centers.[72] Yet the material fabric of these shrines was not the most radical aspect
of the changes happening in Gaul. Rather, the vigorous and widely published powers of the saints, especially in the realm of healing, made the cultic centers engines of holy power within the Christian community. Written
sources produced in the shrines, about the shrines, and for the shrines were
not private documents; they were often on view, they were copied, and they
were excerpted into hagiographic literature which, in its turn, was read
aloud on holy days. The shrine literature that survives still speaks to us
today of the claims that the saints were making on the allegiance of the
community.

Visions in "libri miraculorum"

The cult of the saints would never have achieved the power and visibility
that it did were it not that veneration of the saints was believed to be both
appropriate and effective.[73] In hagiographies and their ancillary literature—
translationes, inventiones, libelli miraculorum—shrine guardians recorded

---

[71] Grabar, *Martyrium*, vol. 2, pp. 129–39.

[72] For example, St. Benignus of Dijon was said to have overseen the construction of a church
dedicated to the nun Paschasia. *GM* 50. The two virgins Maura and Britta instructed a certain
man in a vision to provide shelter for their tombs, and after a vision of his own, Bishop Euphronius of Tours agreed to bless the oratory constructed over them. *GC* 18. More concrete instruction on building techniques was said to have been provided by the Virgin Mary at the
church dedicated to her in Constantinople. *GM* 8.

[73] On healing at Christian shrines see Aline Rouselle, "From Sanctuary to Miracle-Worker:
Healing in Fourth-Century Gaul," in *Ritual, Religion, and the Sacred*, ed. Robert Foster and
Orest A. Ranum, pp. 95–127 (Baltimore, 1982); Rouselle, *Croire et guérir. La foi en Gaule
dans l'antiquité tardive* (Paris, 1990); Edward James, "Miracles and Medicine in the Life
of Gregory of Tours" in *The Culture of Christendom: Essays in Medieval History in Commemoration of Denis L. T. Bethell*, ed. Marc Anthony Meyer, pp. 45–60 (London, 1993);
J. H. Corbett, "The Saint as Patron in the Work of Gregory of Tours," *Journal of Medieval History* 7 (1981), 1–13; Miller, *Dreams*, pp. 106–23; and Van Dam, *Saints and Their Miracles*,
pp. 82–115.

and extolled the benefits showered on some happy individuals and by extension on the community at large, when the saints and their remains were properly cared for. Among the benefits for which medieval saints were most prized was their ability to heal the sick. Medieval authors did not distinguish qualitatively between dream-healings and healings effected through the many other sorts of contact with the saint's presence: potions made from the dust of a saint's tomb, contact with the tomb railings or those around the saint's bed, use of candles or holy oil which had been left at the tomb over night, linen cloths (*brandea*) which had absorbed the relics' holiness, and masses said in the saint's honor. However, for this study it is important to consider how healing dreams and visions were handled by the clergy. Guardianship over saintly relics and the staging of liturgical ritual in the shrines were central ways in which the clergy conceived and displayed their authority in spiritual matters.

The supernatural activity of divine grace, channeled through the saints, was inscribed on the bodies of the healed. But a more permanent form of documentation was necessary if the reputation of a shrine was to last from one generation to another. Ideally, the successful shrine enjoyed the confluence of two impulses: first, lay and clerical piety which recognized in the alleviation of suffering the boon of their saintly patron, and second, the determination of the clergy to record miracles and publish them (that is, make public readings from them and display them). There were thus two authors of the medieval cult: the saint whose power was attested by the people, and the clergy who, convinced by reports of miraculous healings and apparitions, believed that there was a need to document the saint's activity.[74] Thus our view of activity at Gallic shrines is colored by the clerical perspective of the documents which record them, and the visionary accounts which sometimes accompanied these marvels were likewise imprinted with the values and expectations of their authors.

The clerics and monks who oversaw the shrines were responsible for generating a "positive" history of the saint's interraction with his devotees.[75] In

---

[74] Augustine soberly noted in his *De cura* 19, 20, that he doubted that martyrs have any control over or interest in, the living. Cases where it appeared that martyrs intervened in human affairs, he averred, must be the result of angelic powers which assumed the martyr's physical appearance. Augustine revised these views in later life and accorded the saints a more personalized habit of intervention. In cultic concerns, as in many matters, early medieval churchmen were slow to absorb Augustine's tempered views.

[75] On miracle-lists see Hippolyte Delehaye, "Les premiers 'libelli miraculorum,'" *AB* 29 (1910), 427–34; Delehaye, "Les recueils antiques des miracles des saints. II. Les recueils latins," *AB* 43 (1925), 73–85, 305–25; and Martin Heinzelmann, "Une source de base de la littérature hagiographique latine: le recueil de miracles," in *Hagiographie, cultures et sociétés ive–xiie siècles* pp. 235–57. Études Augustiniennes, (Paris, 1981). See Heinzelmann's discussion on the miracle-lists of Gregory of Tours and the relationship between this genre and hagiography (pp. 57–59). On the ninth century (generally applicable) see Michel Rouche, "Miracles, maladies et psychologie de la foi à l'époque carolingienne en Francie," in *Hagiographie, Cultures et Sociétés* pp. 319–37 (Paris, 1981).

this the Christian shrine was no different from the healing shrines of pagan antiquity which had likewise kept careful records.[76] The practice did not develop immediately in the Christian tradition, however, or rather there was a lag between the time when record keeping was customary and when it became routine. St. Augustine in the early fifth century reveals that in some communities in North Africa it was customary to compose and maintain miracle-lists at the shrines, but with the inference that in his day the practice was localized and discretionary. Of the miracles being attributed to St. Stephen's relics in Uzalis, he writes, "but there the custom of publishing narratives does not obtain."[77] Augustine's own account of the miracles in Uzalis had to be confined to those which had been written for "public recital," which suggests a multitude of unpublished miracles. Augustine undertook to record the martyr's miracles at Hippo: "I desired that narratives might be written, judging that the multitude should not remain ignorant of these things." For some indication of the vigor which some relics displayed, it should be recalled that within two years of the arrival of St. Stephen's relics in Hippo, seventy miracles were already recorded there.[78] Healing shrines that were reportedly successful were often phenomenally so. The length of miracle-lists could be impressive, and indeed this fact alone made some lists themselves a new relic designed to inspire devotion and awe. It was often reported that a saint's *vita* conferred healing or protection when used as a holy talisman.[79] Sometimes the miracle-lists also, like the saint's *vita*, dispensed the saint's power through its healing touch. Paulinus of Périgueux's list of Martin's miracles was laid upon a sick boy who recovered as a result, and Gregory's hope for his own list of Martin's miracles was that it likewise radiate such power.[80]

In sixth-century Gaul miracle-lists were probably kept at most shrines. Gregory of Tours' deacon visited the tomb of St. Nicetius in Lyons on his return from a pilgrimage to Rome, and entering the shrine, he "examined the famous register of the various miracles which had been done there."[81] It no longer exists, but we do have a very impressive example of a miracle-list associated with a famous shrine in Gregory of Tours' *Libri de virtutibus sancti Martini episcopi*. Gregory's four books of miracles recorded that churches dedicated to St. Martin and housing his relics were the scene of many miraculous events, including healings (most plentifully), aversion of storms and epidemics, and deliverances from captivity. The four books of miracles com-

---

[76] On inscriptions recording dedicatory gifts in return for healing see Kee, *Miracle*, chap. 3.

[77] Augustine, *Civ. Dei* 22.8. See also Augustine's *Sermons* 314–324 on St. Stephen, *PL* 38, 1425–54.

[78] *Civ. Dei* 22. 8.

[79] A deacon of Autun placed a papyrus copy of Nicetius of Lyons' *vita* on his eye and was cured of eye disease. *VP* 8.

[80] *Virt. Mart.*, Praef.

[81] *VP* 8.6.

prise a single-authored selection of miracles written within a fairly short period of time, and each book was written at a distinct moment in the cult's
development.[82] Gregory also glossed the list with comments on the meanings
of miracles and, to some extent, the methodology underlying its composition. Gregory's motive for writing the list is very clear; he believed that the
glory and power of St. Martin was manifested through the efficacy of the
saint's remains. Gregory wanted to create a written record for "the memory
of posterity," suitably embarked upon after he had a vision of his mother encouraging him to do so. St. Martin's posthumous miracles under Gregory's
episcopate were to be added to previous lists of miracles at the shrine, and
as an extension to Sulpicius Severus' late fourth-century *vita* of the saint.
"When he was in the world, God worked through him; now God distinguishes his tomb with miracles," wrote Gregory, who may have hoped that
his book would be appended or integrated into the existing corpus of Martinian writings.[83] Paulinus of Périgueux's versified account of St. Martin's
miracles was a traditional resource, and some miracles from it were quoted
in the beginning of Gregory's work. Gregory's request to Venantius Fortunatus that his own miracle list might be turned into verse probably stemmed
from the hope that it might join Paulinus' versified compilation.[84]

Gregory's miracle-list is a rare resource. Most miracle-lists from the Merovingian period have survived only because they were later incorporated into
the hagiographies of the saint in question. Sometimes it was the existence of
an impressive list of miracles which initially inspired the composition of a
Life. In other cases miracle-lists were used to supplement the biographical
portion of a *vita*. Venantius Fortunatus' *Vita sancti Germanii Parisiensis* is a
good example. Venantius claimed to draw on existing documents and oral
sources to fashion his portrait of the bishop of Paris. The lengthy list of miracles which Germanus was recorded as performing during his lifetime, and
which were listed one after the other, comprised the bulk of the *vita* and is
testimony to its origins as a *libellus* which must have been kept at Paris.[85]
The *Vita s. Anstrudis* is an example of another *vita* in which a miracle-list
was incorporated at a later stage into the saint's hagiography, or rather

[82] *Virt. Mart.*, pp. 584–661. Translations used here are from Van Dam, *Saints and Their Miracles*, pp. 199–303. The fourth book was evidently incomplete when the author died. It is shorter and lacks an epilogue. Heinzelmann, "Une source," demonstrated that the books list miracles in chronological order. The second through fourth books can be dated because the miracles recorded were contemporary: book 2 in 573–81; book 3 in 581–87; book 4 in 588–93. Heinzelmann also notes that internal references such as *in eadem festivitate* and *post haec* suggest that the miracles may originally have been dated (p. 240).

[83] *Virt. Mart.*, Praef.

[84] Van Dam, *Saints and their Miracles* p. 200, n. 3; Heinzelmann, "Une source," p. 236. In his *Virt. Mart.*, Gregory identified Sulpicius Severus' *Dialogues* as another type of Martinian miracle-list. A reference to miracles heaped before the congregation's eyes may allude to the presence of Paulinus of Périgueux's list of Martin's miracles in his renovated church. Le Blant, *Inscriptions*, vol. 1, #176.

[85] *Vita s. Germanii Parisiensis*, chaps. 46–185, comprise a distinct list of miracles.

appended to it with little real effort at integration.[86] Indeed the *Vita s. Anstrudis* retains an interesting feature which points to the diachronicity of the document. The biographic portion of the *vita* without exception employs the term "visio" to record the saint's appearances to her suppliants. In the list of posthumous miracles at her tomb, however, her appearances are consistently described as having occurred "in somniis." This difference in vocabulary, I suggest, was not the result of an attempted distinction between visions occurring in the saint's lifetime as opposed to those after her death. Rather the change in terminology reflects the singular preferences of different authors who wrote at different times and is thus a tell-tale sign of the join between two documents. The advantage of miracle-lists within the context of hagiographies is that the dreams, visions, and miracles are occasionally given some context in the life of the saint. The disadvantage is that the miraculous information has been picked over by the hagiographer and presumably chosen to fit a preconceived profile. That is why the few examples of early medieval miracle-lists that have retained their identity as freestanding lists are so valuable. Translations of relics from one location to another were often the occasion for dreams, apparitions, and healing miracles, and, because separate festivities were usually assigned to the day of the relic translation, translation miracles were documented separately from the *vita*. Translation miracles which occurred in the pre-Carolingian period, on the other hand, were often incorporated into hagiographies. In the Carolingian period, miracle-lists generated by relic translations were widely produced and became part of the growth of the supraregional expansion of a public cult.[87]

Thus, preparatory to using surviving miracle-lists for the investigation of healing dreams (whether as freestanding documents or interwoven into the saint's hagiography), it is important to keep some considerations in mind. Neither Augustine nor any other commentator on the practice indicates what, if any, guidelines determined the choice of entries. In general, narratives of healing were succinct, tending to focus on the discernible, palpable signs of the marvelous rather than on the broader concerns of the recipient, who was often anonymous or else portrayed exclusively in terms of his affliction. We know that not all miracles accredited to a shrine were included in these lists. The compilers of the lists often stated that the lists were merely representative of the power of the saint, and that they could have chosen many other examples but for their concern not to bore the reader (a conventional comment, but one which gave an expansive sense of the saint's munificence). In cases of very active shrines such as St. Martin's tomb in Tours, some of the beneficiaries of the saint's power simply got away before

---

[86] *Vita Anstrudis abbatissae Laudunensis*, ed. Wilhelm Levison, *MGH, SRM* 6 (1913), pp. 64–78.

[87] See Heinzelmann, "Une source," for an overview of this development in the Carolingian period, and his *Translationsberichte und andere Quellen des Reliquienkultes*, Typologie des sources du moyen âge, 33 (Turnhout, 1979), esp. pp. 52–66, 94–99.

they could be questioned. Gregory of Tours bemoaned this fact in his third book of miracles: "When these people have been restored to health by this saint of God, immediately they depart and sometimes leave so quietly that, if it is proper to say so, no one sees them. Whenever a rumour arises that the power of the blessed bishop has appeared, I summon the custodians of the shrine and learn what has happened; but I do not always learn the names from these custodians. But often I do record by name those people whom I was able to see or with whom I talked." [88] The extent of biographical information on the sick and healed depended on the compiler's knowledge of the pilgrim community. Gregory of Tours, for example, sought to discover the religious infractions which he believed had caused the illness to begin with, especially if the transgression indicated that the afflicted person had failed to observe the preaching of bishops. [89]

Did the compilers' selections of miracle stories promote or obscure healings obtained through the agency of visions? This we cannot know. Gregory of Tours does not appear to have had any problems with the concept of healing dreams, for he relates some of the most interesting cases which we have for the sixth century. Of the 232 miraculous healings recorded by him in the *Libri de virtutibus sancti Martini*, 7.3 percent were effected through dreams and visions. [90] Yet the problem of the compilers' modes of selection remains. We know for a later period that certain groups were discouraged or prohibited from approaching shrines: lepers and women, for example. [91] Nor would it be unreasonable to expect that individual clerics had different priorities when selecting and summarizing miraculous occurrences in written form. The choice of data might reflect the compiler's phenomenological interests— his intent to show breadth of saintly power in a wide variety of miracle types or, alternatively, a saint's expertise in one particular aspect of miraculous healing. [92] Or the compiler might want to emphasize healing events that had moralizing capabilities (such as afflictions visited upon peasants who worked on Sundays) or that addressed a particular social constituency. These could then be read aloud on the saint's festivals. Martin of Tours and Germanus of Paris were both specialists in miraculous eye cures (in visions, other saints deferred to their expertise) but their relics had a wide range of efficacy. Certain saints acquired professional dossiers in one or another spe-

---

[88] *Virt. Mart.* 3, 45.

[89] *VM* 4.45.

[90] I have not included cases of demonic possession or miracles drawn from Paulinus of Périgueux, or of animals cured. Of the 232 healings, 215 were without visionary intervention, and seventeen were with visions (7.327 percent). Of those seventeen, twelve were men and five were women.

[91] Rouche, "Miracles, maladies et psychologie," examines a corpus of ninth-century miracle-lists.

[92] On the supernatural "specializations" of saints see František Graus, *Volk, Herrscher und Heiliger im Reich der Merowinger. Studien zur Hagiographie der Merowingerzeit* (Prague, 1965), pp. 51–52.

ciality, but the role of the clerical compiler in shaping that reputation for posterity must have been significant. Thus, in addition to all the winnowing that occurred between the individual's memory of their experience and the version they recounted to the recorder, our documents for dream healings come to us loaded with clerical concerns that we have no means to overcome. In short, the recording cleric fashioned the tools from which the cult was made, and most miracle-lists were compiled in ad hoc fashion, by different clerics at different times, and almost always, from our perspective, anonymously.

With all these caveats, and with all their flaws and uncertainties, the unique importance of these miracle-lists is that they embody both the best and the worst of our documentation on visions at shrines. The focus of the miracle-list (both the way it was composed and the way it was designed to be read) was only tangentially on the recipient of the saint's blessing. Yet though these considerations circumscribe our efforts to draw conclusions from the sources, accounts of miraculous healings at the tombs of the saints offer a special and indeed unique insight into the dreams and visions of the ordinary individual: a view into that space permitted to the ordinary suppliant by the clergy.

Dreams That Healed

Healing visions were generally of two sorts. Either they were a means of communication through which the saint prescribed specific remedies, or the experience of the dream itself was the remedy. There are plentiful examples of the former, fewer of the latter, and as usual Gregory of Tours is our best source for both.

The consultative vision provided the venue for a personal consultation with the saint, which might involve righting a wrong or doing the saint's bidding in some matter overlooked by the petitioner. One of Gregory's servants brought sickness upon his whole family because he had taken a piece of wood from the railings around St. Martin's bed, and they were cured only when a terrifying vision identified the source of the problem.[93] Most commonly, however, the sick reported that a figure in a dream (usually identified as the saint who ultimately provided the cure) directed them to seek out a certain saint's shrine (sometimes involving substantial travel) or identified relics closer to home which would be effective in providing a cure. This type of advice was too common to merit much comment from the person recording it. For example, the grandmother of a sick boy was advised to go to St. Martin's tomb, where her grandson was duly healed.[94] Leudard, a blind slave of a deacon of Nantes, received a cure in like manner after he had been ad-

[93] *Virt. Mart.* 1.35.
[94] *Virt. Mart.* 4.17.

vised in a dream, as did another inhabitant of Tours, blind for twenty-five years.[95] One woman's sickness was caused by sinning on a Sunday, and she was healed on a Sunday after being advised in a dream to go to the shrine of St. Hilary of Poitiers.[96] Occasionally, advisory dreams of this sort were not specific enough to save the suppliant a long journey; one woman who was advised in a dream to go to St. Julian's tomb went to Saintes because she was unaware that there were relics of the saint closer to home.[97]

The remedial dream cured afflictions by giving the suppliant specific directions on how to obtain a "medicinal" remedy. As a very young boy, Gregory of Tours was advised in two dreams how he might provide a cure for his ailing father. The first required a talisman be made and slipped beneath his father's pillow, and the second remedy required burnt fish entrails. Cooked up by his devout mother, the celestial remedy worked (at least temporarily).[98] At the convent of St. John in Arles, less than a century later, a male servant was cured of paralysis after he was advised in his sleep to ask the nuns for the water used to wash the four corners of the pallet upon which their newly deceased abbess Rusticula had died.[99]

Most interesting, however, are the cases in which the experience of the dream or vision itself, usually a dream in which the saint made a personal appearance, sufficed to effect a cure. The afflicted person was not necessarily at St. Martin's church in Tours, but usually some connection between the suppliant and the saint's cult had already been established. Mostly, however, the person had sought proximity to a shrine containing the saint's relics, and was even in some cases at the saint's tomb at night when the dream occurred, perhaps having fallen asleep during a long vigil. Gregory relates how a mute man from Angers was healed by a dream at St. Martin's shrine at Candes. "It happened that suddenly the place was filled with a bright light . . . immediately there appeared to him a man that was clothed in a bishop's robe. This man touched him, made the sign of the cross of Christ on his forehead, and said: 'The Lord has made you healthy. Rise, hurry to the church, and thank your God.'"[100] The mute then cried out for all to hear, and, as often happened, other miracles were reported soon after. Mutes were not rare among the afflicted, and their healing was not always a pleasant experience. In one case a visionary apparition worked through shock therapy: a cleric from Candes named Piolus had suffered various afflictions in his life which had been cured by attending St. Martin's shrine. So when he became mute as a result of a violent illness, he traveled to the saint's shrine at Epiphany and

---

[95] Ibid., 4.20, 2.41.
[96] Fortunatus, *V. Hil.* 24.
[97] *VJ* 47.
[98] *GC* 39; Tobit 11. 11–13.
[99] *V. Rusticulae* 27.
[100] *Virt. Mart.* 3.23.

decided to keep a vigil at the tomb. After midnight he fell asleep, had a terrifying dream, and in his panic called out "Lord Martin, free me!" and was thus cured.[101]

The possibility of miraculous healing at a shrine provided the desperately sick with a focus for hope, but medieval society was not generally tolerant of those marked with visible signs of disease and physical mutilation. The afflicted might suffer social ostracism, and even disinheritance on account of their condition, as in the case of a deaf mute from Angers.[102] Many roamed the roads of Gaul as beggars, clapping wooden boards to attract attention, pity, and alms. Having undergone significant reversals in their lives, having lost the familial environment that was rightfully theirs, they found that the process of healing after lengthy disability could itself be a traumatic experience.[103] In some cases an individual's whole identity might become so tied to their affliction that it took a saintly visitation to validate a remission, both to vindicate the affliction as having been genuine and grant the suppliant "permission" to be healed. One man who was cured of tertian fever after being administered a dust potion from St. Martin's tomb by Gregory of Tours needed further saintly assurance that he was indeed over his sickness and to remove the traumatic memory of his affliction. In a vision before dawn, a hideous person appeared to him to remind him that it was time for his sickness to resume: "Behold, the time for your tremor has already arrived. Why are you pretending? Do what you usually do." Then the reassuring presence of the saint appeared in his vision, reminding him of the protection he was under by advising him to make the sign of the Cross over his forehead, and he finally knew that he was cured.[104]

More commonly, however, visionary images supplanted one image of self-hood with another: the healthy person supplanted the sick person. A crippled slave named Veranus lived this transition in his dream, in which "while he asleep, it seemed to him as if he were a man accustomed to stretch his foot on his bed."[105] It was a short step to interject the saint's person into the equation. We see this in a couple of cases in which healing happened in sleep.

A nun named Apra who was severely crippled in one hand and both feet sought St. Martin's intercession through prayer. One night, we are told, "it seemed to her that an old man came to her and gently touched and stroked all her limbs." She awoke from her sleep with her feet healed. After another dream in which she was told to go to St. Martin's church, she was healed of

---

[101] Ibid., 2.26.
[102] Ibid., 3.23. The deaf mute from Angers was dispossessed of his inheritance by his brothers, and spent the next six years of his life as one of the poor registered at St. Martin's shrine at Candes.
[103] Ibid., 3.23.
[104] Ibid., 4.37.
[105] Ibid., 2.4.

the paralysis in her hand. In Apra's dream, the stroking of her afflicted limbs perhaps signaled the return of sensation. She attributed her first cure to her prayers to St. Martin, but second dream directed her to St. Martin's shrine, thus placing the cure of her hand (and by association her earlier cure) in the indisputable context of the supernatural. A similar story is told of a Poitevin woman who had already left St. Martin's shrine without a cure and was on her journey home. She was visited in her sleep by the saint, whom she identified as St. Martin because he was dressed in purple and carried a cross in his hand, and as he moved his fingers among hers, straightening them out, she awoke to find her hand on the mend. In both these cases of dream cures, there was no doubt about the agent of healing: it was the saint who brought supernatural relief. These two accounts are interesting in that they so closely associate the moment of physical healing with the mental, visionary image of the healer. The physical sensation of returning tactility was ascribed to the saint's healing touch, while for the women returning sensation brought the saint's mercy into view.

The healing narratives examined above reveal the intimate connection of mind, imagination, and body in the process and realization of healing. Most significantly, however, they underscore the centrality of liturgical space and liturgical functions provided by the clergy. The posthumous nature of the power of the saint necessitated this mediating function by the clergy. Exhortations to repentance (with public displays of weeping and lamenting), emphasis on all night vigils, fasting, almsgiving, oblations, confession, and the sponsoring of Masses were the sacramental and liturgical underpinnings of the saint's beneficence. Most Masses said in honor of a saint, such as that attended by Ultrogotha at St. Martin's tomb, were probably not votive masses, although that process was just beginning in the late sixth century as Frederick Paxton has shown.[106] The clergy no less than the saint provided their flock with the apparatus of spiritual healing, and also like the saint they provided physical care for the sick. The contented presence of the saint depended on the clergy's providing the proper environment in which the saint flourished and dispensed healing through his relics. Many healing visions noted the smiling radiance of the saint's face, and in sixth-century visions, St. Martin appeared always as a bishop, carrying the emblems of his office. Any suggestion that the saint might not be present at his shrine induced panic among the clergy. Gregory of Tours and his flock experienced a profound shock when they were informed by one of the possessed at the shrine that St. Martin had left his church and was in Rome instead! Gregory persevered, said the Mass, and a paralyzed man named Bonulf became the

---

[106] Frederick Paxton, "Liturgy and Healing in an Early Medieval Saint's Cult: The Mass *in honore sancti Sigismundi* for the Cure of Fevers," *Traditio* 49 (1994), 23–43, traces the early development of votive Masses to a particular saint for a specific ailment, and the "ritual healing by priests in a liturgical setting."

happy instrument of relief: his healing confirmed the continuing presence of the saint at his shrine.[107]

* * *

At the healing shrines of the saints the Gallic clergy displayed most visibly their commitment to advertising a wide spectrum of vision recipients. Primarily, however, clerics promoted the efficacy of the petitioning rituals orchestrated at the shrine. Living saints who displayed thaumaturgical powers and communicated divine powers through visions posed a potential threat to the spiritual authority of the clergy.[108] Dead saints and their relics, however, brought liturgical and thus clerical powers into view. Relics required intercessory ritual from the clergy and contrition from the suppliant. Thus clerical writers were sometimes probably quick to assign piety to those who attended the shrine services which they provided. It was not just the saint's efficacy but that of the clergy which must be manifested through supernatural events at the shrine. Yet in the sources there was always room for the saint to be seen to extend his mercy to the least deserving of his suppliants.

[107] *Virt. Mart.* 2.25.
[108] See Chapter 2. In the discussion segment of Heinzelmann's paper "Une source," F. Dolbeau noted that the Bollandists had made a distinction between a saint's posthumous miracles and those performed while he was alive, especially as they related to ecclesiastical authority.

5 Visionary Journeys
to the Otherworld

Scholars disagree about how to situate Merovingian literature of travels to the otherworld in the wider development of a visionary "genre." Discussion has centered on whether such tales in the seventh century constituted a substantially new genre, a recognizable modification of an older literary tradition, or perhaps not even a tradition at all. In her study of the influence of Gregory the Great's *Dialogues* on visionary literature, Maria Pia Ciccarese describes the corpus of texts as "un vero e proprio filone letterario."[1] Walter Berschin's view agrees with this characterization but with the qualification that although seventh-century visionary texts such as the *Visio Baronti* and the *Visio Fursei* mark a watershed in the genre, the original form of this literature is to be found in Hellenistic precedents.[2] By contrast, Yitzhak Hen doubts that these two seventh-century Merovingian texts and the "scattering of texts" prior to them could be said to comprise a genre at all, questioning whether it is meaningful to designate a visionary genre before the more plentiful texts of the Carolingian age.[3]

Scholars generally agree, however, that the seventh century is a watershed

[1] Maria Pia Ciccarese, "La *Visio Baronti* nella tradizione letteraria dell *Visiones* dell'aldilà," *Romanobarbarica* 6 (1982), 25–52, esp. 26, and her "Le visioni dell'aldilà come genere letterario: fonti antiche e sviluppi medievali," in *Le "Visiones" nella Cultura Medievale*, ed. Peter Dinzelbacher, Maria Pia Ciccarese, Yves Christe, and Walter Berschin, pp. 266–77, *Scede Medievali*, 19 (1990). See also Arnold Angenendt, "Theologie und Liturgie der mittelalterlichen Toten-Memoria," *Memoria der geschichtliche Zeugniswert des liturgischen Gedenkens im Mittelalter*, in ed. Karl Schmid and Joachim Wollasch, pp. 79–199, esp. pp. 86–99 (Munich, 1984).

[2] Berschin, *Biographie und Epochenstil*, vol. 2, pp. 104–9, cites the *Visio Isaiae* and the *Visio Pauli* as examples of Hellenistic "kleinliteratur." He also cites the emergence of vision collections such as the *Vita Columbani*, book 2, and the *Vita Aldegundis* as breakthroughs in the genre of visionary literature.

[3] Yitzhak Hen, "The Structure and Aims of the 'Visio Baronti,'" *Journal of Theological Studies*, n.s. 47 (1996), 477–97, esp. 485.

in the development of visionary literature. Claude Carozzi notes that despite occasional anticipation of otherworldly journeying earlier, the true starting point for medieval accounts is the seventh century, and Jocelyn N. Hillgarth likewise asserts that the rise of a Christian visionary literature was largely a product of the seventh-century West.[4] Peter Brown adds that although Christian views of the afterlife prior to the seventh century appear "exotic" to modern eyes, the view of the otherworld presented in texts after 700, after "the very end of late antiquity," seem familiar.[5] Clearly something new and important was happening in the seventh century. One important aspect of the change was the moral status of the visionary traveler. Saints Paul and Peter were compassionate observers of the otherworld. In the seventh century visionary journeys were undertaken by avowed sinners whose fearful experiences prompted them to penance and to impart messages of penance to others. Partly in consequence of their penitential form, their visionary stories were disseminated with a degree of clerical approbation that was new. Before the seventh century, as we saw in Chapter 1, it occasionally happened that an ordinary Christian had a vision while a priest who was also present saw nothing. Such situations perplexed prominent churchmen such as Gregory of Tours, especially when the visions occurred in venues of high visibility such as churches and other cultic arenas. Yet when avowed sinners journeyed to the otherworld to be judged and punished, no comparable anxiety was expressed by seventh-century clerics. Furthermore, because of their moralizing tone and their attention to the benefits of sacramental services, these visionary tales must have appeared eminently suitable for wider audiences than the monastic milieu which gave them voice. Consequently, although from a later medieval perspective Merovingian otherworld journeys seem few, still the sixth and seventh centuries are an important juncture in the integration of such visionary accounts into early medieval religious views.

Still, while acknowledging the importance of the seventh century in the development of the genre, in keeping with the overall thrust of this study it is important to recognize the importance of a longer perspective on what was happening in this period. In earlier chapters we observed that clerics accepted that ordinary Christians had divine dreams, especially in cultic contexts. This clerical acceptance far predates the seventh century. Thus Merovingian visions of the otherworld are only one symptom, albeit a dramatic and colorful one, of the much longer process by which religious authorities

[4] Carozzi, *Le voyage de l'âme*, pp. 4, 635; Jocelyn N. Hillgarth, "Eschatological and Political Concepts in the Seventh Century," in *The Seventh Century: Change and Continuity*, ed. Jacques Fontaine and J. N. Hillgarth, pp. 212–31 (London, 1996) (see also discussion following the paper, pp. 231–35).

[5] Peter Brown, *The End of the Ancient Other World: Death and Afterlife between Late Antiquity and the Early Middle Ages*, 1996 Tanner Lectures at Yale (University of Utah Press). I would like to thank Professor Brown for making his manuscript available to me prior to publication.

accepted and incorporated ancient traditions about open access to visions—traditions epitomized by the sinful slave author of *The Shepherd of Hermas*, who was made privy to spiritual truths about the governance of the Church.[6] It is in this longer tradition that we see continuity in the early Christian ideal of a community instructed and guided in spiritual matters by means of dreams and other types of revelation.

Nevertheless we may ask what conditions encouraged the emergence of this literature in this particular time and place. For if we look at the religious culture of the seventh century, we can see the convergence of influences both internal and external to Frankish society which nurtured a still-developing literature of the otherworld. Thus though it is important to guard against linking spiritual and eschatological developments too closely with social and political ones, it is common to discern two external, historical conditions at work in the Merovingian north which influenced the form and contributed to the popularity of this literature. I further suggest a third.

The first of these influences on the Merovingian visions, largely seen as a literary influence, is the work of Pope Gregory the Great (590–604).[7] The literary stamp of Gregory's writings—both his *Dialogues* and his *Homilies on the Gospels*—on visionary tales of the seventh century has been well documented in scholarly literature.[8] The vibrant depictions of the afterlife contained in the fourth book of his *Dialogues* soon worked their way into the imagination of his readers. With their sensory details these stories intensified earlier images of the afterlife, and their focus on the death of the ordinary sinner in the "interim period between death and resurrection" has been seen as a turning point in Western vision narratives.[9] However, my concern here is not so much with literary influences as it is with the way Gregory's work intersected with prevailing institutional attitudes in Gaul. For Gallic clerics who had long accepted the dreams and visions of ordinary visionaries at cultic sites as useful for understanding the relationship between man and God through his saints, it was now a short step to accepting visions as a medium for knowledge of the afterlife.

Gregory the Great's readers acknowledged their debt to him. The *Dia-*

---

[6] *The Shepherd of Hermas* was known in Gaul in the fifth century when it was among the works "non recipiendi" listed in the Pseudo-Gelasian *Decretum*: "Liber qui appellatur Pastoris, apocryphum." *PL* 59, 157–66. There are medieval manuscripts from the sixth and ninth centuries. Theodore Bogdanos, "'The Shepherd of Hermas' and the development of Medieval Visionary Allegory," *Viator* 8 (1977), 33–46, discusses the transmission of the Mother Ecclesia figure to the middle ages through Boethius' use of the *Shepherd* in his *Consolation of Philosophy*.

[7] Gregory, *Dialogues*. Text, translation and commentary by Adalbert de Vogüé, *SC*, 251, 260, 265 (1978–80); Latin text also in Umberto Morrica, *Gregorii Magni Dialogi libri IV* (Rome,1924). Especially useful is Joan Petersen, *The Dialogues of Gregory the Great in their Late Antique Cultural Background* (Toronto, 1984).

[8] See especially Ciccarese, "La *Visio Baronti*," which focuses on Gregory's fourth *Dialogue* as "il modello e lo stimulo che ha dato il via a tutta una serie di narrazioni di visioni, più o meno elaborate e fedeli all'originale" (26).

[9] Carol Zaleski, *Otherworld Journeys: Accounts of Near-Death Experience in Medieval and Modern Times* (Oxford, 1987), p. 30.

logues was read not only in Italy and Gaul but also in Spain.[10] Gregory's compilation of visionary stories, tales that claimed to inform on the nature of death and the afterlife, appears to have invigorated clerical storytelling in those areas where he was read. But it was his willingness to use visionary stories to assert a view of the afterlife as if it had the force of doctrine, which was even more influential. In his *Dialogues*, Gregory regarded visions as a persuasive and compelling argument for validating ecclesiastical teachings and rituals. Naturally this had an impact on the theological and ritual scope of subsequent visionary stories. Specifically, we see in visionary accounts written in late Merovingian Gaul an increasing ease in linking liturgical practices to visions that related a specific outcome in the afterlife.[11]

Gregory the Great's *Dialogues* were especially important in promoting the efficacy of clerical services and the liturgy at the moment of death. Here Gregory related visionary stories that "proved" the Mass benefited the redeemable soul after death and others in which the deceased made requests of the living for prayers in order to secure their soul's release from torment in the afterlife.[12] For those writers who assembled similar stories after Gregory's time, it was not inconsequential that these stories came from a pope.[13]

The second impetus for religious change in the seventh century was the influence of Irish monasticism on the Continent, which introduced ascetic ideals focusing on personal culpability and the efficacy of penance.[14] Both

[10] Indeed, the earliest citation of Gregory's *Dialogues* is in the *Vitas sanctorum patrum Emeretensium* (The Lives of the Father of Mérida, hereafter, *VPE*), ed. A. Maya Sanchez, CC 116 (Turnhout, 1992), composed early in seventh-century Visigothic Spain. The preface refers to the task "qua sanctissimus egregiusque uates, Romane presul urbis, Gregorius inflammatus paracliti carismate Spiritus Dialogorum in libris veridico edidit prenotationis stilo." Visions in the *VPE* show signs of Gregorian influence.

[11] In what was perhaps a logical extension of the idea that visionary information and the liturgy could be connected, in ninth-century Spain a cleric named Eldefonsus justified the weight and marking which he inscribed on the Host by means of a vision. The information in his vision was his authority to change an aspect of clerical ritual. Eldefonsus, *Revelatio*, PL 106, 881–90. The vision is dated 845, but the author, a Spanish "bishop," has not been identified.

[12] Gregory, *Dial.* 4.48; 4.42. On the connection between Masses for the dead and release from purgatory see R. R. Atwell, "From Augustine to Gregory the Great: An Evaluation of the Emergence of the Doctrine of Purgatory," *Journal of Ecclesiastical History* 38 (1987), 173–86.

[13] Gregory's views on visions did not carry the official force of a decretal, but his personal authority was important.

[14] Scholarship on medieval penitential practice and literature is vast. Important for this study are Henry Gabriel Justin Beck, *The Pastoral Care of Souls in South-East France During the Sixth Century*, Analecta Gregoriana, vol. 51 (Rome, 1950); John Thomas McNeill and Helena Margaret Gamer, *Medieval Handbooks of Penance: A Translation of the Principal 'Libri Poenitentiales' and Selections from Related Documents* (New York, 1990; reprt. of 1938 edition); Cyrille Vogel, *La discipline pénitentielle en Gaule des origines à la fin du viie siècle* (Paris, 1952), and *Les "Libri Paenitentiales,"* Typologie des sources du moyen âge occidental, 27 (Turnhout, 1978); and Jean Chélini, *L'aube du moyen âge. Naissance de la chrétienté occidentale. La vie religieuse des laïcs dans l'europe carolingienne (750–900)* (Paris, 1991; 2d ed. 1997), pp. 360–70. See also Hubertus Lutterbach's two articles, "Intentions-oder Tafhaftung? Zum Bußverständnis in den frühmittelalterlichen Bußbüchern" (esp. on the *Christus medicus* theme), and "Die Bußordines in den iro-fränkischen Paenitentialien. Schlüssel zur Theologie und Verwendung der mittelalterlichen Bußbücher," in *Frühmittelalterliche Studien* 29 (1995), 120–43, and 30 (1996), 150–72.

seventh-century visionary journeys examined below were in communities which had been touched by Irish ideals and Irish penitentialism. The rise of penitential literature among the Irish and the propagation of that literature on the Continent in the seventh century are often seen as a watershed in Continental religious attitudes toward the afterlife. Furthermore, the otherworld visions examined below often occurred at the deathbed, when penitential practices alongside prayers for the dying and the dead were important influences.[15] A heightened penitentialism is certainly evident in visionary narratives stemming from the Irish orbit. Visions now increasingly stressed sins weighed and penances provided for.[16] However, it would be more accurate to say that the influx of these new ideas promoted a shift in emphasis, not a revolution, for penitential provisions held an important place in Gallic Christianity before the seventh century.

In the fourth and fifth century, penances were used relatively sparingly since it was held that the sinner could avail himself of this ritual of reconciliation only once[17] and since penance entailed a public visibility that was unattractive to most. But by the sixth century, confession and penance became more frequent over a person's lifetime and perhaps more commonly requested at the deathbed, "in extremis."[18] By the seventh century, and largely as a result of Irish practices, penances were dispensed by priests (not exclusively by bishops as earlier) and were "private" and "auricular." A tendency toward more elaborate systems of private penance was not an exclusively Irish phenomenon. Continental penitentialism appears to have been moving in the same direction, dictated in part by the need to provide penitential practices for clerics and monks who were barred from public penance, and to offer more immediate absolution from sin.[19] But the Irish influence accelerated and heightened an already existing disposition toward penance and personal accountability in Gaul. The heightened penitentialism of the sev-

---

[15] On the liturgy for the dead see Damien Sicard, *La liturgie de la mort dans l'église latine des origines à la réforme carolingienne*, Liturgiewissenschaftliche Quellen und Forschungen, 63 (Münster,1978).

[16] The Germanic custom of composition and *wergild* probably facilitated the religious variant on compensatory payment. See Chélini, *L'aube du moyen âge*, p. 368.

[17] Vogel, *Discipline pénitentielle en Gaule*, p. 26.

[18] As suggested by Beck, *Pastoral Care*, p. 221–22. On penance "in extremis" see Vogel, *Discipline pénitentielle en Gaule*, pp. 47–54. Vogel also notes that penance was sometimes imposed by bishops coercively (p. 157).

[19] Regarding Continental penitentialism, Beck, *Pastoral Care* p. 221, reminds us that Celtic penitentialism had its roots in fifth-century Gaul and that in his sermons 60 and 179, Caesarius of Arles set out a rudimentary tariff of penance based on categories of sin. Ian Wood, "The *Vita Columbani* and Merovingian Hagiography," *Peritia* 1 (1982), 63–80, esp. 73–74, likewise notes that "in practice the bishops of Gaul had already arrived at the solution of Columbanus and his disciples over the cure of souls." Elsewhere Wood notes that the influence of literature from the Eastern Empire on Gallic penitentialism cannot be discounted. "A Prelude to Columbanus," pp. 9, 23, n. 59. Chélini, *L'aube du moyen âge*, pp. 366–68, indicates that a collection of penitential practices must have been first worked out for monks (who could not undertake the once-only public penance), and from thence passed to lay use.

enth century undoubtedly strengthened the connection between penance and visions of the afterlife, but the assumption of personal responsibility was already in place.[20]

To the influences of Pope Gregory and the Irish, which are generally recognized, we must now add a third—the importance of clerical attitude towards visionary access. This influence has not been adequately appreciated hitherto. Yet it must color the success and significance of the earlier two. If we want to explain the favorable clerical ambiance which permitted Gregorian and Irish influences to blossom in Gaul, we must keep in mind that the clergy had long accepted that ordinary Christians and sinners had visions which were authentic. In their acceptance of visionary journeys to the otherworld as valuable to the Christian life, the Merovingian clergy built on a long tradition of visions heard and assessed in a pastoral and cultic context. In seventh-century visionary literature we are merely confronted with the results of that groundwork. For example, it has been noted that Pope Gregory's stories drew on visionaries from many spheres of life. But Gallic clerics had already accepted a socially diverse range of legitimate visionaries and provided appropriate venues in which such visions could be explored. Pope Gregory's interest in doctrinally significant visions undoubtedly encouraged clerical approval in Gaul too, but it must be remembered that such advances could only take root because movement toward the legitimation of clerical authority in visions in other contexts had already begun. The religious culture of Romano-Gallic and Frankish Gaul was acclimated to the visionary claims of ordinary people and readily embraced Pope Gregory's work. Thus it is to the long-term and already developed religious attitudes toward dreams and visions that we must attribute the success of such literature in Frankish circles.[21]

The "Postmortem" Journey of the Soul

Perhaps the most important way in which Merovingian visionary journeys to the otherworld differed from the dreams and visions examined thus far was the intervention of death. In 2 Corinthians 12.1–4, and the *Visio Pauli*

---

[20] On penance in Gaul prior to the seventh century see Beck, *Pastoral Care*, pp. 187–222, and Vogel, *Dicipline pénitentielle en Gaule*. Those undergoing penance were distinguished by having their hair shorn, wearing a hair shirt and other penitential clothing, fasting and living celibately, undertaking certain chores within the church, kneeling separately from the rest of the congregation during services, and being denied access to the Eucharist. Reconciliation to the Church did not restore the penitent fully to his prepenitential state; among other restrictions he could not hold public or religious office, serve in the army, or marry. However, penitential practices in Gaul varied regionally and according to the rigor of the individual bishop.

[21] Using a different argument, Peter Brown tends in this same direction in his *End of the Ancient Other World*. He notes that in the seventh century a new style of "otherworldliness" was adopted with gusto by a new class of super-*potentes*.

which drew on the passage, the apostle Paul did not die in order to see his vision of the third heaven.[22] By contrast, Merovingian journeys to the heavens were generally depicted as postmortem events during which the visionary's soul left his body at death, traveled to the otherworld, and then (usually on the orders of St. Peter or some other celestial authority) returned to his body, causing his corpse to revive.

In almost all accounts of Merovingian visionary travel, death was requisite for the soul's release.[23] In part this convention was a theological necessity. Patristic writers asserted that the soul could not leave the body in dreams and therefore it could not travel to a world which was believed to exist elsewhere in time and space.[24] "The operation of death is plain and obvious: it is the separation of body and soul," wrote Tertullian.[25] Thus the visionary's journey began at death and ended when his soul was returned to his body.[26] The extraordinary, even miraculous, reanimation of the corpse was further proof of the visionary's claim to have visited the otherworld. Astonished bystanders who witnessed the reanimation of a corpse, often already prepared for burial, have left us their observations. Witnesses to Salvius of Albi's reanimation testified to the erubescence of the pallid corpse: "Salvius' cheeks flushed red again, he stirred himself as if awakened from a deep sleep."[27] And at cock crow, when Fursey's soul was returned to his

[22] *Visio Pauli* 1. Augustine explained Paul's rapture as an internal ecstasy, i.e., one in which the vision was shown to the saint while he was removed from bodily senses but without his soul traveling externally from the body. *De Genesi ad litteram* 12.2. On death-bed visions see Zaleski, *Otherworld Journeys*, esp. pp. 45–52, and *Life of the World to Come: Near-Death Experience and Christian Hope*, Albert Cardinal Meyer Lectures (Oxford, 1996).

[23] Exceptions: Sunniulf of Randan's vision of Hell (sixth century), was described as "per visum" but also as a dream ("somnium"). *HF* 4.33. Abbot Brachio was taken to the presence of God in a dream (sixth century). *VP* 12.3.

[24] Tertullian, *De anima* 44, rejected stories common in his day such as that of Hermotimus, whose soul was said to have traveled outside his body in sleep, and whose body was burned by his enemies before his soul could return. Despite patristic opposition to the idea of soul-travel in dreams, the possibility nevertheless remained a widely held assumption in the middle ages. In his *History of the Lombards* 3.34, Paul the Deacon told a story of the Frankish king Guntramn whose reptile-like soul exited his mouth as he slept and discovered long-buried treasure. *Paul the Deacon: History of the Lombards*, ed. Edward Peters (Philadelphia, 1994). The peasants of Montaillou told similar stories of the soul leaving the body in dreams and getting caught away from the body. Emmanuel Le Roy Ladurie, *Montaillou: Cathars and Catholics in a French Village 1294–1324* (Harmondsworth, 1980), pp. 351–52.

[25] Tertullian, *De anima* 51, trans. Peter Holmes. Tertullian rejected the idea that the soul remained with the body at death and considered stories of corpses moving their hands into devotional postures as a miraculous rather than natural occurrence. In common with many churchmen of his age, Gregory the Great assumed a living connection between the martyr and his body, for while the martyr's soul was in heaven, the body displayed the martyr's "life" through miraculous healings. Expressing death as a separation of the soul from the body is widely witnessed in epigraphic sources. See Richmond Lattimore, *Themes in Greek and Latin Epitaphs* (Urbana, Ill., 1962), pp. 304–6.

[26] Traditional stories of mistaken identity in which a namesake was called to the afterlife by mistake and was later returned to life strengthened the view of the otherworld as a "place" to which one traveled and from which one could return. See Gregory the Great, *Dial.* 4.37.

[27] *HF* 7.1, trans. Lewis Thorpe.

body after being taken up by angels, "his face was suffused with a rosy colour."[28] The visionary's extracorporeal experience was thus integral to the broader significance of the story as one in which the ordinarily impenetrable barrier of death was temporarily breached. A mini-resurrection had occurred, followed later by a second death at which the sinner hoped to have profited from his experience. Thus the postmortem vision of the revived visionary, echoing the parable of Dives and Lazarus in the New Testament, offered "proof" of Christian teachings and confirmed the resurrection of the dead.

The experience of otherworldly travel was thus placed firmly at the deathbed, a poetically and theologically appropriate place for visions of the afterlife to occur. Yet the deathbed was not a private zone; it was often a public space where family, clerics, and a lifetime's clutter of mental images of the afterlife converged. Images of the afterlife related by the revived visionary, whether understood symbolically or concretely, reproduced what for that time was a familiar landscape. In late antiquity, it was often an assemblage of oneiric scraps drawn from a variety of sources—Near Eastern, Graeco-Roman, and Jewish[29]—and it was always a landscape which was populated. The otherworldly landscape of late antiquity focused primarily on two destinations: the pleasant place (*locus amoenus*) and the place of pain (*locus poenalis*). The idea of a third place of temporary purification which existed in time between the first resurrection and the second did not attract much descriptive attention before the seventh century.[30] Whether heavenly or in-

[28] *Vita sancti Fursei*, 4. I use Maria Pia Ciccarese's edition in "Le Visioni de S. Fursa," *Romanobarbarica* 8 (1984–85), 231–303, text 279–303.
[29] For a discussion of these images of the afterlife, which in time became common for Christian writers, see Nancy Gauthier, "Les images de l'au-delà durant l'antiquité chrétienne," *Revue des études augustiniennes* 33 (1987), 3–22.
[30] The development of a third "place" or "stage" in the afterlife, where souls underwent purgation, developed slowly in the early middle ages. In the *Passion of SS. Perpetua and Felicity* 7–8, Perpetua's brother Dinocrates was in a place of suffering until Perpetua's prayers released him to a happier state. In *Enchiridion* 69, Augustine pondered a purgatorial fire for those who had committed minor sins, and stated that between death and resurrection the soul "dwells in a hidden retreat, where it enjoys rest or suffers affliction just in proportion to the merit it has earned by the life which it led on earth" (109). See Joseph Ntedika, *L'évolution de la doctrine du purgatoire chez saint Augustine* (Paris, 1966), and Arnold Angenendt, "Theologie und Liturgie der mittelalterlichen Toten-Memoria," *Memoria. Der Geschichtliche Zeugniswert des liturgischen Gedenkens im Mittelalter*, ed. Karl Schmid and Joachim Wollasch, pp. 79–199, esp. pp. 81–86 (Munich, 1984). Pope Gregory promoted the idea that minor sins would be purged by fire in the afterlife to ready the soul for its ultimate acceptance into heaven. *Dial.* 4.39. Later Merovingian and Carolingian stories were influenced by Pope Gregory's conviction that prayers for the dead could aid the departed who had landed in this purgatorial fire, and related that the prayers of the pious, especially relatives, could release the sinner's soul from torment, as in the case of the nun Deurechild at Burgundofara's convent, who won salvation for her less pious mother. *Vita Columbani* 2.15; as explained to the Northumbrian layman Drythelm, c. 696–705, *Vision of Drythelm*, Bede, *Historia ecclesiastica gentis Anglorum*, ed. B. Colgrave and R. Mynors (Oxford, 1969); and in 824 in the *Vision of Wetti*, ed. E. Dümmler, *MGH, Poetae* 2, pp. 267–334. On Merovingian developments see Aubrun, "Caractères et portée religieuse." Jacques Le Goff, *The Birth of Purgatory*, trans. Arthur Goldhammer (Chicago, 1984; first pub-

fernal, these images presented a positivistic idea of the afterlife as a destination. Late fourth-century Christians such as Augustine of Hippo's friend and confidant Evodius of Uzalis expressed the view that some kind of immediate life beyond death was preferable to the vacancy of even temporary extinction: "The thought disturbs me that the soul should take upon itself a kind of sleep, that it becomes like one who sleeps while still within the body, as if buried, and living only in hope: in the future having nothing, knowing nothing; the more so if it is not brushed by a dream. Such a thing is very frightening, and shows the soul as if it were extinguished." [31] In such terms did Christian writers articulate their worst fear of death; that there might be a time when there was no continuity of existence, personality, and identity. The peopling of the otherworld was an intrinsic component of the happiness or sadness that awaited the soul. For Evodius, as for pagans before him and Christians after him, fear of the cold, quiet nullity of personality in the grave would negate all that was good in the world: the embrace of family and the recollection of friends. [32] The desire to meet friends and family in the next life was a common concern. In his *Dialogues*, Pope Gregory was asked by his deacon Peter whether the deceased would recognize each other in heaven, to which he responded that "not only those whom they knew on earth, but many saintly men and women whom they had never seen before will appear to them as old friends." [33] Not surprisingly, Christians, like pagans before them, imagined the afterlife as a place where good things such as friendship and *convivium* might be regained in the hereafter. [34] Roman visions empha-

---

lished as *La naissance du purgatoire*, 1981) minimized the importance of early medieval evidence for belief in this third destination as a place: "Purgatory did not exist before 1170 at the earliest" (p. 135). Claude Carozzi, "La géographie de l'au-delà et sa signification pendant le haut moyen âge," *Popoli e paesi nella cultura altomedierae*, Settimane di Studio, 19 (1983), 423–81, has challenged this view and affirmed the existence of purgatory in early medieval texts even if the term "purgatorium" was not used. R. R. Atwell, "From Augustine to Gregory the Great: An Evaluation of the Doctrine of Purgatory," *JEH* 38 (1987), 173–86, notes that the movement toward a specific connection for eucharistic offerings for the dead with the concept of purgatorial fire seen in Gregory the Great's writings was "an important catalyst in the development of the doctrine of Purgatory." Peter Brown argues in *End of the Ancient Otherworld* that the emergence of purgatory feeds on the juxtaposition of two imaginative structures: the purgation of the soul and the idea of God's amnesty. See also the discussion by Brian Patrick McGuire, "Purgatory, the Communion of Saints, and Medieval Change," *Viator* 20 (1989), 61–84.

[31] "Satis autem me perturbat, si soporem quemdam accipit animus ipse, ne talis sit, qualis cum dormit in corpore constitutus, quasi sepultus, et in spe tantum vivens: caeternum nihil habens, nihil sciens; maxime si somnio nullo pulsetur. Quae res vehementer terret, et quasi exstinctum indicat animum." Evodius, *Ep.* 158.7.

[32] Evodius wanted to believe that the soul, "in tranquillitate sine tentatione positus, videat quod desideravit, amplexetur quod amavit. Recordetur quoque et amicorum, et quos iam praemisserat." Ibid.

[33] *Dial.* 4. 34, trans. O. J. Zimmerman.

[34] Banqueting scenes are often seen on Christian tombs. Whether the scenes represent the banqueting of the dead in the afterlife or the banqueting of the living at the tomb, the continued participation by the dead in such social practices was an important part of the Christian afterlife. Paul-Albert Février, "La tombe chrétienne et l'au-delà," in *Le temps chrétien de la fin de l'antiquité au moyen âge, iiie–xiiie siècles*, Colloques internationaux du CNRS, no. 164 (Paris,

sized bonds of *amicitia*, expressing the hope that one might rejoin not only loved ones but one's chosen religious fellowship in the next world.[35] Roman epitaphs expressed hopes for reunion with loved ones and commended to the living the virtue (*merita*) and good memory of the deceased.[36]

In the Germanic north, the afterlife was where one met with one's ancestors. The prospect of not seeing his ancestors in the Christian heaven discouraged at least one prospective convert to Christianity.[37] For those who did convert, Germanic culture brought to Christian graves concrete views of the afterlife in which a warrior continued to need food, fine glass vessels, and even weapons.[38] The afterlife which these furnished graves suggest—they mirrored in ideal form the conditions of the living—was not a destination as much to be feared as to be prepared for. For Merovingian Christians, whether Romano-Gallic or Germanic in origin, preparation for death, whether introspective or social, allowed the dying to anticipate that in death they would continue to experience human values of warmth, beauty, friendship, and kinship in the pastures and palaces of the hoped-for otherworld.

By the sixth century, Gallic clerics were becoming very interested in the deathbed as an ecclesiastical venue. The presence of clergy and the developing ritual they dispensed comforted the dying and their loved ones with images of the soul's happy departure. Liturgical prayers at the deathbed and the gravesite voiced the hope that the soul of the departed would make a safe transition past the portals of hell to reach heaven and the company of the saints. At the convent of St. John in Arles, the *Te Domine sancte* prayer of the Gallican rite was intoned over the nun's corpse before burial: "To you Lord, holy father, ominipotent and eternal God, we humbly pray for this the spirit of your handmaiden, whom you have called to you out of the abyss of

---

1984), pp. 163–83, esp. p. 165. Otto Gerhard Oexle notes the memorializing dimension of meals at graves. "Die Gegenwart der Toten," in *Death in the Middle Ages*, ed. Herman Braet and Werner Verbecke pp. 19–77, esp. pp. 48 ff., (Leuven, 1983). Schmitt, *Ghosts in the Middle Ages*, p. 17, comments that memorialization, as a rite of separation, allowed the living also to *forget* the dead.

[35] In the vision of Saturus, friends and co-martyrs meet in heaven: "There we found Jocundus and Saturninus and Artaxius who in the same persecution had suffered . . . and Quintus, a martyr also." *Passio Perpetuae et Felicitatis* 11. Translation by W. H. Shewring.

[36] Heinzelman, *Bischofsherrschaft in Gallien*, p. 44, discusses virtues commonly listed in the funerary *laudatio*; they include *integritas*, *auctoritas*, and *iustitia*. He proceeds to discuss the pagan and Christian common culture of a "theology of merits" (pp. 87 ff). Lattimore provides examples in *Themes*, pp. 336–39. In a Merovingian example, an inscription on the tomb of Pionius reads that he was of good memory, "bonae memorie." Heidrich, "Südgallische Inschriften," 167–83, esp. 179.

[37] The Frisian duke Rathbod stepped away from the baptismal font when he learned from Wulframn that his unbaptized ancestors were condemned to hell. *Vita Vulframni Episcopi Senonici*, chap. 9, ed. Wilhelm Levison, *MGH, SRM* 5 (1910), pp. 657–73.

[38] On the cultural meaning of the grave goods in the later Merovingian period, and the problems of linking their disappearance to Christianity, see Edward James, *The Franks* (Oxford, 1988), pp. 137–45; Bonnie Effros, "Symbolic Expressions of Sanctity: Gertrude of Nivelles in the Context of Merovingian Mortuary Custom," *Viator* 27 (1996), 1–10; and Bailey K. Young, "Paganisme, christianisme et rites funéraires," *Archéologie Médievale* 7 (1977), 5–81.

this world. May you see fit, Lord, to grant her a place of refreshment and quiet. Permit her to pass by the doors of hell and the paths of darkness and reside in the mansions of the saints and in the holy light which you promised to Abraham and to his seed."[39] This prayer is a good example of the oft-commented-upon confidence and optimism about Christian hopes for the afterlife in the early Christian funeral liturgy.[40] At death the Christian could expect his soul to undertake a journey that would bring him into the company of saints and martyrs. Deathbed visions of the afterlife extended this simple hope into complex travel narratives, while often reversing the basic narrative structure so that the soul did not simply pass by the portals of hell but entered them after visiting the mansions of the righteous.

Deathbed visions, like the prayers intoned in the liturgy, focused on the soul's peril as it journeyed from life to afterlife. Certainly in monasteries, and perhaps among the prominent in the secular community also, the dying were surrounded by family and representatives of the religious community. The struggle for breath and the fear of suffocation was witnessed by bystanders who interpreted it as the soul's struggle with the demons which every Christian believed to inhabit the airy spaces. Passage to the other side was difficult, except for the holy whose departure might be smoothed by heavenly singing and sweet odor.[41] Despite patristic disapproval, Christians continued to believe that difficulties attended those who did not make the transition successfully (say, for want of burial). For Christians, religious rituals promised to ease this transition, although they may not have been readily available to all in the Christian community. In monastic communities, though, we see a gradual movement toward sacramentalizing the deathbed, and this is reflected in the deathbed visions of the afterlife of the period.[42]

---

[39] "Te domine sancte pater omnipotens aeterne Deus supplices deprecamur pro spiritu famulae tuae ill. quam de voraginibus huius saeculi ad te arcessire praecepisti. . . . Ut digneris domine dare ei locum refrigerii et quietis. Liceat ei transire portas infernorum et vias tenebrarum maneatque in mansionibus sanctorum et in luce sancta quam olim Abrahae promisisti et semini ejus." Sicard, *La liturgie de la mort*, pp. 265–66. This prayer was one of six prayers appended to the *Regula ad virgines* and was probably, like the Rule itself, authored by Bishop Caesarius of Arles for his sister's convent in the early sixth century. Sicard suggests that Caesarius may have been in part responsible for the composition of the old Gallican rite (p. 279).

[40] Gauthier, notes that "la liturgie de la mort est une liturgie de la joie." "Les images de l'au-delà," p. 5. See also Paxton, *Christianizing Death*, pp. 43–44.

[41] Gregory the Great, *Dial* 4.15 ff., related that heavenly singing prevented the dying from experiencing pain at the soul's separation from the body.

[42] The extent to which clerics were involved at the deathbed and in the commemoration and burial of ordinary Christians is disputed. For the religious elite (clerics, monks, and nuns), the evidence is fuller; visionary accounts in hagiography indicate that in monasteries monastic clerics were an important presence at the deathbed and that it was customary for psalms to be sung. Bonnie Effros, "Beyond Cemetery Walls: Early Funerary Topography and Christian Salvation," *Early Medieval Europe* 6 (1997), 1–23, examines the funerary ritual for the Merovingian period. Manuscripts containing liturgical prayers for the dead and the dying are sparse until the eighth century, when Roman sacramentaries began to appear in Francia. Paxton, *Christianizing Death*, pp. 61 ff. By the Carolingian period canonical texts required that a priest attend the deathbed. Paul-Albert Février, "La mort chrétienne," in *Segni e riti nella chiesa altomedieval occidental*, Settimane di studio 33 (1987), 881–942, esp. 888.

Death and the process of dying became increasingly a liturgical event with prayers and psalms sung over the sick, and with final offerings being made and received.[43] At times death came too soon, before the dying person could be joined one last time to the Church through taking the Eucharist, but miraculously the dead nun or saint might be revived temporarily in order to take communion.[44]

Deathbed visions reminded even healthy bystanders of their mortality. Ascetic training embraced active thinking about death; monks were taught that death was an instruction in how to live, and salutary reflections on mortality were encouraged in ascetic literature as a spur to timely repentance and penance. The *Benedictine Rule*, for example, advised its adherents "to fear the Day of Judgement, to be in dread of hell, to desire eternal life with all the passion of the spirit, to keep death daily before one's eyes."[45] Lengthy penitential provisions reminded the sinner that appropriate penance could be a time-consuming business and should not be postponed. Indeed it was revealed to some that time was too short for sufficient penance.[46] However, visions did not always benefit the visionary. Gregory the Great related that the sinner Reparatus' vision was not granted for his own sake but for those who heard it.[47] Didactic concerns were promoted furthermore by supernatural injunctions that the visionary relate publicly what he had seen. Here we see a change from the code of secrecy that had often characterized early Christian visions. Some saints in Merovingian hagiography were still governed by such concerns. Merovingian visionaries of the seventh and eighth centuries, by contrast, not only desired publication of their experiences but even on occasion remitted messages from the afterlife to the living.[48]

From the perspective of the clerical hierarchy, visions received in the context of death and revivification were not "divinatory" (in the sense that a visionary seer claimed personal spiritual authority from having had contact

[43] The order of prayers, the reading of the Gospel account of the passion, communion, and psalm singing in the final rite were not firmly established in early liturgical texts. See Sicard, *La liturgie* pp. 31 and 33 (tables) on variations and correspondences in the Roman *ordines*.

[44] Odilia was rejoicing in the company of St. Lucy when she was brought back to life by the prayers of her nuns, concerned that she had not received last rites. *Vita s. Odiliae abbatissae Hohenburgensis* 22, ed. W. Levinson, *MGH, SRM* 6 (1913), pp. 24–50. As Aldegund lay mortally sick, a nun of Maubeuge reported seeing a vision in which the mortally sick Aldegund took communion supernaturally when she could not receive it physically. *Vita Aldegundis* 1.25.

[45] *Benedictine Rule*, 4.44–47, trans. Justin McCann, *The Rule of St. Benedict* (London, 1970).

[46] Jonas, *Vita Columbiani* 2.10, 11, 12, ed. Bruno Krusch, *MGH, SRM* 4 (1902), pp. 112–52.

[47] *Dial.* 4.32.

[48] Circa 716 the monk of Wenlock was instructed that "he was not to hesitate to tell all that had been revealed to him to believers and to those who should question him with a pious purpose." Boniface, *Letter* 2 to Eadburga, trans., intro. Ephraim Emerton, *The Letters of Saint Boniface* (New York, 1940), pp. 25–31. By contrast, 150 years earlier St. Salvius of Albi lamented of his vision, "Woe is me that I had dared to reveal such a mystery." *HF* 7.1. In the seventh and eighth centuries, messages to the living generally advised penance. The monk of Wenlock was instructed to reveal to a certain woman her sins, and suggest to her how she might absolve them.

with the divine). In cosmic journeying the soul was an active but largely unwilling player in the events described. Visionary journeys to the otherworld,
which were almost always sobering accounts of individual failings, allowed
for an outpouring of personal recrimination resulting in what may be called,
somewhat anachronistically, "confessional literature." By this I do not mean
that they were written from encounters with the liturgical practice of confession, but rather from an impulse to lay bare the most unflattering depths
of personality. This characteristic was intensified when the accounts were
narrated in the first person. Far from being meritorious, most travelers to the
otherworld were avowed sinners whose chastisement in the afterlife became
the subject of edifying reflections on the nature of religious transgression.
Thus, generally speaking, these visionary accounts were not written to promote the reputation of the visionary as a prospective holy person.[49] They circulated independently from hagiographic or other cultic literature, and were
products, like the apocalypses to which they were related, of an elite scribal
culture interested in showcasing abstract soteriological issues as much as
the fate of a mere single individual—even if the ostensibly autobiographical
form was the immediate vehicle for that discussion.[50] To these first-person
narratives were added editorial discourses that supplemented the confessional and autobiographical, and it is this combination of personal experience and editorial commentary which justifies these texts' being accorded
significance in the wider cultural and religious arena. In the form in which
they have been handed down, these visionary stories inform us of theological, political, and intellectual concerns alongside the purely spiritual ones
which ostensibly gave rise to them.

Merovingian Visions of the Afterlife

Some of the major themes that have attracted attention from Merovingian
scholars in seventh-century visions of the afterlife were in fact anticipated in
the sixth. Before Fursey and Barontus traveled to heaven and to hell, Sunniulf of Randan and the holy Salvius experienced similar visions of the afterlife. Their experiences provide sixth-century precedents for seventh-century
developments which are important to this study because they were written
independently of the Gregorian and Irish traditions that are generally held
to have had a significant impact on later examples of the genre. Furthermore,

[49] The *Life of Fursey* is an exception. Fursey became a saint long after the events described
in his vision, but even he was imperiled and wounded in the afterlife for having accepted a gift
from a sinner. Later travelers to the afterlife—the seventh-century Barontus, the eighth-century
monk of Wenlock, and the ninth-century monk Wetti—were not venerated as saints.

[50] Barontus' story is told in the first person, as an autobiographical account. Yet at the beginning and end of the work, and a few times in between, a redactor commented on Barontus'
experience.

visions describing the topography of the afterlife are not numerous in sixth-century Gallic writings, so these two narratives merit special attention here.

Abbot Sunniulf of Randan's Vision of Hell

We owe our knowledge of Sunniulf's vision to Gregory of Tours, who included the account of his contemporary in his *History*.[51] Sunniulf was the well-regarded abbot of the monastery of Randan near Clermont. Gregory tells us, however, that he had one fault as abbot: he was too lenient with the monks under his care. In the 560s this fault precipitated an admonitory vision:

> He used himself to tell how once he was shown in a vision a certain river of fire, into which men, assembling together on one part of the bank, were plunging like so many bees entering a hive. Some were submerged up to the waist, some up to the armpits, some even up to the chin, and all were shouting out that they were being burned very severely. A bridge led over the river, so narrow that only one man could cross at a time, and on the other side there was a large house all painted white. Then Sunniulf asked those who were with him what they thought this meant. "From this bridge will be hurled headlong anyone who is discovered to have been lacking in authority over those committed to his charge," they answered. "Anyone who has kept good discipline may cross without danger and will be welcomed joyfully in the house which you see opposite." As he heard these words, Sunniulf awoke.[52]

Thenceforth Sunniulf was more severe with his monks.

It has long been noted that images of hell were not highly developed in early Christian literature and art.[53] There was little concrete information in the scriptures to shape early Christian views of hell, and thus early medieval images were largely appropriated from other sources. Sunniulf's vision of hell brought together a number of elements that were to become important to the medieval view of the infernal regions. Some of these were traditional to pagan literature. Virgil's description of Aeneas' journey to the underworld was an important influence on the Christian conception of hell's Stygian gloom.[54] The tortures experienced by the damned in Sunniulf's vision (such as graded submersion in a river of fire) are reminiscent of those described in

---

[51] *HF* 4.33. Latin text with notes and Italian translation in Maria Pia Ciccarese, *Visioni dell'aldilà in occidente. Fonti modelli testi* (Florence, 1987), pp. 149–65. See also Carozzi, *Le voyage de l'âme*, p. 63.

[52] *HF* 4.33, trans. Lewis Thorpe.

[53] Gauthier, "Les images de l'au delà," and Henricus Fros, "L'eschatologie médiévale dans quelques écrits hagiographiques (IV–IX s.)," in *The Use and Abuse of Eschatology in the Middle Ages*, ed. Werner Verbeke, Daniel Verhelst, Andries Welkenhuysen, pp. 212–20 (Leuven, 1988).

[54] Virgil, *Aeneid*, book 6.

the *Apocalypse of Peter* and the *Vision of Paul*.[55] Other elements were new. For example, in earlier accounts no bridge spanned the fiery river. Indeed, Sunniulf's description anticipated, possibly by decades, the more widely known soldier's vision related by Gregory the Great in his *Dialogues*.[56] Such tales had doubtless circulated orally for some time, but the abbot's description of hell with its tortures and its bridge over the fiery river was new to Gallic texts. By contrast, other sixth-century accounts from Gaul refer only vaguely to the geography of hell. For example, a tax collector who took sheep belonging to the shrine of St. Julian of Brioude was smitten by a fever and cried out that he was on fire because of the martyr's power:

> Although at first he kept quiet, after the flames of judgement had been applied to his soul he confessed his crimes, and with whatever sound he was capable of he begged that water be sprinkled on him. But even though water was brought in a vessel and often sprinkled on him, smoke poured from his body as if from a furnace. Meanwhile his suffering limbs, as if on fire, turned black and produced such a stench that scarcely any of the bystanders could tolerate it.[57]

The man died soon after, but despite the confession of his crimes, Gregory commented that "there is no doubt about what place the man who departed from here with such a judgement occupied there [hell]."[58] Other images of the afterlife echoed biblical vagueness, referring to "jaws of the underworld"[59] (*inferni faucibus*) or even more simply the "places of darkness" (*obscuris locis*),[60] although on the periphery of the known world at the island monastery of Iona, St. Columba wrote a poem to Pope Gregory which foreshadowed the bishop of Rome's own view of the infernal regions: "No one seems to doubt the presence of an inferno somewhere deep in the earth. In that place there are darkness, worms and terrible beasts. There is burning sulphur glowing with the hungry flames. There are the bestial screams of men, the weeping and gnashing of teeth. There is the wailing of Gehenna,

---

[55] In the *Apocalypse of Peter*, 6, sinners stood in a fiery river "to everyman according to his deeds." Montague Rhodes James, *The Apocryphal New Testament* (Oxford, 1924; reprt., 1955), pp. 504–21; in the *Visio Pauli* 10 the level of the river on the sinner's body indicated the *locus* of transgression. See also Gregory the Great, *Dial.* 4.45.

[56] *Dial.* 4.37. Gregory of Tours added his account of Sunniulf's vision to his *History* under events occurring in the 560s when the abbot died. Strictly, the *terminus ad quem* for the story is Gregory of Tours' death, c. 594. Gregory the Great, who was still completing his *Dialogues* in 593, related that the soldier's vision had taken place during the plague years in Rome three years earlier, c. 590. Thus I propose that Gregory of Tours' account of Sunniulf's vision could have predated Gregory the Great's account of the soldier's vision. The bridge became a common motif in visions thereafter; for example, a bridge conducted the souls of the holy in the vision of the monk of Wenlock, c. 716, described by Boniface in his letter to Eadburga, Letter 2, pp. 25–31.

[57] *VJ* 17.

[58] Ibid.

[59] *Virt. Mart.* 4.30.

[60] Sulpicius, *VM* 7.1–5.

that terrible and ancient noise. There is the flamelike burning of a horrible hunger and thirst."[61] To these details, Pope Gregory's stories added something more than the purely visual. Gregory's visionaries reported odors both fragrant and pungent, temperatures steamy and cold, and ascensions smooth and vertiginous. Artistic representations of hell undoubtedly mirrored such imaginings.[62]

In ancient apocalypses such as the *Vision of Paul*, the compelling issue was the "justice" of divine judgment. Mortal visitors to the otherworld in late Roman texts often found their views and systems of justice at variance with those of the divinity. As visionary travelers observed the torments of the damned and lamented at their suffering, they had constantly to be reminded by angelic voices or their guide that God is just.[63] In the sixth century, protection against this perilous "justice" was expressed in terms of the powers and intercession of the saints more than it was through a reliance on the sacraments, as was the case a century later. "We do not doubt not only that we are worthy to acquire this remission for our sins through their prayers, but also that we are saved from the infernal torments through their intervention" wrote Gregory, and furthermore, "each person rejoices under the protection of his own patron."[64] Gregory of Tours liked to imagine that his own patron saint, St. Martin, would protect him on that sombre day: "And when in accordance with the judge's decision I am to be condemned to the infernal flames, he will protect me with the sacred shroud that shields him from boasting and reprieve me from this punishment," so that Gregory would be "freed from the threatening agents of the underworld."[65] Gregory hoped that his devotion to his patron saint in life would earn him the saint's protection in death. In seventh-century visions, new variants on supernatural protection for the pious began to appear: individuals were returned temporarily to the living in order to have a second chance at making appropriate amends. The hagiographer Jonas related a number of such incidents which happened at Burgundofara's convent in the seventh century. The nun Sisetrude, for example, was already joyfully dancing among the angels when at her tribunal the Judge ordered that she be returned to life for three days so as to complete the Lenten fast and prepare for her death. And Gibitrude,

[61] Columba, *Altus Prosator*, trans. Harold Isbell, *The Last Poets of Imperial Rome* (Harmondsworth, 1971).

[62] Prudentius' *Tituli historiarum* included a rubric for a painting of Christ treading the pit, evidence that hell was depicted in early Gallic art. We do not know whether the paintings which Prudentius listed were ever executed. Prudentius, *Tituli historiarum*, ed. Johannes Bergman, *CSEL* 61 (1926), 435–47.

[63] *Apocalypse of Peter*, 3; *Visio Pauli* 6.

[64] *Virt. Mart.* 6, Prologue.

[65] Ibid., 2.60. Gregory may have had in mind the story told of St. Martin by Sulpicius, *VM* 7.1–5, in which a catechumen died and came before the Judge. He was destined for "obscuris locis." When two angels intervened and informed the Judge that this was the man for whom St. Martin prayed, the catechumen was returned to life.

another sister in the convent, was returned to life from the heavenly tribunal to make amends to the three sisters she had wounded spiritually before she also departed again six months later.[66] In the seventh century, God's justice and man's had come into closer harmony as mortals were able to negotiate God's anger through penance.

Yet neither Sunniulf nor Salvius was brought before a tribunal in their visions. Their visions displayed the consequences of their deeds and emphasized duties yet to be accomplished. Sunniulf was a holy man whose self-discipline was not at issue. Rather, his vision expressed concern regarding Christian leadership and the perils of leniency toward monks. Abbots' responsibilities extended beyond their own salvation to those of their monks, as Benedict's rule made clear: "Let the abbot always bear in mind that at the dread Judgement of God there will be an examination of these two matters: his teaching and the obedience of his disciples." As loving father of his monks, the abbot was to recall the biblical injunction, "Beat your son with the rod and you will deliver his soul from death." And finally, "Let him know, then, that he who has undertaken the government of souls must prepare himself to render an account of them. Whatever number of brethren he knows he has under his care, he may be sure beyond doubt on Judgement Day he will have to give the Lord an account of all these souls, as well as of his own soul." [67] A lax abbot was no true father to his charges. Indeed, severity to the point of cruelty might be justified, as Gregory of Tours indicated when he related with approval the severity of Brachio's measures against those who broke his community's rule.[68] Sunniulf's vision of the narrow bridge over a river of fire indicated that his lenient leadership imperilled the safe passage of his monks to the mansions of the righteous which should have been their reward.[69]

St. Salvius of Albi's Vision of Heaven

Like Sunniulf, Salvius (d. 584), who later became bishop of Albi, was regarded by Gregory as a holy man. Salvius had a long secular career before he turned to the ascetic life in middle age. He joined a monastery where he became a recluse with a reputation for healing. Then he died—or so the monks believed. His body was placed on the funeral bier and an all-night vigil was kept. In the morning he suddenly revived and told his astonished brethren of his experience. He told of how he had been taken up by angels;

---

[66] Jonas, *Vita Columbani* 2.11, 12, ed. Bruno Krusch, *MGH*, *SRM* 4 (1902), pp. 112–52.
[67] *Benedictine Rule*, chap. 2.
[68] *VP* 12.3.
[69] The theme of the good abbot's responsibility for his monks was reprised in the vision of the monk of Wenlock, in which a good abbot's soul was seized by demons but then rescued by his pupils who had preceded him to the afterlife.

carried to the highest pinnacle of heaven, until I seemed to have beneath my feet not only this squalid earth of ours, but the sun and the moon, the clouds and the stars. Then I was led through a gate which shone more brightly than our sunshine and so entered a building where all the floor gleamed with gold and silver. The light was such as I cannot describe to you, and the sense of space was quite beyond our experience.[70]

In the foreground was a throng of people "neither men nor women," and in the distance Salvius saw a place over which "hung a cloud more luminous than any light and yet no sun was visible, no moon and no star." The angels helped push Salvius through the crowd toward a company of priests, martyrs, and other holy people, who all treated him with courtesy. He was nourished there by a fragrant perfume.

Then I heard a voice [from the luminous cloud] which said: "Let this man go back to the world, for our churches have need of him." I heard the Voice; but I could not see who was speaking. Then I threw myself flat on the ground and wept. "Alas! Alas! Lord," I said. "Why have you shown me these things only to take them away from me again? You cast me out today and send me back again to a worldly existence which has no substance, powerless as I am ever to return on high. I entreat You, Lord, do not turn Your mercy aside from me. Let me stay here, I beseech You, lest, falling once more to earth, I perish." The Voice which spoke to me said: "Go in peace. I will watch over you, until I bring you back again to this place." Then my guides left me and I turned back through the gate by which I had entered, weeping as I went.[71]

The encompassing theme in this vision, as in Sunniulf's, is the service which the prominent Christian was expected to render to the faithful. The monk Salvius discovered that it was his further duty to serve the Church as bishop, and indeed, as bishop of Albi, Salvius was courageous in face of plague and military attack.[72] This motif reflects a sixth-century preoccupation, although it does not disappear entirely thereafter. Gregory of Tours' telling of the visions complemented his own disposition which upheld service to the Christian community as an important spiritual and social value. High status and officeholding bound the individual to certain community obligations. Being a community leader entailed doing for the community. Thus community service as much as personal qualities provided the yardstick by which the prominent Christian's merits were measured.

In the sixth century, visions of the otherworld were generally experienced by pious men who possessed a reasonable hope of spiritual amendment and redemption. Gregory of Tours, who is our primary source for the visions of

[70] *HF* 7.1. trans. Lewis Thorpe.
[71] Ibid.
[72] Ibid.

heaven and hell in sixth-century Gaul, had no time for spiritual slackers, and little confidence in the redeeming value of the deathbed vision. In Gregory's world, the wicked experienced undignified and bloody deaths in keeping with their earthly crimes, and they were presented in his writings as untouched by belated conscience or remorse. On those few occasions when the wicked did express remorse on their deathbeds, Gregory did not believe their belated sentiments were effective. The referendary Mark, who misappropriated taxes to his own profit, was tonsured and confessed his sins before death, but Gregory's comment was that he took nothing with him but the eternal damnation of his soul.[73] This was a discourse very different from that characterized later by Gregory the Great and his seventh-century successors, for whom fear of death and deathbed visions were held to have a purgative value.[74] For Gregory of Tours, death was the passage to one's ultimate destiny, not a process designed for self-awareness. Confrontation with death was never the stated motive for a change in spiritual direction, for in Gregory's eyes it was a life well lived that brought salvation. When the Devil tempted the holy hermit Patroclus to leave his hermitage and reenter the world, an angel appeared to him and presented him with a column from the top of which he could see the evils of the world, its crimes, and its sins. Patroclus made the right decision and returned to the desert, a worthy beneficiary of divine intervention. He was eventually venerated as a saint.[75] By contrast, the wicked referendary Mark described above had spent a lifetime indulging his greed for gold, and it was that life, not his last minute repentance, which determined his fate.

The preoccupations of seventh-century visions express some of the same concerns in a rather different way, revealing salvation to be focused more on individual doing than community doing. The Christian was expected to undertake minute examination of personal transgression with all its messy nuances of intention, motivation, culpability, and personal responsibility. This was followed by penance. Thus the unfinished business to which seventh-century sinners returned was usually preparation for death rather than external obligations.[76] Certainly the importance of service to the Church and the community as an indicator of spiritual merit continued as a pervasive theme in the seventh century, especially in the call to preach and undertake missionary work, but one senses that by then the centrality and definition of spiritual performance, and thus merit, had shifted. Spiritual merit in the

---

[73] HF 6.28. Paxton, *Christianizing Death*, p. 51, notes a similar reluctance in Caesarius of Arles to believe that deathbed penitence was effective.

[74] *Dial.* 4.48. Most of Pope Gregory's visionaries were monks whose life of ongoing penance distinguished them from Gregory of Tours' account of the secular penitent, the referendary Mark.

[75] VP 9.2.

[76] Raymond A. Moody, Jr., *Life after Life: The Investigation of a Phenomenon—Survival of Bodily Death* (New York, 1976), pp. 21–23, notes the "unfinished business" motif in modern near-death descriptions; cited by Zaleski, *Life of the World to Come*, p. 19.

sixth century was at least in part an extension of social responsibility, but in the seventh it was increasingly determined by the quality of the inner life, which was seen "per introspectivo oculo" as Merovingian texts tell us. Personal purity was measured by the increasingly elaborate tariffs of sin, and penances were prescribed in accordance with the degree and nature of the transgression.

Seventh-century visions are a witness that the exhortatory role of the clergy in community affairs had extended to management of the deathbed. Since most seventh-century visions of the afterlife occurred at the deathbed, and were voiced in the presence of monastic clerics, what might be considered a private, family-centered event in the secular environment had a broader meaning in the cloister. Clerical presence at the deathbed of monks and nuns and the interest of monastic communities in recording the last moments of the dying account for the survival of such narratives.

St. Fursey's Visions of Heaven and Hell

The Irish monk Fursey accomplished most of his missionary work in Ireland and had his famous visions there. He then moved to Anglia from whence, after some political troubles, he moved on to northern France and founded the monastery of Lagny-sur-Marne in the vicinity of Faremoutiers and Jouarre. His self-imposed exile in Neustria paralleled the stream of Irish who were making their way to the Continent in the seventh century in imitation of Columbanus.[77] Fursey was generously received by the Neustrian mayor Erchinoald who, with his own Anglo-Saxon connections, was known for sponsoring Irish reform monasticism. Eventually Fursey died in Neustria in 649–50. His body was laid to rest at the monastery of Péronne, where his cult was nurtured and where the story of his life and visions was composed in 656 or 657.[78] Eventually his brothers Foillan and Ultan followed him to Neustria.[79]

[77] On Columbanus's missions see the collection of papers in H. B. Clarke and M. Brennan, eds., *Columbanus and Merovingian Monasticism*, British Archeological Reports, International Series, 113 (Oxford, 1981).

[78] *Vita Sancti Fursei*, ed. Bollandus, *AASS* Ian. ii, pp. 35–41; Bruno Krusch, *MGH, SRM* 4 (1902), pp. 423–49 (with an extract from the *Additamentum Nivialense de Fuilano*, pp. 449–51), does not include the visions. The edition used here is from Ciccarese, "Le Visioni di S. Fursa." See also Latin text supplied by Carozzi, drawn from different manuscripts, in *Le voyage de l'âme*, pp. 677–92, and his discussion of Fursey's vision, pp. 99–138. Works that shed light on Fursey as missionary and on his hagiography include Alain Dierkens, "Prolégomènes à une histoire des relations culturelles entre les îles britanniques et le continent pendant le haut moyen âge" in *La Neustrie*, vol. 2, ed. Harmut Atsma, pp. 371–94, esp. 385 ff., and his *Abbayes et Chapitres entre Sambre et Meuse (VIIe–XIe siècles) Francia*, 14 (1985), p. 71, n. 7, p. 304, n. 147; Pádraig ó Riain, "Les Vies de saint Fursey: les sources irlandaises," *Revue du Nord* 68: 269 (1986), 405–12, and discussion by Dierkens and Michel Rouche, 412–13.

[79] Foillan founded the monastery of Fosses on land donated by Pippinid, Itta. The change of patronage and the politics behind it are discussed by Fouracre and Gerberding, *Late Merovingian France*, pp. 100–101, 3–4.

Fursey's *vita* records two visions, of which the second was the more detailed.[80] Both visions were set in Ireland. In the first, an illness which afflicted Fursey as he was returning home from one of his monasteries became so debilitating that he arrived "as if already dead." According to his hagiographer, as Fursey lay on his deathbed a dark mist began to envelop him, and four hands stretched out toward him, grasping him by the arms. Fursey had difficulty making out the exact shape of the angels, who shone with very bright light, but a third angel was armed with a white shield and a shining sword. Fursey heard a song which he did not recognize, sung by many thousands of angels; the only words he could make out were "they will come out to meet Christ." The faces of the angels, as far as he could see them, all appeared the same, although he saw no corporeal form. Then one of the crowd of armed angels ordered that Fursey be returned to his body. Fursey replied that he did not want to leave them, but the angel replied, "We will come back to get you when you have completed the aforementioned responsibilities." In what manner his soul was able to reenter his body he claimed not to know, but at the birds' chorus he began to come to. Those who were tending the corpse, observing his movements, removed the cloth which had been placed over his face. Reflecting on the vision's warning about his duties, Fursey resolved not to be unprepared when the angels next came to fetch him. He requested and took communion. He survived his sickness that day and the next. However, on the third night, as friends and family visited him, the darkness began once again to enclose him, and, stretching out his hands he gladly "caught at death" (*laetus excepit mortem*).

The lengthy description of the second vision comprises the remainder of the text of Fursey's *vita*. The second vision reprised the major theme of the first, namely that Fursey had duties and responsibilities yet to perform. Fursey's second journey was far more eventful than his first, for he was now attacked by squalls of wailing demons and by fiery arrows.

This second vision comprised five basic scenes. In the first scene, Fursey espied a dark valley in which four fires burned, stoked by the four sins of mendacity, covetousness, discord, and cruelty. In the second, angels and demons engaged in an extended debate regarding the nature of God's justice and the remissibility of sins once the sinner had departed the world. In the third scene, Fursey asked about the end of the world. In the fourth, he reported an extended monologue about the particular responsibilities attendant on teachers of the faith and rulers of the Christian people. The shortcomings of the unworthy teacher were listed at length with the conclusion that the lax teacher "is to be judged as the enemy of souls." In the final scene Fursey met two clerics known to him, Beoanus and Meldanus. He was then

---

[80] Bede's retelling of the story in his *Historia ecclesiastica* 3.19. was prefaced by another vision which impelled Fursey to establish a monastery on land granted to him by King Sigbert of East Anglia at a place called Cnobheresburg. Fursey fled East Anglia ahead of Penda's incursions.

conducted home, but not before one of the damned was slung at him out of the fire, leaving burn marks on his shoulder and jaw. The unfortunate soul was a man from whom Fursey had once accepted an article of clothing. For that reason it was Fursey's lot to share in the punishment meted out to the wretch. Fursey's revulsion at returning to his own corpse is described in some detail, and once he awoke *ex profunda mortis quiete*, he was discovered to bear the burn scars of his encounter with the damned man.

Fursey's vision has much in common with that of Salvius as related by Gregory of Tours. The narrator carefully presented the postmortem nature of the experience and the soul's attendant difficulties of "reentry." Like both Salvius and Sunniulf, Fursey was told to consider his leadership responsibilities, and like Salvius he was promised eventual return to heaven. Unlike Salvius and Sunniulf, however, Fursey received an interim judgment and punishment in this second vision. His transgression in accepting an article of clothing from a sinful man was punished through burns and permanent scars. In late antique apocalypses, the nature of God's justice was an insistent theme; here the theme of justice was debated by demons and angels. Yet Fursey did not come before a heavenly tribunal. Rather his sins judged him, for we are told that hell's fires only burn those who have sinned. Fursey's penances were the burns which he must bear in mortal life and his memory of the frightening encounter which, Bede tells us, used to make him sweat in fear. Fursey's interim punishment in the afterlife was a new feature. Rather than simply observing the affliction of those who had already passed on, shielded physically if not emotionally from the spectacle, he was physically touched by hell's torture. In his advance suffering for his sin, Fursey's example showed the importance of penance, for transgression in the present life was seen to be directly connected with the nature and duration of his expected punishment in the next.

Since Fursey's visionary experiences occurred in Ireland, it may be argued that Irish religious culture defined the tradition in which his work was written. Yet the work was not written in Ireland but on the Continent, at Péronne, hence the immediate context for Fursey's visions was the Continental tradition of journeys to heaven and hell combined with residual apocalyptic elements.[81] The striking penitentialism of this transformation of Christian eschatology may have arisen not from unmediated Irish thinking, but rather, like the penitentials themselves, from the confluence of Irish and Continental influences. Although Fursey's vision was soon known in England (Bede synopsized the visions in his *Ecclesiastical History* composed in 731), its most immediate and lasting impact was on the Hiberno-Frankish culture of northern France. Fursey's visions were an important influence on the vision

---

[81] Fursey learned that the end of the world, though close, was not imminent, and that famine and deadly plagues would first afflict the human race. His vision had cosmic elements; for example, he saw the entire world from afar (his panoramic vision of the valley of four fires), thus experiencing the true relationship of creation to its creator.

of Barontus in 678–79, and must share the *Visio Baronti*'s acknowledged debt to the *Dialogues* of Gregory the Great.

The Vision of the Monk Barontus

Within a short time of the composition of Fursey's vision, a Frankish monk at an Irish-influenced Continental monastery also reported having a vision of heaven and hell. The *Vision of Barontus* related the experience of a wealthy, aging nobleman only recently converted to the ascetic life who had entered the monastery of St. Peter's at Lonrey (today St. Cyran-en-Brenne) where his son Aglioaldus was also a monk.[82] After a severe and sudden illness on March 25, 678–79, Barontus' soul left his body and traveled to the otherworld.[83] Of Barontus himself we know nothing for certain, although a generation earlier an aristocrat of that same name (perhaps an older male relative) made a name for himself in that part of the kingdom. This earlier Barontus was a *vir illuster*, first count and then duke in King Dagobert I's Aquitainian lands. In 631–32 he seized and appropriated a portion of King Charibert's treasure, which he was apparantly able to retain.[84] The visionary Barontus lived about forty years after the activities of this earlier magnate, and although St. Peter's monastery (near Bourges) was geographically quite far removed from the orbit of the duke Barontus' activities in and around Toulouse, it was within the same political boundaries and the ducal family may have held lands where St. Peter's was situated. Although the connection between these two namesakes is speculative, the insistence in Barontus' vision on his wealth and the need for its disposition may indicate sensitivity about the dishonorable source of the family's riches.

The account of Barontus' vision appears to have been written down soon after it took place, perhaps by a monk at the neighboring monastery of Méobecque.[85] Situated in the diocese of Bourges, Méobecque was probably founded, like St. Peter's of Lonrey where Barontus lived, by St. Sigiramnus (St. Cyran) along the lines of the Irish reform movement. Wilhelm Levison,

---

[82] The monastery of Lonrey was founded by a cleric and archdeacon of Tours named Sigiramnus (c. 632), and it eventually took its founder's name. See the *Vita Sigiramni abbatis Longoretensis*, ed. Bruno Krusch, *MGH, SRM* 4 (1902), pp. 603–25. The monastery was one of a number of Neustrian foundations influenced by Columbanus, including Méobecque, its sister foundation. See Prinz, *Frühes Mönchtum*, p. 136, 140–41.

[83] *Visio Baronti monachi Longoretensis*, ed. Wilhelm Levison *MGH, SRM* 5 (1910), pp. 368–94. Levison dated the vision 678–79. Jocelyn N. Hillgarth, ed., *Christianity and Paganism, 350–750. The Conversion of Western Europe* (Philadelphia, 1969), pp. 195–204, provides an English translation. However, all translations of the *Visio Baronti* in this chapter are my own. Recent discussions of this work include Ciccarese, "La *Visio Baronti*"; Carozzi, "La géographie de l'au-delà," esp. pp. 440–45, and *Le voyage de l'âme*, pp. 139–86; Hen, "The Structure and Aims of the 'Visio Baronti'"; and Zaleski, *Otherworld Journeys*, esp. pp. 45–52, 70–72.

[84] Horst Ebling, *Prosopographie der Amtsträger des Merowingerreiches von Chlothar II (613) bis Karl Martell (741)*, Francia, 2 (1974), pp. 71–73 # 63.

[85] See Levison, *Visio Baronti*, p. 268.

who edited the *Visio Baronti* for the *Monumenta* edition in 1910, compared the work unfavorably with Fursey's vision, seeing in its focus on personal issues and its earthbound imagination evidence of Frankish artlessness and want of refinement.[86] The Latinity is poor, but the work is original, as Ciccarese has argued, particularly in its description of heaven.[87] Just as importantly, however, the work retains the seams of its compositional stages and is thus important in helping us understand how visionary narratives were used in monastic circles, how they came to be written down, and how and to what purpose such narratives were disseminated. The immediate audience for the work appears to have been monastic, for the work is addressed to "fratres karissimi," presumably the bretheren of Méobecque or Lonrey.[88] As an oral account, however, it may have become much more widely known. For unlike the text of Fursey's visions, but very like the form in which we have the *Visio Pauli*, Barontus' account of his vision is largely written in the first person, with the recensor's introduction and conclusion framing the narrative.[89] Whatever the failings of the *Visio Baronti* with regard to reflective and soteriological sophistication, it appears not so ill-adapted when considered in the light of previous and subsequent developments in the visionary genre.

The journey of Barontus' soul is a Merovingian odyssey dovetailed into an eschatological epic. From the very start of his adventure, Barontus's soul was in danger as two black demons attacked him, strangling him and intending to drag him off to hell with them, until at the third hour the archangel Raphael came to his resue. Raphael and the demons began to argue over who should take his soul, a struggle which lasted the whole day until at the evening hour a compromise was reached. Raphael suggested that he would take Barontus' soul before the court of the eternal Judge but leave his spirit in his body.[90] This compromise required that Barontus believe in (or conceive of) the independence and divisibility of spirit and soul. It might be that the compromise was rendered necessary by the monk's experience in which he did not in fact die. Yet the early medieval visionary journeys described thus far did not require the author to go to such lengths; in a society which believed in miraculous deaths and resurrections, the postmortem vision had a ready audience. So what explains this belief in the divisibility of soul and spirit? In fact it was a theological idea which was not very well developed in

---

[86] Ibid., p. 369.

[87] Ciccarese, "La *Visio Baronti*," pp. 43 ff.

[88] *Visio Baronti* 1.

[89] Ibid., 20. Editorializing crept into the text at points, leading to changes in the narrative person. For example, the narrative shifts from the first to the third person for a sentence in chapter 16.

[90] Ibid., 3. Based on theological considerations expressed by Jerome in *Ep.* 120.12, Levison rendered the contraction "spm" in the manuscript as "spem," or "hope," p. 380, n. 2. Earlier editors such as Henschenius had rendered it as "spiritum," and that is the reading I have preferred here since it is consistent with earlier visionary literature such as like the *Visio Pauli*.

Christian doctrine, but was demonstrably expressed in early visionary
accounts such as the *Apocalypse of Peter*, and in the *Vision of Paul* in which,
in the afterlife, the spirit operated independently of the soul.[91] In consequence of this compromise by which Barontus' spirit would remain in his
body, Barontus was enabled to experience the consequences of death without literal expiration.

As Barontus' narrative continued, he explained that Raphael touched his
throat and he felt his soul being removed from his body. "And I saw my soul,
as far as I could see in my vision, to be a small thing. Thus it seemed to me
to be a small thing like a little baby bird, such as it is when it comes out of
its egg. And it had a little head, eyes, and other limbs, and it carried with it
intact the senses of sight, hearing, taste, smell, and touch; but it could hardly
talk." This description of the soul has elements which are at once ancient
and innovative.[92] The primary image is of birth, or more precisely a scriptural and patristic image of spiritual rebirth.[93] The soul is described as a little
bird, yet unlike conventional descriptions of the soul as a dove, this fledgling
was not able to fly by itself. The bird was dark, not white, indicating its sin-
fulness.[94] Yet it was like a living thing, with all the human senses it would
need to negotiate and experience the other world.[95] At some point in the
story Bartontus acquired a celestial body, "an airy body of light" in which
to travel, for when he was deprived of it on his return, his fledgling soul
could not move effectively even though it still had all its sensations.[96]

Barontus' account of his soul's return to his body after his travels to the
otherworld is no less striking than his account of his soul's initial removal.
Indeed the vertiginous ascent and descent narrative is startling in this early
context, though characteristic of later medieval visions. Back on earth, and
without the aid of his airy body, Barontus began to drag his soul along the
ground, until a divine wind lifted him up and carried him to the roof over
his dead body. From this vantage point Barontus saw the brethren gathered

[91] *Apocalypse of Peter* 4: "And soul and spirit shall the great Uriel give them"; *Vision of Paul* 5. In his *De anima*, Tertullian had repudiated any idea of the divisibility of the soul, yet the concept was not unknown to ancient theologians. Much later, the sixteenth-century heretical miller
"Menochio" asserted his belief in a distinction between soul and spirit reverse to that in church
teaching: "When the body dies the soul dies but the spirit remains." Quoted in Carlo Ginzburg,
The Cheese and the Worms: The Cosmos of a Sixteenth-Century Miller, trans. John and Anne
Tedeschi (New York, 1989; orig. publ. in Italian, 1976), p. 71.
[92] Ciccarese, "La *Visio Baronti*," cites references to bird imagery common in antique literature, p. 40. n. 44. I propose that the psalms were important influences on this avian image—
see discussion below, pp. 428–29.
[93] Augustine, *Enchiridion* 75, connects the scriptural injunction to be "born again" with the
giving of alms.
[94] Black and nocturnal birds were associated with sin and the Devil. See VR 2.19 ("nocturna
avis") and the vision of the monk of Wenlock where the souls of sinners in hell looked like black
birds, clinging to the sides of the fiery pits.
[95] This description is somewhat reminiscent of Tertullian's unorthodox belief in the corpore-
ality of the soul: "It, too, has eyes and ears of its own, by which Paul must have heard and seen
the Lord; it has moreover, all the other members of the body." *De anima* 9.
[96] *Visio Baronti* 18–19.

around his body, including his son Aglioaldus asleep with his hand on his chin. "Then with another gust of wind, I entered my body through the mouth and my first words were in praise of God: 'Gloria tibi, Deus.'"⁹⁷

On his journey to the celestial realms, Barontus encountered the traditional gateways that were believed to mark off regions of heaven. In ancient visionary literature, these gateways were guarded by sentinels who restricted access to the realms above. In pagan and gnostic literature, the gateways, or tolls, to the many levels of heaven numbered as many as seven, eight, or nine.⁹⁸ However, since the apostle Paul recounted in the book of Acts that he was taken up to the third heaven, and especially given Augustine's commentaries on that passage, Christian texts generally accepted that there were three grades in heaven.⁹⁹ Barontus, though, encountered four, and he was quite explicit on this point. Indeed, there is a suggestion that there may have been more, for Barontus noted that he and Raphael were not permitted to proceed further on their journey.¹⁰⁰ As they ascended, they came first to the first door of paradise where they saw assembled many brethren from St. Peter's monastery, awaiting the day of judgment when they would receive eternal joy in full measure. At the second door of paradise they saw thousands of infants dressed in white, praising God in unison. They then ascended by a narrow path to reach the next door, but they were surrounded by so many virgins that only God could see them all. The third door of paradise was like glass, and within were a multitude of crowned saints, with shining faces seated on thrones in splendid mansions, giving constant praise to God. Barontus saw gold-bricked mansions and more in the process of being built, one of which was being prepared for their abbot Francardus.¹⁰¹ Finally, they came to the fourth door of paradise where they met Betolenus, a cripple who used to writhe in pain at the monastery threshold but who was now living in joy. The fourth region of heaven was also the area where Raphael engaged in conversation with St. Peter. In another region between heaven and hell Barontus saw a very beautiful old man with a long beard seated quietly on a high seat. Raphael explained: "It is our father Abraham, and you, brother, should always pray to God that when you die you may live peacefully in the bosom of Abraham."¹⁰² Finally, with his escort, Barontus, arrived in hell. He

---

⁹⁷ Ibid., 19.

⁹⁸ Alan F. Segal discusses the five heavens of 3 Baruch in "Heavenly Ascent in Hellenistic Judaism, Early Christianity, and Their Environment," *Aufsteig und Niedergang* 2. Principat 23.2, 1333–94, esp. 1365. Michael E. Stone discusses the seven heavens described in 4 Ezra in "The Metamorphosis of Ezra: Jewish Apocalypse and Medieval Vision," *JTS*, n.s., 33 (1982), 1–18, and James Stevenson examines the medieval posterity of the seven heavens of the gnostic *Apocalypse of Paul* in "Ascent through the Heavens, from Egypt to Ireland," *Cambridge Medieval Celtic Studies* 5 (1983), 21–35. On nine heavens see Cicero, *De republica* 6.17.

⁹⁹ 2 Cor. 12.1–4; Augustine, *De Gen. ad litt.* 12.4.

¹⁰⁰ *Visio Baronti* 11.

¹⁰¹ Reminiscent of Gregory the Great, *Dial.* 4. 37.9.

¹⁰² *Visio Baronti* 16 echoing the liturgical hope that the Christian's soul will rest in Abraham's bosom. See Sicard, *La liturgie de la mort*, p. 89; on Abraham's bosom see Philippe

could not see within clearly because of the gloomy shades and smoke, but he offered to relate as best he could what he saw there: "I saw many thousands of men bound and constricted by demons, moaning, and like bees returning to their hive."[103]

Elizabeth Petroff has suggested that for women, who were generally denied formal intellectual outlets, visions were often a way in which theological beliefs could be worked out.[104] Barontus' elevated status and the societal expectations of Frankish men in secular careers may likewise have limited his capacity for entering fully into the discourse of more educated Christians. His vision, with its strange combination of conventionality and originality, is testimony to the occasional power of visionary narratives to give voice to personal imaginings.

Barontus' account exhibits the imprint of his monastic environment. His new ascetic world, with its explicit promises of preferential salvation, is clearly reflected in his vision. Many of the people he saw on his travels were connected in some way with St. Peter's of Lonrey. For example, on the first leg of their travel, Barontus and Raphael soared over the monastery's woods until they came to the monastery of Méobecque (Millebecus), twelve miles away—reached in a single moment. There, as at St. John's, vespers was being celebrated. Looking down, Barontus saw people he knew celebrating the office, and a man carrying fresh vegetables to the monastery kitchens. Raphael explained that they were there to visit the humble abbot Leodoald, whose good works singled him out from other inhabitants of Bourges. The abbot was close to death, but now as a result of Raphael's visit he sustained a miraculous recovery.[105]

Méobecque was probably connected to St. Peter's through their mutual founder, Sigiramnus, and this connection may explain Raphael's concern for Méobecque and its holy abbot. Later in the account, at the first door of heaven, Barontus encountered many brethren from his own monastery, some of whom had passed away since his joining the community. He recognized the priests Corbolenus and Fraudolenus, the deacon Austrulfus, and the lectors Leodoaldus and Ebbo. Leodoaldus wanted to know from what monastery Barontus came, and what great sin he had committed that the demons claimed so much power over him. Barontus replied, "I come from the monastery of St. Peter's of Lonrey, and I do not deny that everything which I now suffer is due to my faults." When Leodoaldus discovered that Barontus was from his monastery, he moaned and cried out that no demon had yet taken any soul from St. Peter's. The brethren began to pray and implore Raphael that their brother should not be devoured by the Devil. At

---

Ariès, "Une conception ancienne de l'au-delà," in Braet and Verbeke, *Death in the Middle Ages* pp. 78–87.

[103] *Visio Baronti* 17.

[104] Elizabeth A. Petroff, *Medieval Women's Visionary Literature* (Oxford, 1986), pp. 8–9.

[105] *Visio Baronti* 6. This miracle was later confirmed by Leodoaldus, who claimed to have seen Raphael in his cell.

the fourth door of paradise Barontus encountered another brother from the monastery, the former cripple Betoleno, who was now in charge of all the church lights in the whole world, and who asked him why the lights were not on in his own monastery at night.[106] Later in the story, after Barontus had been ordered to visit hell, it was decided by the brethren that he be escorted there by a former monk, Framnoaldus, who had died as a boy. They promised Framnoaldus that if he undertook the unpleasant task of escorting Barontus to the infernal regions, Barontus would clean his tomb every Sunday and sing "Miserere mei" over it. This was of concern to the young monk because his body lay buried at the threshold of the church and had been much neglected. Barontus acceded to the promise.

Although he could not see hell clearly because of the gloomy shades and smoke, Barontus saw the damned seated on leaden seats. The sin of each group was explained. They included the prideful, the lascivious, perjurers, murderers, detractors, and traitors.[107] Likewise in that place Barontus saw innumerable clerics who had tainted themselves through contact with women, and they screamed in great pain. Among the tortured, Barontus saw the bishop of Bourges, Vulfoleodus (a deceiver), and bishop Dido of Poitiers.[108] There he also saw foolish virgins who were without good works. But those who had done some good deeds in life were offered manna each day at the sixth hour as a refreshment.[109]

A striking feature of the text is its emphasis on penance. By Barontus' time, Irish penitential literature had made its mark on many northern Frankish monasteries. The institution of penance was already entrenched, of course, but its litigiousness was new, and northern. Barontus was a sinner, not in the general sense that all men were considered to be, but in some very specific ways. As the demons revealed before St. Peter, Barontus was guilty of "mortal vices" (which, it was believed, damned a man eternally if not properly expiated).[110] The demons said of Barontus: "He had three wives, which is not allowable; and he perpetrated other adulteries." Barontus continued his recollection: "They recalled one by one the other sins which I had committed since infancy, and others which I no longer remembered."[111] In response to this assault, St. Peter reminded the demons of the Church's

---

[106] Ibid., 11.

[107] The redactor of the *Visio Baronti* referred the reader to Gregory's *Dialogues* where it is mentioned that sinners were grouped into bundles according to their sins. *Visio Baronti* 17.

[108] Bishop Dido of Poitiers was a Neustrian aristocrat who, in association with the Austrasian mayor Grimoald I, was responsible for abducting and exiling the rightful Merovingian king, Dagobert, to Ireland in 656. We may assume that the author of the *Visio Baronti*, who placed Dido in Hell, was not a supporter of Grimoald's coup. However, it is also possible that more local grievances against the bishop were being expressed. See Jean-Michel Picard, "Church and Politics in the Seventh Century: The Irish Exile of Dagobert II," in *Ireland and Northern France A.D. 600–850*, ed. Jean-Michel Picard, pp. 27–52 (Dublin, 1991).

[109] The refreshment offered in Barontus' vision is reminiscent of the once-weekly respite from suffering offered in the *Visio Pauli* 11, later interpreted as a Sunday respite.

[110] "Crimina capitalia" required official penitence. Chélini, *L'aube du moyen âge*, p. 367.

[111] *Visio Baronti* 12.

teaching on the giving of alms and the performance of penance: "Although
he has done some wrong, he has given alms (for alms liberate from death),
and his sins have been confessed to a priest and he has done penance for
that sin, and moreover he is tonsured in my monastery and has left all his
possessions behind for God and has handed himself over to Christ's service.
Thus all these wrongs which you claim are recalculated to the good." Then
taking up his three keys St. Peter struck the demons, and they fled. St. Peter
turned to Barontus and said, "Ransom yourself, brother." He replied,"What
can I give, good shepherd, for I have nothing in my possession." But Peter
(who had presumably tricked the demons) knew that Barontus had hoarded
twelve *solidi* and told him to hurry to donate them. Starting on the kalends
of April and for each month for twelve months, Barontus was commanded
to give one *solidus* into the hands of a pauper, weighed out and marked by
a priest so that he had legitimate witness of his penance.

Almsgiving, in this case essentially money payment for sin, provided a
simple and effective message to Merovingian noblemen who sought to remedy lives lived counter to the precepts of the Church. Other penitential
activities were encouraged, such as visiting the sick, offering hospitality to
strangers, and ascetic practices, but almsgiving was the most important.[112]
Furthermore, Barontus was instructed to have his almsgiving certified by a
priest, for it was before the eyes of the clergy, as Peter's representatives, that
Barontus' penance had to be completed. When asked if this would suffice
for the forgiveness of Barontus' sins, St. Peter replied: "If he gives what I
have instructed him to give, immediately his sins are forgiven," and "This is
the price of the rich man and the poor man, twelve solidi given in alms."[113]
What the Church offered through penances and expiation was access to an
ongoing process of salvation.

A prominent and wealthy man like Barontus was quite a catch for a small
community like St. Peter's. In taking the tonsure, Barontus made visible his
shift of allegiance from the Merovingian to the heavenly king. In return for
this spiritual realignment, monastic life, with its focus on the psalms, offered
Barontus a language of transcendence: a vocabulary of spiritual striving to
set alongside the more prosaic grammar of confession and absolution. Thus
it was that, whether from his own recollection or inserted by his amanuensis, Barontus' visionary tale was carefully grafted to the poetry of the psalms
and the liturgical rhythms of the day. This liturgical framework was a new

[112] Chélini, *L'aube du moyen âge*, p. 367. Augustine argued that almsgiving was not confined
to monetary payment but also included charitable activities, and he required the giver to be in
a godly relationship to himself and others. *Enchiridion* 72 ff. Barontus gave away much of his
property on entering the monastery, but he had not, as Augustine required, been "born again."
Barontus' vision of new birth was accompanied by full repentance.

[113] *Visio Baronti* 13. Despite St. Peter's assurance, Barontus' penance was not yet complete.
He was also required, in exchange for a guide through hell, to clean the tomb of a young monk
whose remains lay at the threshold of Lonrey's monastic church. Performing janitorial services
for the Church was one of the ways in which the penitent made public restitution. See Beck, *Pastoral Care*, p. 194. This penitential service is evidenced in many saints' *vitae* as an ascetic virtue.

feature in accounts of visionary journeys to the otherworld (although it had long featured in dreams and visions in cultic contexts). The daily performance of offices provided the skeleton upon which the monk draped all other experiences.[114] Barontus' struggle with the demons began after he had celebrated lauds with the brethren and lasted until vespers, when Raphael succeeded with the aid of the monks' prayers to pull him free and as the church bells began to chime for the evening service. As they reached Méobecque, Raphael prayed lengthily concluding with the final lines of Psalm 102: "In all the places of his dominion, bless the Lord, O my soul."[115]

Psalms occupy a central position in the *Visio Baronti*, numerous fragmentary quotations being interwoven with the dramatic events. In accordance with monastic funeral custom, the author of the *Visio Baronti* related that the brethren sang psalms over Barontus' prostrate body.[116] In the Gallican rite, the psalms and litanies chosen for funerals varied, although later (Carolingian) evidence is that seven penitential psalms were customary in monastic circles.[117] Did the words of the psalms filter in to Barontus's consciousness as he lay supine, or were the quotations suggested by the events Barontus later told and incorporated by the editor? In Psalm 102, whose final lines were intoned by Raphael, earlier lines called upon the soul to bless God "who redeems your life from the Pit . . . so that your youth is renewed like the eagle's."[118] It is tempting to read in Barontus' own vision of his puny, birdlike soul a tragicomic reflection on his lack of eagle-strength. The bird imagery is reminiscent of Psalm 101, where the psalmist sang the lament of a suffering soul: "Hear my prayer, O Lord; let my cry come to thee . . . I am like a vulture of the wilderness, like an owl of the waste places; I lie awake, I am like a lonely bird on the housetop."[119] Or perhaps Barontus was thinking of the fable of the eagle and his young, which was held to communicate a spiritual truth: the eagle taught its young to look directly into the sun and rejected any eaglet that did not.[120] A Priscillianist text extended the Chris-

[114] In the *Vision of Wetti*, the visionary was taught by the angel in his vision to repeat Psalm 118 in particular, and he requested his fellow monks to intone the antiphons and psalms to accompany his exit from the present life. In the later middle ages, when the visions of lay men and women were recorded, the liturgical calendar provided context, opportunity, and inspiration for their visionary tales as parishioners periodically cycled in and out of church for feasts and high holidays. For example, the peasant Thurkill's vision (c. 1206) occurred between the nights of October 27 and November 1 (All Soul's Day). *Visio Thurkilli*, ed. Paul Gerhard Schmidt (Leipzig, 1978). Many of Margery Kempe's visions were direct responses to her attendance at services on Holy Thursday, Palm Sunday, Good Friday, and Candlemas. *The Book of Margery Kempe*, trans. Barry Windeatt (Harmondsworth, 1985).

[115] Ps. 102.22.

[116] In the Old Roman liturgy for the dead, and the Old Gelasian liturgy quoted below, the *subvenite* was chanted over the dying: "Ut suscipi iubeas animam famuli tui illius per manus sanctorum angelorum deducendam in sinu amici tui patriarchae abrahae." Sicard, *La liturgie de la mort*, p. 89.

[117] Sicard, *La liturgie de la mort*, pp. 43 ff.; Février, "La mort chrétienne," pp. 886 ff.; Paxton, *Christianizing Death*, pp. 38–43.

[118] Ps. 102.4–5

[119] Ps. 101.6–7.

[120] Tertullian, *De anima* 8.

tianized metaphor: "By the eagle God the Father is signified; the chick is Adam's kind."[121] Regardless of when the psalms entered the narrative, the vision of Barontus was a reminder that the duty to sing the psalms was one of the foremost responsibilities of the monk and that the images therein lent themselves readily to ascensional themes.

Although the visionary tale was largely a paean to the value of monasticism, Barontus was quite plain about the value of the clerics whom he encountered in the otherworld. Hillgarth notes the contrast between Barontus' praise for the good abbots of his own times with the wicked bishops of Bourges and Poitiers.[122] But did this really indicate a preferential valuing of monks over clerics? Barontus speaks of the role of clerics a number of times: at the third gate of paradise the mansions built of gold bricks were being prepared for "a multitude of clerics of the highest merit."[123] Further on, as Barontus was about to embark on his frightening journey to hell, he and the rest of the brethren went to ask the former monk and now cleric Ebbo to make the sign of the Cross over the candle so it would not go out. When they arrived, Ebbo was engaged in celebrating the mysteries of the apostles in church. Ebbo's clerical duties, then, continued in heaven. And as he signed the Cross, they saw a wondrous light radiating from his arms and fingers. Barontus tells us a little about this man. Ebbo had been a man of high birth who had given up all his goods, was tonsured, and became a minister of Christ. His elevated merit was due to his almsgiving, and his arms and fingers, which had been the instruments of that charity, radiated as a sign. We have already noted that Barontus' almsgiving was to be administered through a priest. All expectations of a repentant sinner had to be channeled through the services of the clergy.[124]

Although not as sophisticated as the *Vision of Fursey*, Barontus' vision expressed quite readily the theological, institutional, and liturgical concerns of a monastic neophyte. But what was its audience? The clarity, detail and assurance of Barontus' visionary journey, told in the first person, suggests that in Hiberno-Frankish monasteries such tales were used actively as a didactic tool for prospective or recent converts.[125] The fact that Barontus' vision was written down and preserved is likewise testimony to the value given to this kind of text. In the introduction to his edition of the vision, Wilhelm Levison noted that the work was intended for personal reading rather than for reading aloud because the text included a description of St. Peter's keys ac-

---

[121] "Aquila deus pater significatur; pullus genus adae." From a Priscillianist text quoted by Donatien de Bruyne, "Fragments retrouvés d'apocryphes priscillianistes," *Revue Bénédictine* 24 (1907), 318–35.

[122] Hillgarth, *Christianity and Paganism*, p. 182.

[123] *Visio Baronti* 10: "multitudo sacerdotum excelsi meritorum."

[124] *Visio Baronti* 15 calls Ebbo a "minister Christi," not the more usual "presbyter." In the vision of the monk of Wenlock priests were also portrayed positively—the monk was directed to the priest Begga for penance and spiritual direction. Boniface, *Ep.* 22.

[125] We may assume that there was some editorial glossing. The introduction and conclusion were clearly later additions.

companied by illustrations.[126] However, in addressing the reader's attention to illustrations, the recensor did not preclude an oral life for the text. In monastic communities readings of this type enjoyed particular favor. The Merovingian editor's intertextual comments that certain scenes recalled visions in Gregory the Great's *Dialogues* suggest not only that the latter work was common reading in the monastery but that it would have been familiar to a recent convert like Barontus. Likewise reminiscences of the *Visio Pauli* suggest a culture of visionary storytelling. This point is significant because although it is not difficult to assert that visionary stories of this sort had a didactic value, it is a different matter to assert that visions were *used* for didactic purposes and that they produced didactic results. Barontus' vision, with its familiarity with earlier visionary literature, surely witnessed the impact that such visionary stories had on the minds of those who came late to the ascetic life in the heartland of Gaul.

Accommodating Clerical Attitudes

Merovingian visions of the afterlife are clearly important for the study of shifts in religious and cultural attitudes in that society. Clerical dispensation of the sacraments offered opportunities for the cleric to be at the bedside of the dying, and by the later Merovingian period clerics were especially sensitive to the opportunity offered by deathbed visions for verifying and publishing the efficacy of the sacraments. To a great extent this was because these clerics were often also monks whose immediate audience was the monastic community. Clericalization of monasteries brought the services of the clergy to the ascetic community. Thus it would be inaccurate to consider seventh-century visions exclusively as an expression of ascetic concerns.

The influence of Gregory the Great's writings and Irish penitentialism on later Merovingian visions of the otherworld are undeniable. However, receptivity to such cultural and literary influences in Gaul did not happen in a vacuum. Nor did Gregory's *Dialogues* and Irish penitential manuals arise in a vacuum. Gregory the Great wrote visionary stories to make theological and religious points because the tradition of broad access to divine visions had never really disappeared, as we noted in Chapter 1. In Gaul, without knowledge of the theoretical literature on dreams available to Pope Gregory, Gregory of Tours found himself trying to explain, not always very convincingly, how it was that sinners and "ordinary Christians" had important visions. Left to provide theological explanations for traditions of access that were deeply embedded in Roman Christian culture, Gregory found the elitist rhetoric which he inherited from his episcopal culture inadequate and inconsistent. At the same time he had natural sympathies for that older tradition, as did other clerics at that time.

Thus in keeping with the argument of the book as a whole, I propose that

---

[126] Levison, *Visio Baronti*, p. 368.

we must also understand the flowering of visionary tales of the otherworld in the seventh century in the wider context of clerical sympathies toward accommodating the unexpected, sinful visionary. For over the preceding centuries, as we have seen, the clergy had furthered the tradition in which God was not limited to communicating with the meritorious but spoke to all Christians, expressing the infusion of creation by divine power. Clerical sympathies had laid the groundwork for these seventh-century accounts by permitting a populist element in the visions. Sinners' visions of divine mysteries gave filtered expression to the clergy as representatives and mediators for the entire Christian community. The impact of Gregory the Great's writings in Gaul and of the penitential movement on visionary dramas must therefore be placed in the context of the long history of the Gallo-Merovingian clergy's accommodation of a spiritually meaningful tradition of dreams in the community. Yet ultimately the literary genre of visionary journeys was also the product of clericalized monastic elites from the seventh century who, influenced by penitentialism and the doctrinal and didactic potential of the visions of sinners, were able to benefit from a tradition in which sinful Christians had access to visions of divine things. These accounts of visionary journeys had the capacity to become vehicles for religious and political criticism (in the future they often criticized royal and episcopal authority), but they were not subversive to the religious authority of the Church in the way that once, in the second century, "open access" to visions had had the power to be.

Part 3

DREAMS AND VISIONS IN MEROVINGIAN HAGIOGRAPHY

I̶t is impossible to consider the place of visions in the Merovingian world without considering the nature of the hagiographic literature from which so much of our evidence derives.[1] Hagiography and its cultic auxiliaries (*inventiones*, *translationes*, *libri miraculorum*, and so forth) comprise our most significant and abundant textual source for the religious values of the Merovingian age. The clerics, monks, and nuns who manufactured this religious literature were deeply immersed in a religious tradition which saw the *gestae* of the saints as edifying if not readily imitable exempla of the holy life. Their products were not, and were not intended to be, biographic in the modern sense. In hagiography, the saint's accomplishments were viewed as remarkable and spiritually profitable according to their conformity with a long-established tradition of holiness. The hagiographer presented to the reader, in the life of the extraordinary and lackluster protagonist alike, a stimulus for pious reflection and meditation. This didactic context permitted the Merovingian religious community to conceive and live within para-

[1] On Merovingian hagiography see Patrick Geary, "Saints, Scholars and Society: The Elusive Goal," in Sandro Sticca, *Saints: Studies in Hagiography*, pp. 1–22; (Binghamton, N.Y., 1996); Fouracre, "Merovingian History"; Felice Lifshitz, "Beyond Positivism and Genre: 'Hagiographical' Texts as Historical Narrative," *Viator* 25 (1994), 95–113; Gabrielle M. Spiegel, "History, Historicism, and the Social Logic of the Text in the Middle Ages," *Speculum* 65 (1990), 59–86; Jacques Dubois and Jean Loup Lemaitre, eds. *Sources et méthodes de l'hagiographie médiévale* (Paris, 1993); Friedrich Prinz, "Gesellschaftsgeschichtliche Aspekte frühmittelalterlicher Hagiographie," *Zeitschrift für Literatur-Wissenschaft und Linguistik* 3:2 (1973), 17–36; Martin Heinzelmann, "Neue Aspekte der biographischen und hagiographischen Literatur in der lateinischen Welt (1.-6. Jahrhundert)," *Francia* 1 (1973), 27–44; Sophia Boesch Gajano, *Agiographica altomedioevale* (Bologna, 1976); Dieter von der Nahmer, *Die lateinische Heiligenvita. Eine Einführung in die lateinische Hagiographie* (Darmstadt, 1994); Joseph-Claude Poulin, *L'ideal de sainteté dans l'Aquitaine carolingienne d'après les sources hagiographiques 750–950*, (Quebec, 1995); Friedrich Lotter, "Methodisches zur Gewinnung historischer Erkentnisse aus hagiographischen Quellen," *Historische Zeitschrift* 229 (1979) 298–356; Berschin, *Biographie und Epochenstil*; and Graus, *Volk, Herrscher und Heilige*.

digms of holiness represented by the human form of the saint. The high status of hagiography in communicating religious values has been well expressed by Marc van Uytfanghe's comment that hagiography is "une espèce de bible secondaire, une bible locale et contemporaine, pour ainsi dire 'actualisée.'"[2]

Of course hagiography was not the only Merovingian literature in which dreams and visions were accorded spiritual import; as we have seen, visions were documented in cultic literature such as petitions recorded at the shrines of the saints. Some nonsaintly visionaries had their experiences recorded in contexts other than the shrine, as well, in the visionary travel literature which had always found a place in the Christian tradition and which was reinforced by the popularity of Gregory the Great's *Dialogues*. The vision of the sinful monk Barontus examined in the previous chapter falls into that category, and was recorded by the monks of St.-Cyran because of its strong didacticism and emphasis on institutional identity. But visions were most commonly narrated in hagiography, and they acquired much of their meaning from this context.

How one reads the place of dreams and visions in Merovingian hagiography, and the hagiographer's purpose in recording them, however, depends on how one views the thorny issue of authenticity. Most hagiographies of Merovingian saints have been preserved in Carolingian manuscripts, leading to the suspicion voiced by positivist historians of the nineteenth century that what purported to be Merovingian hagiographies were in fact Carolingian falsifications.[3] Many Merovingian Lives have since been saved from such ignominy and reassigned by scholars to the Merovingian era based on orthography, religious practices consistent with an earlier date, and a more complex understanding of the way texts were handled by posterity. Nevertheless scholars still differ on the "reliability" of certain texts, and on specific portions of texts.[4] I have drawn on a wide array of Gallo-Roman and Merovingian hagiographies for my discussion. As far as possible, I have selected *vitae* which are Merovingian compositions or which include Merovingian material. Any exceptions to this rule are noted in the text of the next chapter, and discussions of date and authenticity of texts are to be found in the notes.

Paul Fouracre has observed that in order to understand the historicity and social context of hagiography we must also understand the relationship "be-

[2] Marc van Uytfanghe, "La bible dans les vies de saints merovingiens. Quelques pistes de recherche," in *La christianisation des pays entre Loire et Rhin (IVe–VIIe siécle)* ed. Pierre Riché p. 105 (Paris, 1993).

[3] Bruno Krusch, who edited many Merovingian texts for the *Monumenta* series, was critical of their value as sources for the Merovingian period.

[4] Ian Wood, "Forgery in Merovingian Hagiography," *Fälschungen im Mittelalter: Internationaler Kongress der Monumenta Germaniae Historica*, Munich, 16–19 September 1996, *MGH Schriften* vol. 33, *Fingierte Briefe, Frömmigkeit und Fälschung Realienfälschungen* (Hanover, 1988), pp. 369–84.

tween the conventional and the unconventional in the genre."[5] Visionary narratives drew on both the conventional and the extraordinary in Merovingian expectations of a saint. However, in the next two chapters I have sought to address these two issues independently. Chapter 6 highlights the "conventional" place of visions in Merovingian hagiography, collectively, as a structuring motif in the literature of the genre. The chapter concludes with a study of the hagiographer Baudonivia's use of visions in her portrait of Radegund of Poitiers. Chapter 7 is an examination of an exceptional woman, the visionary Aldegund of Maubeuge. Her visions were said to have been recorded according to her own account.

[5] Fouracre, "Merovingian History," p. 8.

6 Visions and the Hagiographer in Merovingian Sources

In a letter to Paulinus of Nola and his wife Therasia, Augustine pragmatically commented aloud to God, "we do not always change our plans because of visions and ecstasies: sometimes just because circumstances arise." [1] Merovingian hagiography seldom embraced such ordinary cause and effect. For Merovingian saints, supernatural dreams and visions were signs that their world was infused with divine purpose, and for their hagiographers, that the saints' success was predetermined. Visions elevated the religious significance of the saints' choices, and postulated the spiritual rewards for the faithful in heaven. In this literature intended for Christian consumption, repetition of a studied repertoire of virtues enhanced by supporting visions aided didactic function. [2] As literature intended to praise and glorify God, the saint's life provided the canvas upon which divine mercy was drawn.

Narrating divine visions was one of the ways a skillful hagiographer could draw the reader into the spiritual theatre of the holy life, dramatizing the progression of the maturing soul. Unlike ancient martyr stories which focused almost exclusively on the drama of persecution, trial, and death, hagiography emerged from the ascetic tradition and focused on the journey of the saint's soul through his or her entire life, beginning at birth (even before birth) and ending not with death but with life beyond death as witnessed miraculously at holy tombs. [3] Decisions which determined the path of that

[1] Augustine, *Ep.* 82.

[2] On hagiography and its audience see Marc van Uytfanghe, "L'hagiographie et son publique a l'époque mérovingienne," *Studia Patristica* 16:2 (1985), 54–62; he terms the genre a "people's catechism." See also Baudoin de Gaiffier, "La lecture des actes des martyrs dans la prière liturgique en occident. A propos du passionnaire hispanique," *AB* 72 (1954), 134–66.

[3] André Grabar, *Martyrium. Recherches sur le culte des reliques et l'art chrétien antique*, vol. 2: *Iconographie* (Paris, 1946), pp. 136–68; he notes that in the Gospels theophanies cluster around the beginning and end of Christ's life (and the Transfiguration between) and contrasts this with martyr stories whose theophanies are generally confined to the events culminating in

journey were often coded in the language of dreams. Thus hagiographers, determined to show their heroes imitating Christ's life, might include divine visions from the beginning of the saint's life to its end.

Though visions were considered significant events in the lives of saints for whom they were reported, they were not required for sanctity in Romano-Gallic and Merovingian hagiography. Whereas miracles were almost universally noted in *vitae*, both during the saint's lifetime and posthumously, only about one-third of Merovingian *vitae* claim that their saint had divinely inspired dreams or visions. Fewer still supply details.

Not all holy people expressed their spirituality in the language of dreams, or chose to have them revealed and recorded. Even if the saint was widely known to have received visionary revelations, a strong tradition of secrecy dictated that such things should not be revealed.[4] Hagiographers often hinted at *caelestia arcana* without any explanation of what these might be. Wandrille of Fontanelle was said to have related to the monks at his deathbed the fruits of his ecstatic vision as, "very many secret and occult mysteries" (plurima misteria secreta et absconsa), but these mysteries were not revealed to the reader. The convention of secrecy made it perfectly acceptable for Merovingian hagiographers to hint at great things while providing little or no information about them.[5] However, for hagiographers who chose to include them in their work, visions of divine assistance and intervention highlighted significant junctures in the holy life. Collectively, visionary accounts in *vitae* announce that which was common to the Merovingian perception of the saint. Yet in a few individual cases, where more information is available to us, we can uncover the specific aims of the hagiographer. Such a case is Baudonivia's *vita* of Radegund of Poitiers, examined below.

Visions in the Lives of Merovingian Saints

Merovingian hagiographers believed that the saint, as imitator of Christ and the prophets of old, was predestined to holiness.[6] God had announced to Jeremiah for example: "Before I formed you in the womb I knew you, and

---

martyrdom. On miracles at saints' tombs witnessing to life beyond death see, among many other examples, *GC* 46, 52, 58; *VP* 2.2.

[4] St. Paul, for example, did not reveal the content of his vision of the third heaven: "he heard things which cannot be told, which man may not utter." 2 Cor. 12.4.

[5] *VR* 2.20. Radegund was said to have kept her visions a secret during her lifetime except from two of her closest friends. See note 48, Chapter 5, for further examples of visionaries' concerns about secrecy.

[6] See Poulin, *L'ideal de sainteté*, p. 101, who notes that Carolingian saints come by their sanctity through inheritance and predestination. Scheibelreiter, *Der Bischof*, pp. 37–41, examines the prophetic births of holy bishops; Graus, *Volk, Herrscher*, pp. 68–69 examines the Old and New Testament precedents for the child chosen by God.

before you were born I consecrated you."[7] It was never too early to manifest this special destiny—if not at the moment of conception, then at least at
the moment when mothers first became aware of new life growing within
them. Occasionally, however, the biological parents of the saint were not always so well informed, as they discovered to their amazement when God
sabotaged their plans. The gestation of St. Germanus of Paris (d. 576) is perhaps the best Merovingian example. Germanus' mother Eusebia, wishing to
avoid having a child so soon after a previous birth, took a potion in an attempt to abort the fetus, and when that did not work, she slept on her stom-
ach hoping to smother the fetus with her body weight: "There ensued a fight
between the woman and her womb." Eusebia suffered some damage from
the experience but the baby was unharmed. "Thus was the future foretold
of the virtues of him who would be born," commented Venantius Fortunatus.[8] But Germanus' case was unusual. Most mothers of future saints were
forewarned. It was revealed to the mother of St. Nicetius, for example, that
her son would be a priest. The mother of the future saint and abbess of
St. John's convent in Arles saw in ecstatic sleep two baby doves suckling at
her breast, one white and the other dark. The deceased Caesarius of Arles
then appeared and claimed the white dove for Christ. Since she had recently
lost one of her babies, a boy, the black dove was taken to be her dead son;
the white dove was her daughter Rusticula, who became a saint.[9] According to Jonas, Columbanus' pregnant mother had a vision of the sun's rays
shining from her bosom, a portentous sign which Jonas explicated at some
length to signify the merits of the righteous and God's priests.[10] Similarly,
when pregnant with the future saint Praejectus of Clermont, his mother Eligia saw in an ecstatic vision her son exit her body from her side (*per latera*),
followed and drenched by a wave of blood.[11] Her brother, the archpriest
Peladius, interpreted the vision as signaling Praejectus' future martyrdom.
That pregnant women, whether fearful or expectant of childbirth, should

[7] Jeremiah 1.5.

[8] "Erat ergo pugna inter mulierem et viscera" and "erat hinc futura praenoscere ante fecisse
virtutem quam nasci contigerit." Venantius Fortunatus, *Vita s. Germani Parisiensis*. 2–4, ed.
Bruno Krusch, *MGH, SRM* 7 (1920), pp. 372–418; *BHL*, 3568; *CPL*, 1039. On this episode
see also Scheibelreiter, *Der Bischof*, p. 39 ff.

[9] Florentius, *Vita Rusticulae* 2, ed. Krusch, *MGH, SRM* 4 (1902), pp. 339–51. The work
is from the seventh century. See Riché, "La *Vita S. Rusticulae*," pp. 369–77; *CPL*, 2136a;
BHL, 7405.

[10] Jonas, *Vita s. Columbani discipulorumque eius Attalae, Eustasii, Burgundofarae et
Bertulfi* 1.1, ed. Krusch, *MGH, SRM* 4 (1902), pp. 64–108; *CPL*, 1115; *BHL*, 1898. The work
is seventh-century and written by a disciple.

[11] "Se vidisse per extasi quasi per latera filium suum egredi, quem post unda sanguinis sub-
secuta perfunderet. At illa in se concussa, visu tremula, cepit hinc inde ullare; quid sibi talia
haberent, cupiebat decerni." *Passio s. Praejecti episcopi et martyris Arvernensis* 1, ed. Krusch
MGH, SRM 5 (1910), p. 226. This is a near contemporary *vita* of a late seventh-century saint
(d. 675), possibly by a local monk. See also *CPL*, 2133; *BHL*, 6915–16. On the history of the
text see Fouracre and Gerberding, *Late Merovingian France*, pp. 254–60.

have dreams of their unborn child hardly needs explanation. One might suppose that such incidents would be even more likely in cases where the baby was especially wanted,[12] or not wanted as in the case of Germanus' mother. The Merovingian penchant for predestined saints made such dreams a hagiographic topos, but in one case at least, there appears to be some substance underlying the description. Eligia's prenatal dream is unusually precise. After her vision of the blood surging from her side, we are informed that, "restless and shaken by the vision, she began to move hither and thither, wailing. What, she wanted to discover, did these portents hold in store for her?" Her brother arrived and "began to search in detail for the reason she was shaking in such an unaccustomed way." Although Eligia's own interpretation of her dream is not mentioned, we learn that she was initially very distresssed. As women who died in childbirth were sometimes given postmortem casesarians from the side, Eligia may have thought her dream meant that she and perhaps her son would die in childbirth. Peladius' assurances that the bloodshed related to her son's glorious future brought her great happiness, we are told.

Once grown, the saints faced the challenge of publicly professing the religious life. The first occasion when their commitment to a religious vocation collided with the expectations of those around them occurred as they were being prepared for marriage. For both men and women the decision to renounce their anticipated social niche and their role within the family often prompted a family crisis with all its various emotions: anger at the foiling of dynastic plans, fear for the future of the elderly and younger siblings, and bewilderment at the determination of the future saint to adopt a life of poverty, chastity, and self-mortification.[13] In some cases the wishes of the family prevailed, and the saint was forcibly married and obliged to comply with dynastic obligations.[14] Others fled their homes to avoid marriage plans or were able to persuade their partners to renounce the world, although often only after children secured the family line.[15] Eventually most families became resigned to the saint's choice, and reconciliation and forgiveness ensued.

For men, the choice of an ecclesiastical career could offer a degree of pres-

[12] See Donald Weinstein and Rudolph M. Bell, *Saints and Society: The Two Worlds of Western Christendom, 1000–1700* (Chicago, 1982), p. 20.

[13] Genovefa's mother tried to box her daughter's ears. *Vita Genovefae virginis Parisiensis 7,* ed. Bruno Krusch, MGH, SRM 3 (1896) pp. 204–38. Rusticula's mother pressured her through intermediaries and gifts to leave the convent. *Vita s. Rusticula 5.*

[14] VR 1.2; *Vita Eustadiola 2–3, AASS* Iunii ii (1698); *Vita Sadalberga abbatissae Laudunensis 6,* 10, ed. Krusch, MGH, SRM 5 (1910), pp. 40–66.

[15] In *Vita sanctae Rictrudis 13–14,* Rictrude refuses a second marriage (Hucbald's version, early 900s, based on earlier texts now lost). *AASS* Maii iii (1680). Radegund tried to escape her pending marriage and persuaded her husband to let her devote herself to the religious life. VR 1.2. 2.4. See also *Vita s. Austreberthae abbatissae Pauliacensis,* ed. Johannes Mabillon, *AASS,* O.S.B. 3, i. (1639), pp. 28–39; *AASS* Feb. ii. (1658), pp. 417–29; Glodesind escaped to asylum in Metz. *Vita s. Glodesindis 8–9, AASS* Iulii vi (1729); *Vita s. Segolenae 5, AASS* Iulii v (1727).

tige and power which mitigated somewhat the radical nature of their decision, but they did not express anxiety in their dreams regarding the choice
between becoming a priest or a monk. In the seventh century especially,
these two areas of life were increasingly less oppositional than they had been
when monasticism was first introduced to Gaul, and the choice of a career
path was more often determined by social status and political connections.[16]
Many bishops were monks by training, and some bishops returned to the
cloister at the end of their lives. Monks took holy orders and priests lived
under monastic rules. St. Amandus (625–75), for example, was a missionary, a bishop, and an active participant in the monastic movement of the period. He had started his religious life as a priest in Aquitaine, but he yearned
for a wider arena in which to show his dedication to God. Unsure about the
religious path he should follow, Amandus took the first step toward finding
out by going to Rome. There, as he sat on the steps of St. Peter's, St. Peter
himself appeared to him and told him to return to Gaul to preach. Amandus
was overjoyed at the command, and after gaining papal blessing he returned
to Gaul to start his mission in the area of modern-day Belgium.[17] Amandus'
choice thus centered not on whether to be a monk or a priest, but rather on
the specific religious mission he should fulfill.

Women did not have the same options for religious service, and so their
religious individuation tended to center more on their choice of monastic life
over family and social obligations. In the case of well-born women especially, additional pressures to marry could stem from political interests—
often, according to the hagiographers, on the orders of the king himself.[18]
Vitae usually stress that these were times of urgent prayer. The virgin Glodesind of Metz (died c. 608) first rebuffed the attempts by King Childeric to
marry her off, and then those of her father, who wanted to take her to his
sister Rotlinde in Trier in the hope that a woman's persuasion could convince
Glodesind to marry. Instead Glodesind fled to Metz, where she took refuge
in the church of St. Stephen. For six days she prayed there without eating or
drinking, and on the seventh day, a Sunday, an unknown man with the face
of an angel came to her and veiled her.[19]

Once chosen by God, the saint had to secure the best way to fulfill the divine mission. For most, spiritual life was synonymous with monastic life.
Aristocratic saints usually founded monastic communities on their estates
and provided a rule to supplement their personal direction. Visions were of-

---

[16] On secular officeholding saints as a reflection of the aristocratic ideals in seventh- and
eighth-century hagiography see Prinz, "Gesellschaftsgeschichtliche Aspekte," and K. Weber,
"Kulturgeschichtliche Probleme der Merovingerzeit im Spiegel frühmittelalterliche Heiligenleben," *Studien und Mitteilungen zur Geschichte des Benediktiner-Ordens* 48 (1930), 347–403.
[17] *Vita Amandi episcopi Traejectensis* 1. 7, ed. Krusch, *MGH, SRM* 5 (1910), pp. 428–83,
composed seventh or eighth century. *CPL*, 2080; *BHL*, 332.
[18] *Vita s. Geretrudis* 1, ed. Krusch, *MGH, SRM* 2 (1888), pp. 447–74; *Vita s. Sadalberga* 10.
[19] *Vita Glodesindis abbatissa Mettis* 1, *AASS*, Iulii vi (1729), pp. 198–210; *BHL*, 3562.
Glodesind died c. 610. Her ninth-century biographer probably drew on an earlier *vita*.

ten cited as the reason for the decision to build in one place rather than another. Odilia of Hohenburg, for example, was instructed by St. John the Baptist in a vision concerning the site upon she was to erect a church in his honor, and Eparchius of Angoulême (sixth century), looking for a secluded spot to settle, walked outside the monastery walls of St. Cyran and dreamed Christ spoke to him. Nivardus, bishop of Rheims, was likewise given divine aid in choosing the site for his foundation Hautvilliers.[20]

Finding a monastic rule appropriate to the founder's needs was a serious undertaking. Many monastic rules circulated in northern France before the Carolingian period, and it is often difficult to know by which rule or collection of rules a monastery was governed. The most widely used rules were those of Benedict and Columbanus, although older rules continued to be popular; Caesarius' rule for monks, his rule for nuns, and the anonymous *regula cuisdam patris* were sometimes used in conjunction with other rules as a *regula mixta*.[21] Praejectus of Clermont, for example, instituted a triple rule for his foundation for nuns at Chamalières, which combined the Benedictine, Caesarian, and Columbanian rules.[22] Donatus of Besançon's rule for nuns likewise combined elements of the Caesarian, Benedictine, and to a lesser extent Columbanian rule.[23] The *Vita Nivardi* tells us that at Hautvilliers both the Benedictine and Columbanian rules were used.[24]

Wandrille of Fontanelle traveled far in his search for a monastic system which was right for him. His quest began when he received an angelic vision: "He was taken up in spirit by a holy angel and led to the monastery of Bobbio in that Lombard region of Italy, showing him (*ostendens ei*) all its cells, their type and how they were arranged."[25] On the strength of this vision Wandrille left everything behind him and set off for Bobbio, taking with him

[20] *Vita s. Odiliae abbatissa Hohenburgensis* 17, ed. Levison, *MGH, SRM* 6 (1913), pp. 24–50. Odilia's *vita* was written down in the form we have it in the ninth century, but the work may have drawn its information from traditional stories about the saint. *BHL*, 6271. Eparchius of Angoulême died in 581, and Gregory of Tours wrote about him in *GC* 99 and *HF* 6.8. His *vita* is first known in a ninth-century version. *Vita Eparchii Ecolismensis* 8, ed. Bruno Krusch, *MGH, SRM* 3 (1896), pp. 553–60; *BHL*, 2559. Nivardus was Bishop of Rheims in the seventh century, although the *vita*, which is known to us in a ninth-century text, is considered by Friedrich Prinz to have some value for the Merovingian period. See Prinz, *Frühes Mönchtum*, p. 137, n. 92; *Vita s. Nivardi episcopi Remensis, auctore Almanno monacho Altivillarensi* 3, ed. Wilhelm Levinson, *MGH, SRM* 5 (1910), pp. 157–71; *BHL*, 6243.

[21] Caesariaus' rules for monks and nuns are in *Oeuvres monastiques* 1, ed. Adalbert de Vogüé and Joël Courreau, *SC* 345 (1988). The *regula cuisdam patris* was also popular for use in conjunction with other rules. *PL* 66, 987–93.

[22] *Passio Praejecti* 15.

[23] Donatus of Besançon, *Regula ad virgines*, *PL* 87, 273–98, written between 630 and 655. See Prinz, *Frühes Mönchtum*, p. 80; *CPL* 1860.

[24] *V. Nivardi* 3.

[25] "Translatus est in spiritu ab angelo sancto, ductus est in monasterio qui vocatur Bobius, in regione Langobardorum qui dicitur Italia, ostendens ei omnis habitacionis eius, quomodo aut qualiter adessent." *Vita Wandregiseli abbatis Fontanellensis* 9, ed. Krusch, *MGH, SRM* 5 (1910), pp. 1–24; *CPL*, 2146; *BHL*, 8804–5.

only three young men and an ass. In a passage that anticipated the enormous influence Irish monasticism was to have on him, his hagiographer described his travels: "He left his homeland, his acquaintances at his father's house and walked, knowing not which path he would take, but through his angel the Lord showed him which path he should take."[26] At last he arrived at Bobbio and recognized it instantly as the place he had seen in his vision. He stayed there a number of years and even considered traveling on to Ireland, although he never did. His self-mortification, including immersion in icy water, witnesses his training in Irish asceticism.

From Bobbio, Wandrille moved on to Romainmoutier in the Jura, governed by its own rule, and after a lengthy stay there returned to northern Gaul to establish a monastery in the forest of Jumièges. We do not know which rule Wandrille eventually chose for his foundation, but it seems likely that he used both the Benedictine and Columbanian rules, perhaps in conjunction with others.[27] His vision of Bobbio before his travels there perhaps reflects his excited state of mind and the fervor that tales of the Irish monastic movement evidently inspired in the Frankish aristocracy, causing them to flock in droves to Irish communities.

In the early days of their foundation, monasteries were especially vulnerable to economic hardship and divisiveness. Many communities disbanded and regrouped on the death of the founder, who had been the focus for his disciples. Promoting the reputation and person of the saint after death by writing his *vita* and guarding his relics was a powerful cohesive force in the perpetuation of these potentially unstable institutions. Alert to the dangers of disintegration, saints and their hagiographers could strengthen the appeal of the monastic institution by emphasizing divine recognition of the community itself and divine guarantee of corporate salvation. Just before he died, Wandrille addressed the monks assembled around his bed. Having just emerged from an ecstatic vision in which he was told many celestial secrets and mysteries, he evidently spoke with divine authority when he promised his monks that should they maintain and obey his pastoral direction, God would always be with them and help them in times of need.[28] His final words asserted that following his lifetime example was their best security for salvation.

[26] "Exibit de terra sua et di cognatione sua et de domu patris sui et ambulabat, nesciens qua viaticum ducerit; sed Dominus per suum angelum demonstrabat ei, qua via pergere deberit." *Vita Wandregiseli* 9.

[27] André Borias argued strongly that the Benedictine rule was used at Fontanelle, in probable conjunction with that of Columbanus. "S. Wandrille, a-t-il connu S. Benoît?," *RB* 89 (1979), 7–28.

[28] *V. Wandregiseli* 18: "Cercius cognuscatis, quod si permanseritis in sermonibus meis et custodieritis, quod ego predixi vobis, ut in unitate atque karitate seu et humilitate fundati sitis, ut inter vos nulla sit dissensio, condicio vestra manere habit in perpetuo recti, et Dominus vobis erit omnibus necessitatibus aderit."

Continuity of the monastic foundation did not depend on the reputation of its founder alone but also on the abilities of his or her successors. Often founders were involved in the selection of their successor. According to most monastic rules, abbatial elections were conducted by the entire community. There were always cases, however, when the incumbent holy person wanted to make certain of being succeeded by someone who would govern the community according to his or her wishes. The founder's preference often found divine approval in a well-timed vision. Wandrille's *vita*, for example, made the succession issue clear—he was told by an angel that Godo, his nephew, would be his eventual successor.[29] Conversely, a vision could be used to attempt to upset a succession issue which had been already decided, as when Praejectus publicly related his mother's vision in an attempt to claim the bishopric of Clermont for himself over the agreed-upon candidate, Garivald.[30] In this case, however, the publication of Praejectus' vision was no match against the publication of a legal document which he himself had previously signed agreeing on Garivald. Whether such stories stemmed from the hagiographer's attempts to smooth over contentious elections after the fact, visionary narratives with elections as their focus indicate a high degree of institutional investment in the divine properties of dreaming.

As death approached, Merovingian saints looked to their ultimate union with God and their soul's release from the captivity of the body.[31] In firmly Platonic language, Venantius Fortunatus noted that in death Germanus of Paris's soul was "snatched from the body's chains" (*raptus corporeo vinculo*).[32] Likewise Balthild's hagiographer recorded that as she raised her eyes and hands to heaven, "the saint's soul was peacefully released from the body's chain."[33] Similarly, Nivardus of Rheims saw the mortal condition as the prison of the soul: "Lord God . . . take me from this vale of tears."[34] The soul was also compared to the Israelites in exile and then liberated from Egypt (a popular allusion in works of this period).[35] Audoenus, it was

[29] Ibid., 12.

[30] *Passio Praejecti* 12–13.

[31] On death, its rituals, and its language, see Alfred C. Rush, *Death and Burial in Christian Antiquity*, Studies in Christian Antiquity, 1 (Washington D. C., 1941); Philippe Ariès, *Western Attitudes toward Death from the Middle Ages to the Present*, Johns Hopkins Symposia in Comparative History, trans. Patricia M. Ranum (Baltimore, 1974), and *The Hour of Our Death*, translation of *L'homme devant la mort* by Helen Weaver (Knopf, 1981; Oxford, 1991); Braet and Verbeke, *Death in the Middle Ages*; Frederick S. Paxton, *Christianizing Death: The Creation of a Ritual Process in Early Medieval Europe* (Ithaca, N.Y., 1990).

[32] *V. Germani Paris* 205.

[33] *V. Balthildis* 14, ed. Bruno Krusch, *MGH, SRM* 2 (1888), pp. 475–508. Balthild died c. 680, and the first version of her *vita* was probably written within a decade of her death. See the introduction to the new translation of her *vita* in Fouracre and Gerberding, *Late Merovingian France*, pp. 97–118.

[34] "O domine Deus . . . eripe me de convalle lacrimarum." *V. Nivardi* 11.

[35] In an allusion hardly flattering to the Franks, Fortunatus likened the devastation of the Thuringians and Radegund's capture by King Chlothar to the exile of the Israelites into captivity. *VR* 1.2.

recorded, prayed often on his deathbed that his soul might be liberated from his body, and on his death his hagiographer commented: "Therefore, returning to Israel from Egypt, the saint's soul was carried up by angels and flew to the Lord." [36]

Deathbed visions, whether in the words of the dying saint or witnessed by those attending the scene, drew heavily on traditional images of celestial transport: the soul as dove, winging its way heavenward, and, very popular in Merovingian texts, the spirit's reception by a ball of fire hovering over the dying person's cell, commonly thought to represent Christ or his angels. Likewise, saints envisioned the ancient cosmological motif of a ladder connecting earth with heaven. Balthild saw such a ladder whose top touched the heavens in front of the altar dedicated to the Virgin Mary, and she saw herself ascending it as if accompanied by angels. [37] We see a variant on this theme in England, where at a convent at Barking a nun saw a shining figure being raised on cords brighter than gold, perhaps a reminiscence of the golden chains of Homer. [38] It was postulated that the dying person's deceased friends would be present at death to facilitate the soul's reception into heaven, and Balthild's hagiographer mused on the possibility that her soul was received by her almoner, friend, and supporter Genesius. [39] The monk Barontus, however, needed the assistance of the archangel Raphael as he passed through the demon-infested zones. [40] Having discarded the chains of the body and negotiated the treacherous journey heavenward, the soul achieved communion with God. So, while the monks around Wandrille's

[36] "Igitur rediens versus Israhel de Aegypto, anima sancta deportata ab angelis volavit ad Dominum." *Vita s. Audoini episcopi Rotomagensis* 15, ed. Wilhelm Levison, *MGH, SRM* 5 (1910), pp. 536–67; *CPL*, 2088; *BHL*, 750. According to Fouracre and Gerberding, *Late Merovingian France*, pp. 133–34, the work is probably from the seventh century even though preserved earliest in late eighth- or early ninth-century versions.

[37] *V. Balthildis* 13. The perils of climbing the ladder are described in *Passio ss. Perpetua et Felicitatis* 1,3. Mircea Eliade examined these images, especially the ladder, in his *Images and Symbols: Studies in Religious Symbolism*, trans. Philip Mairet (Princeton, 1991) pp. 48–50, 163 (originally published as *Images et Symbols* [Gallimard, 1952]). The ladder motif was also used to represent the stages of contemplative ascent to God: *VP* 10, Praef.

[38] *HE* 4, 9, ed. B. Colgrave and R. Mynors (Oxford, 1969). Shining cords are also mentioned in Pseudo-Dionysius the Areopagite, *The Divine Names* 3, trans. C. E. Rolt, Translations of Christian Literature. Series 1: Greek Texts (London, 1920). Reference to a divine cord or chain is made by Homer, *Iliad* 8.19, ed. Alexander Pope (London, 1967); Macrobius wrote that "from the Supreme God even to the bottommost dregs of the universe there is one tie, binding at every link and never broken. This is the golden chain of Homer which, he tells us, God ordered to hang down from the sky to the earth." *Somnium Scipionis* 14.15, trans. W. H. Stahl.

[39] *V. Balthildis* 14. It is indicative of the tendency for revisionist hagiographers to amplify their texts that this whimsical suggestion is related as a bona fide vision in the later version of the *vita* (B). On Balthild and Genesius see Janet Nelson, "Queens as Jezebels: The Careers of Brunhild and Balthild in Merovingian History" in *Medieval Women*, ed. Derek Baker, pp. 31–77, Studies in Church History, Subsidia 1 (Oxford, 1978), and Eugen Ewig, "Das Privileg des Bischofs Berthefrid von Amiens für Corbie von 664 und die Klosterpolitik der Königin Balthild," *Francia* 1 (1973), 63–114, esp. 107–8 and n. 86.

[40] *Visio Baronti* 4.

deathbed poured out their tears for the separation of the flesh, his hagiographer commented that "the angels exult for the union of the soul."[41]

Conveying the inner spiritual life of the saint was probably the hagiographer's most challenging task. The solution was to record external manifestations of the inner life: tears and groans, solitary prayer, heroic feats of contemplation, and mortification of the body with fasts, vigils, and physical discomforts. In similar ways visionary accounts offered an expressible external dimension to the saint's special relationship with God; they also informed outsiders of the saint's special status. Ecstasy, a removal from bodily sensation, was an obvious expression of the visionary's special if brief union with the divine. Gregory of Tours described how the tardy abbot Venantius stopped short to hear the Mass already in progress in heaven. Once released from his trancelike vision, he stepped forward and groaned.[42] Yet removal from the material world did not require an ecstatic vision because prayer and contemplation could also produce a state of removal. Audoenus, the bishop of Rouen (d. 683), so poured himself out in prayer and meditation that when he contemplated God his disciples saw a light radiating around him.[43] The enveloping sheath of light bespoke not only his privileged bond with God but also his isolation from those around him. The visible radiance of light, like the cell walls of the solitary, suggested a barrier, an intimacy of experience, which the outside observer could never penetrate.

Fortunately for hagiographers (and students of visionary literature), visionaries did sometimes describe their visions. For example, in the epicene medieval imagery of the Song of Songs, the saint enjoyed a connubial connection with the divinity. Male or female, the saint was the bride of Christ, beloved by him and awaited by him.[44] Such a union of love was only possible if a saint had truly surrendered himself or herself to God's will. In Merovingian visions, it was most common for the hagiographer to linger on the loving male God's love for his trembling female bride. Radegund of Poitiers was visited by Christ as bridegroom.[45] Berthila, the late-seventh-century abbess of Chelles, desired from her youth that she would have Christ as her spouse, and there were others like her.[46] Male saints were more likely to see Christ in the role of friend and protector, coming to their aid in times of trouble,

---

[41] *V. Wandregiseli* 20: "angeli exultant pro iunctionem anime."

[42] *Vita Patrum* 16.2.

[43] *V. Audoini* 8.

[44] On the centrality of the Song of Songs to medieval mysticism see Ann W. Astell, *The Song of Songs in the Middle Ages* (Ithaca, N.Y., 1990); Jean Leclercq, *The Love of Learning and the Desire for God: A Study of Monastic Culture* (New York, 1961).

[45] *VR* 2.20.

[46] *Vita Bertiliae abbatissae Calensis* 1, ed. Levison, MGH, SRM 6 (1913), pp. 95–109; BHL, 1287. Berthila lived c. 658–705, and the *vita* was written in the mid to late eighth century. Anstrudis, abbess of Laon, received a ring from her celestial bridegroom which could not be seen with earthly eyes. *Vita Anstrudis abbatissae Laudunensis*, 2, ed. Levison, MGH, SRM 6 (1913), pp. 64–78; BHL, 556.

guiding them in their service to God, and promising them celestial rewards.[47] For both male and female saints, visions were a consolation for a life of service and obedience, and both anticipated the nuptial blessings of the "happier vow" (*felicia vota*).[48]

As Peter Dinzelbacher has noted, vision recipients can be divided into two categories: those for whom visions appeared suddenly, spontaneously, and without expectation of the event, and those for whom visions were the culmination of much grief and prayer. As examples of the first category he mentions only male visionaries, whereas in the second some men, but above all women, have their visions preceded by long periods of prayerful and tearful supplication.[49] To a certain extent this pattern is evident already in the Merovingian period. St. Amandus saw his vision of St. Peter suddenly (*subito*), as did Barontus his vision.[50] It is rare to find examples of women whose visions were expressly said to have appeared suddenly, although they are not unknown. Columbanus' mother's vision of the future of her unborn child came to her in a "sudden sleep." [51] What is the significance of the sudden vision over the protracted wait for a vision? Why should a sudden vision be so rarely reported for female visionaries? Insofar as some saints experienced both sudden visions and long-awaited visions, the distinction may have less to do with the visionary himself than with the context in which the vision was received. One would expect a miracle-vision to appear suddenly in answer to a particular circumstance. As Wandrille arrived at the royal palace in answer to King Dagobert's summons, his clothes soiled from helping a poor man with his cart, an angel suddenly appeared, *statim apparuit*, to clean his clothes for him.[52] Barontus was conducted on a tour of heaven and hell unexpectedly, but he was a sinner who did not relish his experience. Sudden appearances were more likely to be experienced by men because men were more active in the community and there was greater scope for a miracle-vision, although miraculous visions could occur also at convents, like the nun's vision of St. Aldegund at Maubeuge taking communion.[53]

To draw too sharp a distinction between male and female spirituality, however, is to obscure an important aspect of male spirituality. Just as often as for women, visions were the reward of the male saint's lifetime of protracted yearning. For men as for women, strong emotions of love coursed beneath the surface of everyday life, always ready to burst forth in silent mo-

---

[47] See the case of Wandrille, p. 486.
[48] Fortunatus, *Ad Felicem, Carm* 3.8.29, ed. F. Leo, *MGH, AA* 4 (1881), pp. 58–59.
[49] "Von den Visionären und vor allem von den Visionärinnen der zweiten Phase dagegen haben wir nicht selten Zeugnisse daruber, daß sie ihre Visionen sehr wohl erwarteten und erhofften," Peter Dinzelbacher, *Vision und Visionsliteratur im mittelalter* (Stuttgart, 1981), p. 188.
[50] *V. Amandi* 7; *Visio Baronti* 3.
[51] *V. Columbani* 1.1.
[52] *V. Wandregiseli* 7.
[53] *V. Ald.* 1.25.

ments. Nivardus of Rheims, a bishop who had a number of visions, was "assiduous in meditating on God's law, very devoutly intent in prayer and compunction, given to watchful vigils day and night to the Lord." [54]

Descriptions of Wandrille of Fontanelle's ascetic practices depict a man rendered prostrate by his love for God. In addition to sleep deprivation and submergence in icy water, he groaned and shed daily tears. In direct reference to the Magdalene's tears and ministrations to Christ, we are told that, "his soul thrown before Jesus, he washed his feet and dried them with his hair." [55] His vision of an angel telling him that his place was reserved in heaven came to him as he endured in his devout prayers, and as death approached he cried out, "Good Jesus, free me, for I greatly desire to see you." [56] Similar sentiments were expressed by Nivardus of Rheims, who, "with his whole desire wishing to be in heaven, said with heartfelt longing, 'O Lord, my all-powerful God, true light and everlasting joy, take me from this vale of tears and by your gift of grace, allow me to come into your sight.'" [57] By contrast, Aldegund of Maubeuge, perhaps the most prolific of Merovingian visionaries, appeared to come by her experiences almost effortlessly.

Collectively, hagiographers who included dreams and visions in their accounts of saints tended to cluster them around significant junctures in the saint's life. That is not to say that dreams and visions were inserted in *vitae* indiscriminately, or that visionary accounts were necessarily fictions. Visionary fictions were probably not rare. The hagiographer's task, however, was to present visions within the context of the saint's life to address specific areas of audience interest. The visionary accounts in Baudonivia's *Vita Radegundis* are useful for viewing the hagiographer's craft because other sources permit a fairly rounded picture of the hagiographer's royal subject. Individually, however, hagiographers may have had far more complex rationales for including visions in their writings. Hagiographers generally addressed audiences that were informed about the holy person they described. Visionary accounts may have addressed very concrete concerns relating to a prospective saint. Unfortunately, we rarely have sufficient information about the hagiographer and the saint to discern fully what those concerns might have been. Baudonivia's *Vita Radegundis*, however, described a saintly queen whose life is known to us from other sources. The visions told in this *vita* can be linked to specific events in Radegund's life and to audience concern about her monastic foundation. Baudonivia's work reveals that ha-

[54] *V. Nivardi* 3: "in legis Dei meditatione assiduus, orationi et conpunctioni devotissime intentus, excubiis Domini diurnis et nocturnis vigiliis deditus."
[55] *V. Wandregiseli* 8: "mens eius ad Iesum iacebat, pedes rigabat et crine tergebat."
[56] "Cum in oratione devotissime . . . perdurarit"; "O Iesu boni, libera me, quia multum desidero videre te." Ibid., 12, 18.
[57] *V. Nivardi* 11: "toto desiderio cupiens in caelestibus esse, cum maximo affectu cordis loquebatur: 'O domine Deus meus omnipotens, lumen verum et perhenne gaudium, eripe me de convalle lacrimarum et dono gratie tue ad tuum fac desiderabilem pervenire conspectum.'"

giographers were aware that including visionary accounts in hagiography
could greatly enhance their subject's reputation.

The Hagiographer's Craft: Visions in
Baudonivia's *Life of St. Radegund*

Radegund was a princess of the Thuringian royal house who, after some
years as queen of the Franks, retired from public life to found and enter a
convent in Poitiers.[58] The documentation for her life and cult is relatively
abundant, and enables the interests and motives of her two hagiographers to
be known with an unusual degree of clarity. Her visions have received little
scholarly attention, however.[59]

According to Gregory of Tours, the young Radegund was captured by
King Chlothar of the Franks in his war against the Thuringians in 531, and
was subsequently married to him.[60] At the royal palace at Athies, Radegund
was groomed for her future position as queen and educated in letters. Catholic ritual was an important element in her early years, and this influence intensified during her unhappy marriage.[61] After about six years of infertile
marriage to Chlothar, and after the death of her younger brother, possibly
on her husband's orders, Radegund fled the court and was consecrated deaconess by Medardus, bishop of Noyon.[62] For about a year she lived at Saix,

---

[58] See Venantius Fortunatus, *Vita Radegundis* (hereafter *VR* 1), and Baudonivia, *Vita Rade-
gundis* (hereafter *VR* 2), both ed. Krusch, *MGH*, *SRM* 2 (1888), pp. 358–95; and Venantius
Fortunatus, *Opera poetica*, *MGH*, *AA* 4, ed. Fridericus Leo (1881). Studies of the saint include
Brian Brennan, "St. Radegund and the Early Development of Her Cult at Poitiers," *Journal of
Religious History* 13 (1985), 340–54; Wemple, *Women in Frankish Society*; Sabine Gäbe,
"Radegundis: Sancta, Regina, Ancilla. Zum Heiligkeitsideal der Radegundisviten von Fortu-
nat und Baudonivia," *Francia* 16:1 (1989) pp. 1–30; Bonnie Effros, "Images of Sanctity: Con-
trasting Descriptions of Radegund by Fortunatus and Baudonivia and Gregory of Tours,"
UCLA Historical Journal 10 (1990), 38–58; Lynda L. Coon, *Sacred Fictions: Holy Women and
Hagiography in Late Antiquity* (Philadelphia, 1997), 120–41; Etienne Delaruelle, "Sainte
Radegonde, son type de sainteté et la chrétienté de son temps," *Etudes mérovingiennes. Actes
des journées de Poitiers, 1–3 mai, 1952* (Paris, 1953), pp. 65–74; Graus, *Volk, Herrscher*; René
Aigrain, *Sainte Radegonde (vers 520–87)* (Paris, 1918).
[59] Radegund's visions are briefly considered in de Nie, *Views*, pp. 238–33, and Brennan,
"Deathless Marriage and Spiritual Fecundity."
[60] *HF* 3.7.
[61] Fortunatus described Radegund's precocious piety in *VR* 1.2. It is likely that Radegund
was Catholic from birth—there is no mention of conversion from Arianism. See Aigrain, *Ste.
Radegonde*, for a discussion of Radegund's early life, and Ian Wood, "The Frontiers of Western
Europe: Developments East of the Rhine in the Sixth Century," in *The Sixth Century: Production, Distribution and Demand*, ed. Richard Hodges and William Bowden, pp. 231–53, The
Transformation of the Roman World, 3 (Leiden, 1998).
[62] Gregory of Tours contends that Radegund's brother was killed on her husband's orders.
Fortunatus, however, states that Chlothar was innocent of the murder, perhaps in response
to Chlothar's later position as benefactor of Radegund's convent. Aigrain, *Ste. Radegonde*,
pp. 46–47 suggested that Radegund's brother may have been the focus of the ill-fated Thuringian uprising of 555. If this is true, Radegund had reason to fear for her own life as a possible
accomplice. If one accepts this late date for the murder, after which Radegund is said to have

caring for sick women. She progressed on to Tours and the protection of St. Martin's tomb on the news that her husband wished to reclaim her as his wife. Bishop Germanus of Paris was able to convince Chlothar to relinquish his claims, and Radegund retired to Poitiers, where she established a convent endowed by the king. In 569 the convent acquired a relic of the True Cross from Constantinople and was renamed Holy Cross in its honor. Circa 573 her convent adopted Caesarius of Arles' rule for nuns.[63] She lived at the convent for the remainder of her life, observing the strict claustration provided by the rule.

Two hagiographies were composed in the Merovingian period. The first was written by her close friend and future bishop of Poitiers, Venantius Fortunatus, some time after her death in 587. A second was written c. 605 by Baudonivia, a nun at her convent, by request of the abbess. A number of circumstances made a second *vita* desirable. First, Venantius' use of Sulpicius Severus' *Vita Martini* as a model for his *Vita Radegundis* resulted in a focus on eremitic ideals and thus did insufficient justice to Radegund's founding of a bustling monastic community.[64] Baudonivia's *Vita Radegundis* focused more closely on Radegund's life in the convent and supplied information

---

fled court, then the founding of the convent would have to be placed significantly later than the 552–53 date normally ascribed. Radegund's consecration as deaconess was in open violation of the ruling of the Council of Chalcedon and its reiteration in Gallic councils, such as Orleans 2 (533), 17–18. The precise function of deaconesses in the Gallic and Frankish church has been discussed in a number of publications. See Wemple, *Women in Frankish Society*, pp. 127–48, 136–141, on the fluctuation in womens' permitted role in pastoral and liturgical activities; René Metz, *La consacration des vierges* (Paris, 1954), examines the consecration of female religious in the ancient and medieval world; see also Roger Gryson, *The Ministry of Women in the Early Church* (Collegeville, Minn., 1976). Catholic historians traditionally claimed that Radegund's title was strictly honorary, conferred erroneously or under pressure by Medard of Noyon, and did not correspond to any real function within the Church. It should not be overlooked, however, that Radegund's first task after consecration as deaconess was to set up a hospital for poor women. Care for sick women was a central function of deaconesses in the early Church. Radegund kept her focus on women, translated into a strictly monastic form, as expressed in a letter she addressed to seven bishops. *HF* 9.42.

[63] Radegund herself recorded the history of her convent's founding in her letter to seven bishops of the metropolitan district of Tours. *HF* 9.41. The document is sometimes referred to as Radegund's "will" or "testament," although it was clearly written early in her monastic life. Gregory stated that the letter was written on her founding of the convent, but it must be later since it refers to the protection of the Holy Cross, suggesting a date after that relic's acquisition in 573. Her letter also mentions the Caesarian Rule adopted for the community c. 573. It cannot be later than 573 because it was signed by Gregory of Tours' predecessor Euphronius, who died in that year. Dating the letter is further complicated by the fact that it is normally appended to the resolutions of the Council of Tours which met in 567, the last recorded occasion when the bishops mentioned were assembled. There is no reason to believe that the letter was presented to the bishops at that time, and the internal evidence of the letter argues for the later date, probably 573.

[64] Jacques Fontaine, "Hagiographie et politique de Sulpice Sévère à Venance Fortunat," *La christianisation des pays entre Loire et Rhin (ive-viie siècle)*, ed. Pierre Riché, pp. 113–40, Actes du Colloque de Nanterre (3–4 mai, 1974), Histoire Religieuse de la France, vol. 2 (Paris, 1993).

that Fortunatus had omitted, including Radegund's relic acquisitions which were an important part of the convent's endowment and made it a famous pilgrimage site. The second *vita* was also written in response to a scandalous revolt at the convent in 589 which had publicly besmirched the saint's reputation.[65] Radegund's visionary experiences were recorded only in this later *vita*, and they must be seen in the light of subsequent attempts to consolidate spiritual validation for Radegund's foundation.

According to Baudonivia, Radegund had three visions. The first vision occurred c. 552, in the first year of her consecration to the religious life. A priest named Magnus had arrived at Saix, bringing the queen some relics of St. Andrew and other unspecified saints. He placed them on the altar, leaving Radegund to keep a vigil overnight. As she prayed she was overcome by a light sleep (*parvus sopor*) and heard a voice saying to her, "Know this, blessed one: not only are the relics which Magnus brought assembled here, but also those which you collected at Athies." When she opened her eyes she saw the man who had announced the vision, shining splendidly.[66] Although the most beautiful man (*vir splendidissimus*) was not identified, the saint's prayers which preceded the vision suggested that it was a divine figure. Baudonivia's description of the vision, however, is obscure. We are informed that Radegund did not see the splendid figure in her sleep but as she opened her eyes (unless she dreamed that she opened her eyes), but was aware of the voice in her sleep announcing the message. The account in the *vita*—the miraculous reassembly of relics which she had lost at Athies—was related immediately prior to Baudonivia's description of Radegund's initiative, conceived much later in her life, to acquire a relic of Mamas of Caesarea from Jerusalem.[67] Thus the vision announced the importance of relic acquisition to the queen's holy reputation.

The other two visions recorded by Baudonivia are of greater significance to the culture of Merovingian visions. They are important not only in establishing iconographic modalities for visions in Merovingian hagiography but they are also, by virtue of the hagiographer's unique literary transparency, visions whose influences and sources can be reconstructed with a high degree of success. The first vision, of a Christ-ship, occurred during Radegund's time at Saix, which was also in the first year after her conversion. The saint's final vision, of Christ as bridegroom, occurred in 586, one year before her death. The earliest vision authorized her conversion to the monastic life, and the last confirmed the spiritual path she had taken. Both visions promoted the spiritual value of the life she had established at her convent.

---

[65] Gregory of Tours gives a contemporary account of the revolt and its aftermath in *HF* 9.39–42, 10.15–17, 20. Georg Scheibelreiter, "Königstochter im kloster. Radegund (d. 587) und der Nonnenaufstand von Poitiers (589)," *MIÖG* 87 (1979), 9–37, offers the most substantial study.

[66] VR 2.13.

[67] Moreira, "Provisatrix optima," pp. 285–305.

The Christ-ship

"In the first year of her conversion [to the ascetic life], she saw in a vision a ship in the shape of a man, and in each of his members men were seated, and she herself was seated at his knees; he said to her: 'At this moment you sit at my knees, hereafter you will have a seat in my heart.' Thus she was shown the grace she would later enjoy." [68]

This short vision combined two important images which had a long history in patristic literature. The first was the ship, often associated with Christ or the Church, sailing over the stormy sea of the world and its snares. The ship protects the faithful and ensures their salvation.[69] Radegund found herself inside the ship, and so was saved by her monastic profession. This image of the Christ-ship can usefully be compared with another passage in Baudonivia's *vita* which describes the miraculous salvation of Radegund's emissaries who were in danger of shipwreck on their return to Gaul.[70] As the ship was foundering, the envoys cried out to Radegund to save them, since they were engaged on her holy business. At that moment a dove appeared in the middle of the ocean and circled the craft "three times in the name of the Trinity." One of Radegund's men, Banisaios, extended his hand upward and three feathers fell from the dove's tail onto the water, "and a great calm came over the high sea." [71] Radegund's servants, Baudonivia continues, had been brought back to the world of the living from the portals of death (*mortis ianua*).

Baudonivia's story of the hazardous sea journey back to Gaul was crafted to echo the biblical story of Noah and the ark. For like the animals saved in Noah's ark from the perils of the flood, so Christians are saved by the ark of Christ and his Church. In Baudonivia's story the storm at sea lasted forty days and forty nights, like the rain that fed the flood.[72] Then just as the dove brought to the ark evidence of divine clemency, so the dove appeared to the beleaguered ship to calm the sea and bring them safely to land.[73] The dove was also the symbol of the Holy Spirit, "which the saint always loved in her heart."

The second aspect of the image, the mystical body of Christ in which

[68] VR 2.3: "in primo anno conversionis suae, vidit in visu navem in hominis specie, et in totis membris eius sedentes homines, se vero in eius genu sedentem; qui dixit ei: 'Modo in genu sedes, adhuc in pectore meo sessionem habebis.' Ostendebatur ei gratia, qua fruitura erat."

[69] Hugo Rahner, *Symbole der Kirche. Die Ekklesiologie der Väter* (Salzburg, 1964), pp. 504–47.

[70] VR 2.17.

[71] VR 2.17: "et facta est tranquillitas magna in medio mari"; navigation in this period usually relied on keeping sight of land by hugging the coastline. The ship was in great danger "in medio mari."

[72] Genesis 7.4,12.

[73] Genesis 8.8–11. On patristic interpretations of the dove and the raven in the account of Noah see Augustine, *Contra Faustum libri xxxiii* 12.20, ed. Josephus Zycha, *Sancti Aureli Augustini*, CSEL 25 (1891), pp. 249–797, and Tertullian, *De baptismo.* 8.4, ed. A. Reifferscheid and G. Wissowa, *Tertulliani opera*, vol. 1 CSEL 20, (1890), pp 201–18.

Radegund found a place, is also related to the Noah story.[74] Noah's ark was interpreted as Christ's body in patristic exegetical writings.[75] The fifth-century disciple of Augustine, Quodvultdeus, wrote a commentary on the seventh promise in book 1 of his *De promissionibus* which drew together all the elements in Baudonivia's two accounts.[76] He related that the Word of God, Christ, is like the ark, and from the wound in his side issues the blood of salvation, just as from the port of the ark the dove issued forth and returned (unlike the "heretical" crow which did not). In Quodvultdeus' interpretation we encounter all the motifs mentioned in Radegund's vision: the ship, the swelling sea, the redemptive figure of Christ in the form of an ark, and finally the significance of the dove.[77] It is impossible to know whether Baudonivia was familiar with Quodvultdeus' commentary in particular, but she was certainly aware of the symbolic elements in her tale. Radegund's vision of the ship which is the mystical body of Christ and the highly stylized biblical interpretation of the threatened shipwreck suggest that at the very least this kind of devotional literature provided the substance for exercises in meditation for the nuns of the Holy Cross.

But ultimately Radegund's Christ-ship vision was a vision about the body: Radegund's body and Christ's body. Radegund was seated at the knee of the Christ-ship, but was told that later she would be seated in the Christ-ship's heart. Radegund had evidently found salvation from the perils of her worldly existence in her refuge in the church, and her place at the knees of the Christ-ship undoubtedly referred to the penitential life she must henceforth lead, as she embarked on her journey as a nun. Radegund saw herself in Christ's knees because she must do penance on her knees. She would be accepted into Christ's heart because that was what *her* heart desired. The severity of Radegund's bodily self-mortification was renowned. Fortunatus tried to coax her out of its worst excesses, but Radegund's vision reflected a certitude that a more exalted position awaited as a reward of her penitential life. In that hope, Radegund's vision of the Christ-ship defined a horizontal image of spiritual progress which was very different from the more familiar vertical

[74] Leo Steinberg, *The Sexuality of Christ in Renaisssance Art and in Modern Oblivion* (New York, 1983; 2 ed. Chicago, 1996), discusses the mystical body of Christ through the middle ages to Renaissance art.

[75] See Augustine, *Contra Faustum* 12.16, CSEL 25, p. 345; *Civ. Dei* 15.26: "The actual measurements of the ark, its length, height, breadth, symbolize the human body, in the reality of which Christ was to come, and did come, to mankind."

[76] Quodvultdeus, *De promissionibus et praedicationibus Dei*, ed. René Braun, CC 60 (1976). Quodvultdeus' work identified foreshadowings of Christ in the Old Testament. He drew heavily on Augustine for his Christological interpretation of Noah's ark, especially Augustine's *Contra Faustum* 12.20.

[77] *De promissionibus* 1.7: "suspensus in cruce nostrum omne pretium ex suo latere, tamquam per ostium arcae, pretiosum sanguinem fuderit: ex quo columba ecclesia tanto sanguine dotata processit. Per quod et corvuus haereticus exiens humani cadaveris cupiditate naufragus ad arcam ecclesiam redire noluit." The figurative use of the human body was not confined to biblical exegesis. Quodvultdeus, expanding on Augustine, wrote about different heresies as relating to the anatomy of a leper's body. Ibid., 2.6.

images of cosmic ascent. The vision promised that Radegund's spiritual life would be a journey, a pilgrimage. The scene was set for her final vision, in which the promise of the first vision was fulfilled: she would no longer reside in Christ's knees, but in his heart.

Christ the Bridegroom

Baudonivia described Radegund's final vision thus: "A year before her passing, she saw in a vision her place prepared for her. A richly dressed young man came to her, very beautiful, and being of youthful age he gently touched her and spoke to her in soft conversation. She, mindful of her modesty, rejected his blandishments. Then he said to her, 'Why do you cry to me inflamed by desire and with such tears, seeking with groans, petitioning with such fulsome prayers, and afflicting yourself for me with such tortures, when I am always with you? Know this, my precious jewel, that you are the foremost gem in my diadem.' There is no doubt that her visitor was the one to whom she was so devoted while in the flesh, and he showed to her the glory which she would enjoy in heaven."[78]

There are a number of striking elements in this account which bear examination: the physical beauty of the Christ apparition, his youth, and his sartorial sumptuousness. Radegund's vision is fully in keeping with a long-standing tradition which envisioned Christ as physically beautiful. Christ was the spiritual bridegroom yearned for by the saints and by the Church: "My beloved is all radiant and ruddy, distinguished among ten thousand . . . His speech is most sweet, and he is altogether desirable. This is my beloved and this is my friend, O daughters of Jerusalem."[79] Christ embodied all virtues, was the summation of all essence, life, wisdom, light, and beauty. Yet running parallel to this aesthetic of Christ's beauty was a countertradition which emphasized his ugliness.[80] In Isaiah, Christian writers discovered the "Man of Sorrows" whose appearance was "marred, beyond human semblance, and his form beyond that of the sons of men."[81] As in the case of

[78] *VR* 2.20: "Ante annum transitus sui, vidit in visu locum sibi paratum. Venit ad eam iuvenis praedives, pulcherrimus, et quasi iuvenilem habens aetatem, qui suavi tactu blandoque conloquio dum cum ea loqueretur, illa de se zelans, blandiciam ipsam respuebat. Qui dixit ei: 'Quid me desiderio accensa cum tantis lacrimis rogas, gemens requiris, fusis precibus poscis, pro me tanto cruciatu affligis, qui semper tibi assisto? Tu, gemma preciosa, noveris, te in diademate capitis mei primam esse gemmam.' Nulli dubium est, quod ipse eam visitavit, cui se tota devotione tradidit vivens in corpore, et gloriam, qua fruitura erat, ei ostendit."

[79] Song of Solomon 5.10, 5.16.

[80] Leclercq summarized conflicting views on Christ's physical appearance in "Beauté ou laideur du Christ," *DACL* 7:2 (1927), 2397–2400. See also J. Kollwitz, "Christus, Christusbild," in *Lexikon der christlichen Ikonographie*, vol. 1, ed. Engelbert Kirschbaum and Günter Bandman (Rome, 1968), cols. 355–71. Benz, *Die Vision*, pp. 517–39, examined the dual tradition in the visions and art of the high middle ages, and traced the reassertion of the image of the suffering Christ in art and visions of the later period. He linked the supplanting of the beautiful Christ image by the crucified Christ in popular imagination to widespread availability of the account of Martin of Tours' Christ-vision as related in the *Legenda Aurea* (pp. 532–34).

[81] Isaiah 52.14.

prophets, and not a few saints, the embodiment of the conflict between the ways of God and the ways of the world set up a figure to be rejected by his own generation. This theological perspective emphasized Christ's alienation from the aesthetic principles of the world: he had "no form or comeliness that we should look at him, and no beauty that we should desire him." [82]

In the absence of concrete documentation on Christ's physical appearance, and the ambiguity in Old Testament texts which were believed to foreshadow Christ's ministry, Christ's appearance was determined by theological opinion. Both images, of Christ's beauty and his ugliness, were orthodox and both appear in visionary accounts of the late antique period.

Radegund's Christ was richly dressed, and this image was predominant in the vision accounts of the Merovingian period as well as in the art of the eastern and western Mediterranean. [83] In the Gallic context, however, the royal representation of Christ in visions did not go uncontested. The most famous Gallic Christ-vision was St. Martin's, as described by Sulpicius Severus in his *Vita Martini*. That image adhered strongly to an alternative tradition which it is worthwhile to reprise briefly here.

At Amiens, Christ appeared to Martin in the guise of the beggar with whom Martin had shared his cloak. But Martin was also visited by a false Christ. A figure swathed in bright light appeared to him, gloriously attired: "clothed in royal raiment, wreathed with a diadem made of gold and gems, shod in golden shoes, with a serene countenance and joyful face." [84] According to Sulpicius, Martin was at first silent before the apparition, but prompted by the Holy Spirit to discern the true nature of the apparition, he countered, "The Lord Jesus did not foretell that he would come clothed in purple, and with a shining diadem; I shall not believe Christ has come unless he comes in the dress and appearance of his passion, showing the marks of the Cross." Martin exposed the vision as false and seemingly condemned the regal form in which the vision came. For the ascetic, Christ would come bearing the signs of his humility, not in pomp and pride. Radegund's Christ vision, however, appeared in the very image of the demonic figure which Martin had rejected so strenuously. Christ was described as being very rich (*praedives*), and told Radegund that she was the most precious jewel in his crown. The contrasting images of Christ are particularly striking when one considers that the *Vita s. Martini* was the most influential Gallic *vita* of the period. One might ask how, in Baudonivia's work, Radegund could be shown putting her trust in a vision whose outward appearance St. Martin had condemned. But it is clear from Sulpicius' account that Martin was re-

[82] Ibid., 53.2.

[83] Differences in art include a bearded versus unbearded Christ, Christ the shepherd (common to catacomb art), and Christ the king (popular especially in the East). Artistic evidence from Gallic and Frankish churches is almost nonexistent, but literary descriptions of church interiors suggest that Gallic depictions of religious scenes did not vary greatly from those visible today in the sixth-century mosaics of San Vitale in Ravenna.

[84] *VM* 24.4: "veste etiam regia indutus, diademate ex gemmis auroque redimitus, calceis auro inlitis, sereno ore, laeta facie."

acting only to a particular occasion and not making a broad iconological statement. Martin justified his rejection of the vision based on outward dress and appearance, but it was not the external appearance which informed Martin of its demonic origin but his own powers of discernment through the agency of the Holy Spirit. Indeed, one might argue that Martin needed the power of discernment precisely because the vision conformed so precisely to prevailing and accepted depictions of Christ.[85] Indeed, as Sulpicius informs us, the vision had the appearance of anything but the Devil (*ut nihil minus quam diabolus putaretur*).[86] The *Vita s. Martini* did not therefore dismiss one conception of the physical appearance of Christ in favor of another, but rather played off one tradition against another in order to highlight Martin's powers.

Beauty as an attribute of divinity and sanctity was an entrenched idea which pervades Gallic and Merovingian hagiographic literature, even in cases where a saint followed St. Martin in being unkempt in appearance. We are told of the sixth-century saint Sigiramnus that a certain woman who did not receive the disheveled pilgrim into her home later regretted her decision, for as she noted to her husband, although his clothes were contemptible, "outwardly his face shone like the face and countenance of angels."[87] The authors of the second *vita* of Caesarius of Arles recalled that just as his life was holy, so was his appearance pure and sweet, "his face shines as does his soul . . . so that not without merit he might appear outwardly as he bore himself inwardly."[88] Such examples are numerous, and they reflect the belief that purity and beauty are indivisible even at a superficial level.[89]

Perhaps one of the most intriguing attributes of Radegund's Christ is Baudonivia's assertion regarding his youth. This is not the youthfulness of an infant at his mother's knee. The intention appears to have been to describe an adolescent Christ, displaying feminine beauty.[90] This image of a richly dressed youth is very different from that common in the eastern and western Mediterranean art of the period, where Christ was usually depicted in paintings, mosaics, coins, and funeral art as the mature Christ, as teacher and king of heaven. Early Christian images had depicted Christ as a youthful, beardless shepherd, but never bejewelled. Yet it might be argued that Christ's youthfulness was important to convey the innocence of the intimate mo-

---

[85] Prominent examples of Christ depicted in royal purple in the west include a series of mosaics in the basilica of San Apollinare Nuovo and the apse mosaic of San Vitale, both in Ravenna. Even the good shepherd mosaic in Galla Placidia's mausoleum in same city has Christ clothed in purple and gold.

[86] *VM* 24.4.

[87] *V. Sigiramni* 25: "facies tamen eius ac vultus ceu facies angeli resplendebat exterius."

[88] *V.Caesarii* 2.35: "Resplendat cum anima vultus eius . . . ut non inmerito extrinsecus appararet, quod intrinsecus gerebatur."

[89] On medieval aesthetics see Umberto Eco, *Art and Beauty in the Middle Ages* (New Haven, 1986), and Edgar de Bruyne, *Études D'Esthétique Médievale*, 3 vols. (Bruges, 1946).

[90] It was believed by some that Christ bore a resemblance to his mother, especially in the lower part of his face. See Kollwitz, "Christus, Christusbild."

ments he and Radegund shared. Christ's masculinity was more than historical—it was theological. A mature Christ appearing to a nun vowed to chastity and caressing her required more than mere delicacy in the hagiographer's treatment of her material. Consequently Baudonivia portrayed Christ as a youthful figure stripped of the impropriety of his masculinity, a person to excite almost maternal tenderness, in effect a husband innocent of concupiscence.

The youth of the Christ-vision must be seen in the context and dynamics of the vision itself. Radegund's Christ appeared to her as a bridegroom. He approached her speaking softly and caressing her gently. Radegund's first reaction was modesty; she rejected the overtures of the apparition, which she took for *blandicia*.[91] Her actions acknowledged the dangers in acceding too readily to the demands of an apparition. The figure identified himself more clearly, gently chiding her for her many tears. He promised her that she was the finest jewel in his crown, an explicit if somewhat modified echo of her earlier vision of the Christ-ship in which she sat at his knees but was promised a better place in his heart.

Though the youthful, richly adorned bridegroom figure of Christ was not uncommon in later medieval visions of the heavenly bridegroom, it is important to remember how fresh it was to sixth-century aesthetics and theology. Radegund's experience of her bridegroom was of unparalleled intimacy. In most earlier visions Christ was represented as a distant figure, surrounded by ranks of angels, awesome and shielded from view.[92] In Saturus' vision in the *Passio SS Perpetuae et Felicitatis* Christ caressed the martyrs' faces, but he was still a distant figure. By contrast there is domesticity in the cosy little scene in Radegund's cell. Christ's visitation was a private assurance of love for his bride, hardly cataclysmic and hardly an event of historic importance, but nearer to the desire of the ascetic than any flamboyant supernatural experience. As she accepted Christ for who he was, Radegund's modesty vanished in the warmth of her spiritual husband's presence, as his caresses now fell within the permitted scope of their intimacy.

Radegund's visions as recorded by her hagiographer were very much an expression of prevailing theological and scriptural motifs. As we have noted, Baudonivia's description of Radegund's visions was carefully attuned to ecclesiological and Christological images formulated in exegesis. Yet Baudonivia's descriptive narratives also show the influence of more recent, sixth-century literature which we know to have been available to her, and with which Radegund was also probably familiar.

In Gregory of Tours' *Vita Iuliani* it is recorded that a paralyzed woman

---

[91] *Blandicia* had negative theological connotations in patristic and hagiographic literature; it was through the serpent's *blandicia* that Eve fell. Radegund rejected the false flatteries of the world (*mundi falsa blandimenta*). VR 2.5.

[92] VP 12.3: In a dream he saw the seraphim who "shadowed the divine majesty with their wings."

named Fedamia had a vision of St. Julian of Brioude and was cured. As Giselle de Nie has noted, there are similarities among Fedamia's vision, the vision of an anonymous nun at the Holy Cross convent, and Radegund's vision of Christ.[93] Noteworthy in Fedamia's story is her description of the apparition: "She said he was princely in stature, in shining raiment, uncommonly elegant with a smiling face, and long golden hair. He was of easy gait, had a melodious tone, frank speech, and was very softly spoken. And the whiteness of his skin shone greater than lilies, so that of the thousands of men whom she had seen, she had never seen his like."[94] De Nie remarks on the common elements in descriptions of the idealized spiritual bridegroom, especially his manly refinement and kindness which bring the visionary to her "inner centre" which is "the essence of all bridal mysticism."[95] Just as important, however, is the noble quality of this spiritual ideal. The prominence of noble attributes in the Romano-Gallic and Merovingian saintly ideal need not be repeated here; the literature on the subject is extensive.[96] But it is interesting to note how the beauty of the saints and of Christ mirrored ideals of noble beauty which transcended gender. For example, Hilary of Poitiers' proposed bride was described as a noblewoman of exceptional beauty: a woman "whose nobility would reach to the skies, whose beauty would surpass comparison to roses and lilies . . . of unbelievably outstanding wisdom, of such sweetness that golden honey is less highly esteemed, maintaining unblemished modesty and fanning the flames with sweet scent, a treasure without defect."[97] This could be the description of any saint, male or female. Indeed Hilary himself, later venerated as a saint, was described as an "immensely rich, noble, and beautiful youth."[98] Baudonivia's description of Christ's physical appearance was clearly inspired by the androgynous ideals of noble beauty prevalent in the literature of the time.

The vision of an anonymous nun at the Holy Cross convent described by Gregory of Tours in his *Historia Francorum* provides an obvious Frankish

[93] De Nie, *Views*, pp. 237–39.
[94] "Dicebat, eum statura esse procerum, veste nitidum, elegantia eximium, vultu hilarem, flava caesarie, inmixtis canis, incessu expeditum, voce liberum, allocutione blandissimum, candoremque cutis illius ultra lilii nitorem fulgere, ita ut de multis milibus hominum, quae saepe vidisset, nullum similem conspicaret." *Liber de passione et virtutibus sancti Iuliani martyris*, ed. Bruno Krusch, *MGH, SRM* 1.2 (1885), pp. 112–34.
[95] De Nie, *Views* pp. 237–39.
[96] On "Adelsheilige" see Graus, *Volk, Herrscher*; Prinz, *Frühes Mönchtum*, pp. 496–501; Karl Bosl, "Der 'Adelsheilige' Idealtypus und Wirklichkeit, Gesellschaft und Kultur im Merowingerzeitlichen Bayern des 7 und 8 Jhds.," *Speculum Historiale* (1965), 167–87; Scheibelreiter, *Der Bischof*, pp. 16–28. St. Martin provided an alternative model but not one much in evidence in the Merovingian period, in part because of the aristocratic status of those who embraced the ascetic and episcopal life, and in part because of the tendency of hagiographers to ascribe noble birth to saints even when their status was unknown.
[97] Fortunatus, *V. Hilarii* 19: "cuius nobilitas caelos ascenderet, pulchritudo rosarum et lilii comparationem praecederet . . . sapientia incomprehensibilis emineret, dulcedo favi mella postponeret, pudicitia incontaminata persisteret, odor suavitate flagraret, thesauri sine defectione constarent."
[98] Ibid., 18: "iuvenis nobilissimus praedives pulcherrimus."

precedent for the connubial relationship between Christ and Radegund. Although Christ did not make a personal appearance in the vision, he sent a gift to the nun of a "queenly robe" covered with light, gold, and jewels. "It is your husband who sends you this gift." [99] The nun was so affected by her experience that she asked to be walled up inside her cell. Her request was granted, and Radegund led her there by the hand. Another nun, Disciola, who was the niece of the visionary Salvius of Albi, was visited three times by the archangel Michael on the day of her death. [100] The nuns at Holy Cross convent were evidently accustomed to celestial visions. What was special about the Holy Cross nunnery which explains the prominence of such accounts?

About the year 573, Radegund adopted Caesarius of Arles' *Regula ad virgines* for her convent. Caesarius had written the rule as a guide for his sister Caesaria's convent of St. John at Arles. Its prologue gives clear expression to the desire for a visitation from Christ: "Implore by assiduous prayer the visitation of the son of God, so that afterwards you can say with confidence: 'We have found him whom our soul has sought'" They were also exhorted to "shine forth among the most precious gems of the Church." [101] The significance of these words is clear when one considers that the convent's rule would be the single most familiar text to the nuns apart from the scriptures. Elsewhere, in a sermon, Caesarius emphasized the connubial aspect of Christian devotion to Christ for both men and women, religious and lay: they "should not doubt that they may be espoused to Christ. For Christ is to be understood as the spouse, not of bodies, but of souls." [102] This is not to suggest that Caesarius expected or encouraged the nuns to expect supernatural visions, but his insistence that they fix their gaze on a bridal image of Christ during contemplation may have provoked them. No visions of Christ to women in this period reflect the image of Christ crucified.

Baudonivia's hagiographic methodology, which relied heavily on piecing together borrowed phrases from earlier hagiographic writings, allows us to trace her own devotional reading and its influence on her description of the visions. We have already noted Fortunatus' description of Hilary of Poitiers as a "most noble, most rich, most beautiful youth" (*iuvenis nobilissimus praedives pulcherrimus*), which is very close to Baudonivia's description of Christ. (The rest of Baudonivia's *vita* incorporated similar reminiscences from Fortunatus' *Life of Hilary of Poitiers*.) Baudonivia was also very

---

[99] *HF* 6.29.

[100] Ibid.

[101] "Iugiter in monasterii cellula residentes visitationem Filii Dei assiduis orationibus implorate, ut postea cum fiducia possuis dicere: 'Invenimus quem quaesivit anima nostra.' . . . orante pro me sanctimonia vestra, ut inter pretiosissimas Ecclesiae gemmas micantem favor divinus et praesentibus repleat bonis, et dignum reddat aeternis." *Regula ad virgines*, Prologue. The liturgy for the consecration of virgins also stressed the spiritual marriage of the nun to Christ. Metz, *La consacration*, pp. 117–24.

[102] *Sermo* 155.

influenced by Gregory of Tours' depictions of holy people. Her portrayal of a gentle, soft-spoken Christ recalls Gregory's description of St. Julian's very soft speech (*allucutione blandissimum*) and his reference to Brachio the hermit "who was soft in conversation and gentle of manner." [103] These examples alert us to look beyond other vision narratives for direct influence; often, inspiration for ideas and phrasing came from material not directly connected with the visionary subject in hand.

Though her phrasing is often derivative, it is important not to overlook that which is positive and new Baudonivia's work. Intense verbal borrowings are endemic to hagiographic writing in this period and served a valuable purpose. Rather in the manner of footnotes today, verbal reminiscences served to stimulate cross-referencing in the literary corpus, setting up associations between saints and their models of sanctity. Baudonivia's borrowings were as obvious as any, but that should not blind us to the importance of her vision narratives in exploring the saint's relationship with God. The level of personal intimacy in Radegund's Christ vision has a freshness and creativity which transcends its sources.

Finally we must consider how Radegund's visions were appropriate to her personal history and their significance for the monastic community which strove to perpetuate her memory.

Radegund's visions confirmed the decision she had taken to leave the court, abandon her husband against the laws of the Church, embrace the religious life without his permission, and thwart the king's authority in favor of divine authority. Both of Radegund's hagiographers were sensitive to this issue; both stressed her dedication and fidelity to her spiritual husband Christ rather than to her earthly husband (*plus participata Christo, quam sociata coniugio*).[104] Radegund's first hagiographer, Fortunatus, took particular care to justify her actions, focusing not on her fidelity to her marital obligations but rather on her fulfillment of her spiritual ones. In Fortunatus' work she is shown trying to escape her nuptials, and even when forced into marriage she was shown to remain aloof from normal married life. At the royal palace at Athies she gathered together sick women, caring for them and feeding them. She would excuse herself from the dinner table to sing psalms and give food to the poor. She would leave the marriage bed to pray, to the point where Chlothar was told that he had a nun rather than a queen as his wife.[105] When Radegund finally left the court it was as if her earthly marriage was but a brief interlude in a life of continuous fidelity to her heavenly husband. Writing at a later date, Baudonivia circumvented the issue by claiming that Radegund initially assumed the religious life with her husband's full permission; it was the king who, at a later date, changed his mind

---

[103] *VP* 12.3: "qui erat suavis colloquio et blandus affectu."
[104] *VR* 1.3.
[105] Ibid., 1.5: "de qua regi dicebatur, habere se potius iugalem monacham quam reginam."

and set off in pursuit of her.[106] To these modifications Baudonivia added divine approval of the queen's decision through the use of visions. Radegund's vision of the Christ-ship occurred after her initial removal from court but before Chlothar's attempt to regain her. It is possible to see the queen's first Christ-vision as a sign that her decision to enter the religious life was divinely intended. The second was then a confirmation that she was more truly married to Christ than she had been to her husband.

For Radegund's monastic community, the visions had a clear message. Coming at the beginning of Radegund's dedication to God and at the end of her monastic career, they defined the boundaries of her consecrated life. The value of the consecrated life needed particular promotion after the revolt at the convent two years after Radegund's death. The scandalous and licentious behavior of some of the nuns who broke their vow of claustration and consorted with vagabonds was an unfortunate interlude to the fine beginnings of the saint's foundation. For the monastic community for whom the *vita* was intended, Radegund's visions underscored the importance of the monastic life to salvation, and her own special status within that community.

[106] Ibid., 2.3, 4.

7 No Ordinary Visionary:
St. Aldegund of Maubeuge

St. Aldegund of Maubeuge was a seventh-century nun whose spiritual life was charted by her prolific visionary experiences.[1] Her visions were fulsomely described by two early hagiographers who drew on an earlier *vita*, no longer extant, which was a record of her visions probably very much as she related them to her amanuensis, Subnius of Nivelles. Her earliest vitae provide a useful contrast with the more crafted hagiography of the sixth-century queen Radegund examined in the previous chapter.

The complexion of Frankish monasticism was different in the seventh century from what it had been in the sixth. Radegund had been a pioneer in the female monastic movement; her convent at Poitiers made the monastic vocation for women popular and respectable for the Frankish nobility. Her royal status and her convent's strict claustration undoubtedly helped achieve this end. Aquitaine was also a center of monastic activity in the sixth century. Poitiers had a venerable Christian past and its relic-laden churches attracted pilgrims from far and wide. It was also fairly close to Tours and thus to St. Martin's tomb. These religious amenities placed Radegund's foundation at the geographical centre of Gallic spirituality.

The seventh century saw the blossoming of monasticism among the northern Frankish nobility, and the creation of pioneers of a different type.[2] Irish

---

[1] Aldegund of Maubeuge's visions are briefly considered in Suzanne Wemple, "Female Spirituality and Mysticism in Frankish Monasteries: Radegund, Balthild, and Aldegund," in *Medieval Religious Women*, vol. 2, ed. Lillian Thomas Shank and John A. Nichols (Kalamazoo, 1987). See also Michel Rouche's French translation of the Life, with brief notes, *Vie de sainte Aldegonde réécrite par une moniale contemporaine (VIIIe s.)* (Maubeuge, 1988). The economic impact of her miracles on her monastic community has been noted by Jo Ann McNamara, "A Legacy of Miracles: Hagiography and Nunneries in Merovingian Gaul," in *Women of the Medieval World*, ed. Julius Kirshner and Suzanne F. Wemple, pp. 36–52. (Oxford, 1985).

[2] On northern Frankish monasticism, especially in Belgium, see Alain Dierkens, *Abbayes et chapitres entre Sambre et Meuse (VIIe–XIe siècles)*, Beihefte der Francia, 14 (Sigmaringen,

missionaries infused the Frankish church and its people with a new ascetic vigor. Their influence was visible directly in their recruitment of Frankish nobles to join and finance their monastic foundations, and indirectly in the counterinitiatives of the Gallo-Frankish clergy, who increasingly espoused Irish ideas for their own foundations. Unprecedented numbers of nobles, court officials, and their families founded, endowed, and embraced the ascetic life during these years, but the focus of their endeavours was no longer southwest Gaul. The most important foundations of the seventh century were concentrated geographically around the Neustrian court at Paris and on the vast estates of Austrasia in southern Belgium and the Rhineland. Fifth- and sixth-century monasticism in the south and southwest had been largely urban, but in the second half of the seventh century there was a trend among the Frankish aristocracy toward founding monasteries on their rural estates. As Prinz notes, "Monasticism became land-based, just like the Frankish nobility that bore the material burden of the monasteries." The influence of Irish kinship-based monasteries, he further suggests, provided the bridge between the older urban and new rural monastic trends.[3] This confluence of Frankish customs and Irish practices created what Prinz termed "Hiberno-Frankish monasticism," in recognition of the importance of preexisting continental conditions to the success of the Irish initiative.[4] Older urban monasteries continued to be important, of course, but they were often reformed.[5] In the case of female foundations, the stratagem of establishing monasteries on family estates had the advantage of stemming the alienation of family lands through the marriage of daughters—although it also inhibited the consolidation of estates and the cementing of political ties

1985); Léon Van der Essen, *Le siècle des saints (652–739)* (Brussels, 1948), and *Étude critique et littéraire sur les vitae des saints mérovingiens de l'ancienne Belgique* (Louvain, 1907); Édouard De Moreau, *Histoire de l'Église en Belgique des origines au debut du xiie siècle*, vol. 1 (Brussels, 1945); Prinz, *Frühes Mönchtum* and "Die Rolle der Iren beim Aufbau der merowingischen Klosterkultur," in *Die Iren und Europa im früheren Mittelalter*, ed. Heinz Löwe, vol. 1 (Stuttgart, 1982), and *Askese und Kultur* (Munich, 1980), and "Abriß der kirchlichen und monastischen Entwicklung des Frankenreiches bis zum Karl der Grossen" in *Karl der Große—Lebenswerk und Nachleben*, vol. 2, *Das geistige Leben* pp. 290–99, ed. B. Bischoff (Düsseldorf, 1965); Wallace-Hadrill, *Frankish Church*; J. Lestocquoy, "Monachisme et civilisation mérovingienne dans le nord de la France," in *Mélanges Colombaniens*, pp. 55–60, (Paris, 1950); Wemple, *Women in Frankish Society*; and Jane T. Schulenburg, "Women's Monastic Communities, 500–1100: Patterns of Expansion and Decline," *Signs* 14 (1989), 261–92.

[3] Friedrich Prinz, "Columbanus, The Frankish Nobility and the Territories East of the Rhine," in *Columbanus and Merovingian Monasticism*, ed. H. B. Clarke and Mary Brennan p. 77, British Archeological Reports, International Series, 113 (Oxford, 1981).

[4] Ibid., p. 78. The exact parameters of Irish influence on Continental monastic, diocesan, and liturgical practices continue to be much disputed. Dierkens, "Prolégomènes," proposes that insular influence was not as strong as has often been argued, especially in the case of Balthild's church politics: "En somme, le monachisme dit colombanien diffère véritablement fort peu des formes du monachisme attestées dans la première moitié du vii siècle (p. 381)."

[5] Ibid., p. 80. Urban and suburban monasteries continued to be founded in the seventh century, mostly in the first half of the century. Hartmut Atsma estimated that about 60 percent of these were founded by bishops. "Les monastères urbains du nord de la Gaule," 163–87.

through marriage.[6] For those families with considerable landed wealth, however, monastic foundations on their lands added a spiritual dimension to their economic and political power.

Aldegund and her family were in many ways typical of this ascetic movement among the nobility.[7] Her family was wealthy and historically influential at court. Aldegund's father Waldebert had been a *domesticus* at the court of Chlothar II (584–629) but retired to devote the remainder of his life to religion.[8] Two of her uncles held important offices at the Neustrian court of Dagobert I (629–39); Gundelandus and Landeric were kings' warriors (*bellatores*) and both became mayors of the palace.[9] These were years of relative political stability in Neustria. In Aldegund's early years, Neustria was governed by Clovis II (638–57) and the mayor of the palace, Erchinoald. On the death of Clovis, his wife Balthild assumed the regency of the kingdom for their young son, the future Chlothar III, with the help of a council of nobles under the leadership of the new mayor, Ebroin. Balthild and the council, which included the leading churchmen Audoenus of Rouen and Chrodebert of Paris, pursued a concerted religious policy which determined appointees to the most important episcopal and abbatial offices.[10] These appointments

---

[6] Catherine Peyroux, "Gertrude's Furor: Reading Anger in an Early Medieval Saint's Life" in *Anger's Past: The Social Uses of an Emotion*, ed. Barbara H. Rosenwein (Ithaca, N.Y., 1998), examines the political ramifications of Gertrude of Nivelles's decision to eschew the marriage partner chosen for her.

[7] Editions of her first *vita* include J. Mabillon, *AASS, OSB* 2 (Paris, 1668), pp. 806–15; J. Ghesquière, *AASS Belg. Sel.* 4, 6 vols. (Brussels, 1783–94), pp. 315 ff.; abbr. ed., W. Levinson, *MGH, SRM* 6 (1913), pp. 79–90. The second *vita* is in J. Bollandus, *AASS* Ianuarii ii. (1643), pp. 649 ff. Aldegund's monastic foundation, Maubeuge, is mentioned in Anso's *Vita Ursmari* 4, 6, ed. W. Levison, *MGH, SRM* 6 (1913), pp. 445–61. See Appendix B for further discussion of the date and context of Aldegund's medieval *vitae*. There are now a number of important studies on St. Aldegund and her circle: Anne-Marie Helvétius, "Sainte Aldegonde et les origines du monastère de Maubeuge," *Revue du Nord* 74 (1992), 221–37 sheds light on the type of monasticism practiced at Maubeuge; Michel Rouche, *Vie de sainte Aldegonde*, advances the thesis (not universally accepted) that the *vita prima* was written by a nun at Maubeuge; Otto Dittrich, *St. Aldegundis, eine heilige der Franken* (Kevelaer, 1976), is useful on the saint's cult in Continental Europe, listing church dedications (in France, 13; in Belgium, 26; in Holland, 2; in Luxembourg, 2; and in Germany, 11) and providing a history of her relics; Wemple, "Female Spirituality," addresses her visions. See also McNamara, "A Legacy of Miracles" and Prinz, *Frühes Mönchtum*, pp. 130–1, 165. Still essential: Van der Essen, *Étude critique*, pp. 219–31, and Edouard de Moreau, *Historie de l'église en Belgique*, vol. 1 pp. 137–41.

[8] Fredegar, *Chronicarum quae dicuntur Fredegari Scholastici libri IV cum continuationes*, 54, ed. Bruno Krusch, *MGH, SRM* 2 (1888), pp. 1–193; ed. John Michael Wallace-Hadrill, *The Fourth Book of the Chronicle of Fredegar with Its Continuators* (London, 1960) (hereafter, Fredegar, *Chron.*); Prinz, *Frühes Mönchtum*, p. 130. The earliest *vita* to mention Waldebert's high office is the eleventh-century manuscript from the monastery of St. Ghislain. *AASS* Ianuarii ii., pp. 662–65.

[9] *V. Ald.* 1.1. describes her uncles as "scholares" and "bellatores," which suggests that they formed part of the king's own guard. On Landeric as mayor see Fredegar, *Chron.* 25, 26; *Liber Historiae Francorum* 35, 36, 40, ed. Bruno Krusch, *MGH, SRM* 2 (1888), pp. 215–72 (hereafter *LHF*). On Gundelandus, who succeeded him, see *LHF* 40 and Fredegar, *Chron.* 45.

[10] *Vita sanctae Balthildis*, ed. Bruno Krusch, *MGH, SRM* 2 (1888), pp. 475–508. On Balthild's *kirchenpolitik* see Nelson, "Queens as Jezebels"; Fouracre and Gerberding, *Late Merovingian France*, pp. 18–21, 97–118, and the annotated translation of her *vita*, pp. 118–132; and Robert Folz, "Tradition hagiographique et culte de sainte Balthilde, reine des

reflected a commitment to the spirit of the Hiberno-Frankish reform movement which also influenced Aldegund's circle.[11] Although Aldegund and her family lived through the political upheaval which erupted in 675 between the Austrasian and Neustrian mayors, these disruptions were not mentioned in Aldegund's *vitae*.[12]

There are lacunae in our knowledge about Aldegund's convent (for example, we do not know what rule was observed there),[13] but we are fortunate in having two near-contemporary hagiographies which shed light on the saint and her circle. The monastic milieu in which Aldegund and her family undertook their monastic ventures was clearly privileged. She, and thus her foundation, benefited from the friendship and attention of important religious figures in the region. She included among her acquaintance St. Amandus, the "apostle of the Belgians," who may have been personally associated with her foundation, and St. Ursmer abbot of Lobbes, who entrusted his niece to her care.[14] These contacts make it highly likely that Maubeuge was governed according to Irish monastic principles.[15]

Aldegund was also able to rely on the support of her family. Aldegund's elder sister Waldetrude married a nobleman named Vicentius Madelgarius, and both soon established and headed monastic communities of their own. Waldetrude founded Mons (*Altus Mons*) at a fortified site, and her husband retired to Hautmont and, according to his eleventh-century *vita*, founded another community at Soignies. Aldegund avoided marriage altogether.[16] Her convent at Maubeuge (*coenobium Malbodiense*) on the Sambre River was probably a double monastery, perhaps modeled after Nivelles.[17] On the death of her parents, she assembled twelve nuns at the villa Cousolre (*Cur-*

Francs," *Académie des inscriptions et belles-lettres comptes rendus des séances pour 1975* (1976), 369–84.

[11] In "Prolégomènes," Dierkens softens the picture of specifically Irish influence in Balthild's religious policy.

[12] On the political wrangling of these years see Fouracre and Gerberding, *Late Merovingian France*, pp. 1–26; Richard Gerberding, *The Rise of the Carolingians and the Liber Historiae Francorum* (Oxford, 1987); and Eugen Ewig, "Die frankischen Teilreiche im 7. Jahrhundert (613–714)" in his *Spätantikes und frankisches Gallien* 1, ed. Hartmut Atsma, pp. 172–230 (Munich, 1976). On Neustrian politics and culture see the collected essays in Atsma, *La Neustrie*, and Patrick Périn and Laure-Charlotte Feffer, eds., *La Neustrie* (Rouen, 1985).

[13] It is not possible to establish direct links between these foundations and Columbanian monasticism (see Prinz, *Frühes Mönchtum*, p. 130, although it is evident in the *vitae* that Aldegund had ties with Amandus and with Nivelles. We cannot positively ascertain that Nivelles had a joint rule (Columbanian-Benedictine) at that time. See Wood, "The *Vita Columbani*," p. 69. Dierkens, "Prolégomènes," p. 388, throws doubt on Nivelles having the double rule. Helvétius, "Sainte Aldegonde," posits a rather relaxed regime at the convent of Maubeuge and argues against its exclusive use of the joint rule.

[14] Anso, *Vita Ursmari* (written before 776), ed. Wilhelm Levison, *MGH, SRM* 6 (1913), pp. 445–61; Dierkens, *Abbayes et Chapitres*, pp. 95–98, 289–91.

[15] Prinz, *Frühes Mönchtum*, p. 165, n. 78.

[16] According to later *vitae* Aldegund fought her mother's aims to have her marry. The extent of this maternal pressure was vastly exaggerated in the later *vitae* in accordance with the hagiographic fashion.

[17] See Helvétius, "Sainte Aldegonde," pp. 230–31.

tissolra) where they were buried. Aldegund was herself buried there until her relics were translated to the convent of Maubeuge in the ninth century. By that time Aldegund was already the focus of a cult at Maubeuge; already in the eighth century her name was listed in martyrologies.[18] The family monasteries were close to each other, enabling Aldegund and Waldetrude to maintain a close relationship from within their convents, visiting each other periodically. At least one of Waldetrude's daughters, Aldetrude, was educated at Maubeuge under Aldegund's care.[19]

Despite the external conventionality of her monastic milieu, there was nothing conventional in Aldegund's frequent visions, nor in the apparent fidelity and attention to detail with which they were recorded. Moreover, they addressed not only her spiritual maturation but issues of ecclesiastical interest, thus claiming an authority in external affairs which was unusual for women in this period. Simply put, Aldegund is the most important female visionary of the Merovingian age to be recorded in contemporary hagiographic literature, both for her detail-rich visions themselves and because they were said to be copied from her own account to Subnius of Nivelles and another monk.[20] This autograph record of her visions has not survived, nor has the earliest *vita*. However, the first two extant hagiographies (*vita* 1 and 2) were both written soon thereafter: the first c. 715–18, the second in the ninth century.[21] It is likely that both hagiographers independently consulted the list of Aldegund's visions. Together, the visions described in the two *vitae* provide the most comprehensive view of this remarkable visionary.[22]

I approach Aldegund's visions from four perspectives. First is a reading of those visions which recorded the spiritual progress of a woman later venerated as a saint. In these visions scriptural and literary allusions attest to a Frankish culture rooted in broad traditions of antique visual representation. The second section addresses the language of Aldegund's visions. The third and fourth sections consider her visions as vehicles for spiritual and religious

---

[18] She appears in eighth- and ninth-century kalendars on January 30, listed by W. Levison, *MGH, SRM* 6, pp. 79–80.

[19] *V. Ald.* 2.22. Later *vitae* added another daughter, Madelberta, and according to Waldetrude's *vita* she also had two sons, Landricus and Dentlin.

[20] *V. Ald.* 1.18: "Supradicta famula Dei Aldegunda de visionibus atque revelationibus spiritualibus quas Christus sponsus eius revelavit, cuidam viro religioso Subino Abbati de Nivialensi Monsaterio narravit ordinanter, et scribendo tradidit." Nivelles was founded c. 640–47 as a female monastery and became a double monastery after Foillan fled there in 650–51 and set up a male abbey. The community was thus governed by an abbess, though the male portion of the community was governed by identifiable male abbots who were the spiritual directors of the entire community. In the seventh century they included the founder Foillan (also abbot of Fosses), Ultan (abbot of Péronne and possibly Fosses), and Cellán (also abbot of Péronne) (d. 706). The name "Sobinus" in the texts is properly rendered Subnius. See also, Dierkens, "Saint Amand et la fondation de l'abbaye de Nivelles," *Revnue du Nord* 68:269 (1986), 325–32.

[21] Dated by Anne-Marie Helvétius, *Abbayes, éveques et laïques. Une politique du pouvoir en Hainaut au moyen âge (VIIe–XIe siècle)*. Collection Historie in-8, no. 92 (Brussels, 1994).

[22] *Vita* 1 drew on the original Nivelles *vita* and on the list of visions compiled by the saint. *Vita* 2 drew in part on the material in *vita* 1 but also, I argue, independently consulted Aldegund's vision list. See my discussion in Appendix B.

authority, and their significance in the context of contemporary church politics and her own monastic community.[23]

Living in the Palace of Love

The saint's desire is to love and be loved by Christ. For female mystics this love was explicitly connubial, replacing a terrestrial with a celestial husband, a terrestrial home with a heavenly home. From her divine husband the saint expected in transcendent and ideal form those qualities and gifts which an earthly husband might be expected to provide: love, protection, assurance, and status. The nun gave her virginity to her celestial husband upon taking vows, and all her yearning and desire for companionship was directed to her chosen and eternal spouse.

Aldegund's visionary life in many ways exemplified for the Merovingian age the connubial relationship which we saw already glimmering through the Life of Radegund of Poitiers and the nuns at the Holy Cross. In Aldegund's case, however, the sources for our knowledge of her visions are incomparably richer, and we recognize in them a more clearly articulated visual language. Her many visions are an outpouring of spiritual consciousness that is possible only for one long familiar with the imprint of dreams. Aldegund, we are told, had visions from the time when she was a young girl. At her parents' house, her visions centered on the importance of her eschewing earthly marriage for the consecrated life, emphasizing the heavenly rewards that would accompany her steadfast resolve to dedicate her virginity to Christ. Naive and bold, they promised her riches greater than the earthly benefits of an advantageous marriage: "The most blessed girl heard in a vision the high measure of riches she was going to have."[24] At first, she did not understand the vision's meaning until she was granted another in which she saw a mansion with seven columns ornamented with images and steeped in Christ's sweet odor.[25] She then understood that she was being promised heavenly, not earthly riches. The social consequences of this vision were clear when she heard an angelic voice telling her "You will have no husband other than the Lord Christ."[26] Then she saw Christ in the form of a

[23] For the purposes of the following sections, I use the two earliest *vitae*. Combined, they offer as full a record of her visions as is available. Where the two versions have material in common they tend to concur; where they do not I have signaled this in the text or in the notes.

[24] *V. Ald.* 1.5: "audivit Beatissima per visum quodammodo altitudinem divitiarum se habituram." I have translated "per visum" as "vision" although the term was sometimes used to describe a spectral apparition.

[25] *V. Ald.* 1.5; *V. Ald.* 2.5 explains that at first she thought she was being offered earthly riches, but then realized that they were heavenly riches. Writing on columns is also recorded in the *Visio Pauli*, chap. 19: "duas columnas plene litteris."

[26] *V. Ald.* 1.6; *V. Ald.* 2.5 relates that she was exhorted to put aside transient things and not to fear the obstructions of the world, so that she might easily attain heaven. She then heard a voice saying to her, "Do not seek any husband except the Son of God."

very beautiful boy offering her a precious robe, holding a palm in one hand and in the other a crown of woven gold and jewels not made by human hands but shaped by God alone.[27] Aldegund's mother Bertilia pressured Aldegund to accept a husband.[28] But in the meantime her sister Waldetrude, who along with her husband had turned away from worldly affairs, supported the young girl's resolve to deserve "Christ's prize." Of Aldegund's father we hear nothing. Perhaps by this time he had already retired to the ascetic life.[29]

The early visions are very explicit: Aldegund must not vacillate, but take only Christ as her husband. Insightfully her second hagiographer informs the reader that these visions were a spiritual strength to her at a time when her corporeal defenses were not strong.[30] For whosoever sets out firm in faith and perseveres in charity, the second hagiographer maintained, begins to contemplate greater things.

Aldegund's spiritual marriage to Christ is at the heart of her most mystical visions. Love is the insistent theme. The night after Aldegund was warned by the angel to take no other husband but Christ, she had a vision on returning from matins. Christ's angel announced to her, "The more one guards the spark of faith in the soul, the more one will burn with the love of Christ."[31] Then she remembered her vision in which she was dressed in a very precious robe, unlike any earthly garb, standing in the presence of Christ who appeared as a young and beautiful boy. He had told her that the garment which he would give her would shine like the sun and the moon in his kingdom. After speaking further with the angel who identified the vision as Christ, Aldegund saw Christ again holding in his hands a palm and a crown made of gold and gems.[32] This youthful vision bears obvious parallels with Radegund's vision, and the precious robe given to Aldegund reminds us of the vision of an anonymous nun at Radegund's convent.[33] The comparison of the robe's brilliance with that of the sun and the moon anticipates another vision in which the Holy Spirit approached as she prayed at her window.[34]

---

[27] *V. Ald.* 1.7; The second hagiographer further explains that the robe was white and that the palm signified victory. *V. Ald.* 2.5.

[28] The degree of Bertilia's interest in Aldegund's contracting an earthly marriage is different in each recension of the Life. Bertilia is a concerned parent in the first *vita*, but becomes more tyrannical in subsequent recensions. This later development fit hagiographic and romantic models of the saint's trials in renouncing marriage.

[29] The order in which events are presented in the *vita* cannot be used to construct a chronology of the family's lives. Bertilia and Waldebert, Aldegund's parents, are commended for having renounced carnal relations (after the birth of their children), yet it is not clear when this happened, or whether both parents turned to religious life at the same time.

[30] *V. Ald.* 2.5.

[31] *V. Ald.* 1.6: "Quo plus quippe vigilat scintilla fidei, plus accenditur amor Christi." Translation by Wemple, "Female Spirituality," p. 47.

[32] *V. Ald.* 1.7.

[33] *HF* 6.29.

[34] *V. Ald.* 1.11.

Aldegund's visions of Christ's love conferred status. In part this status derived from the authority which her closeness to the supernatural world and her prognostic visions gave her in the eyes of others. However, the visions are also impregnated with iconographic images of spiritual status communicated in the earthly emblems of power: a precious robe, a crown of gold and gems. These are the bridal clothes which accompany the saint's sacrifice of worldly pleasures. The significance of these costly vestments lies not simply in their sumptuousness and their related sense of spiritual treasure. The act of clothing itself is an intimate one, a protective shielding of the saint's body, the wrapping of a precious object. It is an extension of the acts of love, nurture, and guardianship which the visionary sought from her spouse.

Aldegund's visions are crowded places, full of new sights, sounds, and fragrances. She was constantly visited by an angel, by a young girl sent to her by the Virgin Mary, by the Holy Spirit, by the apostle Peter, and by the Devil. Even her vision of Christ was interrupted by an angel making sure that she understood who it was that she saw. In this, Aldegund's visions were very different from Radegund's vision of Christ, which was a very private affair, very confined in its reach, and homely. Yet insofar as the visions spoke to the inner life of the saint alone and not to the wider community, the visions were similar.

Another feature of Aldegund's visions which reminds us of Radegund's is the importance of divine assurance. Assurances of love, salvation, and a place in heaven are common themes in these womens' *vitae*. Like the early visions, the later ones continued the theme of her heavenly rewards, assuring Aldegund that her name was written in the Book of Life, even in the face of demonic temptations.[35] Her last visions comforted her with the promise of her union with the heavenly bridegroom, advising of her mortal demise and her eternal life.

Despite all her joys and consolations, for Christ's bride, marooned by her mortal state on earth and able only rarely to see, savor or smell her husband's presence, her life was one of almost constant yearning. Throughout Aldegund's life, we are told, she received her visions with great spiritual emotion. On being comforted by an angel after her temptation by the Devil, she sang psalms continuously with tears of joy. She prayed to God saying that she would willingly sacrifice to him and acknowledge his name. When would he come to her?[36] Every day, we are told, she strove for and claimed the victory in the spiritual race; every day she prayed, usually alone, and fasted.[37] Meanwhile the saint confronted many obstacles along the way: the Devil attempted to intimidate her, and there was some unspecified persecution which Aldegund was obliged to endure. Yet she persevered with a vir-

[35] Ibid., 1.8. Aldegund's confrontation with the devil has a different tone in *V. Ald.* 2.8, on which see pp. 210–12.
[36] *V. Ald.* 1.8.
[37] Ibid., 1.10, 6, 16.

tuous and saintly disposition. Through all this, Aldegund had a celestial companion to help her, an angel named Glorious.

The *angelus Domini* was perhaps the most familiar figure to appear in visions to saints. When a visionary figure was not otherwise identified but appeared bathed in light, he was generally considered to be an angel. It was the angel who conveyed divine will, and it was through the agency of angels that visions were believed to be manifested.[38] Accounts of angelic visions in hagiography did not report that the identity of the angel was the same across the various experiences; one of the striking features of Aldegund's visionary life is that much of it was communicated by a single angel who acted as her guide.

The angel appeared to Aldegund many times, answering her questions and explaining her visions with *spiritualia verba*.[39] He consoled her after her temptation by the Devil and exhorted her to remain a virgin.[40] He explained to her that the Holy Spirit had come upon her in the form of the rays of the sun and moon. As the angel held out her bridal clothes to her, Aldegund asked him his name, and he replied, "My name is glorious."[41] Near the end of her life, he appeared to her to tell her that she would soon receive her heavenly rewards.[42] The author of the second *vita* claimed that Aldegund asked the angel his name out of sheer familiarity with him.[43] Again and again, he writes, the angel of the Lord advised her on heavenly things. He also informed her who would be bound by punishment and who would be in glory in the afterlife. And in a similar vein, she was informed of "many things" concerning certain clerics.[44]

Aldegund's visions of other figures were not always very clear to her, and she sought clarification from the angel. For example, at first she thought her vision of Christ was a vision of an angel.[45] Sometimes the visions came in symbolic form, as when the Holy Spirit came to her as the sun and moon. Such a vision needed deciphering. Her angel appeared always in recognizable form, was with her as she experienced her other visions, and was her teacher. Together, she, the angel, and Christ formed a holy triad.

Thus far we have noted the spiritual coherence and consistency of a visionary life directed toward spiritual perfection and maturation. Because Aldegund's visions were based on her own account (*quas ipsa descripserat*),[46] they are as close to the "authentic" experience of Merovingian vi-

---

[38] Augustine, *Enchiridion* 59.
[39] *V. Ald.* 1.6.
[40] Ibid., 1.8.
[41] Ibid., 1.13: "Gloriosum est nomen meum."
[42] Ibid., 1.16.
[43] *V. Ald.* 2.6. He also points out the similarity of this incident with the story of Samson's parents who also asked their angelic visitor his name. Judges 13.17.
[44] *V. Ald.* 2.9.
[45] *V. Ald.* 1.7.
[46] Ibid., 1.18.

sions as we get. Yet Aldegund described her visions at the end of her life, after a life of reflection. Aldegund had to find the language and the references with which to communicate her experiences as she remembered them. It is not surprising, therefore, to find the visions rich in religious, cultural, and literary metaphor. The infusion of hagiography by biblical quotation, metaphor, and reminiscence has long been recognized; scholars have begun to determine how this infusion worked.[47] Marc van Uytfange in particular has drawn attention to the "biblical drapery" in which hagiography clothed itself.[48] And indeed Aldegund's visions are in part meditations on biblical injunctions. Her vision of the Virgin's messenger-girl intoned, "You shall love your Lord God with all your heart and with all your soul and with all your might; and you shall love your neighbor as yourself."[49] The language and images by which the visions were given written expression were resolutely biblical. But perhaps more than other form of literature, visions synthesize images and ideas from many sources, conflating and paring in unusual and creative ways. Aldegund's influences were not confined to biblical studies, and not all of these were "tamed" by her hagiographers into scriptural conformity. What follows is an analysis of one of her earliest visions whose depth of imagistic associations is a reminder of the unexpected eclecticism of the visionary event.

This vision appears in both of the earliest *vitae* as Aldegund's first:

> While she was still in her carnal condition, and still in her parents' home, the blessed girl heard in a vision the high measure of riches she would have. Marveling at the vision's showing (*ostensio*), an unaccustomed vision beyond what could be believed, she did not know the meaning of the enigmatic vision (*visio aenigmatica*). Then reflecting on Christ's secrets, she found herself led to the gate of a great house supported on seven columns ornamented with seals, and she looked inside at the bright ornaments and the fragrant aroma, wonderfully steeped in the sweetness of Christ's odor. Thereafter she began to see more clearly, the scales having now fallen from her eyes, and she began to know that a celestial gift was promised to her by him who says: "Come to me all ye who labor and are burdened and I will give you rest."[50]

---

[47] Leclercq, *Love of Learning*, pp. 71–88, highlights the impregnation of medieval monastic culture by biblical reminiscence.

[48] Marc van Uytfange's work has greatly advanced our sensitivity to the scriptural underpinnings of hagiography. See his *Stylisation biblique et condition humaine dans l'hagiographie mérovingienne (600–750)* (Brussels, 1987), and "La Bible dans les vies des saints mérovingiennes," pp. 103–11.

[49] *V. Ald.* 1.10, quoting Matthew 22.37.

[50] *V. Ald.* 1.5: "Dum vero sub carnali conditione maneret, atque in domatibus parentum versaretur, audivit Beatissima per visum quodammodo altitudinem divitiarum se habituram. Cuius visionis ostensionem insolitam mens puellaris supra quam credi potest admirans, quidnam vellet visio aenigmatica ignorabat. Ipsa quoque arcana Christi considerans, quae iam ducta stetit ad ostium domus magnae septem columnis sigillatim subnixae, clara cuncta ornamenta aromatum fragrantia introspexit, miro vapore suavissimoque odore Christi imbuta. Quapropter

The celestial mansion was a common destination for the Christian visionary. Revelation described the heavenly Jerusalem as a cosmic, bejeweled cityscape, a place in which mansions were built for the righteous. Visions relating journeys to the otherworld invariably mentioned the mansions being busily prepared for the saints. Any of these allusions could have been intended by Aldegund. However, the perspective from which Aldegund saw her mansion does not suggest that these were the many mansions of the afterlife. Mansions of the afterlife were generally viewed from afar: from across a burning river as in Pope Gregory's description of a soldier's vision, or at a distance in the vision of Sunniulf of Radan. They were also described from the outside, in the process of construction with bricks of gold. By contrast, the mansion seen in Aldegund's vision presents an interior view. She enters through a great gate to view the splendors within. In her vision she does not simply see the mansion; she experiences it and participates in its space by entering into it. Furthermore, details of the mansion are very specific: it is supported on seven columns, and it is replete with the sweet aroma of Christ. The seven columns are an allusion to Wisdom's abode in Proverbs 9.1: "Wisdom has built her house, she has set up her seven pillars." In Aldegund's vision, I would suggest, it is Christ's palace that is being entered—the palace of the bridegroom, which is also the house of Wisdom. This analysis necessitates another look at the vision's meaning. From what source did the bright ornaments and fragrant aroma of Christ's mansion derive?

At first look the answer is surprising. Its contours, its features, its brightness and sweet odor, are all features of very ancient descriptions of the mythical palaces of love which were evoked to celebrate marriages. The pagan Claudian's *Epithalamium* for the Christian bridal couple Honorius and Maria serves as a good example of this kind of literature and explains how pagan imagery crossed into Christian literature:

> Afar shines and glitters the goddess' many-coloured palace, green gleaming by reason of the encircling grove. Vulcan built this too of precious stones and gold, wedding their costliness to art. Columns cut from rock of hyacinth support emerald beams; the walls are of beryl, the high-builded thresholds of polished jasper, the floor of agate trodden as dirt beneath the foot. In the midst is a courtyard rich with fragrant turf that yields a harvest of perfume; there grows sweet spikenard and ripe cassia, Panchaean cinnamon-flowers and sprays of oozy balm, while balsam creeps forth slowly in an exuding stream.[51]

Venus's bejeweled palace with its perfumed odor and supporting columns provides a very strong association with the theme of celestial love, and the use of this imagery to celebrate a marriage made its appropriation for the

---

coepit clarius videre iam solutis squamis ab oculis, donum caeleste sibi promissum percipere ab illo qui dicit: 'Venite ad me omnes qui laboratis et onerati estis, et ego reficiam vos.' "

[51] Claudian, *Epithalamium of Honorius and Maria*, ed. and trans. Maurice Platnauer, *Claudian* 1, Loeb, 135 (Cambridge, Mass., 1976), p. 249.

description of Aldegund's mystical marriage meaningful. The mansion in Aldegund's vision, however, is the mansion of Christ, of the celestial bridegroom, who also represents love. Allegories concerning love and the soul were popular ways in which ancient fables gained a new lease on life in Christian contexts.[52] For example, in Apuleius of Madaurus' story of the marriage of Cupid and Psyche, Psyche (the soul) was taken to her new home, the palace of her invisible bridegroom Cupid (love). The palace had silver walls, pillars of gold and precious stones underfoot. Aldegund, one senses, peered into Christ's palace of love with something of Psyche's anticipation.[53]

Christian writers were very taken with these images and absorbed much of the pagan aesthetic into Christian works. Aldegund's earliest *vita* contains a number of specific allusions to Virgil, which were quite common in Merovingian hagiography.[54] But there is also perhaps a Christian source for some of the elements in Aldegund's vision: Prudentius' *Psychomachia*, an allegorized "battle of the soul." In this work, the following description resembles Christ's palace in Aldegund's vision: "An inner chamber, too, is constructed, which rests on seven pillars cut from a glassy rock of ice-like crystal.... Here mighty Wisdom sits enthroned."[55] Is this where Aldegund found inspiration for her palace? The context of the soul's battle and Aldegund's struggle to assert her newly found religious vocation appears a neat fit. This kind of literary connection in visionary literature should not surprise us. Aldegund was a noblewoman whose family had connections at court and with Irish monasticism. Though specific attributions of learning cannot be verified, there is reason to think that Aldegund could have had access to at least the rudiments of classical learning.[56] Even while the tendency of ascetic movements was to eschew secular works, the Irish missionary monasteries were pre-

---

[52] The fifth-century mythographer Fulgentius suggested a Christian reading of the widely read and allegorized fable, the marriage of Cupid and Psyche, from Apuleius of Madaura's *The Golden Ass*, ed. Rudolph Helm, *Apulei Platonici Madaurensis Metamorphoseon libri XI* (Leipzig, 1931), but it does not appear to have been influential. *Mythography* 6, trans. Leslie George Whitbread, in *Fulgentius the Mythographer*, pp. 88–90, (Columbus, 1971).

[53] I examine this vision and its palace imagery at further length in "Living in the Palaces of Love: Love and the Soul in a Vision of St. Aldegund of Maubeuge (c. 635–84)," *Quidditas: Journal of the Rocky Mountain Medieval and Renaissance Association* 19 (1999).

[54] See W. Levinson, *MGH, SRM* 6 (1913), 81.

[55] Prudentius, *Psychomachia*, ed. Maurice P. Cunningham, in *Aurelii Prudentii Clementis Carmina* (Turnhout, 1966); Harold Isbell, *The Last Poets of Imperial Rome* (Harmondsworth, 1971). See Anne-Marie Palmer, *Prudentius on the Martyrs* (Oxford, 1989), esp. pp. 202–4, and Macklin Smith, *Prudentius' Psychomachia: A Re-examination* (Princeton, 1976), pp. 199–206.

[56] On aristocratic court and home education (for women as well as men) in Merovingian hagiography, see Martin Heinzelmann, "Studia sanctorum. Éducation, milieux d'instruction et valeurs éducatives dans l'hagiographie en Gaule jusqu'à la fin de l'époque mérovingienne," in *Haut Moyen-Âge*, ed. Michael Sot, pp. 105–38. Heinzelmann cites the Lives of Gertrude, Sadalberga, Segolena, and Eustadiola as examples of female saints whose hagiographers noted their education. See also Pierre Riché, *Education and Culture in the Barbarian West, Sixth through Eighth Centuries* (Columbia, 1976); trans. John J. Contreni of *Education et culture dans l'occident chrétien* (Paris, 1962).

serving them. Classical poetry and literature fared less well than other types of ancient writing; at Bobbio and Luxeuil they were erased so that the parchment could be reused.[57] Yet the survival of pagan stories in oral culture and storytelling is perhaps the most resilient form of cultural transmission. The preservation of descriptive conventions, however, has to do with more than simply the survival of texts; it requires a prevailing aesthetic. Prinz noted in a general way about medieval receptivity to classical culture that "only in a period when the living relationship with Christian late Antiquity had been broken in space and in time . . . only then could there have ensued a more uninhibited turning towards classical culture and its literary and artistic products."[58] He saw the beginning of that process in the early Carolingian renaissance, although as we now know, the last Merovingian century anticipated Carolingian trends.[59] Yet it is important that other types of evidence, like visual memories, be kept in view. For regardless of whether the specific elements of the visionary mansion were provided by Aldegund herself or by her amanuensis Subnius of Nivelles, we should not discount the significance of pagan philosophical images in the making of the Merovingian Christian vision.

* * *

In antithesis to celestial delights stood the Devil and the evil he represented. The place of the demonic in medieval accounts defies simple explanation. In hagiography especially, Satan and his demons played a variety of roles which relied on a contemporary disposition to externalize sources of conflict. For the ascetic demonic trials often included unwanted sickness or other infirmities (although some saints prayed for sickness in order to participate more fully in Christ's suffering). Aldegund encountered the Devil's agency behind a severe illness when, after a night of fever and great thirst, the Devil admitted to her that angels were constraining him from doing her more harm.[60] In hagiography the Devil's primary role was to act as a foil for the saint's training in godliness.[61] However, this was not his only function. One of the other roles the devil played in Gallo-Roman and Merovingian hagiography was interlocutor in theological debate; in Chapter 2 we observed Martin of Tours debating purist "demons" who wanted to exclude lapsed monks from reentry to the monastic community. In the first two *vitae* of

---

[57] Prinz, "Columbanus," pp. 82–83.

[58] Ibid., p. 83.

[59] Fouracre and Gerberding, *Late Merovingian France*, pp. 6–7, note the nascent intellectual movement in and around the year 700 which produced manuscripts and *vitae* that anticipated Carolingian trends.

[60] The first *vita* explained that the Devil's role in Aldegund's sickness was permitted by God so that she would be tested like gold in a furnace. The Devil is ultimately powerless against her, however, since she has angelic help.

[61] Graus notes: "Die Hagiographie spekulierte night über Teufel und monen; für sie waren sie einfach da, die Heiligen ihr siegreicher widerpart." "Hagiographie und Dämonenglauben," p. 112.

Aldegund we find the saint engaged in disputes with the Devil, which likewise throw up theological issues, although in a more abstract manner.

Aldegund's first hagiographer related a confrontation scene which was typical of early Christian hagiography: the malevolent Devil taunts the stalwart Christian.[62] According to hagiographic tradition, the saint's decision to lead a life devoted to God was depicted as arousing the particular fury of the Devil and his minions, and the saint's life was orchestrated around this theme of confrontation. The Devil's frustration and powerlessness drove him to try to tempt the saints with carnal temptations, to pelt them with stones and blast them with an infernal din, to frighten them with gruesome phantoms, and to deceive them in cunning guises.[63] In such confrontations saints prevailed by relying on prayer and the inspiration of the Holy Spirit. St. Anthony of Egypt had taught his followers that the demons need not be feared if they confronted them with faith, for it was by such confrontation that their fear would be overcome.

Aldegund saw the Devil in the form of a rapacious wolf, roaring like a lion, gnashing his teeth.[64] The confrontation which ensued was along traditional lines. The Devil impudently complained that the kingdom he had lost would be given to Aldegund. "I hate your virginity very much, and I tried to snatch it away from you, but to no avail." But Aldegund lashed back angrily at him, stating that the Lord had cast him down at his feet, so that now Satan raged at God's image, mankind. With immense energy and authority she concluded her tirade: "Apostate, I order you in the name of our Lord Jesus Christ, who having conquered you triumphs in heaven with the Father, descend into the prison of Hell!"[65] In typical manner the Devil was said to vanish in confusion.

In contrast to this confrontation scene, which bears the classic signs of an exorcism, Aldegund's second hagiographer depicted a gentler, more reflective visionary encounter. Aldegund was shown the Devil in a vision, and he was very sad. She asked him with concern (*sollicite requisivit*) why he was so stubbornly against the human race, and what profit it was to him that he should take so many thousands down to hell with him. He spitefully replied that he was envious of the sons of Adam, who took his place in heaven while he and his accomplices were ejected. Aldegund's "concerned" response to Satan was evinced in two ways. First, in response to the Devil's sadness she showed love and compassion, a desire to comprehend the psychology of evil, to plumb the depths of the devil's antagonism. Her concern was thus di

---

[62] The theme of aggressive confrontation between saint and devil is developed by Peter Dinzelbacher in "Der Kampf der Heiligen mit den Dämonen," in *Santi e Demoni nell'alto medioevo occidentale (secoli V–XI* vol. 2, pp. 674–95, Settimani di studio 36 (Spoleto, 1989).

[63] See *V. Antonii*, esp. chaps. 8–10, 35–43, 51–53.

[64] See 1 Peter 5.8.

[65] *V. Ald.* 1.8: "Apostata, praecipio tibi in nomine Domini nostri Jesu Christi, qui te exsuperato in caelis triumphat cum Patre, ad inferni claustra descendere."

rected toward Satan's miserable plight. Second, her concern was directed toward herself and the human race as is clear in the substance of her question—the Devil threatens their salvation. The scene has no resolution except in its reiteration of the traditional explanation for the cause of the Devil's malice. Nevertheless the hagiographer's approach is important in its focus on compassion.

If we look at the two demonic visions from the perspective of hagiographic models for women, we see two possible reflections on the female saintly ideal. In the first *vita* Aldegund's righteous fury and her active denunciation of the Devil conformed to the traditional confrontation between the ascetic and her tempter.[66] The duel was between two individuals testing their wills, with Aldegund's virginity the chosen battlefield. In the second *vita* Aldegund's compassionate qualities were reflected on the source of evil, as the confrontation centered on the universal theme of good versus evil, with mankind caught between salvation and damnation. The confrontation was no longer a test of individual wills but rather a theological excursus on Christian dualism.

Aldegund and the Devil were able to engage in this theological debate because, as František Graus has observed, Christian demons believed in God and thus their presence was theologically "sanctioned."[67] This kind of dialogue was also a means for working out conflicting emotions within the Christian tradition, especially those of love and hate. It has been suggested that visions with doctrinal content were particularly suited to female ways of engaging with the liturgy and the Christian message when opportunities for more formal interaction were denied them.[68] In the context of the Romano-Gallic background to Aldegund's vision we must also consider the possible perpetuation of Origenist thinking, perhaps carried through Sulpicius Severus' *Vita Martini*.[69] Martin of Tours had promised that if the Devil would renounce his misdeeds, he could be given mercy.[70] Sulpicius distanced himself from this line of thinking in his *Dialogues*,[71] yet from a philosophical standpoint the issue of the redeemability of the Devil remained theologically unresolved. For a visionary like Aldegund, devoted to the message of Christ's love, we may imagine that the potential of love for conquering evil would have held a particular fascination.

[66] Wemple notes the link between this confrontation and the *virago* motif in Roman literature. "Female Spirituality," p. 47.
[67] Graus, "Hagiographie und Dämonenglauben," p. 113.
[68] Petroff, *Medieval Women's Visionary Literature*, pp. 8–9.
[69] See Henry Chadwick, *The Early Church* (Harmondsworth, 1967), p. 107, on Origen's thinking: "Therefore even Satan himself retains some vestige of power to acknowledge the truth; even he can repent at the very last." In order to accommodate free will, however, there must remain the possibility that the Devil will choose not to be redeemed.
[70] VM 22.5.
[71] *Dialogues* 1.7.

Aldegund's Understanding of Her Visions

Given that the earliest extant manuscript of the *Vita Aldegundis* dates to four hundred years after her death, it is difficult to argue confidently that we can approach Aldegund's authentic expression and understanding of her visions through the sources available to us. However, since the eleventh-century manuscript does retain much of its original Merovingian orthography (see Appendix 2), and since the text claims to use the written description of her visions compiled by Abbot Subnius of Nivelles, it is possible to make some general observations on her visionary experience. Also information from her vision list was incorporated into the two earliest *vitae* en bloc, which suggests that the vision texts underwent less intrusive editorial change than other parts of the *vita*.

Nothing in the earliest visions is inconsistent with a Merovingian context. With the exception of her vision of St. Amandus, which she received in a sleeping state, Aldegund's experiences are all described as visions or apparitions. The visions coincided with times of prayer or fasting, and occurred at night and after the morning office.[72] They delivered verbal messages by trusted figures, such as the pale-faced messenger girl from the Virgin Mary, an angel standing midair, or St. Peter approaching the saint on the road.

There is a transcendent quality to Aldegund's experiences. Many were received in ecstasy. In the first *vita*, we are told that Aldegund, as if raised from the earth, saw a man (angel) standing next to her.[73] In the second, Aldegund saw early visions as if "rapt up high" (*quasi in sublime raperetur*). Yet in neither *vitae* were visions in ecstasy a considered more important than other types of vision. Aldegund's visions of Christ and of the Virgin Mary's messenger girl were not described as ecstatic, yet they were important visionary encounters. The indeterminate value attributed to the ecstatic state is entirely consistent with other hagiographic accounts of the period.

Another feature of the descriptions which is typical of Merovingian accounts is the use of the term "quasi" ("as if") when describing visions. This was a very familiar phrase used by Gregory of Tours to describe visions and apparitions, and it suggests the alternative reality of the dream state. In the first *vita*, for example, Aldegund saw herself *quasi elevata a terra*.[74] The second *vita* used the phrase more often. Aldegund was shown a vision "as if" Amandus was going to heaven. Aldegund also saw an orb of fire coming "as it were" from heaven.[75] Yet in none of these accounts does certainty seem to be at issue, nor does it seem likely that Aldegund's hagiographer wanted to suggest that her vision of Amandus was anything but a meaningful repre-

[72] *V. Ald.* 1.7, 13.
[73] Ibid., 1.6. The term "ecstasy" is not used in the first *vita*.
[74] Ibid., 1.5.
[75] *V. Ald.* 2.8, 12.

sentation of spiritual truth. Rather, "quasi" must be read as a traditional expression to denote supernatural visionary experience and not as an attempt to qualify the experience itself.

Ultimately, of course, it is impossible to attribute specific vocabulary to the saint. We must accept the hagiographer's role in framing the accounts. Still, if it is not always easy to determine at what point the vision narrative reflects the experience of the saint rather than the interpretation or "clarification" of the hagiographer, there are indications within the narratives that the hagiographer preserved from the original text a sense of Aldegund's visionary development; that is, that in addition to transcribing the visions' content, the hagiographer also preserved Aldegund's reaction to and interaction with the visions as they occurred.

In her youth Aldegund had problems understanding her visions. Her first recorded vision was of great riches, but she did not understand its meaning. It was only on seeing the mansion with seven ornamented columns and smelling the aromatic fragrance therein that, we are told, she began to understand that she was being promised celestial gifts. As her hagiographer or perhaps Aldegund explained, she began at that point to see more clearly, the scales having fallen from her eyes (*coepit clarius videre iam solutis squamis ab oculis*).[76] Her transition from literal to spiritual understanding was a critical turning point. That this vision was recorded in the earliest *vitae* suggests that her hagiographers regarded it as the true beginning of her spiritual life.

Despite this newfound understanding, Aldegund did not immediately realize the significance of her visions thereafter, though she understood their divine nature. It was still important to seek an interpretation of the events from an angelic bystander, especially when dealing with symbolic visions. On one occasion Aldegund did not know the meaning of the vision—although she knew it to be from a friendly source (*non dubitat esse benivolum*)—and asked that the angel tell what he saw. The angel replied with "spiritualia verba" that he saw letters encircling her head, a branch reaching up to heaven from her head, and heard a voice from Jerusalem saying that she would be a nun. In answer to further prayers Aldegund was told she must accept no husband other than Christ, to which she replied that she would do as God wished.

On another occasion Aldegund saw a vision of a young boy whom she believed at first to be an angel, but who, it was explained to her, was in fact the living Christ.[77] Later, while Aldegund was alone in her room, the Holy Spirit shone upon her through the windows in the likeness of the sun and the moon. She then saw the angel of the Lord standing in midair, asking her if she didn't see the splendor of the sun and moon shining upon her? She an-

[76] *V. Ald.* 1.5.
[77] In the second *vita* Aldegund could not immediately identify St. Peter until she asked the bystanders in her vision. *V. Ald.* 2.10.

swered that she saw it but did not understand its meaning. The angel then revealed the celestial mystery (*mysterium*) in a mellifluous voice: the sun signified Christ and the moon-rays represented the reward of the righteous.

The search for interpretation within the visionary event itself was a characteristic feature of Aldegund's visions and served a couple of purposes. In the first place, the angelic foil protected Aldegund's humility. More important, however, interpretations worked out within the framework of the vision eliminated the need for a clerical interpretation of the vision. A much later version of Aldegund's *vita* had Aldegund seeking out the hermit Gislanus for an interpretation of her important vision of St. Amandus, but the earliest *vitae* do not suggest that she had to resort to such a course of action.[78]

Aldegund's level of understanding is thus carefully noted in the first two *vitae*. She was illuminated by divine beings when she was in doubt of the vision's meaning, and otherwise the Holy Spirit, which enabled her to see the visions, enabled her also to understand them. Nuns at Aldegund's convent were granted visions which further enriched the reputation of the saint, but they were not in a position to understand the experiences for themselves; the ability to understand a vision was often what distinguished the saint from those around her.[79]

By and large, Aldegund's visions were personal. That is, their purpose was to enhance the saint's spiritual development and her sanctity. The visions did not have the didactic, soteriological purpose which was otherwise a common feature of seventh-century vision narratives. Nor did they make the specific claims for temporal benefits such as land grants and immunities which might be expected from more purely political narratives. The emphasis on love, compassion, and resilience in the face of persecution are all characteristic of the bridal mysticism which was to flower so headily in the central and late middle ages, and in many ways Aldegund's experiences anticipated that movement. Aldegund's mystical experiences brought attention to the convent she founded, and affirmed the value of the spiritual life which she established there, but the benefits she brought to her nuns were only indirectly connected to her visionary life. In only one incident is the visionary experience shown to have an extrinsic value independent of its personal, intrinsic worth. A mortally sick young boy (*puer prope iam mortuus*) was brought to Aldegund, and she ordered that he be placed before the horns of the altar in that place where the Lord had spoken to her.[80] The boy was cured, and Aldegund disclaimed any credit for the healing. However, the boy was cured at the place where she was seen speaking to Christ. In making ex-

---

[78] *V. Ald.* 3.25.

[79] Augustine, *De Genesi ad litteram* 12.9. Joseph interpreted Pharoah's dream, but Daniel saw dreams and interpreted them as well.

[80] *V. Ald.* 1.17: "ante cornu altaris, loco in quo locutus fuerat ei Dominus."

plicit the connection between the place of healing and the place before the altar where Aldegund was believed to have spoken with Christ, her hagiographer suggested that Aldegund's supernatural conversation had brought to the altar an infusion of sacred power intended to benefit all Christians.

Visions of Authority

In previous chapters we observed multiform ways in which visions supported, challenged, and illustrated the Church's endeavors and claims to supreme earthly authority in religious affairs. Compilations of miracle and vision stories by prominent ecclesiastics such as Gregory of Tours and Gregory the Great made the correlation between visionary experiences and the course of church politics seem very apparent. However, the relationship of the individual visionary to ecclesiastical authorities was potentially a sensitive one. Aldegund is a case in point. We do not know the precise nature of her relationship with the ecclesiastics of her day. It is unclear, for example, whether the vision list compiled under the aegis of Abbot Subnius resulted from pastoral concern to oversee the reports of so many visionary experiences, or whether there was a more organized investigation of the saint underway. Reference in the earliest *vitae* to Aldegund's strength and consolation when malicious voices were raised against her suggests that her visionary experiences did not gain immediate acceptance.[81] Nevertheless, Aldegund's earliest *vitae* record visions which were very explicit in making claims for her authority on certain matters of ecclesiastical interest.

Aldegund's visionary association with the society of the saints and her relationship with Christ and his angel were important mainstays of her authority as a saint, as someone who had reached a special degree of spiritual maturity. Her intimacy with Christ promised a relationship to the divine which was eternal and unchanging. Her angel-guide voiced the divine commandments by which she was to conduct her life. But neither of these sources bestowed authority in worldly terms beyond their commendation of her chosen life as a path toward salvation for herself and for her nuns. Aldegund's spiritual authority in ecclesiastical concerns derived rather from her claim, through a vision, to possess the guidance of the Holy Spirit.

In one of the more beautiful and startling of Aldegund's visions, she was at prayer in a room set apart in her house (*in secreto cubiculo domus suae*) when the Holy Spirit in the likeness of the rays of the sun and moon shone upon her through the window.[82] Aldegund was informed that the sun's rays

---

[81]Reference to detractors and malicious voices had become a hagiographic *topos* by this time—a substitute for more concrete evidence of persecution.

[82] *V. Ald.* 1.11: "Spiritus-sanctus per insertas fenestras radios ad similitudinem Solis et Lunae emittebat super eam." In the second *vita*, the same relationship with the Holy Spirit is described. The second hagiographer recorded that frequently she thought that the Holy Spirit spoke to her: "frequenter quoque aestimabat sibi loqui Spiritum sanctum." *V. Ald.* 2.9. The use

signified Christ who is the light of truth, while the rays of the moon represented the rewards of the righteous. The identification of Christ with the sun was of course a very ancient one.[83] The moon's paler, gentler light was a fitting image for redeemed humanity.

The importance of this vision cannot be overestimated. Guidance by the Spirit was the authority by which the Church governed the faithful and by which prophets prophesied. The vision of the descent of the Spirit signaled the beginning of Aldegund's spiritual mission, perhaps directed toward setting up the convent and becoming the spiritual mother of the community of nuns.[84]

The descent of the Spirit imparted to Aldegund a spiritual authority and autonomy which echoed that of the clergy. Consequently her visions included emblems of spiritual authority (the Eucharist, St. Peter) which clerical ritual shared. Even more notably, as we shall see, her hagiographers included an account of a nun's vision which showed Aldegund performing clerical ritual not permitted to her sex at this time.[85]

Both of her earliest *vitae* record visions in which she spoke to Christ in

---

of "aestimare" here might suggest that the hagiographer wished to distance himself from this claim, but his reference to Aldegund further on as "habitaculum Spiritus sancti" (*V. Ald.* 2.27) and his recording of the events below indicates otherwise. In the second *vita*, the description of the descent of the Holy Spirit upon her appears to have combined elements from another vision. Aldegund saw herself in a vision standing in the cloister (*platea*) surrounded by a great crowd when suddenly a fiery orb of very great brightness appeared to come from the sky. When she asked those standing around what it was, the man on her right replied, "Spiritus sanctus superveniet in te, et virtus Altissimi obumbrabit tibi." *V. Ald.* 2.12. Four days after this vision, at about midnight on Sunday, the promise was fulfilled. Aldegund arose to keep the morning vigil, and as she entered the church one of the sisters left it to see a very great shining light in the same place where Aldegund's vision had taken place.

[83] "Sol dominus Iesus Christus, quia fulgeat terris . . . Luna ecclesia, eo quod in hac mundi nocte resplendeat." Eucherius of Lyons, *Formulae* 2, ed. Karl Wotke, *Sancti Eucherii Lugdunensis Formulae spiritalis intelligentiae*, CSEL 31 (Vienna, 1894). In *De somniis*, Philo explains how the sun is likened to God: "And marvel not if the sun, in accordance with the rules of allegory, is likened to the Father and ruler of the Universe (chap. 73). . . . [Moses] gave the figurative title of 'Sun' to the Universal Father, to whose sight all things are open, even those which are perpetrated invisibly in the recesses of the understanding" (chap. 90). On manifestations of the Holy Spirit in the late medieval and early modern periods see Benz, *Die Vision*, pp. 563–73; Franz Joseph Dölger, *Sol Salutis*, 2d ed. (Munster, 1925). In antique and Carolingian art the sun and moon were depicted at the top of crucifixion scenes representing the eclipse. Such iconography would have further strengthened the cosmic association. I would like to thank Genevra Kornbluth for discussing this imagery with me.

[84] It is difficult to determine a clear chronology in the visions. The second *vita* indicates that the visions it recorded were experienced at Aldegund's parents' home, but it is evident that some of the later visions referred to a time of communal living. The explanation may be that communal living began at Aldegund's paternal home before her foundation of Maubeuge; we know that she established twelve nuns at the site of her parents' tomb, and she herself chose to be buried there.

[85] Wemple, *Women in Frankish Society*, pp. 141–43, has argued that the seventh-century blossoming of monasticism coincided with increased female authority in the Church. The seventh- and eighth-century missionary movement often gave women greater spiritual and quasi-clerical responsibilities. In Aldegund's vision of Amandus she is identified with this missionary movement.

front of the altar. The first *vita* mentioned Aldegund's vision in the context of a healing miracle performed at the very same spot. The second offered two occasions when this happened. After her final temptation by the Devil, Aldegund was consoled by a vision of someone standing in front of the altar in priestly garb whom she recognized to be the Lord. She approached to adore him and to ask that she might remain sheltered by his love to the end.[86] The second occasion was when a nun reported her own vision of Christ talking to Aldegund before the altar.[87] In situating Aldegund's meetings with Christ before the church altar, the hagiographer claimed that Aldegund was able to realize in visible form the God to whom every petitioner prayed at the altar. Those who described visions of Christ in the privacy of saints' cells emphasized the intimacy of the visionary's relationship with God, a relationship which bypassed the channels normally open to the faithful. But a vision of Christ before the altar, such as Aldegund reportedly received, appropriated public liturgical space.[88] That Aldegund saw Christ directly suggested that she was not dependent on priestly intervention to aid her closeness to God. Visions reported at the altar emphasized that this was a place where God was actually present, especially during the celebration of Mass. Aldegund was depicted as having a special relationship with Christ, but when her visions occurred in church they underscored the sacral nature of the altar area and the mystical nature of the rite of communion. When it was later reported that a mortally sick boy was healed at the very spot where Aldegund had seen Christ before the altar, the connection between Aldegund's vision and the divine grace such a vision represented would have seemed confirmed.

In another vision recorded in the second *vita* and alluded to in the first, Aldegund saw the gleaming figure of St. Peter from whose hands she received white (communion?) bread. We are not told whether this vision took place in the church, but once again there are the two elements outlined above; Aldegund receiving communion directly from heaven, and the vision underscoring the importance of the church as an institution through the tradition of St. Peter. The spiritual reciprocity between the saint who prays and the God who hears and instructs is a recurring motif in Aldegund's visionary experiences.

Perhaps the clearest example of Aldegund's appropriation of church ritual is in the description of a miracle-vision reported to have taken place during her final illness. As Aldegund lay dying, one of the nuns had a vision of Aldegund standing in front of the altar "in loco sacerdotis." The nun saw Aldegund break the Mass offering (the Host)[89] into a chalice, and turning to the nun Aldegund told her to inform the priest that he should sing the Mass over the chalice, because due to her illness she had been unable to take communion the day before. As day broke and the priest sang Mass, the chalice

---

[86] *V. Ald.* 2.10: "ut in amore tuo permaneam usque in finem."
[87] Ibid., 2.13.
[88] *V. Ald.* 2.13.
[89] The second *vita* referred to the offering as Christ's body.

was seen to rise from its place, suspended in the air, and then settle back down in its place. When Aldegund was told of the vision and the miracle, we are told, she kept quiet, knowing that it presaged her death.

In many respects this miracle-vision is typical of the deathbed miracles of the saints. However, certain aspects of the nun's vision are quite extraordinary. First, Aldegund was seen standing in the priest's place before the altar, even though in this period female religious were often not permitted even to approach the altar, let alone touch sacred vessels.[90] Second, Aldegund crumbled the Host into the chalice with her own hands and later received communion from it supernaturally; that is, she dispensed communion to herself with divine aid, bypassing the offices of the cleric in charge. Furthermore, she handled the Eucharist in the face of conciliar legislation sought to prevent women from touching the communion bread. The priestly functions that Aldegund was seen to perform in this vision may be indicative of a thaw in the seventh century recognized by some historians, during which women appeared to have been permitted a more active role in church services than had earlier been the case.[91] What is perhaps even more remarkable is that this story was incorporated into her *vita* and that it survived the Carolingian age during which clerics once again took firm measures to exclude women from such a role. The nun's report even survived in the eleventh-century recensions of her first and second *vitae*.

Visions that appropriated the symbols and space of ecclesiastical ritual, especially those centered on the Eucharist, illustrate the importance of those symbols and rituals in conveying ideas of spiritual authority to their audience. Not only did the spiritual meaning underlying clerical rituals give them authority, but also clerical performance of them at specific times and in specific spaces gave them meaning. Yet whereas spiritual authority in private affairs was claimed for female saints, ecclesiastical authority was not. Aldegund's visions did not impart to her real authority in the arena in which her visions took place; that is to say, they did not provide her, or any who came after her, with the authority to perform the specifically male clerical functions that she was seen to assume in the visions. Some of Aldegund's reported visions did play an immediate role in the activities of the Church, but as we shall see, in these cases the functions of the clerical office itself were not involved.

Aldegund's Visions and Seventh-Century *Kirchenpolitik*

The seventh and early eighth centuries saw the apogee of the Merovingian monastic movement, both in terms of its expansion and its vibrancy, infused

[90] Synod of Auxerre (561–605) chap. 36: "Non licet mulieri nudam manum eucharistiam accipere"; chap. 37: "Non licet, ut mulier manum suam ad pallam Dominicam mittat." CC 147A (1963), p. 269.
[91] Wemple, *Women in Frankish Society*, pp. 141–43.

as it was by the challenging Irish and later Anglo-Saxon missionary reform. The Frankish church was reforming itself, and the ascetic movement was consolidating its hold on the more ancient spiritual centers of the Neustrian kingdom, especially in the environs of Paris. It was to the north of the Frankish kingdom that the most promising Aquitainian ecclesiastics and would-be missionaries directed their attention, and from these ranks the "apostle to the Belgians," St. Amandus, came.[92] Aldegund and her circle identified their own endeavors with this missionary saint.

The missionary activity of St. Amandus (625–75) spread precisely from that area where Aldegund and her family founded their monastic establishments. Aldegund was bound to him, we are told, by ties of spiritual friendship (*amicitia spirituali familiaritate adnexus*).[93] Her second hagiographer, who felt the need to provide a short historical introduction to a vision so important to the flourishing cult of St. Amandus, described him as a man who brought many people to Christ from surrounding nations and who founded many monasteries for monks and nuns.[94] According to a later *vita*, Aldegund took the initiative to receive consecration on hearing that Amandus, bishop of Tongres-Maastricht (bishop c.647) and Autberthus, bishop of Arras and Cambrai (third quarter of the seventh century), were on their way to visit her sister's foundation at Mons.[95] (Waldetrude had been consecrated by Autberthus.)[96]

On the day of Amandus' death Aldegund was shown a vision of the missionary ascending to heaven. In her dream-vision Aldegund saw Amandus being crowned by the Lord, surrounded by a large company of souls. Angels explained that this was the reward for preaching, and Aldegund was happy to see the salvation of her friend.[97] This all-too-brief description was supplemented modestly in the second version of the *vita*, with its meaning more carefully spelled out. In this second version Amandus was seen ascending to

[92] On Amandus see *Vita Amandi*, Jonas, *Life of Columbanus*, De Moreau, *Histoire de L'église en Belgique*, vol. 1 (Brussels, 1945), esp. pp. 78–92; Van der Essen, *Études*; and Alain Dierkens, "Saint Amand" and *Abbayes et Chapitres*. At first Amandus was a preaching bishop (*episcopus ad praedicandum*), but in 647 he was appointed bishop of Maastrict by the Austrasian mayor Grimoald. Other prominent missionary bishops operating within the established church were Eligius of Noyon-Tournai, Nicetius of Trier, Remaclus of Stavelot-Malmedy, and Achar of Tounai, who was a former monk from Luxeuil. The Aquitainian element in the missionary movement in Austrasia and beyond is clearly mapped by Prinz, *Frühes Mönchtum*, map 8; its members included saints Filibert, Amandus, Vedastus, Silvinus, Eligius, Bercharius, Salvius, Remaclus Nicetius, and Hadelin. On the long history of shared interests between Austrasian lands and Aquitaine see Eugen Ewig, "L'Aquitaine et les pays Rhénans au haut moyen âge," *Cahiers de civilisation médiévale* 1 (1958), 37 ff.
[93] *V. Ald.* 1.14.
[94] *V. Ald.* 2.8. This reference to colleges of canons, a later monastic form which does not date to the seventh century, is anachronistic—a sign that the vocabulary of the work was updated when it was copied in the eleventh century.
[95] *V. Ald.* 3.13.
[96] *V. Ald.* 1.4.
[97] Ibid., 1.14.

heaven and Aldegund saw herself in that retinue. Amandus then received a crown because of the many people he had brought to Christ, just as Aldegund herself, the hagiographer comments, would deserve a crown for the many women she brought to her spiritual husband.[98]

Aldegund's vision of Amandus entering heaven was an important contribution to Amandus' cult. The vision not only claimed his immediate entrance to the society of the saints, but it also endorsed his missionary activity by showing him to be worthy of exalted status in heaven. The suggestion in the second *vita* that spiritual merit accumulated according to the number of people one brought to the Christian fold was not new; a similar idea is found in the fifth-century *Life of St. Honoratus of Arles*.[99] Missionary activity on the scale undertaken by Amandus and his associates, however, was new. Aldegund's vision of Amandus' apotheosis was important to the legitimation of an activity which was a far cry from the introspection and *stabilitas* of the Benedictine ideal. That Aldegund saw herself in the vision as part of the company who followed Amandus suggests that she and those connected with her closely identified with Amandus and his activities. It should be remembered that Aldegund herself traveled around, from her convent at Maubeuge to her foundation at the site of her parents' tomb and her sister's convent at Mons. Hers was not the cloistered life that Radegund had chosen.[100] It is not inappropriate, therefore, that the second hagiographer, perhaps echoing the sentiment of the convent, interpreted Aldegund's place in Amandus' retinue as a real association of mission. Through her monastic foundations Aldegund had indeed brought many women to Christ, and she no doubt saw her efforts as a real mission for the salvation of women. It is interesting that whereas her second hagiographer was willing to note Aldegund's place in the vision as indicating a comparison between the saint's achievements and those of Amandus, her later hagiographers did not accept this interpretation. Clearly these activities did not conform to later medieval ideals of female sanctity. According to Aldegund's third hagiographer, writing in the ninth or early tenth century, the hermit Gislanus provided the vision with the interpretation according to which Aldegund's place in the retinue indicated her own imminent death.[101] The interpretation made sense in the third *vita* only because the account of Amandus' death was placed at the end of the work, shortly before Aldegund's own. In the first two *vitae*, however, the vision of Amandus was described relatively early in the narrative.

[98] *V. Ald.* 2.8.

[99] Hilary of Arles, *Sermo de vita s. Honorati* 2.

[100] Radegund was also said to have converted many by her preaching. *GC* 104. In her letter to the bishops she reveals a deep desire to further the lot of women. *HF* 9.42. She lived in different times, however, and relied on her reputation and that of her relic acquisitions to attract new entrants. There is no mention of relics at Maubeuge except those provided by Aldegund's clothing on her death and in the eighth century those provided by the translation to Maubeuge of the saint's bodily remains.

[101] *V. Ald.* 3.25.

Indeed, Amandus died nine years earlier than the date generally accepted as that of Aldegund's own death.[102]

If Aldegund's vision of Amandus reflected the increasing importance of the missionary ideal to seventh-century claims to sanctity, so her visions and her own foundations mirrored the warming of relations between the Frankish church and the papacy. Church dedications are often useful to trace cultic fashions, which are themselves expressions of new religious and sacral allegiances. For example, the expansion of the cult of St. Martin in the fifth and sixth centuries can be traced in the proliferation of churches and altars dedicated to him.[103] In the seventh century, especially in the northeast regions of the Merovingian empire, there was an explosion of dedications to St. Peter.[104] This pattern of cultic dedication can also be traced in Aldegund's visions.

St. Peter appears to Aldegund in visions in both early *vitae*. In them his role is both pastoral and clerical. In the first *vita* Aldegund is told that she is counted among the blessed and that she should not fear: St. Peter has the power to bind and loose (*ligandi atque solvendi habens potestatem*).[105] In the second *vita* St. Peter warns her about the kingdom of God, and she later accepts communion from him.[106] Visions of St. Peter are not common in hagiographic literature before the seventh century. Earlier visions, like earlier church dedications, were of St. Martin or other local saints. The role played by St. Peter in Aldegund's visions, therefore, reflects the cultic patterns of her day, and especially a vigorous association of salvation and absolution with St. Peter, and by extension, with his representative on earth, the Pope.

We know that Waldetrude's convent church was dedicated to St. Peter, for it is the site of a miracle for the two sisters.[107] On going to the church to pray, the sisters found the doors locked against them. The doors then miraculously opened and they were able to say their prayers.[108] The miracle of an opening door was appropriate to St. Peter's role as doorkeeper of heaven, and as a reference to his miraculous escape from captivity related in Acts 12.10. Another miracle took place at another church dedicated to St. Peter at Nivelles. On the day of Aldegund's death, a great light was seen to enter

[102] I have followed van der Essen, *Étude*, p. 220, for the date 684.
[103] On Martin's cult see Eugen Ewig, "Der Martinskult im Frühmittelalter," pp. 371–92, and "Le culte de saint Martin à l'époque franque," pp. 355–70, both in *Francia* 3.2 (1979); and Etienne Delaruelle, "La spiritualité des pélerinages à saint Martin de Tours du Ve au Xe siècle," in *Pellegrinaggi e culto dei santi in Europa fino alla Ia crociata*, pp. 201–43, Convegni del Centro di studi sulla spiritualità medievale, vol. 4 (Todi, 1963).
[104] Eugen Ewig, "Der Petrus- und Apostelkult in spätrömischen und frankischen Gallien," *Zeitschrift für Kirchengeschichte* 71 (1960), 215–51.
[105] *V. Ald.* 1.10.
[106] *V. Ald.* 2.6, 10.
[107] There was also a chapel dedicated to St. Vaast at Mons, where Waldetrude was consecrated to the religious life.
[108] *V. Ald.* 1.22, 2.18. The church is identified only in the second *vita*. There was also a church dedicated to St. Peter at Lobbes.

the church where St. Gertrude was buried.[109] We do not know the dedication of Aldegund's own convent churches from the first *vita*, though later *vitae* indicate that one of them was dedicated to the Virgin Mary.

In her visions of St. Amandus and St. Peter, Aldegund's hagiographers depicted her as aware of, and influenced by, the major monastic and clerical forces of her day. Regardless of how the hagiographers chose to interpret Aldegund's role in her vision of St. Amandus, all the versions of her *vita* record it. Indeed her later hagiographers came from Amandine foundations, which in part explains the popularity of her *vita*. Her visions of St. Peter, the rock upon which the Church and the papal tradition were founded, underscored the importance of the Church's role in keeping the promise of heaven before the eyes of its flock and the place of communion in maintaining the link between heaven and earth.

It was one thing to have visions which bolstered the reputations of established male saints; it was quite another to claim access to divine knowledge and revelation on matters of ecclesiastical import, especially those potentially critical of the Church. The first hint that Aldegund possessed such authority came from the second *vita*, which may have referred back to an original source, as ambitious claims of this kind were generally excised from subsequent revisions. In the second *vita* it is averred that through communication from the Holy Spirit Aldegund knew not only the fate of those close to her but also of ecclesiastics.[110]

One can imagine the impact such a claim could have on the well-connected society to which she belonged. By such claims Aldegund reached beyond her monastic community to enter into the ecclesiastical politics of her day. It is a pity that her vision list has not survived; it is possible that her pronouncements were more explicit there. That her claim to such knowledge was a sensitive issue is witnessed by references in both early *vitae* to malicious voices arrayed against the saint.[111] It is possible that opposition toward her was fueled by reports of her visionary experiences and particularly her claimed access to divine information. The words of her detractors tortured her soul, we are told, and so Aldegund was comforted by her angel with a vision of her exalted place in heaven and the infernal punishment that awaited her detractors.[112] This vision of final revenge points to the ultimate power of the visionary: to imagine a more fitting final outcome.

[109] *V. Ald.* 1.29, 2.24.
[110] *V. Ald.* 1.9: "Insuper et de quibusdam suis propinquis intimatum erat Virgini Christi, qualiter unus et qualiter alter haberet: quem poena constringebat, et quem gloria decorabat. Nec non de viris ecclesiasticis multa detulerat sibi Angelus."
[111] Reference to Aldegund's enemies is also in the first *vita*, but there it is couched in the language of the psalms.
[112] *V. Ald.* 1.8.

Conclusion

This book opened in the world of late antiquity, which had long believed that dreams were a gateway to divine power and divine knowledge. Early Christians shared this basic assumption with their non-Christian neighbors, and in early Christian literature dreams and visions were cherished as moments when ordinary Christians were made extraordinary through a gift of the Holy Spirit. Christian thinkers began to meld scientific and philosophical ideas with theological concepts in a quest to understand how dreams worked. They believed dreams were connected to the intellect and the soul, the spiritual zones of the body. Yet by the end of the fourth century, some churchmen were reevaluating the place of the charismatic tradition within ancient Christianity; the belief that all Christians might look to their dreams and visions for an understanding of divine things was challenged and circumscribed in some quarters by prominent clerics concerned about eradicating heresy and desirous of establishing strong models of clerical leadership within the community. Furthermore, Christians increasingly desired to differentiate themselves from pagan practices and modes of thinking. Thus by the end of the fourth century the Christian tradition of broad access to divine knowledge through dreams appeared to be seriously threatened, and in hagiography especially an elitist rhetoric of merit had been adopted to bolster this trend.

As we have seen, however, the demise of the ordinary Christian visionary did not occur. Rather, in Romano-Gallic and Merovingian territories there was a clerical tendency to direct lay devotion and lay dreams toward the intercessory figure of the saint: to control, not eliminate, the ordinary dreamer. Clerics who actively fostered devotion to the saints and who took a personal role in tending their shrines were foremost in granting audience to, and recording examples of, oneiric connections between the ordinary Christian and the "special dead."

Thus in studying communities of the Romano-Gallic and Merovingian periods we see some of the ways in which an ancient metareligious phenomenon was reconciled within Christian culture. Step by step, religious leaders and thinkers enabled a Christian culture of dreaming to develop and flourish without compromising either religious orthodoxy or the primacy of clerical authority.

At the level of Christian practice, dreamers often found a sympathetic audience at cultic venues, especially at the shrines of the healing saints. Ascetic visionaries in the primitive monasteries of Gaul slowly but steadily moved toward conformity with clerical views concerning institutional and religious authority, and by the seventh century, in the monastic literature of otherworldly travel, the ascetic turned arch-sinner shined the high beam of celestial and infernal imaginings onto personal spiritual inadequacies, which could be remedied completely only through penance.

The theological implications of a Christian community which dreamed divine dreams were not as highly developed or as visibly debated in Gaul as they had been in the writings of Tertullian, Augustine, and Gregory the Great. Yet the tension between two ideas of access was acted out in Gallic communities every time a dream was reported. The dissonance of clerical opinion, the judicious interplay of merit and grace, and the perplexed ruminations of Gregory of Tours concerning visionary access are evidence of an underlying discomfort with the idea of professionalizing a class of dreamers, even if they were clerics. Whether consciously articulated or not, the idea of universal access to the divine was the ideological penumbra which underlay the demographic spectrum of visionaries recorded in the writings of Merovingian Gaul.

In the end, however, I do not want to intimate that the churchmen of the Gallo-Merovingian period were equal-opportunity, communitarian figures who denied that merit and privilege determined access to the supernatural. Indeed, Gregory of Tours was so wedded to the notion of merit that he was unable to jettison the language of privilege even when it was irreconcilable with the evidence of his own eyes. Clerics and monks are our main source for the literature that survives from these centuries, and they obviously privileged some dreamers, and some sources of information, over others. We might reasonably assume that such a winnowing process would tend to privilege clerical visions over lay, and certainty of explanation over perplexity, yet even the highly select sample of literature that we have examined preserves a discursive friction.

Why did churchmen not simply impose one particular way of thinking about visionary access? I believe the answer is simple. A flexible approach just made sense. Some dreams were clearly fanciful. Others appeared to be divinely prescient. Some visionaries, by status or circumstance, appeared spiritually deserving of legitimate visions. Others did not. Clerics viewed themselves as the guardians of the Christian community, of scriptural interpretation, and of Christian history. Their position gave them some advantage in controlling the interpretation of visions. But they never truly controlled the person of the dreamer. Thus they listened to the experiences of their flocks, and they tendered their opinion case by case, taking into account their knowledge of the individual and the community and their conceptions of an acceptable Christian oneiric landscape. For ultimately, clerical ambivalence, far from being a symptom of ecclesiastical thinking in distress, proved to be a measure of its true strength. Flexible attitudes toward dreams rewarded those in religious leadership with a measure of personal discretion, autonomy, and authority. No Christian theology ever solved fully the problem of assessing visionaries—of creating objective criteria for assessing dreams. Rather, case by case, subjectively, and in tiny increments, the dreams and visions of the broader Christian community filtered through individual clerics, and shaped a Christian community which believed it continued to be guided and protected by divinity through dreams.

APPENDIX A

Otherworld Visions
and Apocalypses

The relationship between medieval tales of otherworldly travel and ancient Christian and Jewish apocalypses is complex. Nevertheless it is generally agreed that medieval soul-journeying visions derived from this earlier literature.[1] In what ways did Christian visionary literature differ from Jewish apocalypticism?

First, though Jewish and Christian apocalypses were clearly related, their objective was different. Both Jewish and Christian apocalyptic authors claimed to have seen a future time when the world of man's present experience would dissolve away and a new world would be established in its place. That other world was described as a future event, a historical development in which a time of destruction would be followed by a time of peace. This expectant literature, especially in its Jewish from, is often argued to have arisen from periods of political stress when disintegrating hopes for the present were transmuted into hopes for the future.[2] Yet, as Bernard McGinn has argued, the popularity of Christian apocalypticism did not necessarily coincide with times of social crisis. The Christian apocalyptic author Lactantius, for example, wrote at a time of relative political and economic secur-

---

[1] The literature on apocalypticism and its genre is vast. Important here are the studies by Bernard McGinn, especially *Visions of the End: Apocalyptic Traditions in the Middle Ages* (New York, 1979) and "The End of the World and the Beginning of Christendom" in *Apocalypse Theory and the Ends of the World*, ed. Malcolm Bull (Oxford, 1995). See also the collection of essays in Richard K. Emmerson and Bernard McGinn, eds., *The Apocalypse in the Middle Ages* (Ithaca, N.Y., 1992). McGinn's work has refined and expanded Cohen's important *Pursuit of the Millenium*. Other important studies of apocalypticism include Stone, "The Metamorphosis of Ezra," and Christopher Rowland, *The Open Heaven: A Study of Apocalyptic in Judaism and Early Christianity* (London, 1982); Verbeke, Verhelst, and Welkenhuysen, *Use and Abuse of Eschatology*; Ernst Käsemann, "The Beginnings of Christian Theology" in *Apocalypticism*, ed. Robert W. Funk (New York, 1969); and Walter Schmithals, *The Apocalyptic Movement: Introduction and Interpretation*, trans. John E. Steely (Nashville, 1975).

[2] Cohen, *Pursuit of the Millenium*, pp. 19–29.

ity.³ While Jewish apocalypticism waned, Christianity was "born apocalyptic," and so apocalyptic visions never lost their appeal.⁴ For example, Latin scribes of the fifth- and sixth-century West continued to copy the late fourth-century *Vision of Paul* which had so worried Augustine. Indeed it was probably known to seventh-century Hiberno-Frankish communities.⁵ Still, educated opinion was often disapproving of this literature in the early middle ages, despite its appeal.⁶

Second, Christian visionary literature was distinct from Jewish apocalypses because it focused on the spiritual fate of the soul. From Augustine's time, expectation for the future was increasingly wedded to (interiorized notions) of the soul and its moral life.⁷ Like their political predecessors, Christian apocalypses were rooted in a particular understanding of history and contemporary events. But rather than looking purely to the future, Christian texts reflected new concerns about how the present life of the soul related to its future salvation, and addressed the fate of individual souls at death, as opposed to the collective fate of humanity.⁸ Christian visions of the soul promoted the otherworld as both a present, contemporaneous level of existence and the soul's destination upon leaving its corporeal anchor to the material world.

Finally, as Bernard McGinn felicitously notes, medieval visionary literature, though in some sense a "twin offspring" of Christian apocalypticism, was a distinct literary genre.⁹ Medieval visionary journeys were not pseudo-

---

³ McGinn, *Visions of the End*, pp. 23–25, and intro. to Lactantius and text in Bernard McGinn, *Apocalyptic Spirituality* (New York, 1979), pp. 17–80.

⁴ McGinn, *Visions of the End*, p. 11.

⁵ On the history of medieval redactions of the *Visio Pauli* see Silverstein, *Visio Sancti Pauli*. The influence of the *Visio Pauli* is evident in the seventh-century *Visio Baronti*. Apocalypses of more modest dimensions such as the fifth-century Spanish production, pseudo-Jerome's *Indiculum de adventum Enoc et Elie adque Antichristi libris duobus*, continued to be copied. See P. Angel Custodio Vega, "El 'liber de haeresibus' de San Isidoro de Sevilla y el 'Códice Ovetense,'" *La Ciudad de Dios* 171 (1958), 241–61, text pp. 262–68, commentary pp. 258–70. The Syriac text of Pseudo-Methodius' *Revelations* was translated into Latin in the seventh century and was known in Merovingian territories by the eighth. McGinn, *Visions of the End*, p. 72.

⁶ A number of "revelationes" were condemned in the fifth-century Gallic pseudo-Gelasian decretal, a list of accepted and unaccepted books including the revelations of Paul, Thomas, and Stephan. *PL* 62, 537–40, and *PL* 59, 162. Also condemned was Sulpicius Severus' *Dialogues* because in it Martin of Tours expressed a belief in the imminent millenium; later medieval manuscripts of the *Dialogues* censored this passage. Frederick Russell Hoare, *The Western Fathers. Being the Lives of SS. Martin of Tours, Ambrose, Augustine of Hippo, Honoratus of Arles, and Germanus of Auxerre* (New York, 1954; reprt. 1965), p. 121, n. 1. See also Jos Vaesen, "Sulpice Sévère et la fin des temps," in Verbeke, Verhelst, and Welkenhuysen, *The Use and Abuse of Eschatology*, pp. 49–71.

⁷ "Augustine immanentized eschatology by moving the meaning of history within the soul." McGinn, "The End of the World," p. 62.

⁸ Both *St. Peter's Apocalypse* (in James, *Apocryphal New Testament* [1955], pp. 504–21) and the *Vision of Paul* (Silverstein, *Visio Santi Pauli*) represented the fate of sinful souls in the afterlife.

⁹ McGinn, *Visions of the End*, p. 15. The phrase intentionally extends Käsemann's metaphor that "apocalyptic was the mother of all Christian theology." Elsewhere McGinn notes that me-

nymous productions as most antique apocalypses had been, nor were they intended to promote pseudobiblical revelations concerning the end. Rather, they were increasingly concerned with issues of personal identity and responsibility. From the seventh century, visionary accounts were wedded to the biographical form, permitting travelers to the otherworld to be identified by name and confronted with their failings.[10] These visionary travelers were also humble people, not biblical heroes.[11] Still, biographical visionary literature continued to share characteristics with apocalyptic literature: the idea of ascension, the need for a celestial guide to the otherworld, a panoramic view of the cosmos, and the expectation of trial and judgment.

---

dieval visions are a new "non-apocalyptic genre" because they do not address the end of history. "The End of the World," p. 64.

[10] Berschin, *Biographie und Epochenstil*, pp. 104–9.

[11] Zaleski, *Otherworldly Journeys*, p. 31, notes the swing away from biblical protagonists to ordinary Christians as one of the ways in which Pope Gregory's accounts differed from apocalyptic texts.

The Earliest *Vitae* of Aldegund of Maubeuge

There are a number of extant versions of the *Vita Aldegundis* which derive more or less from the earliest account of her life and the description of her visions compiled by Abbot Subnius of Nivelles and another unnamed monk.[1] The earliest extant *vita* (*vita* 1) was probably written soon after the saint's death, possibly 715–18.[2] The full text is in J. Mabillon's *Acta Sanctorum, OSB*, vol. 2, published in 1668.[3] The author of this *vita* claimed personal experience for some of the events described in addition to the testimony of reliable witnesses—*iuxta id quod vidimus, aut per idoneos testes audivimus.*[4] The hagiographer also claimed to have consulted the list of visions: "The aforementioned handmaid of God Aldegund related to a certain monk, abbot of Nivelles monastery, the visions and spiritual revela-

---

[1] Editions of the *Vita Aldegundis*: Mabillon, *AASS, OSB* 2 (Paris, 1668), pp. 806–15; J. Bollandus, *AASS* Ian. ii., pp. 649 ff.; J. Ghesquière, *AASS Belg. Sel.* 4 (Brussels, 1783–94), pp. 315 ff.; abbr. ed., W. Levison, *MGH, SRM* 6 (1913), pp. 79–90.

[2] The historicity of this *vita* has been much debated. Van der Essen dated it to the early eighth century based on its Merovingian style and orthography. *Étude critique et littéraire sur les Vitae des saints mérovingiens de l'ancienne Belgique* (Louvain, 1907), pp. 220–31, esp. p. 222. Based on the eleventh-century manuscript's distinctive Carolingian orthography, Levison, *MGH, SRM*, pp. 79–85, postulated a ninth-century date for the work. De Moreau, *Histoire*, p. 138, n. 2, followed Van der Essen in ascribing an earlier date for the *vita*'s composition. More recently Anne-Marie Helvétius has dated the *vita* to 715–18. *Abbayes, éveques et laïques*, p. 141. See entry in *Index Scriptorum Operumque Latino-Belgicorum Medii Aevi. Nouveau répertoire des oeuvres médiolatines belges*, ed. L. Genicot and P. Tombeur, in *Première partie: VIIe-Xe siècles*, ed. A. Stainier (Brussels, 1973), pp. 33–35.

[3] Unfortunately Wilhelm Levison chose not to include Aldegund's visions in his edition. Consequently I have relied on the text of Aldegund's visions as they appear in J. Mabillon's edition (reprinted in 1936). This same text was reproduced by J. Ghesquière in his *Acta Sanctorum Belgii selecta* 4, p. 315 ff.

[4] *V. Ald.* 1.18.

tions which her bridegroom Christ showed to her, in order, and which she wrote down."[5]

Vita 1 was a commissioned work.[6] We do not know whether it was intended for Maubeuge or Nivelles, however; since the second version of the *vita* was written for Maubeuge it seems likely that *vita* 1 was written for Nivelles.[7] The *vita* has distinct blocks of subject matter. The first four chapters describe Aldegund's highborn family, her parents' piety, and her decision to eschew marriage for the consecrated life. They also relate the decision of Aldegund's sister Waldetrude and her husband to establish and retire to their monasteries. Chapters 5–17 are exclusively concerned with Aldegund's visions. They are listed one after the other with no pause for any other type of narrative. In chapter 18 the author relates that he has used the information provided by Abbot Subnius of Nivelles, that is, the visions dictated by Aldegund herself. Chapters 19–29 address Aldegund's final illness, and include miracles witnessed by nuns at the convent, Waldetrude, an officiating priest, and the author himself. It is likely that a block of visions from the dictated list was transposed directly into the *vita* in chapters 5–17. This argues strongly for the author's reliance on a text whose integrity was considered worthy of preservation and gives credence to the author's claim to have relied on the vision list. Furthermore, the author did not transcribe the whole text, but rather selected a few choice visions.[8] This selectivity is important when considering the value of *vita* 2.

The second surviving *vita* has value independent of the first, although to a large extent it relies on the earlier text edited by J. Bollandus. The anonymous author wrote the *vita* for the convent of Maubeuge. We know this because the author addressed its members toward the end of the work: "Rejoice and be exulted, O monastery of Maubeuge . . . be happy in the Lord for you have the blessed Virgin Aldegund, beloved by God, to pray for your offences and a reconcilor of your crimes."[9] The author prefaced the visions by noting: "Now we come to the visions . . . which she herself described, and

<hr>

[5] Ibid.: "Supradicta famula Dei Aldegunda de visionibus atque revelationibus spiritualibus quas Christus sponsus eius revelavit, cuidam viro religioso Subino Abbati de Nivialensi Monasterio narravit ordinanter, et scribendo tradidit."

[6] *V. Ald.* 1.18: "petitionibus vestris obediens scribere conabor."

[7] Van der Essen considered this to be the case, but De Moreau believed it was written for Maubeuge. *Histoire*, p. 138.

[8] *V. Ald.* 1.18.

[9] *V. Ald.* 2.26: "Gaude et exulta coenobium Malbodiense . . . laetare in Domino habens beatam Virginem Aldegundem Deo dilectissimam oratricem pro tuis criminibus, et reconciliatricem pro tuis sceleribus." Michel Rouche, *Vie de sainte Sainte Aldegonde réécrite par une moniale contemporaine (VIIIe siècle)* (Maubeuge, 1988), p. vii, suggests that the second *vita* may have been written by a nun at Maubeuge. This seems unlikely since in the passage cited above the author uses "your", as opposed to "our", which one would expect if the author were addressing her own community.

were written down by certain abbot named Subnius, of the monastery of Nivelles, and to another brother, whose name we do not know; and who wrote down an account of her visions and her life." [10] Thus *vita* 2 used *vita* 1 in addition to the vision list. It is also possible that the author referred to a *vita* even more ancient than *vita* 1, perhaps the one sketched by Subnius to accompany his vision text. Such a text would be the source for both *vita* 1 and 2, thus accounting for the textual coincidences between the two.

But did the author of *vita* 2 really have access to the original list of visions dictated by Aldegund as he claimed? Van der Essen argued that the second hagiographer's fertile imagination accounted for the additional visions in the work, making *vita* 2 no more than an amplification of the first.[11] Édouard De Moreau, citing the work of D. A. Stracke, did not discount the possibility that the second *vita* had some independent value, but he did not elaborate.[12] But there are good reasons why one should not discount the second version summarily. *Vita* 2 was prepared for Aldegund's own community at Maubeuge, and we may imagine that the author had access to the community's documents. Would a community support a *vita* which did not correspond to its own written record? The author included other documents which were not used in the first *vita*, such as Maubeuge's inauthentic charter of foundation.[13] Thus perhaps the author sought out additional documentation on the visions. Even if Subnius' vision list existed in only one copy, at Nivelles rather than at Maubeuge, a likely candidate for the second *vita*'s authorship is in any case a monk of Nivelles.

The second consideration must be the visions themselves as they appear in the two texts. In those cases where the two texts related the same visions, neither the textual order nor the substance of the visions themselves was violated, although ancillary details varied and sometimes the author's interpretation also. In many cases the visions were copied verbatim or simply rephrased. Sometimes the second *vita* summarized a vision that received more extensive coverage in the first. Such summaries tended to be accurate within the limitations of brevity. The second *vita* gave greater detail to some visions mentioned in the first, and included some not mentioned at all. Far from being fanciful accretions, however, these additional vision texts are notably sober. The first *vita* had claimed to offer a selection of Aldegund's vi-

[10] *V. Ald.* 2.5: "Nunc veniendum est ad visiones . . . quas ipsa descripserat, et tradiderat cuidam religioso Abbati, nomen Sobino, de monasterio Nivellensi, et alteri Fratri, cuius nomen ignoramus; quique scripsit visiones eius et vitam."

[11] Van der Essen, *Étude*, p. 224.

[12] De Moreau, *Histoire*, p. 140, n. 2, noted that Stracke made a comparison between the two texts. "Een oud-frankische Visioenenboek uit de zevende eeuw," *L'Historisch Tijdschrift* 7 (1928), 361–87, and 8 (1929), 18–38, 167–82, 340–71. De Moreau agreed with Stracke's findings that suggest the two *vitae* had independent access to the original vision text. I have been unable to consult the work, and De Moreau does not indicate the basis upon which Stracke's assertion was made. Those arguments for the validity of the second *vita* which I present are independently arrived at.

[13] *V. Ald.* 2.27.

sions, and not a full text. The second *vita* did not repeat visions from the first *vita* unless they were of particular importance, such as Aldegund's vision of St. Amandus ascending to heaven.

The structure of the first *vita* with its list of visions in a block is replicated in the second *vita*. However in *vita* 2 the block of visions distort the narrative flow. Chapters 1–4 introduces the saint and her family up to the time she was ready to eschew marriage for Christ. Chapters 5–13 record a list of the visions she received during her lifetime (not just those received at her parents' house as the hagiographer indicates). Chapters 14–16 return to her struggles with her mother concerning her monastic vocation. Chapters 17–19 record miracles and other details of her life in the convent. Chapters 20–27 record visions with Aldegund as their subject as received by the priest, a novice, a senior nun, and Waldetrude—visions presaging her death, glorious afterlife, and the translation of her remains. It is clear from the way the *vita* is constructed that the later hagiographer brought together documents or descriptions without dismantling their order. Thus the biographic narrative was not always chronological. There was no attempt to do what later medieval versions of the *vita* were to do, namely to rearrange the visions to comply with a supposed chronology of the saint's life.

Finally, the second *vita* makes certain claims for Aldegund's authority in spiritual matters. *Vita* 2 claims that Aldegund knew the eternal destiny not only of those close to her but also of ecclesiastics. Such claims were potentially disruptive, and opposition may have been voiced during her lifetime. Churchmen did not feel comfortable when female visionaries started becoming involved, even if only in their dreams and visions, with ecclesiastical politics. Additionally, the second *vita* retained those powerful images of the first, such as the descent of the Holy Spirit on Aldegund and the favorable interpretation of Aldegund's place in her vision of Amandus.

The *Acta Sanctorum* edition also includes two later versions. One *vita* was attributed questionably to Hucbald (d. 930).[14] Another was preserved in a manuscript from the monastery of St. Ghislain. Except for her vision of Amandus, Aldegund's visions are almost entirely excised. Further later versions survive, but only the first two *vitae* are directly relevant to discussion of Merovingian material.

---

[14] Scholars are divided on the attribution of the *vita* to Hucbald, first made by Surius and reproduced in the *Acta Sanctorum*. In his edition for the *Monumenta*, Levison doubted that Hucbald was the author, noting that no manuscripts make the attribution and that there are textual similarities between it and the eleventh-century *Vita Gisleni*. Van der Essen contended that the borrowing could as likely be in the other direction and noted similarities between this *vita* and another by Hucbald, that of Rictrude. *Études*, p. 225.

Selected Bibliography

Primary Sources

Ambrose of Milan. *Letters*. Trans. Sister Mary Melchior Beyenka. Fathers of the Church, 26. New York: Fathers of the Church, Inc., 1954.

————. *De excessu fratris*. Ed. Otto Faller, *Sancti Ambrosii opera, pars septima, CSEL* 73. 1955; trans. H. de Romestin, *St. Ambrose: Select Works and Letters*. Select Library of Nicene and Post-Nicene Fathers. Vol. 10. Edinburgh: T & T Clark, 1989.

Ambrosiaster. *Commentary on the Pauline Letters*. Ed. Henry Joseph Vogels, *Ambrosiastri qui dicitur commentarius in epistulas Paulinas, CSEL* 81.ii. Vienna: Hoelder, Pichler, Tempsky, 1968.

Anso. *Vita Ursmari*. Ed. Wilhelm Levison, *MGH, SRM* 6. 1913.

Apophthegmata: William Bousset, *Apophthegmata. Studien zur Geschichte des ältesten Mönchtums* Tübingen: J. C. B. Mohr (Paul Siebeck),1923; Jean Dion and Guy Oury, *Les sentences des pères du désert: les apophtegmes des pères (recension de Pélage et Jean)* Introduction by Lucien Regnault, Sablé-sur-Sarthe: Solesmes, 1966; Lucien Regnault, *Les sentences des pères du désert: Série des anonymes*. Sablé-sur-Sarthe, Bégrolles-en-Mauge: Solesmes, Bellefontaine, 1985.

Apostolic Tradition. Trans. Gregory Dix, *The Treatise on the Apostolic Tradition of St. Hippolytus of Rome, Bishop and Martyr*. London: SPCK, 1968.

Apuleius of Madaura. *The Golden Ass (Metamorphoses)*. Ed. Rudolph Helm, *Apulei Platonici Madaurensis Metamorphoseon libri XI*. Leipzig: B. G. Teubner, 1931.

Artemidorus. *The Interpretation of Dreams: Oneirocritica*. Trans. Robert J. White. Park Ridge, N.J.: Noyes Press, 1975.

Athanasius. *Life of St. Anthony*. Ed. Jacques Noret, *Vitae duae antiquae sancti Athanasii Athonitae, CC*, Series graeca 9. 1982; Migne, *PG* 26. 1887; trans. Robert T. Meyer, *St. Athanasius, Life of St. Anthony*. Ancient Christian Writers, 10. Westminster, Md.: Newman Press, 1950; ed. and trans. G. J. M. Bartelink, *Althanasius. Vie d'Antoine, SC* 400. 1994.

Augustine. *Contra Faustum libri xxxiii*. Ed. Josephus Zycha, *Sancti Aureli Augustini. CSEL* 25. 1891.

————. *De cura pro mortuis gerenda*. Ed. Joseph Zycha, *CSEL* 41. Vienna: F. Tempsky, 1900; Migne, *PL* 40. 1845; trans. H. Browne, Select Library of Nicene and Post-Nicene Fathers. Vol. 3. Edinburgh: T & T Clark. 1887.

———. *Enchiridion*. Ed. E. Evans. CC 46. 1969; trans. J. F. Shaw, Select Library of Nicene and Post-Nicene Fathers. Vol. 3. Edinburgh: T & T Clark, 1887.

———. *Epistulae*. Ed. Alois Goldbacher, *CSEL* 34, 44, 57, 58, 63. Vienna: F. Tempsky, 1895–1923; ed. Ioannes Divjak, *CSEL* 84. 1971.

———. *De fide rerum invisibilium*. Ed. M. P. J. Van den Hout. CC 46. 1969.

———. *De Genesi ad litteram*. Ed. Joseph Zycha, *Aurelii Augustini Opera, Pars. III*. *CSEL* 28. Vienna: Tempsky, 1894; trans. with notes, John Hammond Taylor, *Ancient Christian Writers* 41, 42. New York: Newman Press, 1982.

———. *In Johannis Evangelium tractatus ccxxiv*. Ed. Radbod Willems, CC 36. 1954.

———. *De natura et origine animae libri quattuor*. Ed. Carolus Urba and Joseph Zycha, *CSEL* 60. Vienna: F. Tempsky, 1913; trans. Peter Holmes and Robert Ernest Wallis, Select Library of Nicene and Post-Nicene Fathers. Vol. 5, *St. Augustine*. Edinburgh: T & T Clark, 1887.

———. *Two Books on Genesis against the Manichees*. Trans. Roland J. Teske. Fathers of the Church, 84. Washington, D.C.: Catholic University of America Press, 1991.

Avitus of Braga. *Epistula ad Palchonium episcopum Bracarensem de reliquiis s. Stephani*. PL 41, 805–16.

Avitus of Vienne. *Contra Eutychianam heresim libri II*. Ed. R. Peiper, *MGH, AA* 6.ii.

Baudonivia. *Vita Radegundis*. Ed. Bruno Krusch, *MGH, SRM* 2. 1888.

Bede. *Historia ecclesiastica gentis Anglorum*. Ed. B. Colgrave and R. Mynors. Oxford: Clarendon Press, 1969.

Benedict of Nursia. *Rule for Monks*. Ed. Rudolphus Hanslik, *Benedicti Regula. CSEL* 75. 1960; ed. Adalbert de Vogüé and Jean Neufville, *La règle de saint Benoit*. SC 181, 182, with commentaries by Adalbert de Vogüé, SC 184, 185, 186. 1971–7; trans. J. McCann, *The Rule of St. Benedict*. London: Sheed and Ward, 1970.

Boniface. *Letters*. Trans. and intro. Ephraim Emerton, *The Letters of Saint Boniface*. New York: Columbia University Press, 1940.

Caesarius of Arles. *Opera*. Ed. G. Morin, *S. Caesarii Opera omnia*. 2 vols. Maredsous, 1937–42; ed. G. Morin, *Caesarius Arelatensis Sermones*, CC 103, 104. 1953.

Cassian of Marseilles. *Conlationes*. Ed. and trans. with comm. Eugene Pichery, *Jean Cassien, Conférences*. SC 42, 54, 64. 1955–9; ed. Michael Petschenig, *CSEL* 13. 1886.

———. *Institutiones*. Ed. and trans. with comm. Jean-Claude Guy, *Jean Cassien, Institutions cénobitiques*. SC 109. 1965; ed. Michael Petschenig. *CSEL* 17. 1888.

Cicero, *De re publica*. Trans. Clinton Walker Keyes. *Loeb*. 1977.

Claudian. *Epithalamium of Honorius and Maria*. Text and trans. Maurice Platnauer, *Claudian* 1. *Loeb* 135. 1976.

Clement of Alexandria. *Paedagogus*. Trans. William Wilson, *Writings of Clement of Alexandria*. Vol. 1. Ante-Nicene Christian Library, 4. Edinburgh: T&T Clark, 1871.

———. *Stromates*. Ed. A. Le Boulluec and P. Voulet, SC 278. 1981.

Columba. *Altus Prosator*. Trans. Harold Isbell, *The Last Poets of Imperial Rome*. Harmondsworth: Penguin, 1971.

Concilia Africae a.345–a.525. Ed. C. Munier, CC 259. 1974.

Concilia Galliae a.314–a.506. Ed. C. Munier, CC 148. 1963.

Concilia Galliae a.511–a.695. Ed. C. de Clercq, CC 148A. 1963.

Constantius of Lyon. *Vita Germani ep. Autissiodorensis*. Ed. R. Borias, SC 112. 1965.

Cyprian of Carthage. *Letters (1–81)*. Trans. Sister Rose Bernard Donna, Fathers of the Church, 51, Washington: Catholic University of America Press, 1965.

Eldefonsus. *Revelatio*. PL 106, 881–90.

Epiphanius of Salamis. *Panarion*. Ed. Ronald E. Heine, *The Montanist Oracles and Testimonia*. Patristic Monograph Series, 14. Macon, Ga.: Mercer University Press, 1989.

Eucherius of Lyons. *Formulae*. Ed. Karl Wotke, *Sancti Eucherii Lugdunensis Formulae spiritalis intelligentiae*. CSEL 31. Vienna: F. Tempsky, 1894.

Eusebius. *The Ecclesiastical History.* Trans. Kirsopp Lake and J. E. L. Oulton. 2 vols. New York: Putnam, 1926–32.
———. *Vita Constantini.* Trans. Ernest Cushing Richardson, Nicene and Post-Nicene Fathers, second series 1. Grand Rapids, Mich.: Eerdmans, 1904.
Evagrius Ponticus. *153 Chapters on Prayer.* Trans. John Eudes Bamberger, *Evagrius Ponticus: The Praktikos, Chapters on Prayer.* Kalamazoo, Mich.: Cistercian Publications, 1981.
———. *Praktikos.* Ed. A. and C. Guillaumont, *Évagre le Pontique, Traité practique ou le moine. SC* 170, 171. 1971.
Evagrius Scholasticus. *Historia ecclesiastica. PG* 86.
Evodius of Uzalis. *Ep.* 158. Ed. Alois Goldbacher, *S. Aureli Augustini Hipponiensis episcopi epistulae III. CSEL* 44. Vienna: F. Tempsky, 1904.
Fortunatus, Venantius. "Ad Dynamium Massiliensem." *Carmina* 6.9. Ed. Fridericus Leo, *MGH, AA* 4.1. 1881; trans. Judith George, *Venantius Fortunatus: Personal and Political Poems.* Translated Texts for Historians 23. Liverpool: Liverpool University Press, 1995.
———. "Ad Felicem episcopum Namneticum. In laude." *Carm* 3.8.29. Ed. Fridericus Leo, *MGH, AA* 4. 1881.
———. "Ad Iustinum et Sophiam Augustos." *MGH, AA* 4.1. 1881.
———. *Liber de virtutibus s. Hilarii.* Ed. Bruno Krusch, *MGH, AA* 4.2. 1885.
———. *Opera Poetica.* Ed. Fridericus Leo, *MGH, AA* 4.1. 1881.
———. *Vita s. Germani ep. Parisiensis.* Ed. Bruno Krusch, *MGH, SRM* 7. 1920.
———. *Vita s. Martini.* Ed. Fridericus Leo, *MGH, AA* 4.1. 1881.
———. *Vita s. Radegundis.* Ed. Bruno Krusch, *MGH, SRM* 2. 1888.
Fredegar. *Chronicarum quae dicuntur Fredegari Scholastici libri IV cum continuationes.* Ed. Bruno Krusch, *MGH, SRM* 2. 1888; ed. and trans. John Michael Wallace-Hadrill, *The Fourth Book of the Chronicle of Fredegar with its Continuations.* London: Nelson, 1960.
Fulgentius. *Mythography.* Trans. Leslie George Whitbread, *Fulgentius the Mythographer.* Columbus: Ohio State University, 1971.
Pseudo-Gelasius. *Decretal.* Ed. E. von Dobschütz, *TU* 38, 4. 1912; *PL* 59, 162; *PL* 62, 537–40.
———. *Decretum. PL* 59, 157–66. Ed. E. von Dobschütz, "Das Decretum Gelasianum de libris recipiendis et non recipiendis.' *TU* 38 (1912).
Gennadius, *De viris inlustribus.* Ed. E. Richardson, *TU* 14, 1. 1896.
Gregory the Great. *Dialogorum libri IV.* Ed. Adalbert de Vogüé, *SC* 251, 260, 265. 1978–80; Umberto Morrica, *Gregorii Magni Dialogi libri IV.* Rome: Tip. del Senato, 1924; trans. Odo John Zimmerman; *Gregory the Great: Dialogues.* New York: Fathers of the Church, 1959.
———. *Moralia in Job.* Ed. Marc Adriaen, *CC* 143. 3 vols. 1979–85; trans. André de Gaudemaris and A. Bocognano, intro. Robert Gillet, *Grégoire le Grand, Morales sur Job. SC,* 32, 212, 221. 1952–75; Trans. J. Bliss, *Morals on the Book of Job.* 3 vols. Oxford: John Henry Parker, 1844–50.
Gregory of Nyssa. *Canonical Epistle of St. Gregory of Nyssa to Letoïus, Bishop of Melitene.* Ed. Henry R. Percival, *The Seven Ecumenical Councils.* A Select Library of Nicene and Post-Nicene Fathers. Vol. 14. Edinburgh: T & T Clark, 1899.
Gregory of Tours, *Vitae patrum.* Ed. Bruno Krusch, *MGH, SRM* 1.2. 1885; intro. and trans. Edward James, *Gregory of Tours: Life of the Fathers.* Translated Texts for Historians, Latin Series, 1. Liverpool: Liverpool University Press, 1985; 2d ed. 1991.
———. *Gloria confessorum.* Ed. Bruno Krusch, *MGH, SRM* 1.2. 1885; trans. Raymond Van Dam, *Glory of the Confessors.* Translated Texts for Historians, 4. Liverpool: Liverpool University Press, 1988.
———. *Historia Francorum.* Ed. Bruno Krusch and Wilhelm Levison, *MGH, SRM* 1.1. 1937–42.

————. *Liber de passione et virtutibus sancti Iuliani martyris.* Ed. Bruno Krusch, *MGH,*
  SRM 1.2. 1885.
————. *Liber in gloria martyrum.* Ed. Bruno Krusch, *MGH, SRM* 1.2. 1885.
————. *De virtutibus s. Martini.* Ed. Bruno Krusch, *MGH, SRM* 1.2. 1885.
Hilary of Arles. *Sermo de vita s. Honorati.* Ed. Marie-Denise Valentin, *SC* 235. 1977.
Hilary of Poitiers. *Contra Constantium Imperatorem.* Ed. A. Rocher, *SC* 334. 1987.
Hippolytus. *The Apostolic Tradition.* Trans. Gregory Dix. 2d ed. London: SPCK, 1968.
Homer, *Iliad.* Trans. Alexander Pope. London: Methuen, 1967.
Hucbald, *vita s. Rictrudis. AASS* Maii iii (1680) pp. 79–89.
Isidore of Seville. *De ecclesiasticis officiis.* Ed. Christopher M. Lawson, *Sancti Isidori epis-*
  copi Hispalensis de ecclesiasticis officiis. CC 113. 1989.
————. *Etymologiae.* PL 82, 74–728.
————. *Sententiarum libri tres.* PL 83, 537–738.
Jerome, *Adversus Jovinianum libri duo.* PL 23, 211–352.
————. *Contra Vigilantium.* PL 23, 354–68.
————. *Vita s. Pauli.* PL 23, 17–30.
Pseudo-Jerome, *Indiculum de adventum Enoc et Elie adque Antichristi libris duobus.*
  P. Angel Custodio Vega, "El 'liber de haeresibus' de San Isidoro de Sevilla y el 'Códice
  Ovetense.'" *La Ciudad de Dios* 171 (1958), 241–61.
Jonas of Bobbio. *Vita s. Columbani discipulorumque eius Attalae, Eustasii, Burgundo-*
  farae et Bertulfi. Ed. Bruno Krusch *MGH, SRM* 4. 1902.
Julianus Pomerius. *De vita contemplativa.* PL 59, 415–520; trans. M. J. Suelzer, Ancient
  Christian Writers, 4. Westminster: Newman Press, 1947.
Lausiac History. See Palladius.
Letter to Diognetus. Trans. Kirsopp Lake, *Apostolic Fathers.* Vol. 2. Loeb 25. 1913.
Liber Historiae Francorum. Ed. Bruno Krusch, *MGH, SRM* 2. 1888; ed., trans., and
  intro. Bernard S. Bachrach. Lawrence, Ks.: Coronado Press, 1973.
Liber Sacramentorum Gellonensis. Ed. Antoine Dumas, CC 159, 159A. 1981.
Life of Onnophrius. Trans. and intro. T. Vivian. Kalamazoo: Cistercian Publications,
  1993.
Lucian, presbyter. *Revelationem sancti Stephani.* See Avitus of Braga.
Macrobius. *Commentary on the Dream of Scipio.* Ed. F. Eyssenhardt, *Macrobius.* Leip-
  zig, 1893; trans. William Harris Stahl. New York: Columbia University Press, 1952.
Marcus Aurelius. *Meditations.* Trans. Maxwell Staniforth. Harmondsworth: Penguin,
  1964.
Margery Kempe. *The Book of Margery Kempe.* Ed. Barry Windeatt. Harmondsworth:
  Penguin, 1985.
The Nag Hammadi Library in English. Ed. James M. Robinson. 3d ed. San Francisco:
  Harper and Row, 1988.
Oeuvres monastiques. Ed. Adalbert de Vogüé and Joël Courreau, *SC* 345. 1988.
Origen of Alexandria. *Contra Celsum.* Trans. Frederick Crombie, *Writings of Origen,* 2.
  Ante-Nicene Christian Library, 23. Edinburgh: T & T Clark, 1872.
————. *De Principiis.* Trans. Frederick Crombie, *Writings of Origen,* 1. Ante-Nicene
  Christian Library, 10. Edinburgh: T & T Clark, 1871.
Otloh of St. Emmeran. *Liber visionem.* PL 146, 341–88.
Palladius. *Lausiac History.* Cuthbert Butler, *The Lausiac History of Palladius.* 2 vols.
  Texts and Studies, 6. Cambridge, 1898–1904.
Paphnutius. *Histories of the Monks of Upper Egypt.* Trans. and intro. T. Vivian. Kala-
  mazoo, Mich.: Cistercian Publications, 1993.
Passio s. Leudegarii ep. et martyris Augustodunensis, I. Ed. Bruno Krusch, *MGH, SRM* 5.
  1910.
Passio SS. Perpetuae et Felicitatis. Ed. and trans. W. H. Shewring. London: Sheed and
  Ward, 1931.

Passio s. Praeiecti episcopi et martyris Arvernensis. Ed. Bruno Krusch, *MGH, SRM* 5. 1910.

Paul the Deacon. *History of the Lombards.* Trans. William Dudley Foulke, ed. with intro. Edward Peters. Philadelphia: University of Pennsylvania Press, 1974.

Paulinus of Milan, *Vita s. Ambrosii. PL* 14.

Pausanias. *Descriptio Graeciae.* Trans. Peter Levi, *Pausanias: Guide to Greece.* Harmondsworth: Penguin, 1979.

Philo of Alexandria. *Allegorical Interpretation of Genesis.* Trans. F. H. Colson and G. H. Whitaker, *Philo I.* Loeb 226. 1929.

———. *De somniis.* Trans. F. H. Colson and G. H. Whitaker, *Philo* 5. Loeb 275. 1929.

Plato, *Republic.* Trans. P. Shorey. *Loeb* 276. 1935.

———. *Timaeus.* Trans. Donald J. Zeyl, *Plato: Complete Works.* Ed. John M. Cooper. Indianapolis: Hackett, 1997.

Priscillian, *Tractates.* Ed. George Schepss, *Opera quae supersunt. CSEL* 18. 1889.

Prudentius. *Liber Cathemerinon.* Ed. Ioannes Bergman, *CSEL* 61. 1926; trans. Harold Isbell, *The Last Poets of Imperial Rome.* Harmondsworth: Penguin, 1971.

———. *Psychomachia.* Ed. Maurice P. Cunningham, *Aurelii Prudentii Clementis Carmina.* Turnhout: Brepols, 1966; ed. Ioannes Bergman, *CSEL* 61 (1926). Trans. Harold Isbell, *The Last Poets of Imperial Rome.* Harmondsworth: Penguin, 1971.

———. *Tituli historiarum.* Ed. Ioannes Bergman, *CSEL* 61. 1926.

Pseudo-Dionysius the Areopagite. *The Divine Names.* Trans. C. E. Rolt, Translations of Christian Literature. Series 1: Greek Texts. London: SPCK, 1920.

———. *Mystical Theology.* Trans. C. E. Rolt, Translations of Christian Literature. Series 1: Greek Texts. London: SPCK, 1920.

Quodvultdeus. *De promissionibus et praedictionibus Dei.* Ed. René Braun, *Opera Quodvultdeo Carthaginiensi episcopo tributa.* CC 60 (1976), pp. 1–223.

Les règles des saints pères. Ed. A. de Vogüé, *SC* 297, 298. (1982).

Règles monastiques d'occident ive—vie siècle. D'Augustin à Ferréol. ed. V. Desprez and A. de Vogüé. Bégrolles-en-Mauges: Abbaye de Bellefontaine, 1980.

Regula Magistri. Ed. Adalbert de Vogüé, *SC* 105, 106.

Rule of Donatus of Besançon. PL 87, 273–98.

The Shepherd of Hermas. Trans. and intro. G. F. Snyder, London, 1968; trans. Kirsopp Lake, *Loeb* 25. 1913.

Sidonius Apollinaris. *Epistulae et Carmina.* Ed. Christianus Luetjohann, *MGH, AA* 8. 1887; trans. W. B. Anderson, *Poems and Letters. Loeb.* 1936.

Somnia Danielis. Steven Fischer. *The Complete Medieval Dreambook: A Multilingual Alphabetical Somnia Danielis Collation.* Bern: Peter Lang, 1982.

Sulpicius Severus. *Vita Martini.* Ed. Carolus Halm, *Sulpicii Severi libri qui supersunt. CSEL* 1. Vienna: Geroldi Filium Bibliopolam Academiae, 1866; trans. and intro. Jacques Fontaine, *Sulpice Sévère, Vie de St. Martin. SC* 133–35. 1967–9.

Synesius of Cyrene. *De insomniis. PG* 66, 1281–1320.

Tacitus. *Germania.* Ed. Karolus Müllenhoff, *Germania Antiqua.* Berlin, 1873.

Tertullian. *De anima.* Ed. Jan Hendrik Waszink, *Tertulliani Opera, pars 2. Opera Montanistica.* CC 2. 1954; trans. Peter Holmes, *The Writings of Tertullian* 2. Ante-Nicene Christian Library. Vol. 15. Edinburgh: T & T Clark, 1874.

———. *De baptismo.* Ed. Augusti Reifferscheid and Georgii Wissowa, *Tertulliani Opera, pars 1. CSEL* 20. Vienna: F. Tempsky, 1890.

———. *De praescriptione haereticorum.* Ed. R. F. Refoulé, CC 1. 1954.

———. *De pudicitia.* Ed. Charles Munier and Claudio Micaelli, *SC* 394, 395. 1993; ed. Eligius Dekkers, CC 2. 1954; ed. Augusti Reifferscheid and Georgii Wissowa, *Tertulliani Opera.* Vol. 1. CSEL 20. Vienna: F. Tempsky, 1890.

Victricius of Rouen. *De laude sanctorum.* Ed. R. Demeulenaere, CC 64. 1985; *PL* 20, 443–58.

Visio Baronti monachi Longoretensis. Ed. Wilhelm Levison, *MGH, SRM* 5. 1910; trans. Jocelyn N. Hillgarth, *Christianity and Paganism, 350–750: The Conversion of Western Europe*. Philadelphia: University of Pennsylvania Press, 1969.

Visio Sancti Pauli: The History of the Apocalypse in Latin, Together with Nine Texts. Ed. Theodore Silverstein, Studies and Documents, 4. 1935.

Vision of Drythelm. See Bede, *Ecclesiastical History*.

Vision of the Monk of Wenlock. Trans. and intro. Ephraim Emerton, *The Letters of Saint Boniface*. New York: Columbia University Press, 1940.

Vision of Peter. (Apocalypse of Peter). Trans. Montague Rhodes James, *The Apocryphal New Testament*. Oxford: Clarendon Press, 1924.

Vision of Thurkill. Ed. Paul Gerhard Schmidt, *Visio Thurkilli relatore, ut videtur , Radulpho de Coggeshall*. Leipzig: B. G. Teubner, 1978.

Vision of Wetti. Ed. E. Dümmler, *MGH, Poetae Latini Aevi Carolini* 2. 1884; trans. David A. Traill, *Walahfrid Strabo's Visio Wettini: Text, Translation and Commentary*. Bern: Peter Lang, 1974.

Vita s. Aldegundis. Ed. J. Bollandus, *AASS* Ianuarii. ii. 1643; J. Mabillon, *AASS, OSB* 2. 1668; J. Ghesquière, *AASS Belgica Selecta* 4. 6 vols. Brussels, 1783–94; Abbrev. ed., Wilhelm Levison, *MGH, SRM* 6. 1913.

Vita s. Ambrosii. See Paulinus of Milan.

Vita s. Aniani ep. Aurelianensis. Ed. Bruno Krusch, *MGH, SRM* 3. 1896.

Vita s. Antonii. See Athanasius.

Vita s. Anstrudis abbatissae Laudunensis. Ed. Wilhelm Levison, *MGH, SRM* 6. 1913.

Vita s. Austreberthae abbatissae Pauliacensis. Ed. J. Mabillon, *AASS, OSB* 3, i. 1639.

Vita s. Balthildis. Ed. Bruno Krusch, *MGH, SRM* 2. 1888.

Vita s. Bertiliae abbatissae Calensis. Ed. Wilhelm Levison, *MGH, SRM* 6. 1913.

Vitae s. Caesarii Episcopi Arelatensis, libri duo. Ed. Bruno Krusch, *MGH, SRM* 3. 1896.

Vita s. Columbani. See Jonas of Bobbio.

Vita et virtutes Eparchii reclusi Ecolismensis. Ed. Bruno Krusch, *MGH, SRM* 3. 1896.

Vita s. Eustadiola. *AASS* Iun ii. 1698.

Vita s. Fursei. *AASS* Ian ii. 1643; ed. Bruno Krusch, *MGH, SRM* 4. 1902 (does not include the visions); M. P. Ciccarese, "Le Visioni di S. Fursa." *Romanobarbarica* 8 (1984–85), 231–303.

Vita s. Geretrudis Nivialensis. Ed. Bruno Krusch, *MGH, SRM* 2. 1888.

Vita s. Glodesindis, *AASS* iulii vi. 1729.

Vita s. Nivardi episcopi Remensis. Ed. Wilhelm Levison, *MGH, SRM* 5. 1910.

Vita s. Odiliae abbatissae Hohenburgensis. Ed. Wilhelm Levison, *MGH, SRM* 6. 1913.

Vita s. Praejecti. See *Passio s. Praejecti*.

Vita s. Radegundis. See Baudonivia and Fortunatus.

Vita s. Rictrudis. See Hucbald.

Vita s. Rusticulae sive Marciae abbatissae Arelatensis auctore Florentio. Ed. J. Mabillon *AASS, OSB*. Vol. 2. Paris, 1669; repr. *AASS* Augusti ii. 1735; abbrev. ed., Bruno Krusch, *MGH, SRM* 4. 1902.

Vita s. Sadalberga abbatissae Laudunensis. Ed. Bruno Krusch, *MGH, SRM* 5. 1910.

Vita s. Segolenae vidua. *AASS* iulii v. 1727.

Vita s. Sigiramni abbatis Longoretensis. Ed. Bruno Krusch, *MGH, SRM* 4. 1902.

Vita s. Ursmari. See Anso.

Vita s. Vulframni episcopi Senonici. Ed. Wilhelm Levison, *MGH, SRM* 5. 1910.

Vita s. Wandregiseli abbatis Fontanellensis. Ed. Bruno Krusch, *MGH, SRM* 5. 1910.

Vitas sanctorum Patrum Emeretensium. Ed. A. Maya Sanchez, *CC* 116. 1992.

Vitae Patrum Jurensium. Ed. François Martine, *SC* 142. 1968; ed. Bruno Krusch, *MGH, SRM* 3. 1896.

Secondary Sources

Adam, J.-P., G. Aubin, J.-F. Baratin et al. *Les premiers monuments chrétiens de la France.* Vol. 2, *Sud-Ouest et Centre.* Paris: Picard, 1996.

Aigrain, René. *Sainte Radegonde (vers 520–87).* Paris: Librairie Victor Lecoffre, 1918.

Alexandre, Monique. *Le commencement du livre Genèse I–V.* Christianisme antique, 3. Paris: Beauchesne, 1988.

Alsup, J. *The Post-Resurrection Appearance Stories of the Gospel Tradition: A History-of-tradition Analysis.* Stuttgart: Calwer-Verlag, 1975.

Amat, Jacqueline. *Songes et visions. L'au-delà dans la littérature latine tardive.* Paris: Études Augustiniennes, 1983.

Angenendt, Arnold. *Heilige und Reliquien. Die Geschichte ihres Kultes vom frühen Christentum bis zur Gegenwart.* Munich: C. H. Beck, 1994.

———. "Theologie und Liturgie der mittelalterlichen Toten-Memoria." In *Memoria. Der geschichtliche Zeugniswert des liturgischen Gedenkens im Mittelalter,* ed. Karl Schmid and Joachim Wollasch, pp. 79–199. Munich: Wilhelm Fink Verlag, 1984.

Arbesmann, Rudolph. "Fasting and Prophecy in Pagan and Christian Antiquity." *Traditio* 7 (1949–51), 1–71.

Ariès, Philippe. "Une conception ancienne de l'au-delà." In *Death in the Middle Ages,* ed. Herman Braet and Werner Verbeke, pp. 78–87. Leuven: Leuven University Press, 1983.

———. *The Hour of Our Death.* Trans. of *L'homme devant la mort* by Helen Weaver. New York: Alfred J. Knopf, 1981.

———. *Western Attitudes toward Death from the Middle Ages to the Present.* Johns Hopkins Symposia in Comparative History, trans. Patricia M. Ranum. Baltimore: Johns Hopkins University Press, 1974.

Ash, James, L. "The Decline of Ecstatic Prophecy in the Early Church." *Theological Studies* 37 (1978), 227–52.

Astell, Ann W. *The Song of Songs in the Middle Ages.* Ithaca, N.Y.: Cornell University Press, 1990.

Atsma, Hartmut. "Les monastères urbains du nord de la Gaule." In *La christianisation des pays entre Loire et Rhin (ive–viie siècle),* ed. Pierre Riché pp. 163–87. Paris: Éditions du Cerf, 1993.

———. Ed. *La Neustrie: Les pays au nord de la Loire de 650 à 850; colloque historique international.* Beihefte der Francia, 16. Sigmaringen: Jan Thorbecke Verlag, 1989.

Atwell, R. R. "From Augustine to Gregory the Great: An Evaluation of the Emergence of the Doctrine of Purgatory." *Journal of Ecclesiastical History* 38 (1987), 173–86.

Aubrun, Michel. "Charactères et portée religieuse et sociale des 'visiones' en Occident du vie au xie siècle." *Cahiers de civilisation médiévale* 23 (1980), 109–30.

Auerbach, Erich. *Literary Language and Its Public in Late Latin Antiquity and the Middle Ages.* New York: Pantheon, 1965.

Babut, E.-C. *Priscillien et le Priscillianisme.* Paris: Bibliothèque de l'école de hautes études, 1909.

Bachrach, Bernard S. *Early Medieval Jewish Policy in Western Europe.* Minneapolis: University of Minnesota Press, 1977.

Bagliani, Agostino Paravicini and Giorgio Stabile, eds. *Träume im Mittelalter. Ikonologische Studien.* Stüttgart: Belser, 1989.

Barnes, Timothy D. *Tertullian: A Historical and Literary Study.* Oxford: Clarendon Press, 1971.

Barraclough, Geoffrey. "The Making of a Bishop in the Middle Ages." *Catholic Historical Review* 19 (1933–34), 275–319.

Bautier, Anne-Marie. "Typologie des ex-voto mentionnés dans des textes antérieurs a 1200." In *La piété populaire au moyen âge,* pp. 237–282. Actes du 99e Congrès National des Sociétés Savantes. Vol. 1. Paris: Bibliothèque Nationale, 1977.

Baynes, N. H. "The Icons before Iconoclasm." *HTR* 46 (1951), 93–106.

Beaujard, Brigitte "Dons et piété à l'égard des saints dans la Gaule des ve et vie siècles," In *Haut moyen-âge: Culture, éducation et société*, ed. Michel Sot, pp. 59–67. Études offertes à Pierre Riché. Nanterre: Éditions Publidix, 1990.

Beck, Henry Gabriel Justin. *The Pastoral Care of Souls in South-east France during the Sixth Century*. Analecta Gregoriana. Vol. 51. Rome: Gregorian University, 1950.

Benson, Robert. *The Bishop-Elect: A Study in Medieval Ecclesiastical Office*. Princeton: Princeton University Press, 1968.

Benz, Ernst. *Die Vision. Erfahrungsformen und Bilderwelt*. Stuttgart: Ernst Klett Verlag, 1969.

Berschin, Walter, *Biographie und Epochenstil im lateinischen Mittelalter*. Vol. 2, *Merowingische Biographie, Italien, Spanien und die Inseln im frühen Mittelalter*. Quellen und Untersuchungen zur lateinischen Philologie des Mittelalters, 9. Stuttgart: Anton Hiersemann Verlag, 1988.

Binns, John. *Ascetics and Ambassadors of Christ: The Monasteries of Palestine, 314–631*. Oxford: Clarendon Press, 1994.

Bitel, Lisa. "In Visu Noctis: Dreams in European Hagiography and Histories, 450–900." *History of Religions* 31 (1991), 39–59.

Bitterman, Helen Robbins. "The Council of Chalcedon and Episcopal Jurisdiction." *Speculum* 13 (1938), 198–203.

Bjorck, G. "Onar idein. De la perception du rêve chez les anciens." *Eranos Jahrbuch* 44 (1946), 306–14.

Blumenkranz, Bernhard. *Juifs et chrétiennes dans le monde occidental 430–1096*. Paris: Mouton & Co., 1960.

Boesch Gajano, Sophia. *Agiographica altomedioevale*. Bologna: Il Molino, 1976.

Bogdanos, Theodore. "'The Shepherd of Hermas' and the Development of Medieval Visionary Allegory." *Viator* 8 (1977), 33–46.

Borias, André. "S. Wandrille, a-t-il connu S. Benoît?" *RB* 89 (1979), 7–28.

Bosl, Karl. "Der 'Adelsheilige' Idealtypus und Wirklichkeit, Gesellschaft und Kultur im Merowingerzeitlichen Bayern des 7 und 8 Jhds." In *Speculum Historiale. Geschichte im Spiegel von geschichtsschreibung und geschichtsdeutung*, ed. C. Bauer, L. Boehn, and M. Müller, pp. 167–87. Freiburg: Karl Alber Verlag, 1965.

Bousset, William. *Apophthegmata. Studien zur Geschichte des ältesten Mönchtums*. Tübingen: J. C. B. Mohr, 1923.

Braet, Herman, and Werner Verbeke, eds. *Death in the Middle Ages*. Leuven: Leuven University Press, 1983.

Bregman, Jay. *Synesius of Cyrene: Philosopher-Bishop*. Berkeley: University of California Press, 1982.

Brennan, Brian. "The Conversion of the Jews of Clermont." *JTS* n.s. 36 (1985), 321–37.

———. "Deathless Marriage and Spiritual Fecundity in Venantius Fortunatus' *De Virginitate*." *Traditio* 51 (1996), 73–97.

———. "'Episcopae': Bishop's Wives Viewed in Sixth-Century Gaul." *Church History* 54 (1985), 311–23.

———. "Senators and Social Mobility in Sixth-Century Gaul." *Journal of Medieval History* 11 (1985), 145–61.

———. "St. Radegund and the Early Development of Her Cult at Poitiers." *Journal of Religious History* 13 (1985), 340–54.

Breukelaar, Adriaan H. B. *Historiography and Episcopal Authority in Sixth-Century Gaul: The Histories of Gregory of Tours in Their Historical Context*. Amsterdam: Vandenhoeck & Ruprecht, 1994.

Brown, Peter Robert Lamont. "Approaches to the Religious Crisis of the Third Century A.D." *English Historical Review* 83 (1968), 542–58.

———. *Augustine of Hippo: A Biography*. London: Faber & Faber, 1967.

———. *Authority and the Sacred: Aspects of the Christianization of the Roman World.* Cambridge: Cambridge University Press, 1995.

———. *The Body and Society: Men, Women, and Sexual Renunciation in Early Christianity.* New York: Columbia University Press, 1988.

———. *The Cult of the Saints: Its Rise and Function in Late Antiquity.* Chicago: University of Chicago Press, 1981.

———. *The Making of Late Antiquity.* Carl Newell Jackson Lectures. Cambridge, Mass.: Harvard University Press, 1978.

———. "The Notion of Virginity in the Early Church." In *Christian Spirituality: Origins to the 12th Century*, ed. Bernard McGinn, John Meyendorff, and Jean Leclercq, pp. 427–43. World Spirituality, 16. New York: Crossroad, 1986.

———. "The Rise and Function of the Holy Man in Late Antiquity." *Journal of Roman Studies* 61 (1971), 80–101.

———. *Society and the Holy in Late Antiquity.* Berkeley: University of California Press, 1982.

Bruyne, Donatien de. "Fragments retrouvés d'apocryphes priscillianistes." *Revue Bénédictine* 24 (1907), 318–35.

Bruyne, Edgar de. *Études d'esthétique médiévale.* 3 vols. Bruges: De Tempel, 1946.

Bugge, John. *Virginitas: An Essay in the History of a Medieval Idea.* The Hague: Martinus Nijhoff, 1975.

Bull, Malcolm, ed. *Apocalypse Theory and the Ends of the World.* Oxford: Blackwell, 1995.

Butler, Cuthbert. *Benedictine Monachism.* London: Longmans, 1919.

Cahn, Walter. "Ascending to and Descending from Heaven: Ladder Themes in Early Medieval Art." In *Santi e Demoni nell'alto medioevo occidentale (secoli v–xi)*, vol. 2., pp. 697–724. Settimane di studio, 26. Spoleto: Presso La Sede del Centro, 1989.

Cameron, Averil. "The Byzantine Sources of Gregory of Tours," *JTS* n.s. 26 (1975), 421–26.

Campenhausen, Hans F. von. *Ecclesiastical Authority and Spiritual Power in the Church of the First Three Centuries.* Trans. J. A. Baker. London: A. and C. Black, Ltd., 1969.

Carozzi, Claude. "La géographie de l'au-delà et sa signification pendant le haut moyen âge." *Popoli e Paesinella Cultura Altomedievale* Settimane di studio. 19 (1983), 423–81.

———. *Le voyage de l'âme dans l'au-delà d'après la littérature latine (ve–xiiie siècle).* Collection de l'École Française de Rome, 189. Rome: École Française de Rome, 1994.

Chadwick, Henry. *The Early Church.* Harmondsworth: Penguin, 1967.

———. "Priscillian of Avila: Occult and Charisma in the Ancient Church." *Studia Patristica* 15:1 (1984), 3–12.

———. *Priscillian of Avila: The Occult and the Charismatic in the Early Church.* Oxford: Clarendon Press, 1976.

Chélini, Jean. *L'aube du moyen âge. Naissance de la chrétienté occidentale. La vie religieuse des laïcs dans l'europe carolingienne (750–900).* Paris: Picard, 1991. 2d edition, 1997.

Cheyette, Fredric L. ed. *Lordship and Community in Medieval Europe: Selected Readings.* New York: Holt, Rinehart and Winston, 1968.

Chitty, Derwas James. *The Desert a City: An Introduction to the Study of Egyptian and Palestinian Monasticism under the Christian Empire.* Oxford: Blackwell, 1966.

Ciccarese, Maria Pia. "La *Visio Baronti* nella tradizione letteraria delle *Visiones* dell'aldilà." *Romanobarbarica* 6 (1982), 25–52.

———. "Le visioni dell'aldilà come genere letterario: fonti antiche e sviluppi medievali." In *Le "Visiones" nella Cultura Medievale*, ed. Peter Dinzelbacher, M. P. Ciccarese, Yves Christe, and Walter Berschin, *Scede Medievali* 19 (1990), 266–77.

————. *Visioni dell'aldilà in occidente. Fonti modelli testi.* Florence: Nardini Editore, 1987.

Clarke, H. B., and M. Brennan, eds. *Columbanus and Merovingian Monasticism.* British Archeological Reports, International Series 113. Oxford, 1981.

Claude, D. "Die Bestellung der Bischofe im Merowingische Reiche." *Zeitschrift der Savigny-Stiftung für Rechtsgeschichte, kanonistische Abteilung* 49 (1963), 1–75.

Cochini, Christian. *Apostolic Origins of Priestly Celibacy.* Trans. Nelly Marans. San Francisco: Ignatius Press, 1990.

Cohen, Norman. *The Pursuit of the Millennium: Revolutionary Millenarians and Mystical Anarchists of the Middle Ages.* Oxford: Oxford University Press,1957.

Colish, Marcia L. *The Stoic Tradition from Antiquity to the Early Middle Ages.* 2 vols. Studies in the History of Christian Thought, 34–35. Leiden: E. J. Brill, 1985.

Collins, Roger. *Early Medieval Spain: Unity in Diversity, 400–1000.* London: Macmillan, 1983.

Coon, Lynda L. *Sacred Fictions: Holy Women and Hagiography in Late Antiquity.* Philadelphia: University of Pennsylvania Press, 1997.

Corbett, J. H. "The Saint as Patron in the Work of Gregory of Tours." *Journal of Medieval History* 7 (1981), 1–13.

Courcelle, Pierre. "De Platon à saint Ambroise par Apulée. Parallèls textuels entre le 'De excessu fratris' et le 'De Platone.'" *Revue de Philologie* 87 (1961), 15–28.

————. *Late Latin Writers and Their Greek Sources.* Trans. Harry E. Wedeck. Cambridge: Harvard University Press, 1969.

Courtois, Christian. "Die Entwicklung des Mönchtums in Gallien vom heiligen Martin bis zum heiligen Columban." In *Mönchtum und Gesellschaft im Frühmittelalter*, ed. Friedrich Prinz, pp. 13–36. Wege der Forschung, 312. Darmstadt: Wissenschaftliche Buchgesellschaft, 1976.

Cox, Patricia. *Biography in Late Antiquity. A Quest for the Holy Man.* Berkeley: University of California Press, 1983.

Cracco, G. "Gregorio e l'oltre-tomba," In *Grégoire le grand*, ed. J. Fontaine, R. Gillet and S. Pellistrandi, pp. 255–66. Paris: CNRS, 1986.

Dassman, Ernst, and Karl Suso Frank, eds. *Pietas. Festschrift für Bernhard Kötting.* Jahrbuch für Antike und Christentum, Ergänzungsband, 8. Münster: Aschendorff, 1980.

————. "La spiritualité des pélerinages à saint Martin de Tours du ve–xe siècles," In *Pellegrinaggi e culto dei santi in Europa fino alla Ia crociata*, pp. 201–43. Convegni del Centro di studi sulla spiritualità medievale, 4. Todi: Presse l'Accademia Tudertina, 1963.

Delaruelle, Étienne. "Sainte Radegonde, son type de sainteté et la chrétienté de son temps." In *Études Mérovingiennes*, pp. 65–74. Paris: Picard, 1953.

————. "Les premiers 'libelli miraculorum.'" *AB* 29 (1910), 427–34.

————. "Les recueils antiques des miracles des saints. II. Les recueils latins," *AB* 43 (1925), 73–85 and 305–25.

Delehaye, Hippolyte. *Sanctus. Essai sur le culte des saints dans l'antiquité.* Subsidia Hagiographica, 17. Brussels: Société des Bollandistes, 1927.

De Nie, Giselle. *Views from a Many-Windowed Tower: Studies of Imagination in the Works of Gregory of Tours.* Studies in Classical Antiquity, 7. Amsterdam: Editions Rodopi B. V. 1987.

————. "Un avatar du mythe de la caverne." In *Homenage a Fray Justo Perez de Urbel.* Vol. 2, 19–24. Burgos: Abadía de Silos, 1976.

De Vogüé, Adalbert. *Community and Abbot in the Rule of St. Benedict.* Cistercian Studies, 5. 2 vols. Kalamazoo, Mich.: Cistercian Publications, 1979–88.

————. "Grégoire la Grand et ses 'Dialogues' d'après deux ouvrages récents." *RHE* 83 (1988), 281–348.

Dierkens, Alain. *Abbayes et chapitres entre Sambre et Meuse (viie–xie siècles)*, Francia, 14 Sigmaringen: Jan Thorbecke Verlag, 1985.

————. "Prolégomènes à une histoire des relations culturelles entre les îles britanniques et le continent pendant le haut moyen âge." In *La Neustrie: Les pays au nord de la Loire de 650 à 850; colloque historique international*, ed. Hartmut Atsma, pp. 371–94. *Francia* 16, 2. Sigmaringen: Jan Thorbecke Verlag, 1989.

————. "Saint Amand et la fondation de l'abbaye de Nivelles." *Revue du Nord* 68 (1986), 325–32.

Dill, Samuel. *Roman Society in Gaul in the Merovingian Age*. London: Macmillan, 1926.

————. "Der Kampf der Heiligen mit den Dämonen." In *Santi e Demoni nell'alto medioevo occidentale (secoli V–XI)* vol. 2, pp. 647–95. Settimane di studio 36. Spoleto: Presso La Sede del Centro, 1989.

Dinzelbacher, Peter. *Vision und Visionsliteratur im Mittelalter*. Monographien zur Geschichte des Mittelalters, 23. Stuttgart: Anton Hiersemann, 1981.

Dinzelbacher, Peter, Maria Pia Ciccarese, Yves Christe, and Walter Berschin, eds. *Le "Visiones" nella cultura Medievale*. Scede Medievali 19 (1990).

Dittrich, Otto. *St. Aldegundis, eine heilige der Franken*. Kevelaer: Butzon und Bercker, 1976.

Dodds, E. R. *The Greeks and the Irrational*. Berkeley: University of California Press, 1951.

————. *Pagan and Christian in an Age of Anxiety: Some Aspects of Religious Experience from Marcus Aurelius to Constantine*. Cambridge: Cambridge University Press, 1965.

Dölger, Franz Joseph. *Sol Salutis*. 2nd ed. Münster/Westfalen: Aschendorff, 1925.

————. *Die Sonne der Gerechtigkeit und der Schwarze. Eine religionsgeschichtliche studie zum taufgelöbnis*. Liturgiewissenschaftliche Quellen und Forschungen, 14. Münster/Westfalen: Aschendorff, 1971. Orig. pub. 1918.

Dronke, Peter. *Women Writers of the Middle Ages: A Critical Study of Texts from Perpetua (d. 203) to Marguerite Porete (d. 1310)*. Cambridge: Cambridge University Press, 1984.

Dubois, Jacques, and Jean Loup Lemaitre, eds. *Sources et méthodes de l'hagiographie médiévale*. Paris: Editions du Cerf, 1993.

Dulaey, Martine. *Le rêve dans la vie et la pensée de saint Augustin*. Paris: Études Augustiniennes, 1973.

Durliat, J. "Les attributions civiles des évêques mérovingiens: L'exemple de Didier, évêque de Cahors (630–55)." *Annales du Midi* 91 (1979), 237–54.

Dutton, Paul Edward. *The Politics of Dreaming in the Carolingian Empire*. Lincoln: University of Nebraska Press, 1994.

Duval, Yves, and J.-Ch. Picard, eds. *L'inhumation privilégiée du ive au viiie siècle en occident*. Actes du colloque tenu à Créteil les 16–18 mars 1984. Paris: De Boccard, 1986.

Ebling, Horst. *Prosopographie der Amtsträger des Merowingerreiches von Chlothar II (613) bis Karl Martell (741)*. Francia 2 Munich: Artemis Verlag, 1974.

Eco, Umberto. *Art and Beauty in the Middle Ages*. New Haven: Yale University Press, 1986.

Effros, Bonnie. "Beyond Cemetery Walls: Early Funerary Topography and Christian Salvation." *Early Medieval Europe* 6 (1997), 1–23.

————. "Images of Sanctity: Contrasting Descriptions of Radegund by Fortunatus and Baudonivia and Gregory of Tours." *UCLA Historical Journal* 10 (1990), 38–58.

Éliade, Mircea. *Images and Symbols: Studies in Religious Symbolism*. Trans. Philip Mairet. Princeton: Princeton University Press, 1991.

248 | Selected Bibliography

———. *Myths, Dreams, and Mysteries: The Encounter between Contemporary Faiths and Archaic Realities.* Trans. Philip Mairet. New York: Harper Row, 1975.

Elm, Susanna. *Virgins of God: The Making of Asceticism in Late Antiquity.* Oxford: Clarendon Press, 1994.

Emmerson, Richard K., and Bernard McGinn, eds. *The Apocalypse in the Middle Ages.* Ithaca, N.Y.: Cornell University Press, 1992.

Evelyn-White, Hugh Gerard. *The Monasteries of the Wadi 'n Natrun.* Vol. 2, *The History of the Monasteries of Nitria and Scetis.* New York: Metropolitan Museum of Art, 1932.

Ewig, Eugen. "L'aquitaine et les pays rhénans au haut moyen âge." *Cahiers de civilisation médievale* 1 (1958), 37–54.

———. "Le culte de saint Martin à l'époque franque." *Francia* 3:2 (1979), 355–70.

———. "Die fränkischen Teilreiche im 7. Jahrhundert (613–714)." In *Spätantikes und fränkisches Gallien* 1, ed. Hartmut Atsma. Munich: Artemis Verlag, 1976.

———. "Der Martinskult im Frühmittelalter." *Francia* 3:2 (1979), 371–92.

———. "Der Petrus-und Apostelkult in spätrömischen und frankischen Gallien." *Zeitschrift für Kirchengeschichte* 71 (1960), 215–51.

———. "Das Privileg des Bischofs Berthefrid von Amiens für Corbie von 664 und die Klosterpolitik der Königin Balthild." *Francia* 1 (1973), 63–114.

———. "Die Verehrung orientalischen heilige im spätrömischen Gallien und im Merowingerreich." *Francia* 3:2 (1979) 393–410.

Farmer, Sharon. *Communities of St. Martin: Legend and Ritual in Medieval Tours.* Ithaca, N.Y.: Cornell University Press, 1991.

Favez, Charles. *La consolation latine chrétienne.* Paris: Librairie philosophique J. Vrin, 1937.

Favreau, Robert. *Les inscriptions médiévales.* Typologie des sources du moyen âge occidental, 35. Turnhout: Brepols, 1979.

Festugière, André Marie Jean. *Les moines d'orient.* 4 vols. Paris, 1961–5.

Février, Paul-Albert. "La mort chrétienne." In *Segni e Riti nella Chiesa Altomedieval Occidentale,* Settimane di Studio 33, pp. 881–942. Spoleto: Centro Italiano di Studi sull'alto Medioevo, 1987.

———. "La tombe chrétienne et l'au-delà." In *Le temps chrétien de la fin de l'antiquité au moyen âge, iiie–xiiie siècles,* pp. 163–83. Paris: CNRS, 1984.

Filoramo, Giovanni. *A History of Gnosticism.* Trans. Anthony Alcock. Oxford: Blackwell, 1990.

Fischer, Steven R. "Dreambooks and the Interpretation of Medieval Literary Dreams." *Archiv für Kulturgeschichte* 65 (1983), 1–20.

Folz, Robert "Tradition hagiographique et culte de saint Balthilde, reine des Francs." *Academie des inscriptions et belles-lettres* (1976), 369–84.

Fontaine, Jacques. "Hagiographie et politique de Sulpice Sévère à Venance Fortunat." In *La Christianisation des pays entre Loire et Rhin (ive–viie siècle),* ed. Pierre Riché. Actes du Colloque de Nanterre (3–4 mai, 1974), Histoire Religieuse de la France. Vol. 2, pp. 113–40. Paris: Éditions du Cerf, 1993.

Fontaine, Jacques, and Jocelyn N. Hillgarth, eds. *The Seventh Century: Change and Continuity. Studies of the Warburg Institute.* Vol. 42. London: Warburg Institute, University of London, 1992.

Fossier, Robert. *Polyptyches et censiers.* Turnhout: Brepols, 1978.

Foster, Robert, and Orest A. Ranum, eds. *Ritual, Religion and the Sacred.* Selections from the Annales, economies, sociétés, civilisations. Vol. 7. Baltimore: Johns Hopkins University Press, 1982.

Fouracre, Paul. "Merovingian History and Merovingian Hagiography." *Past and Present* 127 (1990), 3–38.

Fouracre, Paul, and Richard A. Gerberding. *Late Merovingian France: History and Hagiography, 640–720.* Manchester: Manchester University Press, 1996.

Fox, Robin Lane. *Pagans and Christians*. Harper and Row: San Francisco, 1986.

Frend, W. H. C. "The Gnostic-Manichaean Tradition in Roman North Africa." *JEH* 4 (1953), 13–26.

———. *Martyrdom and Persecution in the Early Church*. Oxford: Blackwell, 1965.

Fros, Henricus. "L'eschatologie médiévale dans quelques écrits hagiographiques (IV–IX s.)." In *The Use and Abuse of Eschatology in the Middle Ages*, ed. Werner Verbeke, Daniel Verhelst, and Andries Welkenhuysen, pp. 212–20. Leuven: University of Leuven Press, 1988.

Gäbe, Sabine. "Radegundis: Sancta, Regina, Ancilla. Zum Heiligkeitsideal der Radegundisviten von Fortunat und Baudonivia." *Francia* 16:1 (1989), 1–30.

Gaiffier, Baudoin de. "La lecture des actes des martyrs dans la prière liturgique en occident. A propos du passionnaire hispanique." *AB* 72 (1954), 134–66.

Gardiner, Eileen, ed. *Visions of Heaven and Hell before Dante*. New York: Italica Press, 1989.

Geary, Patrick J. *Furta Sacra: Thefts of Relics in the Central Middle Ages*. Princeton: Princeton University Press, 1990.

———. "Saints, Scholars, and Society: The Elusive Goal." In *Saints: Studies in Hagiography*, ed. Sandro Sticca, pp. 1–22. Medieval and Renaissance Texts and Studies,141. Binghamton, N.Y.: Medieval and Renaissance Texts and Studies, 1996.

George, Judith. "Variations on Themes of Consolation in the Poetry of Venantius Fortunatus." *Eranos* 85 (1987), 53–66.

———. *Venantius Fortunatus: A Latin Poet in Merovingian Gaul*. Oxford: Clarendon Press, 1992.

———. *Venantius Fortunatus: Personal and Political Poems*. Translated Texts for Historians, 23. Liverpool: Liverpool University Press, 1995.

Gerberding, Richard. *The Rise of the Carolingians and the Liber Historiae Francorum*. Oxford: Clarendon Press, 1987.

Gilliard, Frank D. "The Senators of Sixth-Century Gaul." *Speculum* 54 (1979), 685–97.

Ginzburg, Carlo. *The Cheese and the Worms: The Cosmos of a Sixteenth-Century Miller*. Trans. John and Anne Tedeschi. New York: Dorset Press, 1989.

Gnuse, Robert Karl. *Dreams and Dream Reports in the Writings of Josephus: A Traditio-Historical Analysis*. Leiden: E. J. Brill, 1996.

Goffart, Walter. "The Conversions of Avitus of Clermont, and Similar Passages in Gregory of Tours." In *To See Ourselves As Others See Us*, ed. J. Neusner and E. S. Frerichs, pp. 473–97. Chico, Calif.: Scholars Press, 1985.

———. "Merovingian Polyptychs: Reflections on Two Recent Publications." *Francia* 9 (1981), 57–77.

———. "Old and New in Merovingian Taxation." *Past and Present* 96 (1982), 3–21.

Grabar, André. *Martyrium. Recherches sur le culte des reliques et l'art chrétien antique*. Paris: Collège de France, 1946.

Graus, František. "Hagiographie und Dämonenglauben—Zur ihren Funktionen in der Merowingerzeit." In *Santi e Demoni Nell'Alto Medioevo Occidentale (Secoli V–XI)*, pp. 93–120. Settimani di studio 36. Spoleto: Presso la Sede del Centro, 1989.

———. *Volk, Herrscher und Heiliger im Reich der Merowinger: Studien zur Hagiographie der Merowingerzeit*. Prague: Nakladatelstvi Ceskoslovenske akademie ved, 1965.

Griffe, Élie. *La Gaule chrétienne à l'époque romaine*. 3 vols. 2d ed. Paris: Letouzey et Ané, 1964–65.

Groh, Dennis E. "Utterance and Exegesis: Biblical Interpretation in the Montanist Crisis." In *The Living Text*, ed. D. E. Groh and Robert Jewett. New York: University Press of America, 1985.

Gryson, Roger. *The Ministry of Women in the Early Church*. Collegeville, Minn.: Liturgical Press, 1976.

Guelphe, Walter. "L'érémitisme dans le sud-ouest de la gaule à l'époque mérovingienne." *Annales du Midi* 98 (1986), 293–315.

Guillaumont, Antoine. *Aux origins du monachisme chrétien. Pour une phénoménologie du monachisme.* Spiritualité orientale, 30. Bégrolles-en-Mauges: Abbaye de Bellefontaine, 1979.

Hagiographie, cultures et sociétés ive–xiie siècles. Actes du colloque organisé à Nanterre et à Paris (2–5 mai 1979). Paris: Études Augustiniennes, 1981.

Heidrich, Ingrid. "Südgallische Inschriften des 5.-7. Jahrhunderts als Historische Quellen." *Rheinische Vierteljahrsblätter* 32 (1968), 167–83.

Heine, Ronald E. *The Montanist Oracles and Testimonia.* Patristic Monograph Series, 14. Macon, Ga.: Mercer University Press, 1989.

Heinzelmann, Martin. *Bischofsherrschaft in Gallien. Zur Kontinuität römischer Führungsschichten vom 4. bis zum 7. Jahrhundert. Soziale, prosopographische und bildungsgeschichtliche Aspekte. Francia* 5 (1976).

———. *Gregor von Tours (538–594): "Zehn Bücher Geschichte." Historiographie und Gesellschaftskonzept im 6. Jahrhundert.* Darmstadt: Wissenschaftliche Buchgesellschaft, 1994.

———. "Neue Aspekte der biographischen und hagiographischen Literatur in der lateinischen Welt (1.-6. Jahrhundert)." *Francia* 1 (1973), 27–44.

———. "Studia sanctorum. Éducation, milieux d'instruction et valeurs éducatives dans l'hagiographie en Gaule jusqu'à la fin de l'époque mérovingienne." In *Haut moyen-âge: Culture, éducation et société,* ed. M. Sot, pp. 105–38. Études offertes à Pierre Riché. Nanterre: Éditions Publidix, 1990.

———. "Une source de base de la littérature hagiographique latine: le recueil de miracles." In *Hagiographie, cultures et sociétés ive–xiie siècles,* pp. 235–57. Actes du colloque organisé à Nanterre et à Paris (2–5 mai 1979). Paris: Études Augustiniennes, 1981.

———. *Translationsberichte und andere Quellen des Reliquienkultes.* Typologie des sources du moyen âge, 33. Turnhout: Brepols, 1979.

Heitz, Carol. "L'hypogée de Mellebaude à Poitiers." In *L'inhumation privilégiée du ive au viiie siècle en occident,* ed. Yves Duval and J.-Ch. Picard, pp. 91–96. Actes du colloque tenu à Créteil les 16–18 mars 1984. Paris: De Boccard, 1986.

———. *Abbayes, évèques et laïques: Une politique du pouvoir en Hainaut au moyen âge (viie-xie siècle).* Collection Histoire in-8, no. 92. Brussels: Credit Communal, 1994.

Helvétius, Anne-Marie. "Sainte Aldegonde et les origines du monastère de Maubeuge." *Revue du Nord* 74 (1992), 221–37.

Hen, Yitzhak. *Culture and Religion in Merovingian Gaul A.D. 481–751.* Leiden: E. J. Brill, 1995.

———. "The Structure and Aims of the 'Visio Baronti'." *JTS,* n.s. 47 (1996), 477–97.

Heuclin, Jean. *Aux origines monastiques de la Gaule du Nord: ermites et reclus du ve au xie siècle.* Lille: Presses Universitaires de Lille, 1988.

Hillgarth, Jocelyn N. "Eschatological and Political Concepts in the Seventh Century." In *The Seventh Century: Change and Continuity,* ed. Jacques Fontaine and Jocelyn N. Hillgarth, pp. 212–31. London: Warburg Institute, 1992.

———. *Visigothic Spain, Byzantium and the Irish.* Collected Studies Series, 216. London: Variorum Reprints, 1985.

———. ed. *Christianity and Paganism, 350–750: The Conversion of Western Europe.* Philadelphia: University of Pennsylvania Press, 1969.

Hoare, Frederick Russell. *The Western Fathers: Being the Lives of SS. Martin of Tours, Ambrose, Augustine of Hippo, Honoratus of Arles, and Germanus of Auxerre.* New York: Sheed and Ward, 1954.

James, Edward. *The Franks.* Oxford: Blackwell, 1988.

———. "Miracles and Medicine in the Life of Gregory of Tours." pp. 45–60. In *The Cul-*

ture of Christendom: Essays in Medieval History in Commemoration of Denis L. T. Bethell, ed. Marc Anthony Meyer, pp. 45–60. London: Hambledon, 1993.

———. "Septimania and Its Frontier: An Archeological Approach." In *Visigothic Spain: New Approaches*, ed. Edward James, pp. 223–41. Oxford: Clarendon Press, 1980.

Jussen, Bernhard. "Über 'Bischofherrschaften' und Prozeduren politisch-sozialer Umordnung in Gallien zwischen 'Antike' und 'Mittelalter.'" *HZ* 260 (1995), 673–718.

Kaiser, Reinhold. "Royauté et pouvoir épiscopal au nord de la Gaule (viie–ixe siècles). Résultats d'une recherche en cours." In *La Neustrie*, ed. Harmut Atsma, pp. 143–60. Sigmaringen: Jan Thorbecke Verlag, 1989.

Kamphausen, Hans Joachim. *Traum und Vision in der lateinische Poesie der Karolingerzeit*. Frankfurt: Peter Lang, 1975.

Kartsonis, Anna D. *Anastasis: The Making of an Image*. Princeton: Princeton University Press, 1986.

Käsemann, Ernst. "The Beginnings of Christian Theology." In *Apocalypticism*, ed. Robert W. Funk. New York: Herder and Herder, 1969.

Katz, Solomon. *The Jews in the Visigothic and Frankish Kingdoms of Spain and Gaul*. New York: Kraus Reprint, 1970.

Kee, Howard Clark. *Miracle in the Early Christian World*. New Haven: Yale University Press, 1983.

Kenney, James Francis. *The Sources for the Early History of Ireland*. Vol. 1. New York: Octagon Books, 1929.

Kirk, Kenneth E. *The Vision of God: The Christian Doctrine of the Summum Bonum*. Longmans, Green: London, 1931.

Kirschner, Julius, and Suzanne Fonay Wemple, eds. *Women of the Medieval World: Essays in Honor of John H. Mundy*. Oxford: Blackwell, 1985.

Klawiter, F. C. "The Role of Martyrdom and Persecution in Developing a Priestly Authority of Women in Early Christianity: A Case Study of Montanism." *Church History* 49 (1980), 251–61.

Klingshirn, William E. *Caesarius of Arles: The Making of a Christian Community in Late Antique Gaul*. Cambridge: Cambridge University Press, 1994.

Kollwitz, J. "Christus, Christusbild." In *Lexikon der christlichen Ikonographie*. Vol. 1. Ed. Englebert Kirschbaum and Günter Bandman, pp. 355–71. Rome: Herder, 1968.

König, Dorothee. *Amt und Askese. Priesteramt und Mönchtum bei den lateinischen Kirchenvätern in vorbenediktinischer Zeit*. Regulae Benedicti Studia, Supplementa 12. St. Ottilien: Eos Verlag, 1985.

Kruger, Steven F. *Dreaming in the Middle Ages*. Cambridge: Cambridge University Press, 1992.

Labriolle, Pierre de. *La crise montaniste*. Paris, Ernest Leroux, 1913.

———. *Histoire de la littérature latine chrétienne*. Paris, 1920.

Ladurie, Emmanuel Le Roy. *Montaillou: Cathars and Catholics in a French Village 1294–1324*. Harmondsworth: Penguin, 1980.

Lattimore, Richmond. *Themes in Greek and Latin Epitaphs*. Urbana: University of Illinois Press, 1962.

Le Blant, Edmond. *Inscriptions chrétiennes de la Gaule antérieures au viii siècle*. 2 vols. Paris, 1856, 1865.

———. *Nouveau recueil des inscriptions chrétiennes de la Gaule antérieurs au viiie siècle*. Paris, 1892.

Leclercq, Henri. "Beauté ou laideur du Christ." *DACL* 7. ii (1927), 2397–2400.

———. "Pèlerinages aux lieux saints." *DACL* 14.i (1939), 65–176.

———. "Perpétue et Félicité." *DACL* 14.i (1939), 393–444.

———. "Poitiers." *DACL* 14.i (1939), 1252–1340.

Leclercq, Jean. *The Love of Learning and the Desire for God: A Study of Monastic Culture*. New York: Fordham University Press, 1961.

Le Goff, Jacques. *The Birth of Purgatory.* Trans. Arthur Goldhammer. Chicago: Chicago University Press, 1984.

———. "Christianity and Dreams (Second to Seventh Century)." In *The Medieval Imagination,* trans. Arthur Goldhammer, pp. 193–231. Chicago: Chicago University Press, 1985.

Lestocquoy, J. "Monachisme et civilisation mérovingienne dans le nord de la France." In *Mélanges Colombaniens,* pp. 55–60. Actes du congrès international de Luxeuil, 20–23 Juillet, 1950. Paris: Alsatia, 1951.

Lewis, Naphtali. *The Interpretation of Dreams and Portents in Late Antiquity.* Wauconda, Ill.: Bolchazy-Carducci, 1996.

Lieu, Samuel N. C. *Manichaeism in the Later Roman Empire and Medieval China: A Historical Survey.* Manchester: Manchester University Press, 1985.

Lifshitz, Felice. "Beyond Positivism and Genre: 'Hagiographical' Texts as Historical Narrative." *Viator* 25 (1994), 95–113.

Lotter, Friedrich. "Methodisches zur Gewinnung historischer Erkentnisse aus hagiographischen Quellen." *HZ* 229 (1979), 298–356.

Lutterbach, Hubertus. "Die Bußordines in den iro-fränkischen Paenitentialien. Schlüssel zur Theologie und Verwendung der mittelalterlichen Bußbücher." *Frühmittelalterliche Studien* 30 (1996), 150–72.

———. "Intentions- oder Tafhaftung? Zum Bußverständnis in den frühmittelalterlichen Bußbüchern." *Frühmittelalterliche Studien* 29 (1995), 120–43.

———. *Monachus factus est. Die Mönchwerdung im frühen Mittelalter.* Beiträge zur Geschichte des alten Mönchtums und des Benediktinertums, 44. Münster: Aschendorf, 1995.

MacMullen, Ramsey. *Christianizing the Roman Empire A.D. 100–400.* New Haven: Yale University Press, 1984.

———. *Paganism in the Roman Empire.* New Haven: Yale University Press, 1981.

Maddicott, J. R. "Plague in Seventh-Century England." *Past and Present* 156 (1997), 7–54.

Madec, Goulven. *Saint Ambroise et la Philosophie.* Paris: Études Augustiniennes, 1974.

Markus, Robert Austin. "From Caesarius to Boniface: Christianity and Paganism in Gaul" In *The Seventh Century: Change and Continuity; Le Septième Siècle: Changements et Continuités,* ed. Jacques Fontaine and Jocelyn N. Hillgarth, pp. 154–72. Studies of the Warburg Institute. Vol. 42. London: Warburg Institute, 1992.

———. "The Cult of Icons in Sixth-Century Gaul." *JTS* n.s. 29 (1978), 151–57.

———. *The End of Ancient Christianity.* Cambridge: Cambridge University Press, 1990.

Martin, Lawrence Thomas. *The 'Somniale Danielis.' An Edition of a Medieval Latin Dream Interpretation Handbook.* Ph.D. diss. University of Wisconsin, 1977.

Mathews, Thomas F. *The Clash of the Gods: A Reinterpretation of Early Christian Art.* Princeton: Princeton University Press, 1993.

Mathisen, Ralph W. "Barbarian Bishops and the Churches 'in barbaricis gentibus' during Late Antiquity." *Speculum* 72 (1997), 664–97.

———. *Ecclesiastical Factionalism and Religious Controversy in Fifth-Century Gaul.* Washington, D.C.: Catholic University of America Press, 1989.

Mathisen, Ralph W., and Hagith S. Sivan, eds. *Shifting Frontiers in Late Antiquity.* Aldershot: Variorum, 1996.

McCarthy, Maria C. *The Rule for Nuns of St. Caesarius of Arles: A Translation with a Critical Introduction.* Washington, D.C.: Catholic University of America Press, 1960.

McCulloh, John M. "Jewish Ritual Murder: William of Norwich, Thomas of Monmouth, and the Early Dissemination of the Myth." *Speculum* 72 (1997), 698–740.

———. "From Antiquity to the Middle Ages: Continuity and Change in Papal Relic Policy from the Sixth to the Eighth Century." In *Pietas. Festschrift für Bernhard Kötting,* eds. Ernst Dassman and Karl Suso Frank, pp. 313–24. Jahrbuch für Antike und Christentum, Ergänzungsband 8. Münster: Aschendorff, 1980.

McGinn, Bernard. *Apocalyptic Spirituality*. New York: Paulist Press, 1979.
———. "The End of the World and the Beginning of Christendom." In *Apocalypse Theory and the Ends of the World*. ed. Malcolm Bull. Oxford: Blackwell, 1995.
———. "Teste David cum Sibylla: The Significance of the Sibylline Tradition in the Middle Ages." In *Women of the Medieval World*, ed. J. Kirschner and S. Wemple, pp. 7–35. New York: Blackwell, 1985.
———. *Visions of the End: Apocalyptic Traditions in the Middle Ages*. New York: Columbia University Press, 1979.
McGuire, Brian Patrick. "Purgatory, the Communion of Saints, and Medieval Change." *Viator* 20 (1989), 61–84.
McNamara, Jo Ann. "A Legacy of Miracles: Hagiography and Nunneries in Merovingian Gaul." In *Women of the Medieval World: Essays in Honour of John H. Mundy*, eds. Julius Kirshner and Suzanne F. Wemple, pp. 36–52. Oxford: Blackwell, 1985.
McNeill, John Thomas, and Helena Margaret Gamer. *Medieval Handbooks of Penance: A Translation of the Principal 'Libri Poenitentiales,' and Selections from Related Documents*. New York: Columbia University Press, 1990.
Meier, C. A. "The Dream in Ancient Greece and Its Use in Temple Cures (Incubation)." In *The Dream and Human Societies*, ed. Gustave Edmund von Grunebaum and Roger Caillois, pp. 303–18. Berkeley: University of California Press, 1966.
Metz, René. *La consecration des vierges dans l'église romaine. Étude d'histoire de la liturgie*. Paris: Presses Universitaires de France, 1954.
Meyer, Marc Anthony, ed. *The Culture of Christendom: Essays in Medieval History in Commemoration of Denis L. T. Bethell*. London: Hambledon, 1993.
Miller, Patricia Cox. *Dreams in Late Antiquity. Studies in the Imagination of a Culture*. Princeton: Princeton University Press, 1994.
Mohrmann, Christine. "Encore une fois: paganus." *Vigiliae Christianae* 6 (1952), 109–21.
Monod, Gabriel Jacques Jean. *Études critiques sur les sources de l'histoire mérovingienne*. 2 vols. Paris: A. Francke, 1872–75. Repr., Geneva: Librairie Slatkine, 1978.
Moreau, Édouard de. *Histoire de l'église en Belgique*. Vol. 1. Brussels: L'édition universelle, 1945.
Moreira, Isabel. "Augustine's Three Visions and Three Heavens in Some Early Medieval Florilegia." *Vivarium* 34 (1996), 1–14.
———. "Living in the Palaces of Love: Love and the Soul in a Vision of St. Aldegund of Maubeuge (c. 635–84)." *Quidditas: Journal of the Rocky Mountain Medieval and Renaissance Association*, forthcoming.
———. "Provisatrix Optima: St. Radegund of Poitiers' Relic Petitions to the East," *Journal of Medieval History* 19 (1993) pp. 285–305.
Moyse, Gérard. "Les origines du monachisme dans le diocèse de Besançon (ve–xe siècles)." *Bibliothèque de L'École des Chartes* 131 (1973), 21–104.
Nagel, Peter. *Die Motivierung der Askese in der alten Kirche und der Ursprung des Mönchtums*. TU 95. Berlin: Akademie Verlag, 1966.
Nahmer, Dieter von der. *Die lateinische Heiligenvita. Eine Einfuhrung in die lateinische Hagiographie*. Darmstadt: Wissenschaftliche Buchgesellschaft, 1994.
Nelson, Janet. "Queens as Jezebels: The Careers of Brunhild and Balthild in Merovingian History." In *Medieval Women*, ed. Derek Baker, pp. 31–77. Studies in Church History, Subsidia 1. Oxford: Blackwell, 1978.
Neusner, Jacob, and Ernst S. Frerichs. Ed. *"To See Ourselves As Others See Us": Christians, Jews, "Others" in Late Antiquity*. Chico, Calif.: Scholars Press, 1985.
Newman, Barbara. *Sister of Wisdom: St. Hildegard's Theology of the Feminine*. Berkeley: University of California Press, 1987.
Ntedika, Joseph. *L'Évolution de la doctrine du purgatoire chez saint Augustine*. Paris: Études Augustiniennes, 1966.

ó Riain, Pádraig. "Les Vies de saint Fursey: les sources irlandaises." *Revue du Nord* 68:269 (1986), 405–12.

Oexle, Otto Gerhard. "Die Gegenwart der Toten." In *Death in the Middle Ages*, ed. Herman Braet and Werner Verbeke, pp. 19–77. Leuven: Leuven University Press, 1983.

Orellius, Io. Casp. *Inscriptionum latinarum selectarum amplissima collectio ad illustrandam Romanae antiquitatis*. Vol. 1. Turin, 1828.

Pagels, Elaine. "Visions, Appearances and Apostolic Authority: Gnostic and Orthodox Traditions." In *Gnosis. Festschrift für Hans Jonas*, ed. B. Aland, pp. 415–30. Göttingen: Vandenhoeck & Ruprecht, 1978.

Palmer, Anne-Marie. *Prudentius on the Martyrs*. Oxford: Clarendon Press, 1989.

Patch, Howard Rollin. *The Other World According to Descriptions in Medieval Literature*. Cambridge: Harvard University Press, 1950.

Paxton, Frederick S. *Christianizing Death: The Creation of a Ritual Process in Early Medieval Europe*. Ithaca, N.Y.: Cornell University Press, 1990.

———. "Liturgy and Healing in an Early Medieval Saint's Cult: The Mass *in honore sancti Sigismundi* for the Cure of Fevers." *Traditio* 49 (1994), 23–43.

Périn, Patrick, and Laure-Charlotte Feffer, eds. *La Neustrie: les pays au nord de la Loire de Dagobert à Charles le Chauve (viie–ixe seicles)*. Créteil, France: Musées et Monuments départmentaux de Seine-Maritime, 1985.

Petersen, Joan. *The Dialogues of Gregory the Great in Their Late Antique Cultural Background*. Toronto: Pontifical Institute for Medieval Studies, 1984.

Petroff, Elizabeth A. *Medieval Women's Visionary Literature*. Oxford: Oxford University Press, 1986.

Peyroux, Catherine. "Gertrude's Furor: Reading Anger in an Early Medieval Saint's *Life*." In *Anger's Past: The Social Uses of an Emotion*. Ed. Barbara H. Rosenwein, pp. 36–55. Ithaca, N.Y.: Cornell University Press, 1998.

Picard, Jean-Michel. "Church and Politics in the Seventh Century: The Irish Exile of Dagobert II." In *Ireland and Northern France A.D. 600–850*, ed. Jean-Michel Picard, pp. 27–52. Dublin: Four Corners Press, 1991.

Pietri, Luce. *La ville de Tours du ive au vie siècle: naissance d'une cité chrétienne*. Rome: École française de Rome, 1983.

Poulin, Joseph-Claude. *L'idéal de sainteté dans l'Aquitaine carolingienne d'après les sources hagiographiques (750–950)*. Quebec: Presses de l'Université Laval, 1975.

Prinz, Friedrich. "Abriß der kirchlichen und monastischen Entwicklung des Frankenreiches bis zu Karl dem Großen." In *Karl der Große. Lebenswerke und Nachleben*, ed. Wolfgang Braunfels. Vol. 2, *Das geistige Leben*, ed. B. Bischoff, pp. 290–99. Düsseldorf: L. Schwann, 1965.

———. *Askese und Kultur vor- und frühbenediktinisches mönchtums an der Wiege Europas*. Munich: Beck, 1980.

———. "Die bischöflische Stadtherrschaft im Frankenreich vom 5. Bis zum 7. Jahrhundert." *HZ* 217 (1974), 1–35.

———. "Columbanus, The Frankish Nobility and the Territories East of the Rhine." In *Columbanus and Merovingian Monasticism*, ed. H. B. Clarke and Mary Brennan, pp. 73–87. British Archeological Reports, International Series 113. Oxford, 1981.

———. *Frühes Mönchtum im Frankenreich. Kultur und Gesellschaft in Gallien, den Rheinlanden und Bayern am Beispiel der monastischen Entwicklung (4. bis 8. Jahrhundert)*. 2d ed. Darmstadt, 1988.

———. "Gesellschaftsgeschichtliche Aspekte frühmittelalterlicher Hagiographie." *Zeitschrift für Literatur-Wissenschaft und Linguistik* 3:2 (1973), 17–36.

———. "Die Rolle der Iren beim Aufbau der merowingischen Klosterkultur." In *Die Iren und Europa im früheren Mittelalter*. Vol. 1, ed. Heinz Löwe, pp. 202–18. Stuttgart: Klett-Cotta, 1982.

——. ed. *Herrschaft und Kirche: Beiträge zur Entstehung und Wirkungsweise episkopaler und monastischer Organisationsformen.* Stuttgart: Hiersemann, 1988.

——, ed. *Mönchtum und Gesellschaft im Frühmittelalter.* Wege der Forschung 312. Darmstadt: Wissenschaftliche Buchgesellschaft, 1976.

Rahner, Hugo. *Symbole der Kirche. Die Ekklesiologie der Väter.* Salzburg: Otto Müller Verlag, 1964.

Reiling, J. *Hermas and Christian Prophecy: A Study of the Eleventh Mandate.* Supplements to Novum Testamentum, 37. Leiden: E. J. Brill, 1973.

Riché, Pierre. *Education and Culture in the Barbarian West, Sixth through Eighth Centuries.* Columbia: University of South Carolina, 1976.

——. "La *Vita s. Rusticulae*: Note d'hagiographie mérovingienne." *AB* 72 (1954), 369–77.

——, ed. *La christianisation des pays entre Loire et Rhin (ive–viie siècle).* Actes du Colloque de Nanterre (3–4 mai, 1974). Histoire Religieuse de la France. Vol. 2. Paris: Éditions du Cerf, 1993.

Richter, Michael. "Urbanitas et rusticitas: Linguistic Aspects of a Medieval Dichotomy." In *The Church in Town and Countryside*, ed. Derek Baker, pp. 149–57. Studies in Church History 16, Oxford: Blackwell, 1979.

Roblin, Michel. "Fontaines sacrées et nécropoles antiques, deux sites fréquents d'églises paroissiales rurales dans les sept anciens diocèses de L'Oise." In *La christianisation des pays entre Loire et Rhin (ive–viie siècle)*, ed. Pierre Riché, pp. 235–51. Actes du Colloque de Nanterre (3–4 mai, 1974). Histoire Religieuse de la France 2. Paris: Éditions du Cerf, 1993.

——. "Paganisme et rusticité: un gros problème, une étude de mots." *Annales: E.S.C.* 8 (1953), 173–83.

Rothaus, Richard. "Christianization and De-paganization: The Late Antique Creation of a Conceptual Frontier." In *Shifting Frontiers*, ed. Ralph W. Mathisen and Hagith S. Sivan, pp. 299–308. Aldershot: Vivarium, 1996.

Rouche, Michel. *L'Aquitaine des Wisigoths aux Arabes 418–781. Naissance d'une région.* Paris, 1979.

——. "Miracles, maladies et psychologie de la foi à l'époque carolingienne en Francie." In *Hagiographie, cultures et sociétés IVe–XIIe siècles*, pp. 319–37. Actes du colloque organisé à Nanterre et à Paris (2–5 mai 1979). Paris: Études Augustiniennes, 1981.

——. *Vie de sainte Aldegonde réécrite par une moniale contemporaine (viiie s.).* Maubeuge: Maulde et Renou-Sambre, 1988.

Rousseau, Philip. *Ascetics, Authority and the Church in the Age of Jerome and Cassian.* Oxford: Oxford University Press, 1978.

——. "Cassian, Contemplation and the Coenobitic Life." *JEH* 26 (1975), 113–26.

——. *Pachomius: The Making of a Community in Fourth-Century Egypt.* Berkeley: University of California Press, 1985.

——. "The Spiritual Authority of the 'Monk-Bishop.' Eastern Elements in Some Western Hagiography of the Fourth and Fifth Centuries." *JTS* n.s. 22 (1971), 380–419.

Rousselle, Aline. *Croire et guérir. La foi en Gaule dans l'antiquité tardive.* Paris: Fayard, 1990.

——. *Porneia. On Desire and the Body in Antiquity.* Oxford: Blackwell, 1988.

——. "From Sanctuary to Miracle-Worker: Healing in Fourth-Century Gaul." In *Ritual, Religion and the Sacred*, ed. Robert Foster and Orest A. Ranum, pp. 95–127. Selections from the Annales, economies, sociétés, civilisations. Vol. 7. Baltimore: Johns Hopkins University Press, 1982.

Rowland, Christopher. *The Open Heaven: A Study of Apocalyptic in Judaism and Early Christianity.* London: SPCK, 1982.

Rush, Alfred C. *Death and Burial in Christian Antiquity.* Studies in Christian Antiquity
  1. Washington D.C.: Catholic University of America Press, 1941.
Scheibelreiter, Georg. *Der Bischof in Merowingischer Zeit.* Vienna: Böhlau,1983.
———. "Königstochter im kloster. Radegund (d. 587) und der Nonnenaufstand von
  Poitiers (589)." *MIÖG* 87 (1979), 9–37.
Scherman, Katherine. *The Flowering of Ireland: Saints, Scholars, and Kings.* London: Vic-
  tor Gollancz, 1981.
Schmid, Karl, and Joachim Wollasch, eds. *Memoria. Der geschichtliche Zeugniswert des
  liturgischen Gedenkens im Mittelalter.* Munich: Wilhelm Fink Verlag, 1984.
Schmithals, Walter. *The Apocalyptic Movement: Introduction and Interpretation.* Trans.
  John E. Steely. Nashville: Abingdon Press, 1975.
Schmitt, Jean-Claude. *Ghosts in the Middle Ages: The Living and the Dead in Medieval
  Society.* Trans. Teresa Lavender Fagan. Chicago: Chicago University Press, 1998.
Schulenburg, Jane T. "Women's Monastic Communities, 500–1100: Patterns of Expan-
  sion and Decline." *Signs* 14 (1989), 261–92.
Segal, Alan F. "Heavenly Ascent in Hellenistic Judaism, Early Christianity and Their En-
  vironment." *ANRW* 2. Principat 23.2 (1980), 1333–94.
Sicard, Damien. *La liturgie de la mort dans l'église latine des origines à la réforme car-
  olingienne.* Liturgiewissenschaftliche Quellen und Forschungen 63. Münster: Aschen-
  dorff, 1978.
Smith, Macklin. *Prudentius' Psychomachia: A Re-examination.* Princeton: Princeton Uni-
  versity Press, 1976.
Sot, Michel, ed. *Haut moyen-âge: Culture, éducation et société.* Études offertes à Pierre
  Riché. Nanterre: Éditions Publidix, 1990.
Spiegel, Gabrielle M. "History, Historicism, and the Social Logic of the Text in the Middle
  Ages." *Speculum* 65 (1990), 59–86.
Stainier, A., ed. *Première partie: viie–xe siècles* of the *Index Scriptorum Operumque
  Latino-Belgicorum Medii Aevi. Nouveau répertoire des oeuvres médiolatines belges,*
  ed. L. Genicot and P. Tombeur. Brussels: Académie Royale de Belgique, 1973.
Stancliffe, Clare E. *St. Martin and His Hagiographer: History and Miracle in Sulpicius
  Severus.* Oxford: Clarendon Press, 1983.
Steinberg, Leo. *The Sexuality of Christ in Renaisssance Art and in Modern Oblivion.* New
  York: Pantheon, 1983; 2d ed. Chicago: Chicago University Press, 1996.
Stevenson, Jane. "Ascent through the Heavens, from Egypt to Ireland." *Cambridge Me-
  dieval Celtic Studies* 5 (1983), 21–35.
Sticca, Sandro ed. *Saints: Studies in Hagiography.* Medieval and Renaissance Texts and
  Studies,141. Binghamton, N.Y.: Medieval and Renaissance Texts and Studies, 1996.
Stone, Michael E. "The Metamorphosis of Ezra: Jewish Apocalypse and Medieval Vi-
  sion." *JTS* n.s.33 (1982), 1–18.
Suso, Frank, P. Ἀγγελιχὸς βιος. *Begriffsanalytische und begriffsgeschichtliche Unter-
  suchung zum 'Engelgleichen Leben' im frühen mönchtum.* Beitrage zur Geschichte des
  alten mönchtums und des Benediktinerordens, 26. Münster, Westfalen: Aschendorff,
  1964.
Taylor, John Hammond. "The Text of Augustine's *De Genesi ad litteram.*" *Speculum* 25
  (1950), 87–93.
Trout, Dennis. "Town, Countryside and Christianization at Paulinus' Nola." In *Shifting
  Frontiers,* ed. Ralph W. Mathisen and Hagith S. Sivan, pp. 175–86. Aldershot: Vivarium, 1996.
Uytfanghe, Marc van. "La bible dans les vies de saints mérovingiens. Quelques pistes de
  recherche." In *La christianisation des pays entre Loire et Rhin (IVe–VIIe) siècle,* ed.
  Pierre Riché, pp. 103–111. Actes du Colloque de Nanterre (3–4 mai, 1974). Histoire
  Religieuse de la France 2. Paris: Éditions du Cerf, 1993.

———. "L'hagiographie et son publique a l'époque mérovingienne." *Studia Patristica* 16:2 (1985), 54–62.

———. *Stylisation biblique et condition humaine dans l'hagiographie mérovingienne (600–750).* Brussels: A.W.L.S.K., 1987.

Vaesen, Jos. "Sulpice Sévère et la fin des temps." In *The Use and Abuse of Eschatology in the Middle Ages,* ed. Werner Verbeke, Daniel Verhelst, and Andries Welkenhuysen, pp. 49–71. Leuven: Leuven University Press, 1988.

Van Dam, Raymond. *Leadership and Community in Late Antique Gaul.* Berkeley: University of California Press, 1985.

———. *Saints and Their Miracles in Late Antique Gaul.* Princeton: Princeton University Press, 1993.

Van der Essen, Léon. *Étude critique et littéraire sur les vitae des saints mérovingiens de l'ancienne Belgique.* Louvain: Bureaux de Recueil, 1907.

———. *Le siècle des saints (625–739).* Brussels: Renaissance du Livre, 1948.

Vega, P. Angel Custodio. "El 'liber de haeresibus' de San Isidoro de Sevilla y el 'Códice Ovetense.'" *La Ciudad de Dios* 171 (1958), 241–70.

Verbeke, Werner, Daniel Verhelst, and Andries Welkenhuysen, eds. *The Use and Abuse of Eschatology in the Middle Ages.* Leuven: Leuven University Press, 1988.

Von Balthasar, H. Urs. *La Gloire et la Croix.* Vol. 1. Paris: Aubier, 1968.

Von Grunebaum, Gustave Edmund, and Roger Caillois, eds. *The Dream and Human Societies.* Berkeley: University of California Press, 1966.

Vogel, Cyrille. *La discipline pénitentielle en Gaule des origines à la fin du viie siècle.* Paris: Letouazey et Ané, 1952.

———. *Les "Libri Paenitentiales."* Typologie des sources du moyen âge occidental, 27. Turnhout: grepols, 1978.

Waddell, Helen. *The Desert Fathers: Translations from the Latin.* London: Constable, 1936.

Wallace-Hadrill, John Michael. *The Frankish Church.* Oxford: Clarendon Press, 1983.

Weber, K. "Kulturgeschichtliche Probleme der Merovingerzeit im Spiegel frühmittelalterliche Heiligenleben." *Studien und Mitteilungen zur Geschichte des Benediktiner-Ordens* 48 (1930), 347–403.

Weidemann, Margerete. *Kulturgeschichte der Merowingerzeit nach den Werken Gregors von Tours.* 2 vols. Mainz: Verlag des Römisches-Germanischen Zentralmuseums, 1982.

Weinstein, Donald, and Rudolph M. Bell. *Saints and Society: The Two Worlds of Western Christendom, 1000–1700.* Chicago: University of Chicago Press, 1982.

Wemple, Suzanne Fonay. *Women in Frankish Society: Marriage and the Cloister 500 to 900.* Philadelphia: University of Pennsylvania Press, 1981.

———. "Female Spirituality and Mysticism in Frankish Monasteries: Radegund, Balthild and Aldegund." In *Medieval Religious Women.* Vol. 2. Ed. Lillian Thomas Shank and John A. Nichols. Kalamazoo, Mich.: Cistercian Publications, 1987.

Wessel, K. "Der nackte Crucifixus." *Rivista di archeologia cristiana* 43 (1967), 333–45.

Wiulleumier, P. *Inscriptions latines des trois Gaules.* 17th supplement to "Gallia." Paris: CNRS, 1963.

Wolfram, Herwig. "The Goths in Aquitaine." *German Studies Review* 2 (1979), 153–68.

Wood, Ian. "The Ecclesiastical Politics of Merovingian Clermont." In *Ideal and Reality in Frankish and Anglo-Saxon Society,* ed. P. Wormauld, D. A. Bullough, and R. Collins, pp. 34–57. Oxford: Blackwell, 1983.

———. "Forgery in Merovingian Hagiography." In *MGH Schriften.* Vol. 33, *Fälschungen im Mittelalter: Internationaler Kongress der Monumenta Germaniae Historica.* Munich 16–19 September 1996. 5: *Fingierte Briefe, Frömmigkeit und Fälschung Realienfälschungen.* Hanover: Hahnsche Buchhandlung, 1988.

———. "The Frontiers of Western Europe: Developments East of the Rhine in the Sixth Century." In *The Sixth Century. Production, Distribution and Demand*, ed. Richard Hodges and William Bowden, pp. 231–53. Transformation of the Roman World, 3. Leiden: E. J. Brill, 1998.

———. "A Prelude to Columbanus: The Monastic Achievement in the Burgundian Territories." In *Columbanus and Merovingian Monasticism*, ed. H. B. Clarke and M. Brennan, pp. 3–32. BAR International Series 113. Oxford: British Archeological Reports, 1981.

———. "The *Vita Columbani* and Merovingian Hagiography." *Peritia* 1 (1982), 63–80.

Wormald, Patrick, Donald Bullough, and Roger Collins, eds. *Ideal and Reality in Frankish and Anglo-Saxon Society*. Oxford: Blackwell, 1983.

Zaleski, Carol. *Life of the World to Come: Near-Death Experience and Christian Hope*. Albert Cardinal Meyer Lectures. Oxford: Oxford University Press, 1996.

———. *Otherworld Journeys: Accounts of Near-Death Experience in Medieval and Modern Times*. Oxford: Oxford University Press, 1987.

Zimmerman, Gerd. *Ordensleben und Lebensstandard. Die cura corporis in den Ordensvorschriften des abendländischen Hochmittelalters*. Beiträge zur Geschichte des alten mönchtums und des Benediktinerordens, 32. Münster/Westfalen: Aschendorff, 1973.

Zuckerman, A. J., and B. S. Bachrach. "The Political Uses of Theology: The Conflict of Bishop Agobard and the Jews of Lyons." *Studies in Medieval Culture* 3 (1970), 23–51.

Index

Abraham, 70, 74, 122; bosom of, 161
Adam's prophetic sleep, 18–37
Afterlife, visions of, 136–68; as literary
    genre, 136–41
Aldegund of Maubeuge, 7, 124, 183, 198–
    223, 231–35; vision of Amandus, 220–
    22; visions of angels, 206, 214; vision
    of celestial mansion, 207–10; visions of
    Christ, 203–10, 214, 217–19; vision
    of Devil, 210–12, 218
Aldetrude, 202
Almsgiving, 164
Amandus of Tongres-Maastricht, 177n, 183,
    201, 220–22
Ambrose of Milan, 16, 28, 87–88
Anatolius, 47, 66
Angels, 63, 206, 214
Anianus of Orleans, 77n
Anonymous nun of Poitiers, vision of, 195
Anstrudis of Laon, 6–7, 128–29
Anthony of Egypt, 41, 43, 49, 60, 65
Antichrist, 66
Apocalypses, 229–31
Apra, 133–34
Aprunclus of Clermont, 91
Apuleius of Madaurus, *Marriage of Cupid
    and Psyche*, 209–10
Arians, 99, 104–6
Armentaria, 82–85
Artemidorus of Daldis, *Oneirocriticon*, 7,
    17n, 95
Asclepius, shrine of, 117n, 119n
Athanasius of Alexandria, 16, 41, 43, 49;
    Life of St. Anthony, 52, 68
Audoenus of Rouen, 180–82, 200
Augustine of Hippo, 1–2, 18, 43, 127, 130,
    160n, 164n, 173, 189n; *Against the*

Manichees, 31; *City of God*, 30; *De fide
    rerum invisibilium*, 37; *De Genesi ad lit-
    teram*, 8, 18n, 29–33; and tripartite vision
    theory, 43
Austrebertha of Pavilly, 176n
Avitus of Braga, 120
Avitus of Clermont, 82–83, 101–3, 112

Balthild, 180–81, 200
Barontus. *See Vision of Barontus*
Baudonivia, 171, 184, 186–97
Bede, 143n, 156–57
Benedictine Rule, 147, 152, 178
Benignus of Dijon, 83, 125n
Berthila of Chelles, 182
Bertram of Bordeaux, 92n
Bird imagery in visions, 160, 165–66
Bobbio, monastery of, 178–79
Brachio, 142n, 152
Brictius of Poitiers, 65, 67
Burgundofara of Faremoutiers, 151

Caesarius of Arles, 50, 192; rule of, 178,
    186, 195
Carthage, council at, 122
Cassian of Marseilles, 40, 50
Cato, 92–93
Cautinus of Cleremont, 78n, 92–93
Celibacy, 43, 93–94, 117–18
Chalcidius, 8
Chilperic I, 96–99
Chlothar II, 98, 200
Christ, visions of, 182–83, 190–97, 203–10
Chrodebert of Paris, 200
Clement of Alexandria, 27n
Clarus, 66
Claudian, 208–10

259